Praise for *The Site Reliability Workbook*

This new workbook will help people to take the sometimes theoretical and abstract concepts covered in *Site Reliability Engineering* out of the special context of the Googleplex and see how the same concepts work in other organizations. I'm especially excited to see more detail in the analysis of toil, how to apply SRE principles to data pipelines, and the case study reports discussing practical service level management.

—*Kurt Andersen, Site Reliability Engineer, LinkedIn*

This practical hands-on guide to implementing SRE is valuable for engineers at companies of all sizes. It's excellent to see this workbook being shared so that we can all move forward and build more reliable systems together. I was impressed with the level of detail shared; you can pick this book up and get started implementing SRE practices today.

—*Tammy Bütow, Principal SRE, Gremlin*

A timely reminder, from the team that made SRE a required practice for everyone operating at scale, that reliability is created by people. This book is full of practical examples of how to optimize for reliability by focusing on the interactions between users and engineers and between technology and tools, without losing sight of feature velocity. The result is a compelling, interesting, and thought-provoking companion to *Site Reliability Engineering.*

—*Casey Rosenthal, CTO, Backplane.io*

Google's first book explained the what and why of SRE. This book shows you how to implement SRE at any company, startup or giant. Great work by the editorial team.

—*Jonah Horowitz, SRE at Stripe*

In 2016, Google dropped *Site Reliability Engineering* on the operations world, and the operations world was never the same. For the first time people had access to over 500 pages of distilled information on what Google does to run its planet-wide infrastructure. Most people liked the book, a handful didn't, but nobody ignored it. It became a seminal work and an important touchstone for how people thought about SRE (especially the Google implementation of it) from that point on. But it was missing something....

Now in 2018, Google returns to fill in a crucial piece of the puzzle: in their first volume they described what they do, but that didn't help those who couldn't see themselves in Google's story. This book aims to demonstrate *how* Google does SRE— and how you can do it, too.

—*David N. Blank-Edelman, editor of* Seeking SRE: Conversations about Running Production Systems at Scale *and cofounder of the global set of SREcon conferences*

The Site Reliability Workbook
Practical Ways to Implement SRE

Edited by Betsy Beyer, Niall Richard Murphy,
David K. Rensin, Kent Kawahara,
and Stephen Thorne

Beijing · Boston · Farnham · Sebastopol · Tokyo

The Site Reliability Workbook

edited by Betsy Beyer, Niall Richard Murphy, David K. Rensin, Kent Kawahara, and Stephen Thorne

Printed in the United States of America.

Published by O'Reilly Media, Inc., 1005 Gravenstein Highway North, Sebastopol, CA 95472.

O'Reilly books may be purchased for educational, business, or sales promotional use. Online editions are also available for most titles (*http://oreilly.com/safari*). For more information, contact our corporate/institutional sales department: 800-998-9938 or *corporate@oreilly.com*.

Acquisitions Editor: Nikki McDonald	**Indexer:** Ellen Troutman-Zaig
Developmental Editor: Virginia Wilson	**Interior Designer:** David Futato
Production Editor: Kristen Brown	**Cover Designer:** Karen Montgomery
Copyeditor: Rachel Monaghan	**Illustrator:** Rebecca Demarest
Proofreader: Kim Cofer	

August 2018:   First Edition

Revision History for the First Edition

2018-06-08:   First Release
2018-06-22:   Second Release
2018-08-10:   Third Release

See *http://oreilly.com/catalog/errata.csp?isbn=9781492029502* for release details.

This work is part of a collaboration between O'Reilly and Google. See our *statement of editorial independence* (*http://www.oreilly.com/about/editorial_independence.html*).

The O'Reilly logo is a registered trademark of O'Reilly Media, Inc. *The Site Reliability Workbook*, the cover image, and related trade dress are trademarks of O'Reilly Media, Inc.

978-1-492-02950-2

[LSCH]

Table of Contents

Foreword I

Mark Burgess

Having introduced the first SRE book for O'Reilly, I am honored to be invited back for the sequel. In this book, the writing team is leaving the history of the first book to speak for itself and reaching out to a broader audience, offering direct experiences, case studies, and informal guidance. The broad themes will be familiar to anyone in IT, perhaps relabeled and reprioritized, and with a modern sense of business awareness. In place of technical descriptions, here we have user-facing services and their promises or objectives. We see human-computer systems originate from within the evolving business, intrinsic to its purpose, rather than as foreign meteorites impacting an unsuspecting and pristine infrastructure. Cooperation of all human-computer parts is the focus. Indeed, the book might be summarized as follows:

- Commit to clear promises that set service objectives, expectations, and levels.
- Assess those promises continuously, with metrics and budgetary limits.
- React quickly to keep and repair promises, be on-call, and guard autonomy to avoid new gatekeepers.

Keeping promises reliably (to all stakeholders) depends on the stability of all their dependencies, of intent, and of the lives of the people involved (e.g., see *Thinking in Promises* (*https://oreil.ly/2snieke*)). Remarkably, the human aspects of human-computer systems only grow alongside the perceived menace of scale: it turns out that automation doesn't eliminate humans, after all; rather, it challenges us to reassert human needs across all scales, from the genesis of an individual idea to the massive deployments on behalf of a global user base.

Teaching these lessons is a service challenge in its own right—and, like any service, hard-won knowledge is an iterative process. We make these lessons our own by questioning, trying, failing, rehearsing, and perfecting them. There's a wealth of material to ponder and adapt in the book, so let's go.

Foreword II

Andrew Clay Shafer

When I found out people were working on a second SRE book, I reached out and asked if I could write a few words. The principles from the first SRE book align so well with what I always imagined DevOps to be, and the practices are insightful, even when they aren't 100% applicable outside of Google. After reading the principles from the first SRE book for the first time—embracing risk (Chapter 3) (*http://bit.ly/2so6uOc*), service level objectives (Chapter 4) (*http://bit.ly/2szBKsK*), and eliminating toil (Chapter 5) (*http://bit.ly/2Lg1TEN*)—I wanted to shout that message from the rooftops. "Embracing risk" resonated so much because I had used similar language many times to help traditional organizations motivate change. Chapter 6 (*http://bit.ly/2KNCD9F*) was always an implicit DevOps goal, both to allow humans more time for creative higher-order work and to allow them to be more human. But I really fell in love with "service level objectives." I love that the language and the process create a dispassionate contract between operational considerations and delivering new functionality. The SRE, SWE (software engineer), and business all agree that the service has to be up to be valuable, and the SRE solution quantifies objectives to drive actions and priorities. The solution—make the service level a target, and when you are below the target prioritize reliability over features—eliminates a classic conflict between operations and developers. This is a simple and elegant reframing that solves problems by not having them. I give these three chapters as a homework assignment to almost everyone I've met since. They are that good. Everyone should know. Tell all your friends. I've told all mine.

The last decade of my career has been focused on helping people deliver software with better tools and process. Sometimes people say I contributed to inventing DevOps, but I was just in the position to borrow and steal successful patterns from across many different organizations and projects. I get embarrassed when people say "DevOps" was invented by anyone, but especially by me. I don't consider myself an expert in anything but being inquisitive. My idealized DevOps always patterned off whatever information I could extract or infer from my friends, and my friends happened to be building the internet. I had the privilege of behind-the-scenes access to people deploying and operating a representative sample of the world's most incredible infrastructures and applications. DevOps symbolizes aspects of the emergent and existential optimizations required to rapidly deliver highly available software over the internet. The shift from software delivered on physical media to software delivered as a service forced an evolution of tools and processes. This evolution elevated operations' contribution to the value chain. If the systems are down, the software has no value. The good news is, you don't have to wait for shipping the next shrink-wrapped box to change the software. For some, this is also the bad news. I simply had the opportunity and perspective to articulate the most successful patterns of the new way to a receptive audience.

In 2008, before we used the word DevOps like we do now, I'd been through the dot-com collapse, grad school, and a couple of venture-funded rollercoaster rides as a developer—searching Google for answers daily the whole time. I was working on Puppet full-time and I was fascinated by the potential for automation to transform IT organizations. Puppet thrust me into solving problems in the operations domain. At this time, Google used Puppet to manage their corporate Linux and OS X workstations at a scale that pushed the capabilities of the Puppet server. We had a great working relationship with Google, but Google kept certain details of their internal operations secret as a matter of policy. I know this because I'm naturally curious and was constantly seeking more information. I always knew Google must have great internal tools and processes, but what these tools and processes were wasn't always apparent. Eventually, I accepted that asking deep questions about Borg probably meant the current conversation wasn't going very far. I would have loved to know more about how Google did everything, but this simply wasn't allowed at the time. The significance of 2008 also includes the first O'Reilly Velocity conference and the year I met Patrick Debois. "DevOps" wasn't a thing yet, but it was about to be. The time was right. The world was ready. DevOps symbolized a new way, a better way. If *Site Reliability Engineering* had been published then, I believe the community that formed would have rallied to fly the "eliminate toil" flag and the term *DevOps* might have never existed. Counterfactuals notwithstanding, I know the first SRE book personally advanced my understanding of the possible, and I already helped many others just with the SRE principles.

In the early days of the DevOps movement, we consciously avoided codifying practices because everything was evolving so rapidly and we didn't want to set limits on what DevOps could become. Plus, we explicitly didn't want anyone to "own" DevOps. When I wrote about DevOps in 2010, I made three distinct points. First, developers and operations can and should work together. Second, system administration will become more and more like software development. Finally, sharing with a global community of practice accelerates and multiplies our collective capabilities. Around the same time, my friends Damon Edwards and John Willis coined the acronym *CAMS* for Culture, Automation, Metrics, and Sharing. Jez Humble later expanded this acronym to *CALMS* by adding Lean continuous improvement. What each of these words might mean in context deserves to be a full book, but I mention them here because *Site Reliability Engineering* explicitly references Culture, Automation, Metrics, and Sharing alongside anecdotes about Google's journey to continuously improve. By publishing the first SRE book, Google shared their principles and practices with the global community. Now I define DevOps simply as "optimizing human performance and experience operating software, with software, and with humans." I don't want to put words in anyone's mouth, but that seems like a great way to describe SRE as well.

Ultimately, I know DevOps when I see it and I see SRE at Google, in theory and practice, as one of the most advanced implementations. Good IT operations has always depended on good engineering, and solving operations problems with software has always been central to DevOps. Site Reliability Engineering makes the engineering aspect even more explicit. I cringe when I hear someone say "SRE versus DevOps." For me, they are inseparable in time and space, as labels describing the sociotechnical systems that deliver modern infrastructure with software. I consider DevOps a loose generic set of principles and SRE an advanced explicit implementation. A parallel analogy would be the relationship between Agile and Extreme Programming (XP). True, XP is Agile, arguably the best of Agile, but not all organizations are capable of or willing to adopt XP.

Some say "software is eating the world," and I understand why they do, but "software" alone is not the right framing. Without the ubiquity of computational hardware connected with high-speed networks, much of what we take for granted as "software" would not be possible. This is an undeniable truth. What I think many miss in this conversation about technology are the humans. Technology exists because of humans and hopefully *for* humans, but if you look a little deeper, you also realize that the software we rely on, and probably take for granted, is largely dependent on humans. We rely on software, but software also relies on us. This is a single interconnected system of imperfect hardware—software and humans relying on themselves to build the future. Reliability is eating the world. Reliability is not just about technology, though, but also about people. The people and the technology form a single technosocial system. One nice feature about having Google share SRE with the rest of the industry is that any excuses about what kind of processes work at scale became invalid. Google set the highest standard for both reliability and scale. There might be valid arguments about why someone can't adopt Google SRE practices directly, but the guiding principles should still apply. As I look at the landscape of possibilities to build the future and the ambition to transform human experience with software, I see a lot of ambitious projects to quite literally connect everything to the internet. My math says that the successful projects will find themselves ingesting and indexing incredible amounts of data. Few, if any, will surpass the scale of Google today, but some will be the same size Google was when they started SRE and will need to solve the same reliability problems. I contend that in these cases, adopting tools and process that look suspiciously like SRE is not optional but existential—though there is no need to wait for that crisis because SRE principles and practices apply at any scale.

SRE is usually framed as how Google does operations, but that misses the bigger picture: SRE in practice enables software engineering, but also transforms architecture, security, governance, and compliance. When we leverage the SRE focus on providing a platform of services, all these other considerations get to have first-class emphasis, but where and how that happens may be quite different. Just like SRE (and hopefully DevOps) shifted more and more of the burden to software engineering, modern architecture and security practices evolve from slides, checklists, and hope to enabling the right behaviors with running code. Organizations adopting SRE principles and practices without revisiting these other aspects lose a huge opportunity to improve, and will also probably meet with internal resistance if the people who consider themselves responsible for those aspects are not converted into allies.

I always enjoy learning. I read every word of the first SRE book straight through. I loved the language. I loved the anecdotes. I loved understanding more about how Google sees itself. But the question for me is always, "What behavior will I change?" Learning isn't collecting information. Learning is changing behavior. This is easy to determine or even quantify in certain disciplines. You have learned to play a new song when you can play the song. You are better at chess when you win games against stronger players. Site Reliability Engineering, like DevOps, should not just be changing titles, but making definitive behavior changes, focusing on outcomes and obviously reliability. *The Site Reliability Workbook* promises to move forward from an enumeration of principles and practices by Google for Google toward more contextual actions and behaviors. Site reliability is for everyone, but reliability doesn't come from reading books. Here's to embracing risk and eliminating toil.

Preface

When we wrote the original *Site Reliability Engineering* book (*http://bit.ly/2kIcNYM*), we had a goal: explain the philosophy and the principles of production engineering and operations at Google. The book was our attempt to share our teams' best practices and lessons with the rest of the computing world. We assumed that the SRE book might appeal to a modest number of engineers working in large, reliability-conscious endeavors, and that both the quantity and the focus of the content would tend to limit the book's appeal.

As it turned out, we were happily mistaken on both counts.

To our surprise and delight, the SRE book was a best-seller in computing for an exhilarating period after its release, and it was not just being sold or downloaded; it was being *read*. We received questions from around the world about the book, the team, the practices, and the outcomes. We were asked to speak about chapters, approaches, and incidents. We found ourselves in the unexpected position of having to turn down outside requests because we were out of cycles.

Like most success disasters, the SRE book created an opportunity to respond with human effort ("Hire more people! Do more speaking engagements!") or with something more scalable. And being SREs, it will surprise few readers that we gravitated toward the latter approach. We decided to write a second SRE book—one that expanded on the content we were most frequently being asked to speak about, and that addressed the most common questions readers had about the first book.

Out of the many different questions, requests, and comments we received about the first SRE book, two themes were particularly interesting to us; if left unaddressed, they were barriers to putting SRE's lessons to productive use. These themes are colloquially summarized as:

- Principles are interesting, but how do I turn them into practice in *my* project/team/company?

- SRE's approach would not work for me; it is feasible only in Google's culture, and makes sense only at Google's scale.

The purpose of this second SRE book is (a) to add more implementation detail to the principles outlined in the first volume, and (b) to dispel the idea that SRE is implementable only at "Google scale" or in "Google culture."

This volume is a *companion* to the previous work—not a new version. The two books should be taken together as a pair. You will get the most from this book if you're already familiar with its predecessor. The first SRE book is available online for free (*http://www.google.com/sre*).

By design, the structure of this book roughly follows the structure of the first volume. We want you to be able to read the chapters in tandem. Each chapter in this volume assumes you're familiar with its counterpart from the previous work; our goal is to allow you to jump back and forth between principle and practice as you go. That way, you can use both volumes as ongoing references.

Next, a word about ethos: We heard from some readers that while describing Google's journey toward better operations we concentrated too much on *just us*. Some readers suggested that we were too removed from the practicalities of the world outside Google, and failed to address the interaction of our ideas (*http://bit.ly/2J5S63y*) with the principles of DevOps. That's an entirely fair criticism that we've tried to take to heart in this volume.

However, we do think that the highly opinionated nature of SRE contributes to its usefulness as a discipline. To us that's a feature, not a bug. We do not advocate that SRE is the only way (or even universally the best way) to build and operate highly reliable systems. It's just the way that has been most successful for us.

We'll also spend a few words talking about how SRE and DevOps relate to each other. The important point to keep in mind is that they are not in conflict.

We'd like to acknowledge up front that this volume is necessarily incomplete. The SRE discipline is a broad field even inside the confines of Google, and it is evolving even faster now that it's practiced widely outside of Google. Rather than go broad and superficial, we focused this volume to answer the most requested implementation details from the first volume.

Finally, this volume and its predecessor are not intended to be gospel. Please don't treat them that way. Even after all these years, we're still finding conditions and cases that cause us to tweak (or in some cases, replace) previously firmly held beliefs. SRE is a journey as much as it is a discipline.

We hope that you enjoy what you read in these pages and find the book useful. Assembling it has been a labor of love. We're delighted that there's a growing and skilled community of SRE professionals with whom we can learn and improve.

As always, your direct feedback is much appreciated. It teaches us something valuable every time you contribute it.

How to Read This Book

This book is the companion volume to Google's first book, *Site Reliability Engineering* (*http://bit.ly/2kIcNYM*). To get the most out of this volume, we recommend that you have read, or can refer to, the first SRE book (available to read online for free at *google.com/sre*). The two works complement each other in the following ways:

- The previous work was an introduction to principles and philosophy. This volume concentrates on how those principles are applied. (In a few areas—particularly configuration management and canarying—we also cover some new ground to provide background for the practical treatment of other subjects.)

- The earlier volume concentrated exclusively on how SRE is practiced at Google. This work includes perspectives from a number of other firms—from traditional enterprises (including The Home Depot and the *New York Times*) to digital natives (Evernote, Spotify, and others).

- The first book didn't directly refer to the larger operations community—especially DevOps—whereas this book speaks directly to how SRE and DevOps relate to each other.

This volume assumes that you will bounce between this volume and its predecessor. You might, for example, read Chapter 4, "Service Level Objectives" (*http://bit.ly/2szBKsK*) in the first book and then read its implementation complement (Chapter 2) in this volume.

This book assumes that every chapter is just the starting point for a longer discussion and journey. Accordingly, this book is intended to be a conversation starter rather than the last word.

—The Editors

Conventions Used in This Book

The following typographical conventions are used in this book:

Italic
    Indicates new terms, URLs, email addresses, filenames, and file extensions.

`Constant width`
    Used for program listings, as well as within paragraphs to refer to program elements such as variable or function names, databases, data types, environment variables, statements, and keywords.

Constant width bold

Shows commands or other text that should be typed literally by the user.

Constant width italic

Shows text that should be replaced with user-supplied values or by values determined by context.

 This element signifies a tip or suggestion.

 This element signifies a general note.

 This element indicates a warning or caution.

Using Code Examples

Supplemental material (code examples, exercises, etc.) is available for download at *http://g.co/SiteReliabilityWorkbookMaterials*.

This book is here to help you get your job done. In general, if example code is offered with this book, you may use it in your programs and documentation. You do not need to contact us for permission unless you're reproducing a significant portion of the code. For example, writing a program that uses several chunks of code from this book does not require permission. Selling or distributing a CD-ROM of examples from O'Reilly books does require permission. Answering a question by citing this book and quoting example code does not require permission. Incorporating a significant amount of example code from this book into your product's documentation does require permission.

We appreciate, but do not require, attribution. An attribution usually includes the title, author, publisher, and ISBN. For example: "*The Site Reliability Workbook*, edited by Betsy Beyer, Niall Richard Murphy, David K. Rensin, Kent Kawahara, and Stephen Thorne (O'Reilly). Copyright 2018 Google LLC, 978-1-492-02950-2."

If you feel your use of code examples falls outside fair use or the permission given above, feel free to contact us at *permissions@oreilly.com*.

O'Reilly Safari

 *Safari* (formerly Safari Books Online) is a membership-based training and reference platform for enterprise, government, educators, and individuals.

Members have access to thousands of books, training videos, Learning Paths, interactive tutorials, and curated playlists from over 250 publishers, including O'Reilly Media, Harvard Business Review, Prentice Hall Professional, Addison-Wesley Professional, Microsoft Press, Sams, Que, Peachpit Press, Adobe, Focal Press, Cisco Press, John Wiley & Sons, Syngress, Morgan Kaufmann, IBM Redbooks, Packt, Adobe Press, FT Press, Apress, Manning, New Riders, McGraw-Hill, Jones & Bartlett, and Course Technology, among others.

For more information, please visit *http://oreilly.com/safari*.

How to Contact Us

Please address comments and questions concerning this book to the publisher:

> O'Reilly Media, Inc.
> 1005 Gravenstein Highway North
> Sebastopol, CA 95472
> 800-998-9938 (in the United States or Canada)
> 707-829-0515 (international or local)
> 707-829-0104 (fax)

We have a web page for this book, where we list errata, examples, and any additional information. You can access this page at *http://bit.ly/siteReliabilityWkbk*.

To comment or ask technical questions about this book, send email to *bookquestions@oreilly.com*.

For more information about our books, courses, conferences, and news, see our website at *http://www.oreilly.com*.

Find us on Facebook: *http://facebook.com/oreilly*

Follow us on Twitter: *http://twitter.com/oreillymedia*

Watch us on YouTube: *http://www.youtube.com/oreillymedia*

Acknowledgments

This book is the product of the enthusiastic and generous contributions of more than 100 people, including authors, tech writers, and reviewers. Each chapter has a byline for the individual authors and tech writers. We'd also like to take a moment to thank everyone not listed there.

We would like to thank the following reviewers for providing valuable (and sometimes pointed) feedback: Abe Hassan, Alex Perry, Cara Donnelly, Chris Jones, Cody Smith, Dermot Duffy, Jarrod Todd, Jay Judkowitz, John T. Reese, Liz Fong-Jones, Mike Danese, Murali Suriar, Narayan Desai, Niccolò Cascarano, Ralph Pearson, Salim Virji, Todd Underwood, Vivek Rau, and Zoltan Egyed.

We would like to express our deepest appreciation to the following people for serving as our overall quality bar for this volume. They made substantial contributions throughout the entire volume: Alex Matey, Max Luebbe, Matt Brown, and JC van Winkel.

As the leaders of Google SRE, Benjamin Treynor Sloss and Ben Lutch were this book's primary executive sponsors within Google; their strong and unwavering belief in a follow-up project that was a worthy companion of the first SRE book was essential to making this book happen.

While the authors and technical writers are specifically acknowledged in each chapter, we'd like to recognize those that contributed to each chapter by providing thoughtful input, discussion, and review. In chapter order, they are:

- **Chapter 2:** Javier Kohen, Patrick Eaton, Richard Bondi, Yaniv Aknin
- **Chapter 4:** Alex Matey, Clint Pauline, Cody Smith, JC van Winkel, Ola Kłapcińska, Štěpán Davidovič
- **Chapter 5:** Alex Matey, Clint Pauline, Cody Smith, Iain Cooke, JC van Winkel, Štěpán Davidovič
- **Chapter 6:** Dermot Duffy, James O'Keeffe, Stephen Thorne
- **Chapter 7:** Mark Brody
- **Chapter 8:** Alex Perry, Alex Hidalgo, David Huska, Sebastian Kirsch, Sabrina Farmer, Steven Carstensen, Liz Fong-Jones, Nandu Shah (Evernote), Robert Holley (Evernote)
- **Chapter 9:** Alex Hidalgo, Alex Matey, Alex Perry, Dave Rensin, Matt Brown, Tor Gunnar Houeland, Trevor Strohman
- **Chapter 10:** John T. Reese

- **Chapter 11:** Daniel E. Eisenbud, Dave Rensin, Dmitry Nefedkin, Dževad Trumić, Edward Wu (Niantic), JC van Winkel, Lucas Pereira, Luke Stone, Matt Brown, Natalia Sakowska, Niall Richard Murphy, Phil Keslin (Niantic), Rita Sodt, Scott Devoid, Simon Donovan, Tomasz Kulczyński

- **Chapter 12:** Ivo Krka, Matt Brown, Nicky Nicolosi, Tanya Reilly

- **Chapter 13:** Bartosz Janota (Spotify), Cara Donnelly, Chris Farrar, Johannes Rußek (Spotify), Max Charas, Max Luebbe, Michelle Duffy, Nelson Arapé (Spotify), Riccardo Petrocco (Spotify), Rickard Zwahlen (Spotify), Robert Stephenson (Spotify), Steven Thurgood

- **Chapter 14:** Charlene Perez, Dave Cunningham, Dave Rensin, JC van Winkel, John Reese, Stephen Thorne

- **Chapter 15:** Alex Matey, Bo Shi, Charlene Perez, Dave Rensin, Eric Johnson, Juliette Benton, Lars Wander, Mike Danese, Narayan Desai, Niall Richard Murphy, Štěpán Davidovič, Stephen Thorne

- **Chapter 16:** Alex Matey, Liz Fong-Jones, Max Luebbe

- **Chapter 17:** Andrew Harvey, Aleksander Szymanek, Brad Kratochvil, Ed Wehrwein, Duncan Sargeant, Jessika Reissland, Matt Brown, Piotr Sieklucki and Thomas Adamcik

- **Chapter 18:** Brian Balser (*New York Times*), Deep Kapadia (*New York Times*), Michelle Duffy, Xavier Llorà

- **Chapter 19:** Matt Brown

- **Chapter 20:** Brian Balser (*New York Times*), Christophe Kalt, Daniel Rogers, Max Luebbe, Niall Richard Murphy, Ramón Medrano Llamas, Richard Bondi, Steven Carstensen, Stephen Thorne, Steven Thurgood, Thomas Wright

- **Chapter 21:** Dave Rensin, JC Van Winkel, Max Luebbe, Ronen Louvton, Stephen Thorne, Tom Feiner, Tsiki Rosenman

We are also grateful to the following contributors, who supplied significant expertise or resources, or had some otherwise excellent effect on this work: Caleb Donaldson, Charlene Perez, Evan Leonard, Jennifer Petoff, Juliette Benton, and Lea Miller.

We very much appreciate the thoughtful and in-depth feedback that we received from industry reviewers: Mark Burgess, David Blank-Edelman, John Looney, Jennifer Davis, Björn Rabenstein, Susan Fowler, Thomas A. Limoncelli, James Meickle, Theo Schlossangle, Jez Humble, Alice Goldfuss, Arup Chakrabarti, John Allspaw, Angus Lees, Eric Liang, Brendan Gregg, and Bryan Liles.

We would like to extend a special thanks to Shylaja Nukala, who generously committed the time and skills of the SRE Technical Writing Team. She enthusiastically supported their necessary and valued efforts.

Thanks also to the O'Reilly Media team—Virginia Wilson, Kristen Brown, Rachel Monaghan, Nikki McDonald, Melanie Yarbrough, and Gloria Lukos—for their help and support making the book a reality in our ambitious timeline.

And an *extra* special thanks to Niall Richard Murphy: despite the fact that he moved on from Google before this book hit the shelves, his continual insights and dedication were crucial for getting a goodly portion of meaningful content over the finish line. His leadership, thoughtfulness, tenacity, and wit are nothing short of inspirational!

Finally, the editors would also like to personally thank the following people:

- **Betsy Beyer:** To Grandmother, my go-to source for encouragement, inspiration, popcorn, pep, and puzzling. You made both this book and my everyday life better! To Duzzie, Hammer, Joan, Kiki, and Mini (note the alphabetical order—ha!) who helped shape me into the obsessive writer slash person I am today. And of course, Riba, for providing the DMD and other provisions necessary to fuel this effort.

- **Niall Richard Murphy:** To Léan, Oisín, Fiachra, and Kay, north stars. To someone whose protestations of self-interest are entirely out of odds with how he acts. To Sharon, more influential than she knows. To Alex, in a light-filled sitting room, with a cup of tea, a book, a box of dice, and thou.

- **Stephen Thorne:** To my mum and dad, who have always encouraged me to push myself. To my wife, Elspeth. To my colleagues who have given me more respect and encouragement than I think I deserve: Ola, Štěpán, Perry, and David.

- **Dave Rensin:** After I wrote my first book, I swore I'd never write another. That was six books ago and I say exactly the same thing each time. To my wife, Lia, who gives me the space to do it and never says "I told you so." (Even though she tells me so.) To my colleagues at Google—and particularly to the family of SRE—who have taught me more these last few years about production engineering at scale than I had learned in the previous 20. Finally, to Benjamin Treynor Sloss, who interviewed me and convinced me to come to Google in the first place.

- **Kent Kawahara:** To my parents, Denby and Setsuko, and my Aunt Asako for helping me get to where I am. To my siblings, Randy and Patti, for their support over the years. To my wife, Angela, and my sons, Ryan, Ethan, and Brady, for their love and support. Finally, to the core team of Dave, Betsy, Niall, Juliette, and Stephen, I feel honored to have worked with you on this project.

## CHAPTER 1

How SRE Relates to DevOps

class SRE implements interface DevOps

*By Niall Richard Murphy,
Liz Fong-Jones, and Betsy Beyer,
with Todd Underwood, Laura Nolan,
and Dave Rensin*

Operations, as a discipline, is *hard*.[1] Not only is there the generally unsolved question of how to run systems well, but the best practices that *have* been found to work are highly context-dependent and far from widely adopted. There is also the largely unaddressed question of how to run operations teams well. Detailed analysis of these topics is generally thought to originate with Operational Research (*http://bit.ly/2HeARLw*) devoted to improving processes and output in the Allied military during World War II, but in reality, we have been thinking about how to operate things better for millennia (*http://bit.ly/2HcEH7R*).

Yet, despite all this effort and thought, reliable production operations remains elusive —particularly in the domains of information technology (*http://bit.ly/2JoeVmi*) and software operability (*http://bit.ly/2Lf1hiQ*). The enterprise world, for example, often treats operations as a cost center,[2] which makes meaningful improvements in out-

---

1 Note that as this discussion appears in a book about SRE, some of this discussion is specific to software service operations, as opposed to IT operations.

2 Mary Poppendieck has an excellent article on this called "The Cost Center Trap (*http://bit.ly/2LRFkHt*)." Another way in which this approach fails is when a very large and improbable disaster completely wipes out the cost savings you made by moving to a low-grade operations model (c.f. the British Airways outage in May 2017 (*https://ind.pn/2LNQflE*)).

comes difficult if not impossible. The tremendous short-sightedness of this approach is not yet widely understood, but dissatisfaction with it has given rise to a revolution in how to organize what we do in IT.

That revolution stemmed from trying to solve a common set of problems. The newest solutions to these problems are called by two separate names—DevOps and Site Reliability Engineering (SRE). Although we talk about them individually as if they are totally separate reactions to the enterprise mentality just described,[3] we hope to persuade you that in fact they are much more alike, and practitioners of each have much more in common, than you might assume.

But first, some background on the key tenets of each.

Background on DevOps

DevOps is a loose set of practices, guidelines, and culture designed to break down silos in IT development, operations, networking, and security. Articulated by John Willis, Damon Edwards, and Jez Humble, CA(L)MS (*https://www.atlassian.com/devops*)—which stands for Culture, Automation, Lean (as in Lean management (*http://bit.ly/2Hd0nkp*); also see continuous delivery (*http://bit.ly/1V7EIyd*)), Measurement, and Sharing—is a useful acronym for remembering the key points of DevOps philosophy. Sharing and collaboration are at the forefront of this movement. In a DevOps approach, you improve something (often by automating it), measure the results, and share those results with colleagues so the whole organization can improve. All of the CALMS principles are facilitated by a supportive culture.

DevOps, Agile, and a variety of other business and software reengineering techniques are all examples of a general worldview on how best to do business in the modern world. None of the elements in the DevOps philosophy are easily separable from each other, and this is essentially by design. There are, however, a few key ideas that can be discussed in relative isolation.

No More Silos

The first key idea is *no more silos*. This is a reaction to a couple ideas:

- The historically popular but now increasingly old-fashioned arrangement of separate operations and development teams

---

3 Of course, there are a number of other potential reactions. For example, ITIL® is another approach to IT management that advocates for better standardization.

- The fact that extreme siloization of knowledge (*http://bit.ly/2J9m5HG*), incentives for purely local optimization, and lack of collaboration (*http://bit.ly/2J80L5D*) have in many cases been actively bad for business[4]

Accidents Are Normal

The second key idea is that accidents are not just a result of the isolated actions of an individual, but rather result from missing safeguards for when things inevitably go wrong.[5] For example, a bad interface inadvertently encourages the wrong action under pressure; a system misfeature makes failure inevitable if the (unarticulated) wrong circumstances occur; broken monitoring makes it impossible to know if something is wrong, never mind *what* is wrong. Some more traditionally minded businesses possess the cultural instinct to root out the mistake maker and punish them. But doing so has its own consequences: most obviously, it creates incentives to confuse issues, hide the truth, and blame others, all of which are ultimately unprofitable distractions. Therefore, it is more profitable to focus on speeding recovery than preventing accidents.

Change Should Be Gradual

The third key idea is that change is best when it is small and frequent (*http://bit.ly/2Js80IK*). In environments where change committees meet monthly to discuss thoroughly documented plans to make changes to the mainframe configuration, this is a radical idea. However, this is not a new idea. The notion that all changes must be considered by experienced humans and batched for efficient consideration turns out to be more or less the opposite of best practice. Change is risky, true, but the correct response is to split up your changes into smaller subcomponents where possible. Then you build a steady pipeline of low-risk change out of regular output from product, design, and infrastructure changes.[6] This strategy, coupled with automatic testing of smaller changes and reliable rollback of bad changes, leads to approaches to change management like continuous integration (CI) (*http://bit.ly/2J9meec*) and continuous delivery or deployment (CD) (*http://bit.ly/1V7EIyd*).

---

4 Note also that because this is a complicated world, there are also positive effects (*http://bit.ly/2JaOddH*) to partitioning (*http://bit.ly/2L9Mw0s*), silos, and the like, but the downsides seem to be particularly pernicious in the domain of operations.

5 See *https://en.wikipedia.org/wiki/Normal_Accidents*.

6 Higher-risk changes, or those unvalidatable by automatic means, should obviously still be vetted by humans, if not enacted by them.

Tooling and Culture Are Interrelated

Tooling is an important component of DevOps, particularly given the emphasis on managing change correctly—today, change management relies on highly specific tools. Overall, however, proponents of DevOps strongly emphasize organizational culture—rather than tooling—as the key to success in adopting a new way of working. A good culture can work around broken tooling, but the opposite rarely holds true. As the saying goes, culture eats strategy for breakfast (*http://bit.ly/2sokzLC*). Like operations, change itself is hard.

Measurement Is Crucial

Finally, measurement is particularly crucial in the overall business context of, for example, breaking down silos and incident resolution. In each of these environments, you establish the reality of what's happening by means of objective measurement, verify that you're changing the situation as you expect, and create an objective foundation for conversations that different functions agree upon. (This applies in both business *and* other contexts, such as on-call.)

Background on SRE

Site Reliability Engineering (SRE) is a term (and associated job role) coined by Ben Treynor Sloss, a VP of engineering at Google.[7] As we can see in the previous section, DevOps is a broad set of principles about whole-lifecycle collaboration between operations and product development. SRE is a job role, a set of practices (described next) we've found to work, and some beliefs that animate those practices. If you think of DevOps as a philosophy and an approach to working, you can argue that SRE implements some of the philosophy that DevOps describes, and is somewhat closer to a concrete definition of a job or role than, say, "DevOps engineer."[8] So, in a way, *class SRE implements interface DevOps.*

Unlike the DevOps movement, which originated from collaborations between leaders and practitioners at multiple companies, SRE at Google inherited much of its culture from the surrounding company before the term *SRE* became widely popularized across the industry. Given that trajectory, the discipline as a whole currently does not

---

7 The history of SRE at Google is that it sprang from a precursor team, which was more operationally focused, and Ben provided the impetus for treating the problem from an engineering standpoint.

8 This is a misnomer in a large number of ways, perhaps the most fundamental being that you can't just hire some people, call them "DevOps engineers," and expect benefits immediately. You have to buy into the whole philosophy of changing how you work in order to benefit. As Andrew Clay Shafer says (*http://bit.ly/2sy7UVI*), "People sell DevOps, but you can't buy it." And, as Seth Vargo points out in "The 10 Myths of DevOps" (*http://bit.ly/2HcHmP1*), you can't "hire a DevOp to fix your organization."

foreground cultural change by default quite as much as DevOps. (That doesn't imply anything about whether cultural change is necessary to do SRE in an arbitrary organization, of course.)

SRE is defined by the following concrete principles.

Operations Is a Software Problem

The basic tenet of SRE is that doing operations well is a software problem. SRE should therefore use software engineering approaches to solve that problem. This is across a wide field of view, encompassing everything from process and business change to similarly complicated but more traditional software problems, such as rewriting a stack to eliminate single points of failure in business logic.

Manage by Service Level Objectives (SLOs)

SRE does not attempt to give everything 100% availability. As discussed in our first book, *Site Reliability Engineering* (*http://bit.ly/2kIcNYM*), this is the wrong target for a number of reasons. Instead, the product team and the SRE team select an appropriate availability target for the service and its user base, and the service is managed to that SLO.[9] Deciding on such a target requires strong collaboration from the business. SLOs have cultural implications as well: as collaborative decisions among stakeholders, SLO violations bring teams back to the drawing board, blamelessly.

Work to Minimize Toil

For SRE, any manual, structurally mandated operational task is abhorrent. (That doesn't mean we don't *have* any such operations: we have plenty of them. We just don't like them.) We believe that if a machine *can* perform a desired operation, then a machine often *should*. This is a distinction (and a value) (*http://bit.ly/2xvlcIa*) not often seen in other organizations, where toil *is* the job, and that's what you're paying a person to do. For SRE in the Google context, toil is *not* the job—it can't be. Any time spent on operational tasks means time not spent on project work—and project work is how we make our services more reliable and scalable.

Performing operational tasks does, however, by "the wisdom of production," provide vital input into decisions. This work keeps us grounded by providing real-time feedback from a given system. Sources of toil need to be identifiable so you can minimize or eliminate them. However, if you find yourself in a position of operational under-

---

9 A service level objective is a target for performance of a particular metric (e.g., available 99.9% of the time).

load, you may need to push new features and changes more often so that engineers remain familiar with the workings of the service you support.

The Wisdom of Production

A note on "the wisdom of production": by this phrase, we mean the wisdom you get from something running in production—the messy details of how it *actually* behaves, and how software should *actually* be designed, rather than a whiteboarded view of a service isolated from the facts on the ground. All of the pages you get, the tickets the team gets, and so on, are a direct connection with reality that should inform better system design and behavior.

Automate This Year's Job Away

The real work in this area is determining what to automate, under what conditions, and how to automate it.

SRE as practiced in Google has a hard limit of how much time a team member can spend on toil, as opposed to engineering that produces lasting value: 50%. Many people think of this limit as a *cap*. In fact, it's much more useful to think of it as a *guarantee*—an explicit statement, and enabling mechanism, for taking an engineering-based approach to problems rather than just toiling at them over and over.

There is an unintuitive and interesting interaction between this benchmark and how it plays out when we think about automation and toil. Over time, an SRE team winds up automating all that it can for a service, leaving behind things that can't be automated (the Murphy-Beyer effect (*http://bit.ly/2Js7hau*)). Other things being equal, this comes to dominate what an SRE team does unless other actions are taken. In the Google environment, you tend to either add more services, up to some limit that still supports 50% engineering time, or you are so successful at your automation that you can go and do something else completely different instead.

Move Fast by Reducing the Cost of Failure

One of the main benefits of SRE engagement is not necessarily increased reliability, although obviously that does happen; it is actually improved product development output. Why? Well, a reduced mean time to repair (MTTR) for common faults results in increased product developer velocity, as engineers don't have to waste time and focus cleaning up after these issues. This follows from the well-known fact that the later in the product lifecycle a problem is discovered, the more expensive it is to fix (*http://bit.ly/2sqVEXL*). SREs are specifically charged with improving undesirably late problem discovery, yielding benefits for the company as a whole.

Share Ownership with Developers

Rigid boundaries between "application development" and "production" (sometimes called programmers and operators) are counterproductive. This is especially true if the segregation of responsibilities and classification of ops as a cost center leads to power imbalances or discrepancies in esteem or pay.

SREs tend to be inclined to focus on production problems rather than business logic problems, but as their approach brings software engineering tools to bear on the problem, they share skill sets with product development teams. In general, an SRE has particular expertise around the availability, latency, performance, efficiency, change management, monitoring, emergency response, and capacity planning of the service(s) they are looking after. Those specific (and usually well-defined) competencies are the bread-and-butter of what SRE does for a product and for the associated product development team.[10] Ideally, both product development and SRE teams should have a holistic view of the stack—the frontend, backend, libraries, storage, kernels, and physical machine—and no team should jealously own single components. It turns out that you can get a lot more done if you "blur the lines"[11] and have SREs instrument JavaScript, or product developers qualify kernels: knowledge of how to make changes and the authority to do so are much more widespread, and incentives to jealously guard any particular function are removed.

In *Site Reliability Engineering* (*http://bit.ly/2kIcNYM*), we did not make it sufficiently clear that product development teams in Google own their service by default. SRE is neither available nor warranted for the bulk of services, although SRE principles still inform how services are managed throughout Google.[12] The ownership model when an SRE team works with a product development team is ultimately a shared model as well.

Use the Same Tooling, Regardless of Function or Job Title

Tooling is an incredibly important determinant of behavior, and it would be naive to assume that the efficacy of SRE in the Google context has nothing to do with the widely accessible unified codebase (*http://bit.ly/2J4jgMi*), the wide array of software and systems tooling, the highly optimized and proprietary (*http://bit.ly/2J6wkkp*) production stack, and so on. Yet we share this absolute assumption with DevOps:

---

10 Of course, not every team does everything, but those are the most common headings under which SRE works.

11 Perform a layering violation, if you think of this as layered stacks.

12 In fact, there's a Production Readiness Review for onboarding *anything*; SRE won't just onboard services from a standing start.

teams minding a service[13] should use the same tools, regardless of their role in the organization. There is no good way to manage a service that has one tool for the SREs and another for the product developers, behaving differently (and potentially catastrophically so) in different situations. The more divergence you have, the less your company benefits from each effort to improve each individual tool.

Compare and Contrast

Looking at the preceding principles, we immediately see quite a lot of commonality in the points outlined:

- DevOps and SRE are both contingent on an acceptance that change is necessary in order to improve. Without that, there's not much room for maneuvering.[14]

- Collaboration is front and center for DevOps work. An effective shared ownership model and partner team relationships are necessary for SRE to function. Like DevOps, SRE also has strong values shared across the organization, which can make climbing out of team-based silos slightly easier.

- Change management is best pursued as small, continual actions, the majority of which are ideally both automatically tested and applied. The critical interaction between change and reliability makes this especially important for SRE.

- The right tooling is critically important, and tooling to a certain extent determines the scope of your acts. Yet we must not focus too hard on whether something is achieved using some specific set of tools; at the end of the day, API orientation for system management is a more important philosophy that will outlast any particular implementation of it.

- Measurement is absolutely key to how both DevOps and SRE work. For SRE, SLOs are dominant in determining the actions taken to improve the service. Of course, you can't have SLOs without measurement (as well as cross-team debate —ideally among product, infrastructure/SRE, and the business). For DevOps, the act of measurement is often used to understand what the outputs of a process are, what the duration of feedback loops is, and so on. Both DevOps and SRE are data-oriented things, whether they are professions or philosophies.

---

13 A service is loosely defined as software running to perform some business need, generally with availability constraints.

14 Within Google, that question is largely settled, and services change state, configuration, ownership, direction, and so on, all the time. To a certain extent, SRE at Google is the beneficiary of the "change is necessary" argument having been fought and won a number of times in the past. But not completely evenly distributed (*http://bit.ly/2J1qnFf*), as William Gibson might say.

- The brute reality of managing production services means that bad things happen occasionally, and you have to talk about why. SRE and DevOps both practice blameless postmortems (*http://bit.ly/2J2Po2W*) in order to offset unhelpful, adrenaline-laden reactions.

- Ultimately, implementing DevOps *or* SRE is a holistic act; both hope to make the whole of the team (or unit, or organization) better, as a function of working together in a highly specific way. For both DevOps and SRE, better velocity should be the outcome.[15]

As you can see, there are many areas of commonality between DevOps and SRE.

Yet there are significant differences as well. DevOps is in some sense a wider philosophy and culture. Because it effects wider change than does SRE, DevOps is more context-sensitive. DevOps is relatively silent on how to run operations at a detailed level. For example, it is not prescriptive around the precise management of services. It chooses instead to concentrate on breaking down barriers in the wider organization. This has much value.

SRE, on the other hand, has relatively narrowly defined responsibilities and its remit is generally service-oriented (and end-user-oriented) rather than whole-business-oriented. As a result, it brings an opinionated intellectual framework (including concepts like error budgets (*http://bit.ly/2so6uOc*)) to the problem of how to run systems effectively. Although SRE is, as a profession, highly aware of incentives and their effects, it in turn is relatively silent on topics like siloization and information barriers. It would support CI and CD not necessarily because of the business case, but because of the improved operational practices involved. Or, to put it another way, SRE *believes in the same things as DevOps but for slightly different reasons.*

Organizational Context and Fostering Successful Adoption

DevOps and SRE have a very large conceptual overlap in how they operate. As you might expect, they also have a similar set of conditions that have to be true within the organization in order for them to a) be implementable in the first place, and b) obtain the maximum benefit from that implementation. As Tolstoy almost but never quite said (*http://bit.ly/2LPfiog*), effective operations approaches are all alike, whereas broken approaches are all broken in their own way. Incentives can in part explain why that is.

If an organization's culture values the benefits of a DevOps approach and is willing to bear those costs—typically expressed as difficulties in hiring, the energy required to maintain fluidity in teams and responsibilities, and increased financial resources

---

15 See relevant research at *https://devops-research.com/research.html.*

dedicated to compensating a skill set that is necessarily more rare—then that organization must also make sure the *incentives* are correct in order to achieve the full benefit of this approach.

Specifically, the following should hold true in the context of both DevOps and SRE.

Narrow, Rigid Incentives Narrow Your Success

Many companies accidentally define formal incentives that undermine collective performance. To avoid this mistake, don't structure incentives to be narrowly tied to launch-related or reliability-related outcomes. As any economist (*http://bit.ly/ 2J7AZhA*) can tell you, if there *is* a numeric measure, people will find a way to game it to bad effect, sometimes even in a completely well-intentioned way.[16] Instead, you should allow your people the freedom to find the right tradeoffs. As discussed earlier, DevOps or SRE can act as an accelerant for your product team in general, allowing the rest of the software org to ship features to customers in a continuous and reliable fashion. Such a dynamic also fixes one persistent problem with the traditional and divergent systems/software group approach: the lack of a feedback loop between design and production. A system with early SRE engagement (ideally, at design time) typically works better in production after deployment, regardless of who is responsible for managing the service. (Nothing slows down feature development like losing user data.)

It's Better to Fix It Yourself; Don't Blame Someone Else

Furthermore, avoid any incentives to pass off the blame for production incidents or system failures onto other groups. In many ways, the dynamics of passing off blame is the core problem with the traditional model for engineering operations, as separating operations and software teams allows separate incentives to emerge. Instead, consider adopting the following practices to combat blame passing at an organizational level:

- Don't just allow, but actively *encourage*, engineers to change code and configuration when required for the product. Also allow these teams the authority to be radical within the limits of their mission, thereby eliminating incentives to proceed more slowly.
- Support blameless postmortems.[17] Doing so eliminates incentives to downplay or cover up a problem. This step is crucial in fully understanding the product and

---

16 See *http://en.wikipedia.org/wiki/Goodhart%27s_law* and *https://skybrary.aero/bookshelf/books/2336.pdf*.

17 See, for example, *https://codeascraft.com/2012/05/22/blameless-postmortems/*.

actually optimizing its performance and functionality, and relies on the wisdom of production mentioned previously.

Allow support to move away from products that are irredeemably operationally difficult. The threat of support withdrawal motivates product development to fix issues both in the run-up to support and once the product is itself supported, saving everyone time. What it means to be "irredeemably operationally difficult" may differ depending on your context—the dynamic here should be one of mutually understood responsibilities. Pushback to other orgs might be a softer, "We think there are higher-value uses of the time of people with this skill set," or framed within the limit of, "These people will quit if they're tasked with too much operational work and aren't given the opportunity to use their engineering skill set." At Google, the practice of outright withdrawing support from such products has become institutional.

Consider Reliability Work as a Specialized Role

At Google, SRE and product development are separate organizations. Each group has its own focus, priorities, and management, and does not have to do the bidding of the other. However, the product development teams effectively fund the growth of SRE with new hires when a product is successful. In this way, product development has a stake in the success of SRE teams, just as SREs have a stake in the success of the product development teams. SRE is also fortunate to receive high-level support from management, which ensures that engineering teams' objections to supporting services "the SRE way" are generally short-lived. You don't need to have an org chart to do things differently, though—you just need a different community of practice to emerge.

Regardless of whether you fork your organizational chart or use more informal mechanisms, it's important to recognize that specialization creates challenges. Practitioners of DevOps and SRE benefit from having a community of peers for support and career development, and job ladders that reward them[18] for the unique skills and perspectives they bring to the table.

It's important to note that the organizational structure employed by Google, as well as some of the aforementioned incentives, is *somewhat* reliant on a sizeable organization. For example, if your 20-person startup has only one (comparatively small) product, there's not much sense in allowing withdrawal of operational support. It's still possible to take a DevOps-style approach,[19] but the ability to improve an operationally poor product is undermined if literally all you can do is help it grow. Usually,

---

18 In orgs that have well-developed cultures of either. Early-stage companies likely do not have established ways to reward these job roles.

19 Indeed, arguably, that's your *only* choice unless you outsource operations.

though, people have more choice than they imagine about how to fulfill those growth needs versus the rate at which technical debt accumulates.[20]

When Can Substitute for *Whether*

However, when your organization or product grows beyond a certain size, you can exercise more latitude in what products to support, or how to *prioritize* that support. If it's clear that support for system X is going to happen much sooner than support for system Y, the implicit conditionality can play much the same role as the choice to *not* support services in the SRE world.

At Google, SRE's strong partnership with product development has proven to be critically important: if such a relationship exists at your organization, then the decision to withdraw (or supply) support can be based on objective data about comparative operational characteristics, thereby avoiding otherwise nonproductive conversations.

A productive relationship between SRE and product development also helps in avoiding the organizational anti-pattern in which a product development team has to ship a product or feature before it's quite ready. Instead, SRE can work with a development team to improve the product before the burden of maintenance shifts away from the people with the most expertise to fix it.

Strive for Parity of Esteem: Career and Financial

Finally, make sure that the career incentives to do the right thing are in place: we want our DevOps/SRE organization to be held in the same esteem as their product development counterparts. Therefore, members of each team should be rated by roughly the same methods and have the same financial incentives.

Conclusion

In many ways, DevOps and SRE sit, in both practice and philosophy, very close to each other in the overall landscape of IT operations.

Both DevOps and SRE require discussion, management support, and buy-in from the people actually doing the work to make serious progress. Implementing either of them is a journey and not a quick fix: the practice of rename-and-shame[21] is a hollow one, unlikely to yield benefit. Given that it is a more opinionated implementation of how to perform operations, SRE has more concrete suggestions on how to change your work practices earlier on in that journey, albeit requiring specific adaptation.

---

20 For a discussion of how to apply SRE principles in different contexts, see Chapter 20.

21 In other words, simply retitling a group DevOps or SRE with no other change in their organizational positioning, resulting in inevitable shaming of the team when promised improvement is not forthcoming.

DevOps, having a wider focus, is somewhat more difficult to reason about and translate into concrete steps, but precisely because of that wider focus, is likely to meet with weaker initial resistance.

But practitioners of each use many of the same tools, the same approaches to change management, and the same data-based decision-making mindset. At the end of the day, we all face the same persistent problem: production, and making it better—no matter what we're called.

For those interested in further reading, the following suggestions should help you develop a wider understanding of the cultural, business, and technical underpinnings of the operations revolution taking place right now:

- *Site Reliability Engineering (http://bit.ly/2kIcNYM)*
- *Effective DevOps (http://bit.ly/1ST4nI5)*
- *The Phoenix Project (http://oreil.ly/1PfgBX8)*
- *The Practice of Cloud System Administration: DevOps and SRE Practices for Web Services, Volume 2 (https://amzn.to/2GZSY86)*
- *Accelerate: The Science of Lean Software and DevOps (https://amzn.to/2LGQ9fK)*

PART I
Foundations

Every implementation guide needs to start with a common base from which to build. In this case, the basic foundations of SRE include *SLOs, monitoring, alerting, toil reduction, and simplicity*. Getting these basics right will set you up well to succeed on your SRE journey.

The following chapters explore techniques for turning these core principles into concrete practices for your organization.

## CHAPTER 2

Implementing SLOs

By Steven Thurgood and David Ferguson
with Alex Hidalgo and Betsy Beyer

Service level objectives (SLOs) specify a target level for the reliability of your service. Because SLOs are key to making data-driven decisions about reliability, they're at the core of SRE practices. In many ways, this is the most important chapter in this book.

Once you're equipped with a few guidelines, setting up initial SLOs and a process for refining them can be straightforward. Chapter 4 (*http://bit.ly/2szBKsK*) in our first book introduced the topic of SLOs and SLIs (service level indicators), and gave some advice on how to use them.

After discussing the motivation behind SLOs and error budgets, this chapter provides a step-by-step recipe to get you started thinking about SLOs, and also some advice about how to iterate from there. We'll then cover how to use SLOs to make effective business decisions, and explore some advanced topics. Finally, we'll give you some examples of SLOs for different types of services and some pointers on how to create more sophisticated SLOs in specific situations.[1]

Why SREs Need SLOs

Engineers are a scarce resource at even the largest organizations. Engineering time should be invested in the most important characteristics of the most important services. Striking the right balance between investing in functionality that will win new customers or retain current ones, versus investing in the reliability and scalability that

---

[1] A note on terminology: throughout this chapter, we use the word *reliability* to talk about how a service is performing with regard to all of its SLIs. This could be indicative of many things, such as availability or latency.

will keep those customers happy, is difficult. At Google, we've learned that a well-thought-out and adopted SLO is key to making data-informed decisions about the opportunity cost of reliability work, and to determining how to appropriately prioritize that work.

SREs' core responsibilities aren't merely to automate "all the things" and hold the pager. Their day-to-day tasks and projects are driven by SLOs: ensuring that SLOs are defended in the short term and that they can be maintained in the medium to long term. One could even claim that without SLOs, there is no need for SREs.

SLOs are a tool to help determine what engineering work to prioritize. For example, consider the engineering tradeoffs for two reliability projects: automating rollbacks and moving to a replicated data store. By calculating the estimated impact on our error budget, we can determine which project is most beneficial to our users. See the section "Decision Making Using SLOs and Error Budgets" on page 37 for more detail on this, and "Managing Risk" (*http://bit.ly/2xzGm83*) in *Site Reliability Engineering*.

Getting Started

As a starting point for establishing a basic set of SLOs, let's assume that your service is some form of code that has been compiled and released and is running on networked infrastructure that users access via the web. Your system's maturity level might be one of the following:

- A greenfield development, with nothing currently deployed
- A system in production with some monitoring to notify you when things go awry, but no formal objectives, no concept of an error budget, and an unspoken goal of 100% uptime
- A running deployment with an SLO below 100%, but without a common understanding about its importance or how to leverage it to make continuous improvement choices—in other words, an SLO without teeth

In order to adopt an error budget-based approach to Site Reliability Engineering, you need to reach a state where the following hold true:

- There are SLOs that all stakeholders in the organization have approved as being fit for the product.
- The people responsible for ensuring that the service meets its SLO have agreed that it is possible to meet this SLO under normal circumstances.
- The organization has committed to using the error budget for decision making and prioritizing. This commitment is formalized in an error budget policy.
- There is a process in place for refining the SLO.

Otherwise, you won't be able to adopt an error budget–based approach to reliability. SLO compliance will simply be another KPI (key performance indicator) or reporting metric, rather than a decision-making tool.

Reliability Targets and Error Budgets

The first step in formulating appropriate SLOs is to talk about what an SLO should be, and what it should cover.

An SLO sets a target level of reliability for the service's customers. Above this threshold, almost all users should be happy with your service (assuming they are otherwise happy with the utility of the service).[2] Below this threshold, users are likely to start complaining or to stop using the service. Ultimately, user happiness is what matters —happy users use the service, generate revenue for your organization, place low demands on your customer support teams, and recommend the service to their friends. We keep our services reliable to keep our customers happy.

Customer happiness is a rather fuzzy concept; we can't measure it precisely. Often we have very little visibility into it at all, so how do we begin? What do we use for our first SLO?

Our experience has shown that 100% reliability is the wrong target:

- If your SLO is aligned with customer satisfaction, 100% is not a reasonable goal. Even with redundant components, automated health checking, and fast failover, there is a nonzero probability that one or more components will fail simultaneously, resulting in less than 100% availability.

- Even if you could achieve 100% reliability within your system, your customers would not experience 100% reliability. The chain of systems between you and your customers is often long and complex, and any of these components can fail.[3] This also means that as you go from 99% to 99.9% to 99.99% reliability, each extra nine comes at an increased cost, but the marginal utility to your customers steadily approaches zero.

- If you do manage to create an experience that is 100% reliable for your customers, and want to maintain that level of reliability, you can never update or improve your service. The number one source of outages is change: pushing new features, applying security patches, deploying new hardware, and scaling up to

---

2 This is distinct from a *service level agreement* (SLA), which is a business contract that comes into effect when your users are so unhappy you have to compensate them in some fashion.

3 For more details about factoring dependencies into your service's reliability, see Ben Treynor, Mike Dahlin, Vivek Rau, and Betsy Beyer, "The Calculus of Service Availability," *ACM Queue* 15, no. 2 (2017), *https://queue.acm.org/detail.cfm?id=3096459*.

meet customer demand will impact that 100% target. Sooner or later, your service will stagnate and your customers will go elsewhere, which is not great for anyone's bottom line.

- An SLO of 100% means you only have time to be reactive. You literally cannot do anything other than react to < 100% availability, which is guaranteed to happen. Reliability of 100% is not an engineering culture SLO—it's an operations team SLO.

Once you have an SLO target below 100%, it needs to be owned by someone in the organization who is empowered to make tradeoffs between feature velocity and reliability. In a small organization, this may be the CTO; in larger organizations, this is normally the product owner (or product manager).

What to Measure: Using SLIs

Once you agree that 100% is the wrong number, how do you determine the right number? And what are you measuring, anyway? Here, service level indicators come into play: an SLI is an *indicator* of the level of service that you are providing.

While many numbers can function as an SLI, we generally recommend treating the SLI as the ratio of two numbers: the number of good events divided by the total number of events. For example:

- Number of successful HTTP requests / total HTTP requests (success rate)
- Number of gRPC calls that completed successfully in < 100 ms / total gRPC requests
- Number of search results that used the entire corpus / total number of search results, including those that degraded gracefully
- Number of "stock check count" requests from product searches that used stock data fresher than 10 minutes / total number of stock check requests
- Number of "good user minutes" according to some extended list of criteria for that metric / total number of user minutes

SLIs of this form have a couple of particularly useful properties. The SLI ranges from 0% to 100%, where 0% means nothing works, and 100% means nothing is broken. We have found this scale intuitive, and this style lends itself easily to the concept of an error budget: the SLO is a target percentage and the error budget is 100% minus the SLO. For example, if you have a 99.9% success ratio SLO, then a service that receives 3 million requests over a four-week period had a budget of 3,000 (0.1%)

errors over that period. If a single outage is responsible for 1,500 errors, that error costs 50% of the error budget.[4]

In addition, making all of your SLIs follow a consistent style allows you to take better advantage of tooling: you can write alerting logic, SLO analysis tools, error budget calculation, and reports to expect the same inputs: numerator, denominator, and threshold. Simplification is a bonus here.

When attempting to formulate SLIs for the first time, you might find it useful to further divide SLIs into *SLI specification* and *SLI implementation*:

SLI specification
  The assessment of service outcome that you think matters to users, independent of how it is measured.

  For example: Ratio of home page requests that loaded in < 100 ms

SLI implementation
  The SLI specification and a way to measure it.

  For example:

  - Ratio of home page requests that loaded in < 100 ms, as measured from the Latency column of the server log. This measurement will miss requests that fail to reach the backend.
  - Ratio of home page requests that loaded in < 100 ms, as measured by probers that execute JavaScript in a browser running in a virtual machine. This measurement will catch errors when requests cannot reach our network, but may miss issues that affect only a subset of users.
  - Ratio of home page requests that loaded in < 100 ms, as measured by instrumentation in the JavaScript on the home page itself, and reported back to a dedicated telemetry recording service. This measurement will more accurately capture the user experience, although we now need to modify the code to capture this information and build the infrastructure to record it—a specification that has its own reliability requirements.

As you can see, a single SLI specification might have multiple SLI implementations, each with its own set of pros and cons in terms of quality (how accurately they capture the experience of a customer), coverage (how well they capture the experience of all customers), and cost.

---

4 If you measure your SLO over a calendar period, such as a quarter-year, then you may not know how big your budget will be at the end of the quarter if it's based upon unpredictable metrics such as traffic. See "Choosing an Appropriate Time Window" on page 29 for more discussion about reporting periods.

Your first attempt at an SLI and SLO doesn't have to be correct; the most important goal is to get something in place and measured, and to set up a feedback loop so you can improve. (We dive deeper into this topic in "Continuous Improvement of SLO Targets" on page 34.)

In our first book (*http://bit.ly/2kIcNYM*), we advise against picking an SLO based upon current performance, because this can commit you to unnecessarily strict SLOs. While that advice is true, your current performance can be a good place to start if you don't have any other information, and if you have a good process for iterating in place (which we'll cover later). However, don't let current performance limit you as you refine your SLO: your customers will also come to expect your service to perform at its SLO, so if your service returns successful requests 99.999% of the time in less than 10 ms, any significant regression from that baseline may make them unhappy.

To create your first set of SLOs, you need to decide upon a few key SLI specifications that matter to your service. Availability and latency SLOs are pretty common; freshness, durability, correctness, quality, and coverage SLOs also have their place (we'll talk more about those later).

If you are having trouble figuring out what sort of SLIs to start with, it helps to start simple:

- Choose one application for which you want to define SLOs. If your product comprises many applications, you can add those later.
- Decide clearly who the "users" are in this situation. These are the people whose happiness you are optimizing.
- Consider the common ways your users interact with your system—common tasks and critical activities.
- Draw a high-level architecture diagram of your system; show the key components, the request flow, the data flow, and the critical dependencies. Group these components into categories listed in the following section (there may be some overlap and ambiguity; use your intuition and don't let perfect be the enemy of the good).

You should think carefully about exactly what you select as your SLIs, but you also shouldn't overcomplicate things. Especially if you're just starting your SLI journey, pick an aspect of your system that's relevant but easy to measure—you can always iterate and refine later.

Types of components

The easiest way to get started with setting SLIs is to abstract your system into a few common types of components. You can then use our list of suggested SLIs for each component to choose the ones most relevant to your service:

Request-driven

The user creates some type of event and expects a response. For example, this could be an HTTP service where the user interacts with a browser or an API for a mobile application.

Pipeline

A system that takes records as input, mutates them, and places the output somewhere else. This might be a simple process that runs on a single instance in real time, or a multistage batch process that takes many hours. Examples include:

- A system that periodically reads data from a relational database and writes it into a distributed hash table for optimized serving

- A video processing service that converts video from one format to another

- A system that reads in log files from many sources to generate reports

- A monitoring system that pulls metrics from remote servers and generates time series and alerts

Storage

A system that accepts data (e.g., bytes, records, files, videos) and makes it available to be retrieved at a later date.

A Worked Example

Consider a simplified architecture for a mobile phone game, shown in Figure 2-1.

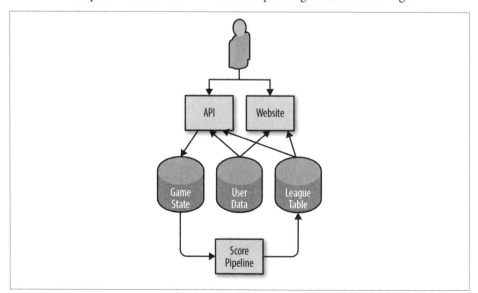

Figure 2-1. Architecture for an example mobile phone game

The app running on the user's phone interacts with an HTTP API running in the cloud. The API writes state changes to a permanent storage system. A pipeline periodically runs over this data to generate league tables that provide high scores for today, this week, and all time. This data is written to a separate league table data store, and the results are available via the mobile app (for in-game scores) and a website. Users can upload custom avatars, which are used both in-game via the API and in the high score website, to the User Data table.

Given this setup, we can start thinking about how users interact with the system, and what sort of SLIs would measure the various aspects of a user's experience.

Some of these SLIs may overlap: a request-driven service may have a correctness SLI, a pipeline may have an availability SLI, and durability SLIs might be viewed as a variant on correctness SLIs. We recommend choosing a small number (five or fewer) of SLI types that represent the most critical functionality to your customers.

In order to capture both the typical user experience and the long tail, we also recommend using multiple grades of SLOs for some types of SLIs. For example, if 90% of users' requests return within 100 ms, but the remaining 10% take 10 seconds, many users will be unhappy. A latency SLO can capture this user base by setting multiple thresholds: 90% of requests are faster than 100 ms, and 99% of requests are faster than 400 ms. This principle applies to all SLIs with parameters that measure user unhappiness.

Table 2-1 provides some common SLIs for different types of services.

Table 2-1. Potential SLIs for different types of components

Type of service	Type of SLI	Description
Request-driven	Availability	The proportion of requests that resulted in a successful response.
Request-driven	Latency	The proportion of requests that were faster than some threshold.
Request-driven	Quality	If the service degrades gracefully when overloaded or when backends are unavailable, you need to measure the proportion of responses that were served in an undegraded state. For example, if the User Data store is unavailable, the game is still playable but uses generic imagery.
Pipeline	Freshness	The proportion of the data that was updated more recently than some time threshold. Ideally this metric counts how many times a user accessed the data, so that it most accurately reflects the user experience.
Pipeline	Correctness	The proportion of records coming into the pipeline that resulted in the correct value coming out.
Pipeline	Coverage	For batch processing, the proportion of jobs that processed above some target amount of data. For streaming processing, the proportion of incoming records that were successfully processed within some time window.

Type of service	Type of SLI	Description
Storage	Durability	The proportion of records written that can be successfully read. Take particular care with durability SLIs: the data that the user wants may be only a small portion of the data that is stored. For example, if you have 1 billion records for the previous 10 years, but the user wants only the records from today (which are unavailable), then they will be unhappy even though almost all of their data is readable.

Moving from SLI Specification to SLI Implementation

Now that we know our SLI specifications, we need to start thinking about how to implement them.

For your first SLIs, choose something that requires a minimum of engineering work. If your web server logs are already available, but setting up probes would take weeks and instrumenting your JavaScript would take months, use the logs.

You need enough information to measure the SLI: for availability, you need the success/failure status; for slow requests, you need the time taken to serve the request. You may need to reconfigure your web server to record this information. If you're using a cloud-based service, some of this information may already be available in a monitoring dashboard.

There are various options for SLI implementations for our example architecture, each with its own pros and cons. The following sections detail SLIs for the three types of components in our system.

API and HTTP server availability and latency

For all of the considered SLI implementations, we base the response success on the HTTP status code. 5XX responses count against SLO, while all other requests are considered successful. Our availability SLI is the proportion of successful requests, and our latency SLIs are the proportion of requests that are faster than defined thresholds.

Your SLIs should be specific and measurable. To summarize the list of potential candidates provided in "What to Measure: Using SLIs" on page 20, your SLIs can use one or more of the following sources:

- Application server logs
- Load balancer monitoring
- Black-box monitoring
- Client-side instrumentation

Our example uses the load balancer monitoring, as the metrics are already available and provide SLIs that are closer to the user's experience than those from the application server's logs.

Pipeline freshness, coverage, and correctness

When our pipeline updates the league table, it records a watermark containing the timestamp of when the data was updated. Some example SLI implementations:

- Run a periodic query across the league table, counting the total number of fresh records and the total number of records. This will treat each stale record as equally important, regardless of how many users saw the data.
- Make all clients of the league table check the watermark when they request fresh data and increment a metric counter saying that data was requested. Increment another counter if the data was fresher than a predefined threshold.

From these two options, our example uses the client-side implementation, as it gives SLIs that are much more closely correlated with user experience and are straightforward to add.

To calculate our coverage SLI, our pipeline exports the number of records that it should have processed and the number of records that it successfully processed. This metric may miss records that our pipeline did not know about due to misconfiguration.

We have a couple potential approaches to measure correctness:

- Inject data with known outputs into the system, and count the proportion of times that the output matches our expectations.
- Use a method to calculate correct output based on input that is distinct from our pipeline itself (and likely more expensive, and therefore not suitable for our pipeline). Use this to sample input/output pairs, and count the proportion of correct output records. This methodology assumes that creating such a system is both possible and practical.

Our example bases its correctness SLI on some manually curated data in the game state database, with known good outputs that are tested every time the pipeline runs. Our SLI is the proportion of correct entries for our test data. In order for this SLI to be representative of the actual user experience, we need to make sure that our manually curated data is representative of real-world data.

Measuring the SLIs

Figure 2-2 shows how our white-box monitoring system collects metrics from the various components of the example application.

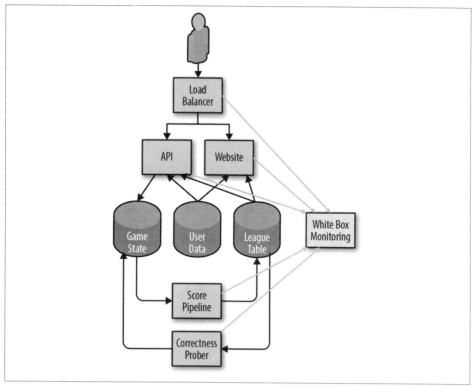

Figure 2-2. How our monitoring system collects SLI metrics

Let's walk through an example of using metrics from our monitoring system to calculate our starter SLOs. While our example uses availability and latency metrics, the same principles apply to all other potential SLOs. For a full list of the metrics that our system uses, see Appendix A. All of our examples use Prometheus notation (*https:// prometheus.io/*).

Load balancer metrics

Total requests by backend (`"api"` or `"web"`) and response code:

```
http_requests_total{host="api", status="500"}
```

Total latency, as a cumulative histogram; each bucket counts the number of requests that took less than or equal to that time:

```
http_request_duration_seconds{host="api", le="0.1"}
http_request_duration_seconds{host="api", le="0.2"}
http_request_duration_seconds{host="api", le="0.4"}
```

Generally speaking, it is better to count the slow requests than to approximate them with a histogram. But, because that information isn't available, we use the histogram provided by our monitoring system. Another approach would be to base explicit slow request counts on the various slowness thresholds in the load balancer's configuration (e.g., for thresholds of 100 ms and 500 ms). This strategy would provide more accurate numbers but require more configuration, which makes changing the thresholds retroactively harder.

```
http_request_duration_seconds{host="api", le="0.1"}
http_request_duration_seconds{host="api", le="0.5"}
```

Calculating the SLIs

Using the preceding metrics, we can calculate our current SLIs over the previous seven days, as shown in Table 2-2.

Table 2-2. Calculations for SLIs over the previous seven days

Availability	`sum(rate(http_requests_total{host="api", status!~"5.."}[7d]))` `/` `sum(rate(http_requests_total{host="api"}[7d])`
Latency	`histogram_quantile(0.9, rate(http_request_duration_seconds_bucket[7d]))` `histogram_quantile(0.99, rate(http_request_duration_seconds_bucket[7d]))`

Using the SLIs to Calculate Starter SLOs

We can round down these SLIs to manageable numbers (e.g., two significant figures of availability, or up to 50 ms[5] of latency) to obtain our starting SLOs.

For example, over four weeks, the API metrics show:

- Total requests: 3,663,253
- Total successful requests: 3,557,865 (97.123%)
- 90th percentile latency: 432 ms
- 99th percentile latency: 891 ms

We repeat this process for the other SLIs, and create a proposed SLO for the API, shown in Table 2-3.

---

5 50 ms because users are unlikely to perceive a 50 ms change in latency, but the appropriate window obviously depends on the service and the users. A reporting service will be different from a real-time game.

Table 2-3. Proposed SLOs for the API

SLO type	Objective
Availability	97%
Latency	90% of requests < 450 ms
Latency	99% of requests < 900 ms

Appendix A provides a full example of an SLO document. This document includes SLI implementations, which we omitted here for brevity.

Based upon this proposed SLI, we can calculate our error budget over those four weeks, as shown in Table 2-4.

Table 2-4. Error budget over four weeks

SLO	Allowed failures
97% availability	109,897
90% of requests faster than 450 ms	366,325
99% of requests faster than 900 ms	36,632

Choosing an Appropriate Time Window

SLOs can be defined over various time intervals, and can use either a rolling window or a calendar-aligned window (e.g., a month). There are several factors you need to account for when choosing the window.

Rolling windows are more closely aligned with user experience: if you have a large outage on the final day of a month, your user doesn't suddenly forget about it on the first day of the following month. We recommend defining this period as an integral number of weeks so it always contains the same number of weekends. For example, if you use a 30-day window, some periods might include four weekends while others include five weekends. If weekend traffic differs significantly from weekday traffic, your SLIs may vary for uninteresting reasons.

Calendar windows are more closely aligned with business planning and project work. For example, you might evaluate your SLOs every quarter to determine where to focus the next quarter's project headcount. Calendar windows also introduce some element of uncertainty: in the middle of the quarter, it is impossible to know how many requests you will receive for the rest of the quarter. Therefore, decisions made mid-quarter must speculate as to how much error budget you'll spend in the remainder of the quarter.

Shorter time windows allow you to make decisions more quickly: if you missed your SLO for the previous week, then small course corrections—prioritizing relevant bugs, for example—can help avoid SLO violations in future weeks.

Longer time periods are better for more strategic decisions: for example, if you could choose only one of three large projects, would you be better off moving to a high-availability distributed database, automating your rollout and rollback procedure, or deploying a duplicate stack in another zone? You need more than a week's worth of data to evaluate large multiquarter projects; the amount of data required is roughly commensurate with the amount of engineering work being proposed to fix it.

We have found a four-week rolling window to be a good general-purpose interval. We complement this time frame with weekly summaries for task prioritization and quarterly summarized reports for project planning.

If the data source allows, you can then use this proposed SLO to calculate your actual SLO performance over that interval: if you set your initial SLO based on actual measurements, by design, you met your SLO. But we can also gather interesting information about the distribution. Were there any days during the past four weeks when our service did not meet its SLO? Do these days correlate with actual incidents? Was there (or should there have been) some action taken on those days in response to incidents?

If you do not have logs, metrics, or any other source of historical performance, you need to configure a data source. For example, as a low-fidelity solution for HTTP services, you can set up a remote monitoring service that performs some kind of periodic health check on the service (a ping or an HTTP GET) and reports back the number of successful requests. A number of online services can easily implement this solution.

Getting Stakeholder Agreement

In order for a proposed SLO to be useful and effective, you will need to get all stakeholders to agree to it:

- The product managers have to agree that this threshold is good enough for users —performance below this value is unacceptably low and worth spending engineering time to fix.

- The product developers need to agree that if the error budget has been exhausted, they will take some steps to reduce risk to users until the service is back in budget (as discussed in "Establishing an Error Budget Policy" on page 31).

- The team responsible for the production environment who are tasked with defending this SLO have agreed that it is defensible without Herculean effort, excessive toil, and burnout—all of which are damaging to the long-term health of the team and service.

Once all of these points are agreed upon, the hard part is done.[6] You have started your SLO journey, and the remaining steps entail iterating from this starting point.

To defend your SLO you will need to set up monitoring and alerting (see Chapter 5) so that engineers receive timely notifications of threats to the error budget before those threats become deficits.

Establishing an Error Budget Policy

Once you have an SLO, you can use the SLO to derive an error budget. In order to use this error budget, you need a policy outlining what to do when your service runs out of budget.

Getting the error budget policy approved by all key stakeholders—the product manager, the development team, and the SREs—is a good test for whether the SLOs are fit for purpose:

- If the SREs feel that the SLO is not defensible without undue amounts of toil, they can make a case for relaxing some of the objectives.
- If the development team and product manager feel that the increased resources they'll have to devote to fixing reliability will cause feature release velocity to fall below acceptable levels, then they can also argue for relaxing objectives. Remember that lowering the SLOs also lowers the number of situations to which the SREs will respond; the product manager needs to understand this tradeoff.
- If the product manager feels that the SLO will result in a bad experience for a significant number of users before the error budget policy prompts anyone to address an issue, the SLOs are likely not tight enough.

If all three parties do not agree to enforce the error budget policy, you need to iterate on the SLIs and SLOs until all stakeholders are happy. Decide how to move forward and what you need to make the decision: more data, more resources, or a change to the SLI or SLO?

When we talk about enforcing an error budget, we mean that once you exhaust your error budget (or come close to exhausting it), you should do something in order to restore stability to your system.

To make error budget enforcement decisions, you need to start with a written policy. This policy should cover the specific actions that must be taken when a service has consumed its entire error budget for a given period of time, and specify who will take them. Common owners and actions might include:

---

6 Disclaimer: there may be more difficult tasks in your future.

- The development team gives top priority to bugs relating to reliability issues over the past four weeks.

- The development team focuses exclusively on reliability issues until the system is within SLO. This responsibility comes with high-level approval to push back on external feature requests and mandates.

- To reduce the risk of more outages, a production freeze halts certain changes to the system until there is sufficient error budget to resume changes.

Sometimes a service consumes the entirety of its error budget, but not all stakeholders agree that enacting the error budget policy is appropriate. If this happens, you need to return to the error budget policy approval stage.

Documenting the SLO and Error Budget Policy

An appropriately defined SLO should be documented in a prominent location where other teams and stakeholders can review it. This documentation should include the following information:

- The authors of the SLO, the reviewers (who checked it for technical accuracy), and the approvers (who made the business decision about whether it is the right SLO).

- The date on which it was approved, and the date when it should next be reviewed.

- A brief description of the service to give the reader context.

- The details of the SLO: the objectives and the SLI implementations.

- The details of how the error budget is calculated and consumed.

- The rationale behind the numbers, and whether they were derived from experimental or observational data. Even if the SLOs are totally ad hoc, this fact should be documented so that future engineers reading the document don't make bad decisions based upon ad hoc data.

How often you review an SLO document depends on the maturity of your SLO culture. When starting out, you should probably review the SLO frequently—perhaps every month. Once the appropriateness of the SLO becomes more established, you can likely reduce reviews to happen quarterly or even less frequently.

The error budget policy should also be documented, and should include the following information:

- The policy authors, reviewers, and approvers

- The date on which it was approved, and the date when it should next be reviewed

- A brief description of the service to give the reader context
- The actions to be taken in response to budget exhaustion
- A clear escalation path to follow if there is disagreement on the calculation or whether the agreed-upon actions are appropriate in the circumstances
- Depending upon the audience's level of error budget experience and expertise, it may be beneficial to include an overview of error budgets.

See Appendix A for an example of an SLO document and an error budget policy.

Dashboards and Reports

In addition to the published SLO and error budget policy documents, it is useful to have reports and dashboards that provide in-time snapshots of the SLO compliance of your services, for communicating with other teams and for spotting problematic areas.

The report in Figure 2-3 shows the overall compliance of several services: whether they met all of their quarterly SLOs for the previous year (the numbers in parentheses indicate the number of objectives that were met, and the total number of objectives), and whether their SLIs were trending upward or downward in relation to the previous quarter and the same quarter last year.

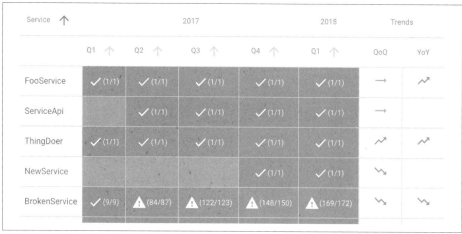

Service ↑	2017				2018	Trends	
	Q1 ↑	Q2 ↑	Q3 ↑	Q4 ↑	Q1 ↑	QoQ	YoY
FooService	✓ (1/1)	✓ (1/1)	✓ (1/1)	✓ (1/1)	✓ (1/1)	→	↗
ServiceApi		✓ (1/1)	✓ (1/1)	✓ (1/1)	✓ (1/1)	→	
ThingDoer	✓ (1/1)	✓ (1/1)	✓ (1/1)	✓ (1/1)	✓ (1/1)	↗	↗
NewService				✓ (1/1)	✓ (1/1)	↘	
BrokenService	✓ (9/9)	⚠ (84/87)	⚠ (122/123)	⚠ (148/150)	⚠ (169/172)	↘	↘

Figure 2-3. SLO compliance report

It is also useful to have dashboards showing SLI trends. These dashboards indicate if you are consuming budget at a higher-than-usual rate, or if there are patterns or trends you need to be aware of.

The dashboard in Figure 2-4 shows the error budget for a single quarter, midway through that quarter. Here we see that a single event consumed around 15% of the error budget over the course of two days.

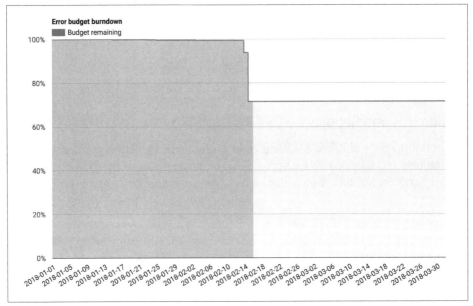

Figure 2-4. Error budget dashboard

Error budgets can be useful for quantifying these events—for example, "this outage consumed 30% of my quarterly error budget," or "these are the top three incidents this quarter, ordered by how much error budget they consumed."

Continuous Improvement of SLO Targets

Every service can benefit from continuous improvement. This is one of the central service goals in ITIL (*https://en.wikipedia.org/wiki/ITIL*), for example.

Before you can improve your SLO targets, you need a source of information about user satisfaction with your service. There are a huge range of options:

- You can count outages that were discovered manually, posts on public forums, support tickets, and calls to customer service.
- You can attempt to measure user sentiment on social media.
- You can add code to your system to periodically sample user happiness.
- You can conduct face-to-face user surveys and samples.

The possibilities are endless, and the optimal method depends on your service. We recommend starting with a measurement that's cheap to collect and iterating from that starting point. Asking your product manager to include reliability into their existing discussions with customers about pricing and functionality is an excellent place to start.

Improving the Quality of Your SLO

Count your manually detected outages. If you have support tickets, count those too. Look at periods when you had a known outage or incident. Check that these periods correlate with steep drops in error budget. Likewise, look at times when your SLIs indicate an issue, or your service fell out of SLO. Do these time periods correlate with known outages or an increase in support tickets? If you are familiar with statistical analysis, Spearman's rank correlation coefficient (*http://bit.ly/1RhdJzE*) can be a useful way to quantify this relationship.

Figure 2-5 shows a graph of the number of support tickets raised per day versus the measured loss in our error budget on that day. While not all tickets are related to reliability issues, there is a correlation between tickets and error budget loss. We see two outliers: one day with only 5 tickets, where we lost 10% of our error budget, and one day with 40 tickets, on which we lost no error budget. Both warrant closer investigation.

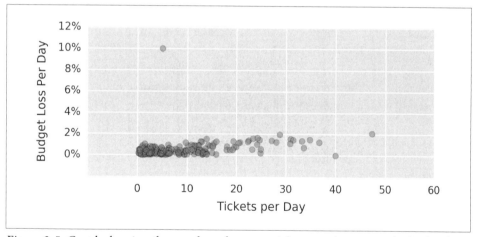

Figure 2-5. Graph showing the number of support tickets per day versus the budget loss on that day

If some of your outages and ticket spikes are not captured in any SLI or SLO, or if you have SLI dips and SLO misses that don't map to user-facing issues, this is a strong sign that your SLO lacks coverage. This situation is totally normal and should be expected. Your SLIs and SLOs should change over time as realities about the service they represent change. Don't be afraid to examine and refine them over time!

There are several courses of action you can take if your SLO lacks coverage:

Change your SLO
> If your SLIs indicated a problem, but your SLOs didn't prompt anyone to notice or respond, you may need to tighten your SLO.

> - If the incident on that date was large enough that it needs to be addressed, look at the SLI values during the periods of interest. Calculate what SLO would have resulted in a notification on those dates. Apply that SLO to your historic SLIs, and see what other events this adjustment would have captured. It's pointless to improve the recall of your system if you lower the precision such that the team must constantly respond to unimportant events.[7]

> - Likewise, for false-positive days, consider relaxing the SLO.

> If changing the SLO in either direction results in too many false positives or false negatives, then you also need to improve the SLI implementation.

Change your SLI implementation
> There are two ways to change your SLI implementation: either move the measurement closer to the user to improve the quality of the metric, or improve coverage so you capture a higher percentage of user interactions. For example:

> - Instead of measuring success/latency at the server, measure it at the load balancer or on the client.

> - Instead of measuring availability with a simple HTTP GET request, use a health-checking handler that exercises more functionality of the system, or a test that executes all of the client-side JavaScript.

Institute an aspirational SLO
> Sometimes you determine that you need a tighter SLO to make your users happy, but improving your product to meet that SLO will take some time. If you implement the tighter SLO, you'll be permanently out of SLO and subject to your error budget policy. In this situation, you can make the refined SLO an *aspirational SLO*—measured and tracked alongside your current SLO, but explicitly called out in your error budget policy as not requiring action. This way you can track your progress toward meeting the aspirational SLO, but you won't be in a perpetual state of emergency.

---

7 *Recall* is the proportion of significantly user-impacting events that the SLI captures. *Precision* is the proportion of events captured by the SLI that were significantly user-impacting.

Iterate

There are many different ways to iterate, and your review sessions will identify many potential improvements. Pick the option that's most likely to give the highest return on investment. Especially during the first few iterations, err on the side of quicker and cheaper; doing so reduces the uncertainty in your metrics and helps you determine if you need more expensive metrics. Iterate as many times as you need to.

Decision Making Using SLOs and Error Budgets

Once you have SLOs, you can start using them for decision making.

The obvious decisions start from what to do when you're not meeting your SLO—that is, when you've exhausted your error budget. As already discussed, the appropriate course of action when you exhaust your error budget should be covered by the error budget policy. Common policies include stopping feature launches until the service is once again within SLO or devoting some or all engineering time to working on reliability-related bugs.

In extreme circumstances, a team can declare an emergency with high-level approval to deprioritize all external demands (requests from other teams, for example) until the service meets exit criteria—typically that the service is within SLO and that you've taken steps to decrease the chances of a subsequent SLO miss. These steps may include improving monitoring, improving testing, removing dangerous dependencies, or rearchitecting the system to remove known failure types.

You can determine the scale of the incident according to the proportion of the error budget it consumed, and use this data to identify the most critical incidents that merit closer investigation.

For example, imagine a release of a new API version causes 100% `NullPointerExcep` `tions` until the system can be reverted four hours later.[8] Inspecting the raw server logs indicates that the issue caused 14,066 errors. Using the numbers from our 97% SLO earlier, and our budget of 109,897 errors, this single event used 13% of our error budget.

Or perhaps the server on which our singly homed state database is stored fails, and restoring from backups takes 20 hours. We estimate (based upon historical traffic over that period) that this outage caused us 72,000 errors, or 65% of our error budget.

---

8 It is worth reiterating here that an error budget is an approximation of user satisfaction. A four-hour outage every 30 days would probably result in fewer unhappy users than four separate one-hour outages every 30 days, which in turn would cause fewer unhappy users than a constant error rate of 0.5%, but our error budget treats them the same. These thresholds will vary between services.

Imagine that our example company had only one server failure in five years, but typically experiences two or three bad releases that require rollbacks per year. We can estimate that, on average, bad pushes cost twice as much error budget as database failures. The numbers prove that addressing the release problem provides much more benefit than investing resources in investigating the server failure.

If the service is running flawlessly and needs little oversight, then it may be time to move the service to a less hands-on tier of support. You might continue to provide incident response management and high-level oversight, but you no longer need to be as closely involved with the product on a day-to-day basis. Therefore, you can focus your efforts on other systems that need more SRE support.

Table 2-5 provides suggested courses of action based on three key dimensions:

- Performance against SLO
- The amount of toil required to operate the service
- The level of customer satisfaction with the service

Table 2-5. SLO decision matrix

SLOs	Toil	Customer satisfaction	Action
Met	Low	High	Choose to (a) relax release and deployment processes and increase velocity, or (b) step back from the engagement and focus engineering time on services that need more reliability.
Met	Low	Low	Tighten SLO.
Met	High	High	If alerting is generating false positives, reduce sensitivity. Otherwise, temporarily loosen the SLOs (or offload toil) and fix product and/or improve automated fault mitigation.
Met	High	Low	Tighten SLO.
Missed	Low	High	Loosen SLO.
Missed	Low	Low	Increase alerting sensitivity.
Missed	High	High	Loosen SLO.
Missed	High	Low	Offload toil and fix product and/or improve automated fault mitigation.

Advanced Topics

Once you have a healthy and mature SLO and error budget culture, you can continue to improve and refine how you measure and discuss the reliability of your services.

Modeling User Journeys

While all of the techniques discussed in this chapter will be beneficial to your organization, ultimately SLOs should center on improving the customer experience. Therefore, you should write SLOs in terms of user-centric actions.

You can use *critical user journeys* to help capture the experience of your customers. A critical user journey is a sequence of tasks that is a core part of a given user's experience and an essential aspect of the service. For example, for an online shopping experience, critical user journeys might include:

- Searching for a product
- Adding a product to a shopping cart
- Completing a purchase

These tasks will almost certainly not map well to your existing SLIs; each task requires multiple complex steps that can fail at any point, and inferring the success (or failure) of these actions from logs can be extremely difficult. (For example, how do you determine if the user failed at the third step, or if they simply got distracted by cat videos in another tab?) However, we need to identify what matters to the user before we can start making sure that aspect of the service is reliable.

Once you identify user-centric events, you can solve the problem of measuring them. You might measure them by joining distinct log events together, using advanced JavaScript probing, using client-side instrumentation, or using some other process. Once you can measure an event, it becomes just another SLI, which you can track alongside your existing SLIs and SLOs. Critical user journeys can improve your recall without affecting your precision.

Grading Interaction Importance

Not all requests are considered equal. The HTTP request from a mobile app that checks for account notifications (where notifications are generated by a daily pipeline) is important to your user, but is not as important as a billing-related request by your advertiser.

We need a way to distinguish certain classes of requests from others. You can use *bucketing* to accomplish this—that is, adding more labels to your SLIs, and then applying different SLOs to those different labels. Table 2-6 shows an example.

Table 2-6. Bucketing by tier

Customer tier	Availability SLO
Premium	99.99%
Free	99.9%

You can split requests by expected responsiveness, as shown in Table 2-7.

Table 2-7. Bucketing by expected responsiveness

Responsiveness	Latency SLO
Interactive (i.e., requests that block page load)	90% of requests complete in 100 ms
CSV download	90% of downloads start within 5 s

If you have the data available to apply your SLO to each customer independently, you can track the number of customers who are in SLO at any given time. Note that this number can be highly variable—customers who send a very low number of requests will have either 100% availability (because they were lucky enough to experience no failures) or very low availability (because the one failure they experienced was a significant percentage of their requests). Individual customers can fail to meet their SLO for uninteresting reasons, but in aggregate, tracking problems that affect a wide number of customers' SLO compliance can be a useful signal.

Modeling Dependencies

Large systems have many components. A single system may have a presentation layer, an application layer, a business logic layer, and a data persistence layer. Each of these layers may consist of many services or microservices.

While your prime concern is implementing a user-centric SLO that covers the entire stack, SLOs can also be a useful way to coordinate and implement reliability requirements between different components in the stack.

For example, if a single component is a critical dependency[9] for a particularly high-value interaction, its reliability guarantee should be at least as high as the reliability guarantee of the dependent action. The team that runs that particular component needs to own and manage its service's SLO in the same way as the overarching product SLO.

If a particular component has inherent reliability limitations, the SLO can communicate that limitation. If the user journey that depends upon it needs a higher level of availability than that component can reasonably provide, you need to engineer around that condition. You can either use a different component or add sufficient defenses (caching, offline store-and-forward processing, graceful degradation, etc.) to handle failures in that component.

It can be tempting to try to math your way out of these problems. If you have a service that offers 99.9% availability in a single zone, and you need 99.95% availability,

---

9 A dependency is critical if its unavailability means that your service is also unavailable.

simply deploying the service in two zones should solve that requirement. The probability that both services will experience an outage at the same time is so low that two zones should provide 99.9999% availability. However, this reasoning assumes that both services are wholly independent, which is almost never the case. The two instances of your app will have common dependencies, common failure domains, shared fate, and global control planes—all of which can cause an outage in both systems, no matter how carefully it is designed and managed. Unless each of these dependencies and failure patterns is carefully enumerated and accounted for, any such calculations will be deceptive.

There are two schools of thought regarding how an error budget policy should address a missed SLO when the failure is caused by a dependency that's handled by another team:

- Your team should not halt releases or devote more time to reliability, as your system didn't cause the issue.

- You should enact a change freeze in order to minimize the chances of future outages, regardless of the cause of that outage.

The second approach will make your users happier. You have some flexibility in how you apply this principle. Depending on the nature of the outage and dependency, freezing changes may not be practical. Decide what is most appropriate for your service and its dependencies, and record that decision for posterity in your documented error budget. For an example of how this might work in practice, see the example error budget policy in Appendix B.

Experimenting with Relaxing Your SLOs

You may want to experiment with the reliability of your application and measure which changes in reliability (e.g., adding latency into page load times) have a measurably adverse impact on user behavior (e.g., percentage of users completing a purchase). We recommend performing this sort of analysis only if you are confident that you have error budget to burn. There are many subtle interactions between latency, availability, customers, business domains, and competition (or lack thereof). To make a choice to deliberately lower the perceived customer experience is a Rubicon to be crossed extremely thoughtfully, if at all.

While this exercise might seem scary (nobody wants to lose sales!), the knowledge you can gain by performing such experiments will allow you to improve your service in ways that could lead to even better performance (and higher sales!) in the future. This process may allow you to mathematically identify a relationship between a key business metric (e.g., sales) and a measurable technical metric (e.g., latency). If it does, you have gained a very valuable piece of data you can use to make important engineering decisions for your service going forward.

This exercise should not be a one-time activity. As your service evolves, so will your customers' expectations. Make sure you regularly review the ongoing validity of the relationship.

This sort of analysis is also risky because you can misinterpret the data you get. For example, if you artificially slow your pages down by 50 ms and notice that no corresponding loss in conversions occurs, you might conclude that your latency SLO is too strict. However, your users might be unhappy, but simply lacking an alternative to your service at the moment. As soon as a competitor comes along, your users will leave. Be sure you are measuring the correct indicators, and take appropriate precautions.

Conclusion

Every topic covered in this book can be tied back to SLOs. Now that you've read this chapter, we hope you'll agree that even partly formalized SLOs (which clearly state your promises to users) offer a framework to discuss system behavior with greater clarity, and can help with pinpointing actionable remedies when services fail to meet expectations.

To summarize:

- SLOs are the tool by which you measure your service's reliability.
- Error budgets are a tool for balancing reliability with other engineering work, and a great way to decide which projects will have the most impact.
- You should start using SLOs and error budgets today.

For an example SLO document and an example error budget policy, see Appendixes A and B.

## CHAPTER 3

SLO Engineering Case Studies

By Ben McCormack (Evernote) and
William Bonnell (The Home Depot)
with Garrett Plasky (Evernote), Alex Hidalgo,
Betsy Beyer, and Dave Rensin

While many tenets of SRE were shaped within the walls of Google, its principles have long lived outside our gates. Many standard Google SRE practices have been discovered in parallel or otherwise been adopted by many other organizations across the industry.

SLOs are fundamental to the SRE model. Since we launched the Customer Reliability Engineering (CRE) team—a group of experienced SREs who help Google Cloud Platform (GCP) customers build more reliable services—almost every customer interaction starts and ends with SLOs.

Here we present two stories, told by two very different companies, that outline their journeys toward adopting an SLO and error budget–based approach while working with the Google CRE team. For a more general discussion about SLOs and error budgets, see Chapter 2 in this book, and Chapter 3 (*http://bit.ly/2so6uOc*) in our first book.

Evernote's SLO Story

by Ben McCormack, Evernote

Evernote is a cross-platform app that helps individuals and teams create, assemble, and share information. With more than 220 million users worldwide, we store over 12 billion pieces of information—a mix of text-based notes, files, and attachments/ images—within the platform. Behind the scenes, the Evernote service is supported by 750+ MySQL instances.

We introduced the concept of SLOs to Evernote as part of a much wider technology revamp aimed at increasing engineering velocity while maintaining quality of service. Our goals included:

- Move engineering focus away from undifferentiated heavy lifting in datacenters and toward product engineering work that customers actually cared about. To that end, we stopped running our physical datacenters and moved to a public cloud.

- Revise the working model of operations and software engineers to support an increase in feature velocity while maintaining overall quality of service.

- Revamp how we look at SLAs to ensure that we increase focus on how failures impact our large global customer base.

These goals may look familiar to organizations across many industries. While no single approach to making these types of changes will work across the board, we hope that sharing our experience will provide valuable insights for others facing similar challenges.

Why Did Evernote Adopt the SRE Model?

At the outset of this transition, Evernote was characterized by a traditional ops/dev split: an operations team protected the sanctity of the production environment, while a development team was tasked with developing new product features for customers. These objectives were usually in conflict: the dev team felt constrained by lengthy operational requirements, while the ops team became frustrated when new code introduced new issues in production. As we swung wildly between these two goals, the ops and dev teams developed a frustrated and strained relationship. We wanted to reach a happier medium that better balanced the varying needs of the teams involved.

We attempted to address the gaps in this traditional dichotomy in various ways over the course of five-plus years. After trying out a "You wrote it, you run it" (development) model, and a "You wrote it, we run it for you" (operations) model, we moved toward an SLO-centric SRE approach.

So what motivated Evernote to move in this direction?

At Evernote, we view the core disciplines of operations and development as separate professional tracks in which engineers can specialize. One track is concerned with the nearly 24/7 ongoing delivery of a service to customers. The other is concerned with the extension and evolution of that service to meet customer needs in the future. These two disciplines have moved toward each other in recent years as movements like SRE and DevOps emphasize software development as applied to operations. (This convergence has been furthered by advances in datacenter automation and the growth of public clouds, both of which give us a datacenter that can be fully controlled by software.) On the other side of the spectrum, full-stack ownership and continuous deployment are increasingly applied to software development.

We were drawn to the SRE model because it fully embraces and accepts the differences between operations and development while encouraging teams to work toward a common goal. It does not try to transform operations engineers into application developers, or vice versa. Instead, it gives both a common frame of reference. In our experience, an error budget/SLO approach has led both teams to make similar decisions when presented with the same facts, as it removes a good deal of subjectivity from the conversation.

Introduction of SLOs: A Journey in Progress

The first part of our journey was the move from physical datacenters to Google Cloud Platform.[1] Once the Evernote service was up and running on GCP and stabilized, we introduced SLOs. Our objectives here were twofold:

- Align teams internally around Evernote SLOs, ensuring that all teams were working within the new framework.
- Incorporate Evernote's SLO into how we work with the Google Cloud team, who now had responsibility for our underlying infrastructure. Since we now had a new partner within the overall model, we needed to ensure the move to GCP did not dilute or mask our commitment to our users.

After actively using SLOs for about nine months, Evernote is already on version 3 of its SLO practice!

Before getting into the technical details of an SLO, it is important to start the conversation from your customers' point of view: what promises are you trying to uphold? Similar to most services, Evernote has many features and options that our users put to use in a variety of creative ways. We wanted to ensure we initially focused on the most important and common customer need: *the availability of the Evernote service for users to access and sync their content across multiple clients.* Our SLO journey started from that goal. We kept our first pass simple by focusing on uptime. Using this simple first approach, we could clearly articulate what we were measuring, and how.

---

1 But that's a story for another book—see more details at *http://bit.ly/2spqgcl.*

Our first SLOs document contained the following:

A definition of the SLOs

This was an uptime measure: 99.95% uptime measured over a monthly window, set for certain services and methods. We chose this number based upon discussions with our internal customer support and product teams and—more importantly—user feedback. We deliberately chose to bind our SLOs to a calendar month versus a rolling period to keep us focused and organized when running service reviews.

What to measure, and how to measure it

What to measure

We specified a service endpoint we could call to test whether the service was functioning as expected. In our case, we have a status page built into our service that exercises most of our stack and returns a 200 status code if all is well.

How to measure

We wanted a prober that called the status page periodically. We wanted that prober to be located completely outside of and independent from our environment so we could test *all* our components, including our load balancing stack. Our goal here was to make sure that we were measuring any and all failures of both the GCP service and the Evernote application. However, we did not want random internet issues to trigger false positives. We chose to use a third-party company that specializes in building and running such probers. We selected Pingdom (*http://www.pingdom.com/*), but there are many others in the market. We conduct our measurements as follows:

- **Frequency of probe:** We poll our frontend nodes every minute.

- **Location of probers:** This setting is configurable; we currently use multiple probes in North America and Europe.

- **Definition of "down":** If a prober check fails, the node is marked as Unconfirmed Down and then a second geographically separate prober performs a check. If the second check fails, the node is marked down for SLO calculation purposes. The node will continue to be marked as down as long as consecutive probe requests register errors.

How to calculate SLOs from monitoring data

Finally, we carefully documented how we calculate the SLO from the raw data we received from Pingdom. For example, we specified how to account for maintenance windows: we could not assume that all of our hundreds of millions of users knew about our published maintenance windows. Uninformed users would therefore experience these windows as generic and unexplained downtime, so our SLO calculations treated maintenance as downtime.

Once we defined our SLOs, we had to do something with them. We wanted the SLOs to drive software and operations changes that would make our customers happier and keep them happy. How best to do this?

We use the SLO/error budget concept as a method to allocate resources going forward. For example, if we missed the SLO for last month, that behavior helps us prioritize relevant fixes, improvements, and bug fixes. We keep it simple: teams from both Evernote and Google conduct a monthly review of SLO performance. At this meeting, we review the SLO performance from the previous month and perform a deep dive on any outages. Based on this analysis of the past month, we set action items for improvements that may not have been captured through the regular root-cause-analysis process.

Throughout this process, our guiding principle has been "Perfect is the enemy of good." Even when SLOs aren't perfect, they're good enough to guide improvements over time. A "perfect" SLO would be one that measures every possible user interaction with our service and accounts for all edge cases. While this is a great idea on paper, it would take many months to achieve (if achieving perfection were even possible)—time which we could use to improve the service. Instead, we selected an initial SLO that covered most, but not all, user interactions, which was a good proxy for quality of service.

Since we began, we have revised our SLOs twice, according to signals from both our internal service reviews and in response to customer-impacting outages. Because we weren't aiming for perfect SLOs at the outset, we were comfortable with making changes to better align with the business. In addition to our monthly Evernote/ Google review of SLO performance, we've settled on a six-month SLO review cycle, which strikes the right balance between changing SLOs too often and letting them become stale. In revising our SLOs, we've also learned that it's important to balance what you would *like* to measure with what's *possible* to measure.

Since introducing SLOs, the relationship between our operations and development teams has subtly but markedly improved. The teams now have a common measure of success: removing the human interpretation of quality of service (QoS) has allowed both teams to maintain the same view and standards. To provide just one example, SLOs provided a common ground when we had to facilitate multiple releases in a compressed timeline in 2017. While we chased down a complex bug, product development requested that we apportion our normal weekly release over multiple separate windows, each of which would potentially impact customers. By applying an SLO calculation to the problem and removing human subjectivity from the scenario, we were able to better quantify customer impact and reduce our release windows from five to two to minimize customer pain.

Breaking Down the SLO Wall Between Customer and Cloud Provider

A virtual wall between customer and cloud provider concerns might seem natural or inevitable. While Google has SLOs and SLAs (service level agreements) for the GCP platforms we run Evernote on, Evernote has its own SLOs and SLAs. It's not always expected that two such engineering teams would be informed about each other's SLAs.

Evernote never wanted such a wall. Of course, we could have engineered to a dividing wall, basing our SLOs and SLAs on the underlying GCP metrics. Instead, from the beginning, we wanted Google to understand which performance charactcristics were most important to us, and why. We wanted to align Google's objectives with ours, and for both companies to view Evernote's reliability successes and failures as shared responsibilities. To achieve this, we needed a way to:

- Align objectives
- Ensure our partner (in this case, Google) really understood what's important to us
- Share both successes and failures

Most service providers manage to the published SLO/SLAs for their cloud services. Working within this context is important, but it can't holistically represent how well our service is running within the cloud provider's environment.

For example, a given cloud provider probably runs hundreds of thousands of virtual machines globally, which they manage for uptime and availability. GCP promises 99.95% availability for Compute Engine (i.e., its virtual machines). Even when GCP SLO graphs are green (i.e., above 99.95%), Evernote's view of the same SLO might be very different: because our virtual machine footprint is only a small percentage of the global GCP number, outages isolated to our region (or isolated for other reasons) may be "lost" in the overall rollup to a global level.

To correct for scenarios like this, we share our SLO and real-time performance against SLO with Google. As a result, both the Google CRE team and Evernote work with same performance dashboards. This may seem like a very simple point, but has proven a rather powerful way to drive truly customer-focused behavior. As a result, rather than receiving generic "Service X is running slow"–type notifications, Google provides us with notifications that are more specific to our environment. For example, in addition to a generic "GCP load balancing environment is running slow today," we'll also be informed that this issue is causing a 5% impact to Evernote's SLO. This relationship also helps teams within Google, who can see how their actions and decisions impact customers.

This two-way relationship has also given us a very effective framework to support major incidents. Most of the time, the usual model of P1–P5 tickets and regular support channels works well and allows us to maintain good service and a good relationship with Google. But we all know there are times when a P1 ticket ("major impact to our business") is not enough—the times when your whole service is on the line and you face extended business impact.

At times like these, our shared SLOs and relationship with the CRE team come to fruition. We have a common understanding that if the SLO impact is high enough, both parties will treat the issue as a P1 ticket with special handling. Quite often, this means that Evernote and Google's CRE Team rapidly mobilize on a shared conference bridge. The Google CRE team monitors the SLO we jointly defined and agreed upon, allowing us to remain in sync in terms of prioritization and appropriate responses.

Current State

After actively using SLOs for about nine months, Evernote is already on version 3 of its SLO practice. The next version of SLOs will progress from our simple uptime SLO. We plan to start probing individual API calls and accounting for the in-client view of metrics/performance so we can represent user QoS even better.

By providing a standard and defined way of measuring QoS, SLOs have allowed Evernote to better focus on how our service is running. We can now have data-driven conversations—both internally, and with Google—about the impact of outages, which enables us to drive service improvements, ultimately making for more effective support teams and happier customers.

The Home Depot's SLO Story

by William Bonnell, The Home Depot

The Home Depot (THD) is the world's largest home improvement retailer: we have more than 2,200 stores across North America, each filled with more than 35,000 unique products (and supplemented with over 1.5 million products online). Our infrastructure hosts a variety of software applications that support nearly 400,000 associates and process more than 1.5 billion customer transactions per year. The stores are deeply integrated with a global supply chain and an ecommerce website that receives more than 2 billion visits per year.

In a recent refresh to our operations approach aimed at increasing the velocity and quality of our software development, THD both pivoted to Agile software development and changed how we design and manage our software. We moved from centralized support teams that supported large, monolithic software packages to a microservices architecture led by small, independently operated software development teams. As a result, our system now had smaller chunks of constantly changing software, which also needed to be integrated across the stack.

Our move to microservices was complemented by a move to a new "freedom and responsibility culture" of full-stack ownership. This approach gives developers freedom to push code when they want, but also makes them jointly responsible for the operations of their service. For this model of joint ownership to work, operations and development teams need to speak a common language that promotes accountability and cuts across complexity: service level objectives. Services that depend upon each other need to know information like:

- How reliable is your service? Is it built for three 9s, three and a half 9s, or four 9s (or better)? Is there planned downtime?
- What kind of latency can I expect at the upper bounds?
- Can you handle the volume of requests I am going to send? How do you handle overload? Has your service achieved its SLOs over time?

If every service could provide transparent and consistent answers to these questions, teams would have a clear view into their dependencies, which allows for better communication and increased trust and accountability between teams.

The SLO Culture Project

Before we began this shift in our service model, The Home Depot didn't have a culture of SLOs. Monitoring tools and dashboards were plentiful, but were scattered everywhere and didn't track data over time. We weren't always able to pinpoint the service at the root of a given outage. Often, we began troubleshooting at the user-facing service and worked backward until we found the problem, wasting countless hours. If a service required planned downtime, its dependent services were surprised. If a team needed to build a three and a half 9s service, they wouldn't know if the service they had a hard dependency on could support them with even better uptime (four 9s). These disconnects caused confusion and disappointment between our software development and operations teams.

We needed to address these disconnects by building a common culture of SLOs. Doing so required an overarching strategy to influence people, process, and technology. Our efforts spanned four general areas:

Common vernacular
Define SLOs in the context of THD. Define how to measure them in a consistent way.

Evangelism

Spread the word across the company.

- Create training material to sell why SLOs matter, road shows across the company, internal blogs, and promotional materials like t-shirts and stickers.

- Enlist a few early adopters to implement SLOs and demonstrate the value to others.

- Establish a catchy acronym (VALET; as discussed later) to help the idea spread.

- Create a training program (FiRE Academy: Fundamentals in Reliability Engineering) to train developers on SLOs and other reliability concepts.[2]

Automation

To reduce the friction of adoption, implement a metric collection platform to automatically collect service level indicators for any service deployed to production. These SLIs can later be more easily turned into SLOs.

Incentive

Establish annual goals for all development managers to set and measure SLOs for their services.

Establishing a common vernacular was critical to getting everybody on the same page. We also wanted to keep this framework as simple as possible to help the idea spread faster. To get started, we took a critical look at the metrics we monitored across our various services and discovered some patterns. Every service monitored some form of its *traffic volume, latency, errors,* and *utilization*—metrics that map closely to Google SRE's Four Golden Signals (*http://bit.ly/2LSLpDQ*). In addition, many services monitored *uptime or availability* distinctly from errors. Unfortunately, across the board, all categories of metrics were inconsistently monitored, were named differently, or had insufficient data.

None of our services had SLOs. The closest metric our production systems had to a customer-facing SLO was support tickets. The primary (and often only) way we measured the reliability of the applications deployed to our stores was by tracking the number of support calls our internal support desk receives.

---

2 Training options range from a one-hour primer to half-day workshops to intense four-week immersion with a mature SRE team, complete with a graduation ceremony and a FiRE badge.

Our First Set of SLOs

We couldn't create SLOs for every aspect of our systems that could be measured, so we had to decide which metrics or SLIs should also have SLOs.

Availability and latency for API calls

We decided that each microservice had to have availability and latency SLOs for its API calls that were called by *other* microservices. For example, the Cart microservice called the Inventory microservice. For those API calls, the Inventory microservice published SLOs that the Cart microservice (and other microservices that needed Inventory) could consult to determine if the Inventory microservice could meet its reliability requirements

Infrastructure utilization

Teams at THD measure infrastructure utilization in different ways, but the most typical measurement is real-time infrastructure utilization at one minute granularity. We decided against setting utilization SLOs for a few reasons. To begin with, microservices aren't overly concerned with this metric—your users don't really care about utilization as long as you can handle the traffic volume, your microservice is up, it's responding quickly, it's not throwing errors, and you're not in danger of running out of capacity. Additionally, our impending move to the cloud meant that utilization would be less of a concern, so cost planning would overshadow capacity planning. (We'd still need to monitor utilization and perform capacity planning, but we didn't need to include it in our SLO framework.)

Traffic volume

Because THD didn't already have a culture of capacity planning, we needed a mechanism for software and operations teams to communicate how much volume their service could handle. Traffic was easy to define as requests to a service, but we needed to decide if we should track average requests per second, peak requests per second, or the volume of requests over the reporting time period. We decided to track all three and let each service select the most appropriate metric. We debated whether or not to set an SLO for traffic volume because this metric is determined by user behavior, rather than internal factors that we can control. Ultimately, we decided that as a retailer we needed to size our service for peaks like Black Friday, so we set an SLO according to expected peak capacity.

Latency

We let each service define its SLO for latency and determine where to best measure it. Our only request was that a service should supplement our common white-box performance monitoring with black-box monitoring to catch issues caused by the network or other layers like caches and proxies that fail outside the microservice. We also decided that percentiles were more appropriate than arithmetic averages. At minimum, services needed to hit a 90th percentile target; user-facing services had a preferred target of 95th and/or 99th percentile.

Errors

Errors were somewhat complicated to account for. Since we were primarily dealing with web services, we had to standardize what constitutes an error and how to return errors. If a web service encountered an error, we naturally standardized on HTTP response codes:

- A service should not indicate an error in the body of a 2xx response; rather, it should throw either a 4xx or a 5xx.

- An error caused by a problem with the service (for example, out of memory) should throw a 5xx error.

- An error caused by the client (for example, sending a malformed request) should throw a 4xx error.

After much deliberation, we decided to track both 4xx and 5xx errors, but used 5xx errors only to set SLOs. Similar to our approach for other SLO-related elements, we kept this dimension generic so that different applications could leverage it for different contexts. For example, in addition to HTTP errors, errors for a batch processing service might be the number of records that failed to process.

Tickets

As previously mentioned, tickets were originally the primary way we evaluated most of our production software. For historical reasons, we decided to continue to track tickets alongside our other SLOs. You can consider this metric as analogous to something like "software operation level."

VALET

We summed up our new SLOs into a handy acronym: VALET.

Volume (traffic)
    How much business volume can my service handle?

Availability
    Is the service up when I need it?

Latency
    Does the service respond fast when I use it?

Errors

Does the service throw an error when I use it?

Tickets

Does the service require manual intervention to complete my request?

Evangelizing SLOs

Armed with an easy-to-remember acronym, we set out to evangelize SLOs to the enterprise:

- Why SLOs are important
- How SLOs support our "freedom and responsibility" culture
- What should be measured
- What to do with the results

Since developers were now responsible for the operation of their software, they needed to establish SLOs to demonstrate their ability to build and support reliable software, and also to communicate with the consumers of their services and product managers for customer-facing services. However, most of this audience was unfamiliar with concepts like SLAs and SLOs, so they needed to be educated on this new VALET framework.

As we needed to secure executive backing for our move to SLOs, our education campaign started with senior leadership. We then met with development teams one by one to espouse the values of SLOs. We encouraged teams to move from their custom metric-tracking mechanisms (which were often manual) to the VALET framework. To keep the momentum going, we sent a weekly SLO report in VALET format, which we paired with commentary around general reliability concepts and lessons learned from internal events, to senior leadership. This also helped frame business metrics like purchase orders created (Volume) or purchase orders that failed to process (Errors) in terms of VALET.

We also scaled our evangelism in a number of ways:

- We set up an internal WordPress site to host blogs about VALET and reliability, outlinking to useful resources.
- We conducted internal Tech Talks (including a Google SRE guest speaker) to discuss general reliability concepts and how to measure with VALET.
- We conducted a series of VALET training workshops (which would later evolve into FiRE Academy), and opened the invite to whomever wanted to attend. The attendance for these workshops stayed strong for several months.

- We even created VALET laptop stickers and t-shirts to support a comprehensive internal marketing campaign.

Soon everybody in the company knew VALET, and our new culture of SLOs began to take hold. SLO implementation even began to officially factor into THD's annual performance reviews for development managers. While roughly 50 services were regularly capturing and reporting on their SLOs on a weekly basis, we were storing the metrics ad hoc in a spreadsheet. Although the idea of VALET had caught on like wildfire, we needed to automate data collection to foster widespread adoption.

Automating VALET Data Collection

While our culture of SLOs now had a strong foothold, automating VALET data collection would accelerate SLO adoption.

TPS Reports

We built a framework to automatically capture VALET data for any service that was deployed to our new GCP environment. We called this framework *TPS Reports*, a play on the term we used for volume and performance testing (transactions per second), and, of course, to poke fun (*http://bit.ly/2J4bGkL*)[3] at the idea that multiple managers might want to review this data. We built the TPS Reports framework on top of GCP's BigQuery database platform. All of the logs generated by our webserving frontend were fed into BigQuery for processing by TPS Reports. We eventually also included metrics from a variety of other monitoring systems such as Stackdriver's probe for availability.

TPS Reports transformed this data into hourly VALET metrics that anyone could query. Newly created services were automatically registered into TPS Reports and therefore could be immediately queried. Since the data was all stored in BigQuery, we could efficiently report on VALET metrics across time frames. We used this data to build a variety of automated reports and alerts. The most interesting integration was a chatbot that let us directly report on the VALET of services in a commercial chat platform. For example, any service could display VALET for the last hour, VALET versus previous week, services out of SLO, and a variety of other interesting data right inside the chat channel.

VALET service

Our next step was to create a VALET application to store and report on SLO data. Because SLOs are best leveraged as a trending tool, the service tracks SLOs at daily, weekly, and monthly granularity. Note that our SLOs are a trending tool that we can

---

3 As made famous in the 1999 film *Office Space* (*http://www.imdb.com/title/tt0151804/*).

use for error budgets, but aren't directly connected to our monitoring systems. Instead, we have a variety of disparate monitoring platforms, each with its own alerting. Those monitoring systems aggregate their SLOs on a daily basis and publish to the VALET service for trending. The downside of this setup is that alerting thresholds set in the monitoring systems aren't integrated with SLOs; however, we have the flexibility to change out monitoring systems as needed.

Anticipating the need to integrate VALET with other applications not running in GCP, we created a VALET integration layer that provides an API to collect aggregated VALET data for a service daily. TPS Reports was the first system to integrate with the VALET service, and we eventually integrated with a variety of on-premises application platforms (more than half of the services registered in VALET).

VALET Dashboard

The VALET Dashboard (shown in Figure 3-1) is our UI to visualize and report on this data and is relatively straightforward. It allows users to:

- Register a new service. This typically means assigning the service to one or more URLs, which may already have VALET data collected.
- Set SLO objectives for any of the five VALET categories.
- Add new metrics types under each of the VALET categories. For example, one service may track latency at the 99th percentile, while another tracks latency at the 90th percentile (or both). Or, a backend processing system may track volume at a daily level (purchase orders created in a day), whereas a customer-serving frontend may track peak transactions per second.

The VALET Dashboard lets users report on SLOs for many services at once, and to slice and dice the data in a variety of ways. For example, a team can view stats for all of their services that missed SLO in the past week. A team seeking to review service performance can view latency across all of their services and the services they depend upon. The VALET Dashboard stores the data in a simple Cloud SQL database, and developers use a popular commercial reporting tool to build reports.

These reports became the foundation for a new best practice with developers: regular SLO reviews of their services (typically, either weekly or monthly). Based upon these reviews, developers can create action items to return a service to its SLO, or perhaps decide that an unrealistic SLO needs to be adjusted.

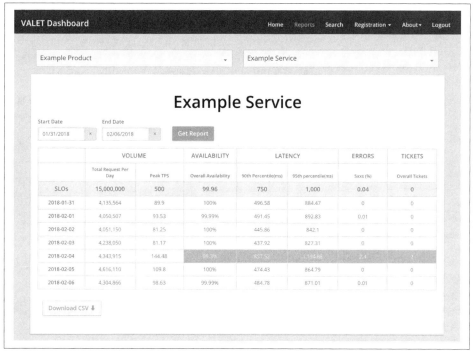

Figure 3-1. The VALET Dashboard

The Proliferation of SLOs

Once SLOs were firmly cemented in the organization's collective mind and effective automation and reporting were in place, new SLOs proliferated quickly. After tracking SLOs for about 50 services at the beginning of the year, by the end of the year we were tracking SLOs for 800 services, with about 50 new services per month being registered with VALET.

Because VALET allowed us to scale SLO adoption across THD, the time effort required to develop automation was well worth it. However, other companies shouldn't be scared away from adopting an SLO-based approach if they can't develop similarly complex automation. While automation provided THD extra benefits, there are benefits to just writing SLOs in the first place.

Applying VALET to Batch Applications

As we developed robust reporting around SLOs, we discovered some additional uses for VALET. With a little adjusting, batch applications can fit into this framework as follows:

Volume
> The volume of records processed

Availability
> How often (as a percentage) the job completed by a certain time

Latency
> The amount of time it takes for the job to run

Errors
> The records that failed to process

Tickets
> The number of times an operator has to manually fix data and reprocess a job

Using VALET in Testing

Since we were developing an SRE culture at the same time, we found that VALET supported our destructive testing (chaos engineering) automation in our staging environments. With the TPS Reports framework in place, we could automatically run destructive tests and record the impact (or hopefully lack of impact) to the service's VALET data.

Future Aspirations

With 800 services (and growing) collecting VALET data, we have a lot of useful operational data at our disposal. We have several aspirations for the future.

Now that we are effectively collecting SLOs, we want to use this data to take action. Our next step is an error budget culture similar to Google, whereby a team stops pushing new features (other than improvements to reliability) when a service is out of SLO. To protect the velocity demands of our business, we'll have to strive to find a good balance between the SLO reporting time frame (weekly or monthly) and the frequency of SLOs being breached. Like many companies adopting error budgets, we're weighing the pros and cons of rolling windows versus fixed windows.

We want to further refine VALET to track detailed endpoints and the consumers of a service. Currently, even if a particular service has multiple endpoints, we track VALET only across the entire service. As a result, it's difficult to distinguish between different operations (for example, a write to the catalog versus a read to the catalog; while we monitor and alert on these operations separately, we don't track SLOs). Similarly, we'd also like to differentiate VALET results for different consumers of a service.

Although we currently track latency SLOs at the web-serving layer, we'd also like to track a latency SLO for end users. This measurement would capture how factors like third-party tags, internet latency, and CDN caching affect how long it takes a page to start rendering and to complete rendering.

We'd also like to extend VALET data to application deployments. Specifically, we'd like to use automation to verify that VALET is within tolerance before rolling out a change to the next server, zone, or region.

We've started to collect information about service dependencies, and have prototyped a visual graph that shows where we're not hitting VALET metrics along a call tree. This type of analysis will become even easier with emerging service mesh platforms.

Finally, we strongly believe that the SLOs for a service should be set by the business owner of the service (often called a product manager) based on its criticality to the business. At the very least, we want the business owners to set the requirement for a service's uptime and use that SLO as a shared objective between product management and development. Although technologists found VALET intuitive, the concept wasn't so intuitive for product managers. We are striving to simplify the concepts of VALET using terminology relevant to them: we've both simplified the number of choices for uptime and provided example metrics. We also emphasize the significant investment required to move from one level to another. Here's an example of simplified VALET metrics we might provide:

- 99.5%: Applications that are not used by store associates or an MVP of a new service
- 99.9%: Adequate for the majority of nonselling systems at THD
- 99.95%: Selling systems (or services that support selling systems)
- 99.99%: Shared infrastructure services

Casting metrics in business terms and sharing a visible goal (an SLO!) between product and development will reduce a lot of misaligned expectations about reliability often seen in large companies.

Summary

Introducing a new process, let alone a new culture, to a large company takes a good strategy, executive buy-in, strong evangelism, easy adoption patterns, and—most of all—patience. It might take years for a significant change like SLOs to become firmly established at a company. We'd like to emphasize that The Home Depot is a traditional enterprise; if we can introduce such a large change successfully, you can too. You also don't have to approach this task all at once. While we implemented SLOs piece by piece, developing a comprehensive evangelism strategy and clear incentive structure facilitated a quick transformation: we went from 0 to 800 SLO-supported services in less than a year.

Conclusion

SLOs and error budgets are powerful concepts that help address many different problem sets. These case studies from Evernote and The Home Depot present very real examples of how implementing an SLO culture can bring product development and operations closer together. Doing so can facilitate communication and better inform development decisions. It will ultimately result in better experiences for your customers—whether those customers are internal, external, humans, or other services.

These two case studies highlight that SLO culture is an ongoing process and not a one-time fix or solution. While they share philosophical underpinnings, THD's and Evernote's measurement styles, SLIs, SLOs, and implementation details are markedly different. Both stories complement Google's own take on SLOs by demonstrating that SLO implementation need not be Google-specific. Just as these companies tailored SLOs to their own unique environments, so can other companies and organizations.

## CHAPTER 4

Monitoring

By Jess Frame, Anthony Lenton, Steven Thurgood,
Anton Tolchanov, and Nejc Trdin
with Carmela Quinito

Monitoring can include many types of data, including metrics, text logging, structured event logging, distributed tracing, and event introspection. While all of these approaches are useful in their own right, this chapter mostly addresses metrics and structured logging. In our experience, these two data sources are best suited to SRE's fundamental monitoring needs.

At the most basic level, monitoring allows you to gain visibility into a system, which is a core requirement for judging service health and diagnosing your service when things go wrong. Chapter 6 (*http://bit.ly/2KNCD9F*) in the first SRE book provides some basic monitoring definitions and explains that SREs monitor their systems in order to:

- Alert on conditions that require attention.
- Investigate and diagnose those issues.
- Display information about the system visually.
- Gain insight into trends in resource usage or service health for long-term planning.
- Compare the behavior of the system before and after a change, or between two groups in an experiment.

The relative importance of these use cases might lead you to make tradeoffs when selecting or building a monitoring system.

This chapter talks about how Google manages monitoring systems and provides some guidelines for questions that may arise when you're choosing and running a monitoring system.

Desirable Features of a Monitoring Strategy

When choosing a monitoring system, it is important to understand and prioritize the features that matter to you. If you're evaluating different monitoring systems, the attributes in this section can help guide your thinking about which solution(s) best suits your needs. If you already have a monitoring strategy, you might consider using some additional capabilities of your current solution. Depending on your needs, one monitoring system may address all of your use cases, or you may want to use a combination of systems.

Speed

Different organizations will have different needs when it comes to the *freshness of data* and the *speed of data retrieval*.

Data should be available when you need it: freshness impacts how long it will take your monitoring system to page you when something goes wrong. Additionally, slow data might lead you to accidentally act on incorrect data. For example, during incident response, if the time between cause (taking an action) and effect (seeing that action reflected in your monitoring) is too long, you might assume a change had no effect or deduce a false correlation between cause and effect. Data more than four to five minutes stale might significantly impact how quickly you can respond to an incident.

If you're selecting a monitoring system based upon this criteria, you need to figure out your speed requirements ahead of time. Speed of data retrieval is mostly a problem when you're querying vast amounts of data. It might take some time for a graph to load if it has to tally up a lot of data from many monitored systems. To speed up your slower graphs, it's helpful if the monitoring system can create and store new time series based on incoming data; then it can precompute answers to common queries.

Calculations

Support for calculations can span a variety of use cases, across a range of complexities. At a minimum, you'll probably want your system to *retain data over a multimonth time frame*. Without a long-term view of your data, you cannot analyze long-term trends like system growth. In terms of granularity, *summary data* (i.e., aggregated data that you can't drill down into) is sufficient to facilitate growth planning. *Retaining all detailed individual metrics* may help with answering questions like, "Has this unusual behavior happened before?" However, the data might be expensive to store or impractical to retrieve.

The metrics you retain about events or resource consumption should ideally be monotonically incrementing counters. Using counters, your monitoring system can calculate windowed functions over time—for example, to report the rate of requests per second from that counter. Computing these rates over a longer window (up to a month) allows you to implement the building blocks for SLO burn-based alerting (see Chapter 5).

Finally, support for a more complete range of statistical functions can be useful because trivial operations may mask bad behavior. A monitoring system that supports computing percentiles (i.e., 50th, 95th, 99th percentiles) when recording latency will let you see if 50%, 5%, or 1% of your requests are too slow, whereas the arithmetic mean can only tell you—without specifics—that the request time is slower. Alternatively, if your system doesn't support computing percentiles directly, you can achieve this by:

- Obtaining a mean value by summing the seconds spent in requests and dividing by the number of requests
- Logging every request and computing the percentile values by scanning or sampling the log entries

You might want to record your raw metric data in a separate system for offline analysis—for example, to use in weekly or monthly reports, or to perform more intricate calculations that are too difficult to compute in your monitoring system.

Interfaces

A robust monitoring system should allow you to concisely display time-series data in graphs, and also to structure data in tables or a range of chart styles. Your dashboards will be primary interfaces for displaying monitoring, so it's important that you choose formats that most clearly display the data you care about. Some options include heatmaps, histograms, and logarithmic scale graphs.

You'll likely need to offer different views of the same data based upon audience; high-level management may want to view quite different information than SREs. Be specific about creating dashboards that make sense to the people consuming the content. For each set of dashboards, displaying the same types of data consistently is valuable for communication.

You might need to graph information across different aggregations of a metric—such as machine type, server version, or request type—in real time. It's a good idea for your team to be comfortable with performing ad hoc drill-downs on your data. By slicing your data according to a variety of metrics, you can look for correlations and patterns in the data when you need it.

Alerts

It's helpful to be able to classify alerts: multiple categories of alerts allow for proportional responses. The ability to set different severity levels for different alerts is also useful: you might file a ticket to investigate a low rate of errors that lasts more than an hour, while a 100% error rate is an emergency that deserves immediate response.

Alert suppression functionality lets you avoid unnecessary noise from distracting on-call engineers. For example:

- When all nodes are experiencing the same high rate of errors, you can alert just once for the global error rate instead of sending an individual alert for every single node.
- When one of your service dependencies has a firing alert (e.g., a slow backend), you don't need to alert for error rates of your service.

You also need to be able to ensure alerts are no longer suppressed once the event is over.

The level of control you require over your system will dictate whether you use a third-party monitoring service or deploy and run your own monitoring system. Google developed its own monitoring system in-house, but there are plenty of open source and commercial monitoring systems available.

Sources of Monitoring Data

Your choice of monitoring system(s) will be informed by the specific sources of monitoring data you'll use. This section discusses two common sources of monitoring data: logs and metrics. There are other valuable monitoring sources that we won't cover here, like distributed tracing (*http://bit.ly/2syvpOw*) and runtime introspection.

Metrics are numerical measurements representing attributes and events, typically harvested via many data points at regular time intervals. *Logs* are an append-only record of events. This chapter's discussion focuses on structured logs that enable rich query and aggregation tools as opposed to plain-text logs.

Google's logs-based systems process large volumes of highly granular data. There's some inherent delay between when an event occurs and when it is visible in logs. For analysis that's not time-sensitive, these logs can be processed with a batch system, interrogated with ad hoc queries, and visualized with dashboards. An example of this workflow would be using Cloud Dataflow (*https://cloud.google.com/dataflow/*) to process logs, BigQuery (*https://cloud.google.com/bigquery/*) for ad hoc queries, and Data Studio (*https://datastudio.google.com/*) for the dashboards.

By contrast, our metrics-based monitoring system, which collects a large number of metrics from every service at Google, provides much less granular information, but in near real time. These characteristics are fairly typical of other logs- and metrics-based monitoring systems, although there are exceptions, such as real-time logs systems or high-cardinality metrics.

Our alerts and dashboards typically use metrics. The real-time nature of our metrics-based monitoring system means that engineers can be notified of problems very rapidly. We tend to use logs to find the root cause of an issue, as the information we need is often not available as a metric.

When reporting isn't time-sensitive, we often generate detailed reports using logs processing systems because logs will nearly always produce more accurate data than metrics.

If you're alerting based on metrics, it might be tempting to add more alerting based on logs—for example, if you need to be notified when even a single exceptional event happens. We still recommend metrics-based alerting in such cases: you can increment a counter metric when a particular event happens, and configure an alert based on that metric's value. This strategy keeps all alert configuration in one place, making it easier to manage (see "Managing Your Monitoring System" on page 67).

Examples

The following real-world examples illustrate how to reason through the process of choosing between monitoring systems.

Move information from logs to metrics

Problem. The HTTP status code is an important signal to App Engine customers debugging their errors. This information was available in logs, but not in metrics. The metrics dashboard could provide only a global rate of all errors, and did not include any information about the exact error code or the cause of the error. As a result, the workflow to debug an issue involved:

1. Looking at the global error graph to find a time when an error occurred.

2. Reading log files to look for lines containing an error.

3. Attempting to correlate errors in the log file to the graph.

The logging tools did not give a sense of scale, making it hard to know if an error seen in one log line was occurring frequently. The logs also contained many other irrelevant lines, making it hard to track down the root cause.

Proposed solution. The App Engine dev team chose to export the HTTP status code as a label on the metric (e.g., `requests_total{status=404}` versus `requests_total {status=500}`). Because the number of different HTTP status codes is relatively limited, this did not increase the volume of metric data to an impractical size, but did make the most pertinent data available for graphing and alerting.

Outcome. This new label meant the team could upgrade the graphs to show separate lines for different error categories and types. Customers could now quickly form conjectures about possible problems based on the exposed error codes. We could now also set different alerting thresholds for client and server errors, making the alerts trigger more accurately.

Improve both logs and metrics

Problem. One Ads SRE team maintained ~50 services, which were written in a number of different languages and frameworks. The team used logs as the canonical source of truth for SLO compliance. To calculate the error budget, each service used a logs processing script with many service-specific special cases. Here's an example script to process a log entry for a single service:

```
If the HTTP status code was in the range (500, 599)
AND the 'SERVER ERROR' field of the log is populated
AND DEBUG cookie was not set as part of the request
AND the url did not contain '/reports'
AND the 'exception' field did not contain 'com.google.ads.PasswordException'
THEN increment the error counter by 1
```

These scripts were hard to maintain and also used data that wasn't available to the metrics-based monitoring system. Because metrics drove alerts, sometimes the alerts would not correspond to user-facing errors. Every alert required an explicit triage step to determine if it was user-facing, which slowed down response time.

Proposed solution. The team created a library that hooked into the logic of the framework languages of each application. The library decided if the error was impacting users at request time. The instrumentation wrote this decision in logs and exported it as a metric at the same time, improving consistency. If the metric showed that the service had returned an error, the logs contained the exact error, along with request-related data to help reproduce and debug the issue. Correspondingly, any SLO-impacting error that manifested in the logs also changed the SLI metrics, which the team could then alert on.

Outcome. By introducing a uniform control surface across multiple services, the team reused tooling and alerting logic instead of implementing multiple custom solutions. All services benefited from removing the complicated, service-specific logs processing code, which resulted in increased scalability. Once alerts were directly tied to SLOs, they were more clearly actionable, so the false-positive rate decreased significantly.

Keep logs as the data source

Problem.   While investigating production issues, one SRE team would often look at the affected entity IDs to determine user impact and root cause. As with the earlier App Engine example, this investigation required data that was available only in logs. The team had to perform one-off log queries for this while they were responding to incidents. This step added time to incident recovery: a few minutes to correctly put together the query, plus the time to query the logs.

Proposed solution.   The team initially debated whether a metric should replace their log tools. Unlike in the App Engine example, the entity ID could take on millions of different values, so it would not be practical as a metric label.

Ultimately, the team decided to write a script to perform the one-off log queries they needed, and documented which script to run in the alert emails. They could then copy the command directly into a terminal if necessary.

Outcome.   The team no longer had the cognitive load of managing the correct one-off log query. Accordingly, they could get the results they needed faster (although not as quickly as a metrics-based approach). They also had a backup plan: they could run the script automatically as soon as an alert triggered, and use a small server to query the logs at regular intervals to constantly retrieve semifresh data.

Managing Your Monitoring System

Your monitoring system is as important as any other service you run. As such, it should be treated with the appropriate level of care and attention.

Treat Your Configuration as Code

Treating system configuration as code and storing it in the revision control system are common practices that provide some obvious benefits: change history, links from specific changes to your task tracking system, easier rollbacks and linting checks,[1] and enforced code review procedures.

We strongly recommend also treating monitoring configuration as code (for more on configuration, see Chapter 14). A monitoring system that supports intent-based

---

1 For example, using promtool to verify that your Prometheus config is syntactically correct.

configuration is preferable to systems that only provide web UIs or CRUD-style (*http://bit.ly/1G4WdV1*) APIs. This configuration approach is standard for many open source binaries that only read a configuration file. Some third-party solutions like grafanalib (*http://bit.ly/2so5Wrx*) enable this approach for components that are traditionally configured with a UI.

Encourage Consistency

Large companies with multiple engineering teams who use monitoring need to strike a fine balance: a centralized approach provides consistency, but on the other hand, individual teams may want full control over the design of their configuration.

The right solution depends on your organization. Google's approach has evolved over time toward convergence on a single framework run centrally as a service. This solution works well for us for a few reasons. A single framework enables engineers to ramp up faster when they switch teams, and makes collaboration during debugging easier. We also have a centralized dashboarding service, where each team's dashboards are discoverable and accessible. If you easily understand another team's dashboard, you can debug both your issues and theirs more quickly.

If possible, make basic monitoring coverage effortless. If all your services[2] export a consistent set of basic metrics, you can automatically collect those metrics across your entire organization and provide a consistent set of dashboards. This approach means that any new component you launch automatically has basic monitoring. Many teams across your company—even nonengineering teams—can use this monitoring data.

Prefer Loose Coupling

Business requirements change, and your production system will look different a year from now. Similarly, your monitoring system needs to evolve over time as the services it monitors evolve through different patterns of failure.

We recommend keeping the components of your monitoring system loosely coupled. You should have stable interfaces for configuring each component and passing monitoring data. Separate components should be in charge of collecting, storing, alerting, and visualizing your monitoring. Stable interfaces make it easier to swap out any given component for a better alternative.

Splitting functionality into individual components is becoming popular in the open source world. A decade ago, monitoring systems like Zabbix (*https://*

---

2 You can export basic metrics via a common library: an instrumentation framework like OpenCensus (*https://opencensus.io/*), or a service mesh like Istio (*https://istio.io/*).

www.zabbix.com/) combined all functions into a single component. Modern design usually involves separating collection and rule evaluation (with a solution like Prometheus server (*https://prometheus.io/*)), long-term time series storage (InfluxDB (*https://www.influxdata.com/*)), alert aggregation (Alertmanager (*http://bit.ly/ 2soB22b*)), and dashboarding (Grafana (*https://grafana.com/*)).

As of this writing, there are at least two popular open standards for instrumenting your software and exposing metrics:

statsd (https://github.com/etsy/statsd)
> The metric aggregation daemon initially written by Etsy and now ported to a majority of programming languages.

Prometheus
> An open source monitoring solution with a flexible data model, support for metric labels, and robust histogram functionality. Other systems are now adopting the Prometheus format, and it is being standardized as OpenMetrics (*https:// openmetrics.io/*).

A separate dashboarding system that can use multiple data sources provides a central and unified overview of your service. Google recently saw this benefit in practice: our legacy monitoring system (Borgmon[3]) combined dashboards in the same configuration as alerting rules. While migrating to a new system (Monarch (*https://youtu.be/ LlvJdK1xsl4*)), we decided to move dashboarding into a separate service (Viceroy (*http://bit.ly/2sqRwad*)). Because Viceroy was not a component of Borgmon or Monarch, Monarch had fewer functional requirements. Since users could use Viceroy to display graphs based on data from both monitoring systems, they could gradually migrate from Borgmon to Monarch.

Metrics with Purpose

Chapter 5 covers how to monitor and alert using SLI metrics when a system's error budget is under threat. SLI metrics are the first metrics you want to check when SLO-based alerts trigger. These metrics should appear prominently in your service's dashboard, ideally on its landing page.

When investigating the cause of an SLO violation, you will most likely not get enough information from the SLO dashboards. These dashboards show that you are violating the SLO, but not necessarily why. What other data should the monitoring dashboards display?

---

3 See Chapter 10 (*http://bit.ly/2svQKYN*) of *Site Reliability Engineering* for Borgmon's concepts and structure.

We've found the following guidelines helpful in implementing metrics. These metrics should provide reasonable monitoring that allows you to investigate production issues and also provide a broad range of information about your service.

Intended Changes

When diagnosing an SLO-based alert, you need to be able to move from alerting metrics that notify you of user-impacting issues to metrics that tell you what is causing these issues. Recent intended changes to your service might be at fault. Add monitoring that informs you of any changes in production.[4] To determine the trigger, we recommend the following:

- Monitor the version of the binary.
- Monitor the command-line flags, especially when you use these flags to enable and disable features of the service.
- If configuration data is pushed to your service dynamically, monitor the version of this dynamic configuration.

If any of these pieces of the system aren't versioned, you should be able to monitor the timestamp at which it was last built or packaged.

When you're trying to correlate an outage with a rollout, it's much easier to look at a graph/dashboard linked from your alert than to trawl through your CI/CD (continuous integration/continuous delivery) system logs after the fact.

Dependencies

Even if your service didn't change, any of its dependencies might change or have problems, so you should also monitor responses coming from direct dependencies.

It's reasonable to export the request and response size in bytes, latency, and response codes for each dependency. When choosing the metrics to graph, keep the four golden signals (*http://bit.ly/2LSLpDQ*) in mind. You can use additional labels on the metrics to break them down by response code, RPC (remote procedure call) method name, and peer job name.

Ideally, you can instrument the lower-level RPC client library to export these metrics once, instead of asking each RPC client library to export them.[5] Instrumenting the

---

4 This is one case where monitoring via logs is appealing, particularly because production changes are relatively infrequent. Whether you use logs or metrics, these changes should be surfaced in your dashboards so they're easily accessible for debugging production issues.

5 See *https://opencensus.io/* for a set of libraries that provides this.

client library provides more consistency and allows you to monitor new dependencies for free.

You will sometimes come across dependencies that offer a very narrow API, where all functionality is available via a single RPC called *Get*, *Query*, or something equally unhelpful, and the actual command is specified as arguments to this RPC. A single instrumentation point in the client library falls short with this type of dependency: you will observe a high variance in latency and some percentage of errors that may or may not indicate that some part of this opaque API is failing entirely. If this dependency is critical, you have a couple of options to monitor it well:

- Export separate metrics to tailor for the dependency, so that the metrics can unpack requests they receive to get at the actual signal.
- Ask the dependency owners to perform a rewrite to export a broader API that supports separate functionality split across separate RPC services and methods.

Saturation

Aim to monitor and track the usage of every resource the service relies upon. Some resources have hard limits you cannot exceed, like RAM, disk, or CPU quota allocated to your application. Other resources—like open file descriptors, active threads in any thread pools, waiting times in queues, or the volume of written logs—may not have a clear hard limit but still require management.

Depending on the programming language in use, you should monitor additional resources:

- In Java: The heap and metaspace (*http://bit.ly/2J9g3Ha*) size, and more specific metrics depending on what type of garbage collection you're using
- In Go: The number of goroutines

The languages themselves provide varying support to track these resources.

In addition to alerting on significant events as described in Chapter 5 you might also need to set up alerting that fires when you approach exhaustion for specific resources, such as:

- When the resource has a hard limit
- When crossing a usage threshold causes performance degradation

You should have monitoring metrics to track all resources—even resources that the service manages well. These metrics are vital in capacity and resource planning.

Status of Served Traffic

It's a good idea to add metrics or metric labels that allow the dashboards to break down served traffic by status code (unless the metrics your service uses for SLI purposes already include this information). Here are some recommendations:

- For HTTP traffic, monitor all response codes, even if they don't provide enough signal for alerting, because some can be triggered by incorrect client behavior.
- If you apply rate limits or quota limits to your users, monitor aggregates of how many requests were denied due to lack of quota.

Graphs of this data can help you identify when the volume of errors changes noticeably during a production change.

Implementing Purposeful Metrics

Each exposed metric should serve a purpose. Resist the temptation of exporting a handful of metrics just because they are easy to generate. Instead, think about how these metrics will be used. Metric design, or lack thereof, has implications.

Ideally, metric values used for alerting change dramatically only when the system enters a problem state, and don't change when a system is operating normally. On the other hand, metrics for debugging don't have these requirements—they're intended to provide insight about what is happening when alerts are triggered. Good debugging metrics will point at some aspect of the system that's potentially causing the issues. When you write a postmortem, think about which additional metrics would have allowed you to diagnose the issue faster.

Testing Alerting Logic

In an ideal world, monitoring and alerting code should be subject to the same testing standards as code development. While Prometheus developers are discussing developing unit tests for monitoring (*http://bit.ly/2JcobXe*), there is currently no broadly adopted system that allows you to do this.

At Google, we test our monitoring and alerting using a domain-specific language that allows us to create synthetic time series. We then write assertions based upon the values in a derived time series, or the firing status and label presence of specific alerts.

Monitoring and alerting is often a multistage process, which therefore calls for multiple families of unit tests. While this area remains largely underdeveloped, should you want to implement monitoring testing at some point, we recommend a three-tiered approach, as shown in Figure 4-1.

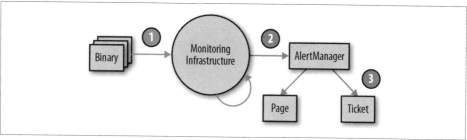

Figure 4-1. Monitoring testing environment tiers

1. **Binary reporting:** Check that the exported metric variables change in value under certain conditions as expected.

2. **Monitoring configurations:** Make sure that rule evaluation produces expected results, and that specific conditions produce the expected alerts.

3. **Alerting configurations:** Test that generated alerts are routed to a predetermined destination, based on alert label values.

If you can't test your monitoring via synthetic means, or there's a stage of your monitoring you simply can't test, consider creating a running system that exports wellknown metrics, like number of requests and errors. You can use this system to validate derived time series and alerts. It's very likely that your alerting rules will not fire for months or years after you configure them, and you need to have confidence that when the metric passes a certain threshold, the correct engineers will be alerted with notifications that make sense.

Conclusion

Because the SRE role is responsible for the reliability of systems in production, SREs are often required to be intimately familiar with a service's monitoring system and its features. Without this knowledge, SREs might not know where to look, how to identify abnormal behavior, or how to find the information they need during an emergency.

We hope that by pointing out monitoring system features we find useful and why, we can help you evaluate how well your monitoring strategy fits your needs, explore some additional features you might be able to leverage, and consider changes you might want to make. You'll probably find it useful to combine some source of metrics and logging in your monitoring strategy; the exact mix you need is highly contextdependent. Make sure to collect metrics that serve a particular purpose. That purpose may be to enable better capacity planning, assist in debugging, or directly notify you about problems.

Once you have monitoring in place, it needs to be visible and useful. To this end, we also recommend testing your monitoring setup. A good monitoring system pays dividends. It is well worth the investment to put substantial thought into what solutions best meet your needs, and to iterate until you get it right.

Alerting on SLOs

By Steven Thurgood
with Jess Frame, Anthony Lenton,
Carmela Quinito, Anton Tolchanov, and Nejc Trdin

This chapter explains how to turn your SLOs into actionable alerts on significant events. Both our first SRE book (*http://bit.ly/2kIcNYM*) and this book talk about implementing SLOs. We believe that having good SLOs that measure the reliability of your platform, as experienced by your customers, provides the highest-quality indication for when an on-call engineer should respond. Here we give specific guidance on how to turn those SLOs into alerting rules so that you can respond to problems before you consume too much of your error budget.

Our examples present a series of increasingly complex implementations for alerting metrics and logic; we discuss the utility and shortcomings of each. While our examples use a simple request-driven service and Prometheus syntax (*https://prome theus.io*), you can apply this approach in any alerting framework.

Alerting Considerations

In order to generate alerts from service level indicators (SLIs) and an error budget, you need a way to combine these two elements into a specific rule. Your goal is to be notified for a *significant event*: an event that consumes a large fraction of the error budget.

Consider the following attributes when evaluating an alerting strategy:

Precision

The proportion of events detected that were significant. Precision is 100% if every alert corresponds to a significant event. Note that alerting can become particularly sensitive to nonsignificant events during low-traffic periods (discussed in "Low-Traffic Services and Error Budget Alerting" on page 86).

Recall

The proportion of significant events detected. Recall is 100% if every significant event results in an alert.

Detection time

How long it takes to send notifications in various conditions. Long detection times can negatively impact the error budget.

Reset time

How long alerts fire after an issue is resolved. Long reset times can lead to confusion or to issues being ignored.

Ways to Alert on Significant Events

Constructing alert rules for your SLOs can become quite complex. Here we present six ways to configure alerting on significant events, in order of increasing fidelity, to arrive at an option that offers good control over the four parameters of precision, recall, detection time, and reset time simultaneously. Each of the following approaches addresses a different problem, and some eventually solve multiple problems at the same time. The first three nonviable attempts work toward the latter three viable alerting strategies, with approach 6 being the most viable and most highly recommended option. The first method is simple to implement but inadequate, while the optimal method provides a complete solution to defend an SLO over both the long and the short term.

For the purposes of this discussion, "error budgets" and "error rates" apply to all SLIs, not just those with "error" in their name. In the section "What to Measure: Using SLIs" on page 20, we recommend using SLIs that capture the ratio of good events to total events. The error budget gives the number of allowed bad events, and the error rate is the ratio of bad events to total events.

1: Target Error Rate ≥ SLO Threshold

For the most trivial solution, you can choose a small time window (for example, 10 minutes) and alert if the error rate over that window exceeds the SLO.

For example, if the SLO is 99.9% over 30 days, alert if the error rate over the previous 10 minutes is ≥ 0.1%:

```
- alert: HighErrorRate
  expr: job:slo_errors_per_request:ratio_rate10m{job="myjob"} >= 0.001
```

 This 10-minute average is calculated in Prometheus with a Recording rule:

```
record: job:slo_errors_per_request:ratio_rate10m
expr:
  sum(rate(slo_errors[10m])) by (job)
  /
  sum(rate(slo_requests[10m])) by (job)
```

If you don't export slo_errors and slo_requests from your job, you can create the time series by renaming a metric:

```
record: slo_errors
expr: http_errors
```

Alerting when the recent error rate is equal to the SLO means that the system detects a budget spend of:

$$\frac{\text{alerting window size}}{\text{reporting period}}$$

Figure 5-1 shows the relationship between detection time and error rate for an example service with an alert window of 10 minutes and a 99.9% SLO.

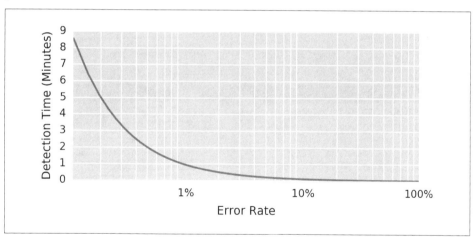

Figure 5-1. Detection time for an example service with an alert window of 10 minutes and a 99.9% SLO

Table 5-1 shows the benefits and disadvantages of alerting when the immediate error rate is too high.

Table 5-1. Pros and cons of alerting when the immediate error rate is too high

Pros	Cons
Detection time is good: 0.6 seconds for a total outage. This alert fires on any event that threatens the SLO, exhibiting good recall.	Precision is low: The alert fires on many events that do not threaten the SLO. A 0.1% error rate for 10 minutes would alert, while consuming *only 0.02% of the monthly error budget.* Taking this example to an extreme, you could receive up to 144 alerts per day every day, not act upon any alerts, and still meet the SLO.

2: Increased Alert Window

We can build upon the preceding example by changing the size of the alert window to improve precision. By increasing the window size, you spend a higher budget amount before triggering an alert.

To keep the rate of alerts manageable (*http://bit.ly/2LQYspl*), you decide to be notified only if an event consumes 5% of the 30-day error budget—a 36-hour window:

```
- alert: HighErrorRate
    expr: job:slo_errors_per_request:ratio_rate36h{job="myjob"} > 0.001
```

Now, the detection time is:

$$\frac{1 - \text{SLO}}{\text{error ratio}} \times \text{alerting window size}$$

Table 5-2 shows the benefits and disadvantages of alerting when the error rate is too high over a larger window of time.

Table 5-2. Pros and cons of alerting when the error rate is too high over a larger window of time

Pros	Cons
Detection time is still good: 2 minutes and 10 seconds for a complete outage. Better precision than the previous example: by ensuring that the error rate is sustained for longer, an alert will likely represent a significant threat to the error budget.	Very poor reset time: In the case of 100% outage, an alert will fire shortly after 2 minutes, and continue to fire for the next 36 hours. Calculating rates over longer windows can be expensive in terms of memory or I/O operations, due to the large number of data points.

Figure 5-2 shows that while the error rate over a 36-hour period has fallen to a negligible level, the 36-hour average error rate remains above the threshold.

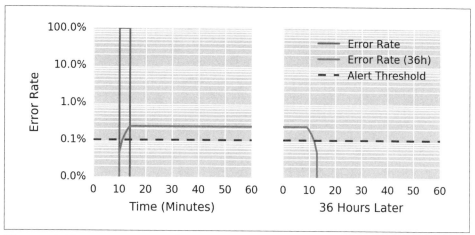

Figure 5-2. Error rate over a 36-hour period

3: Incrementing Alert Duration

Most monitoring systems allow you to add a duration parameter to the alert criteria so the alert won't fire unless the value remains above the threshold for some time. You may be tempted to use this parameter as a relatively inexpensive way to add longer windows:

```
- alert: HighErrorRate
    expr: job:slo_errors_per_request:ratio_rate1m{job="myjob"} > 0.001
    for: 1h
```

Table 5-3 shows the benefits and disadvantages of using a duration parameter for alerts.

Table 5-3. Pros and cons of using a duration parameter for alerts

Pros	Cons
Alerts can be higher precision. Requiring a sustained error rate before firing means that alerts are more likely to correspond to a significant event.	Poor recall and poor detection time: Because the duration does not scale with the severity of the incident, a 100% outage alerts after one hour, the same detection time as a 0.2% outage. The 100% outage would consume 140% of the 30-day budget in that hour.
	If the metric even momentarily returns to a level within SLO, the duration timer resets. An SLI that fluctuates between missing SLO and passing SLO may never alert.

For the reasons listed in Table 5-3, we do not recommend using durations as part of your SLO-based alerting criteria.[1]

---

[1] Duration clauses can occasionally be useful when you are filtering out ephemeral noise over very short durations. However, you still need to be aware of the cons listed in this section.

Figure 5-3 shows the average error rate over a 5-minute window of a service with a 10-minute duration before the alert fires. A series of 100% error spikes lasting 5 minutes every 10 minutes never triggers an alert, despite consuming 35% of the error budget.

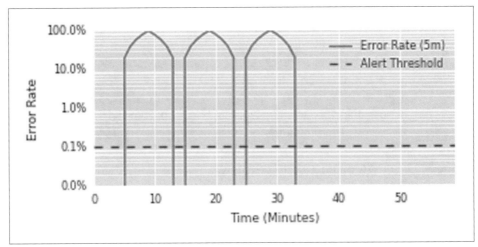

Figure 5-3. A service with 100% error spikes every 10 minutes

Each spike consumed almost 12% of the 30-day budget, yet the alert never triggered.

4: Alert on Burn Rate

To improve upon the previous solution, you want to create an alert with good detection time and high precision. To this end, you can introduce a burn rate to reduce the size of the window while keeping the alert budget spend constant.

Burn rate is how fast, relative to the SLO, the service consumes the error budget. Figure 5-4 shows the relationship between burn rates and error budgets.

The example service uses a burn rate of 1, which means that it's consuming error budget at a rate that leaves you with exactly 0 budget at the end of the SLO's time window (see Chapter 4 (*http://bit.ly/2szBKsK*) in our first book). With an SLO of 99.9% over a time window of 30 days, a constant 0.1% error rate uses exactly all of the error budget: a burn rate of 1.

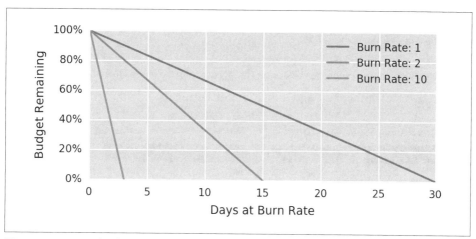

Figure 5-4. Error budgets relative to burn rates

Table 5-4 shows burn rates, their corresponding error rates, and the time it takes to exhaust the SLO budget.

Table 5-4. Burn rates and time to complete budget exhaustion

Burn rate	Error rate for a 99.9% SLO	Time to exhaustion
1	0.1%	30 days
2	0.2%	15 days
10	1%	3 days
1,000	100%	43 minutes

By keeping the alert window fixed at one hour and deciding that a 5% error budget spend is significant enough to notify someone, you can derive the burn rate to use for the alert.

For burn rate–based alerts, the time taken for an alert to fire is:

$$\frac{1 - SLO}{error\ ratio} \times \text{alerting window size} \times \text{burn rate}$$

The error budget consumed by the time the alert fires is:

$$\frac{\text{burn rate} \times \text{alerting window size}}{\text{period}}$$

Five percent of a 30-day error budget spend over one hour requires a burn rate of 36. The alerting rule now becomes:

```
- alert: HighErrorRate
  expr: job:slo_errors_per_request:ratio_rate1h{job="myjob"} > 36 * 0.001
```

Table 5-5 shows the benefits and limitations of alerting based on burn rate.

Table 5-5. Pros and cons of alerting based on burn rate

Pros	Cons
Good precision: This strategy chooses a significant portion of error budget spend upon which to alert.	Low recall: A 35x burn rate never alerts, but consumes all of the 30-day error budget in 20.5 hours.
Shorter time window, which is cheaper to calculate.	Reset time: 58 minutes is still too long.
Good detection time.	
Better reset time: 58 minutes.	

5: Multiple Burn Rate Alerts

Your alerting logic can use multiple burn rates and time windows, and fire alerts when burn rates surpass a specified threshold. This option retains the benefits of alerting on burn rates and ensures that you don't overlook lower (but still significant) error rates.

It's also a good idea to set up ticket notifications for incidents that typically go unnoticed but can exhaust your error budget if left unchecked—for example, a 10% budget consumption in three days. This rate of errors catches significant events, but since the rate of budget consumption provides adequate time to address the event, you don't need to page someone.

We recommend 2% budget consumption in one hour and 5% budget consumption in six hours as reasonable starting numbers for paging, and 10% budget consumption in three days as a good baseline for ticket alerts. The appropriate numbers depend on the service and the baseline page load. For busier services, and depending on on-call responsibilities over weekends and holidays, you may want ticket alerts for the six-hour window.

Table 5-6 shows the corresponding burn rates and time windows for percentages of SLO budget consumed.

Table 5-6. Recommended time windows and burn rates for percentages of SLO budget consumed

SLO budget consumption	Time window	Burn rate	Notification
2%	1 hour	14.4	Page
5%	6 hours	6	Page
10%	3 days	1	Ticket

The alerting configuration may look like something like:

```
expr: (
        job:slo_errors_per_request:ratio_rate1h{job="myjob"} > (14.4*0.001)
      or
        job:slo_errors_per_request:ratio_rate6h{job="myjob"} > (6*0.001)
      )
severity: page

expr: job:slo_errors_per_request:ratio_rate3d{job="myjob"} > 0.001
severity: ticket
```

Figure 5-5 shows the detection time and alert type according to the error rate.

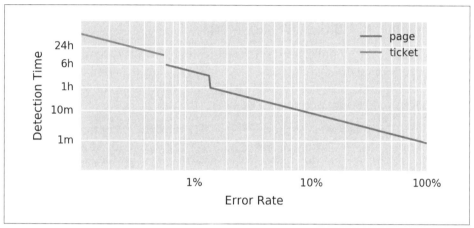

Figure 5-5. Error rate, detection time, and alert notification

Multiple burn rates allow you to adjust the alert to give appropriate priority based on how quickly you have to respond. If an issue will exhaust the error budget within hours or a few days, sending an active notification is appropriate. Otherwise, a ticket-based notification to address the alert the next working day is more appropriate.[2]

Table 5-7 lists the benefits and disadvantages of using multiple burn rates.

---

2 As described in the introduction (*http://bit.ly/2xCtP3S*) to *Site Reliability Engineering*, pages and tickets are the only valid ways to get a human to take action.

Table 5-7. Pros and cons of using multiple burn rates

Pros	Cons
Ability to adapt the monitoring configuration to many situations according to criticality: alert quickly if the error rate is high; alert eventually if the error rate is low but sustained. Good precision, as with all fixed-budget portion alert approaches. Good recall, because of the three-day window. Ability to choose the most appropriate alert type based upon how quickly someone has to react to defend the SLO.	More numbers, window sizes, and thresholds to manage and reason about. An even longer reset time, as a result of the three-day window. To avoid multiple alerts from firing if all conditions are true, you need to implement alert suppression. For example: 10% budget spend in five minutes also means that 5% of the budget was spent in six hours, and 2% of the budget was spent in one hour. This scenario will trigger three notifications unless the monitoring system is smart enough to prevent it from doing so.

6: Multiwindow, Multi-Burn-Rate Alerts

We can enhance the multi-burn-rate alerts in iteration 5 to notify us only when we're *still* actively burning through the budget—thereby reducing the number of false positives. To do this, we need to add another parameter: a shorter window to check if the error budget is still being consumed as we trigger the alert.

A good guideline is to make the short window 1/12 the duration of the long window, as shown in Figure 5-6. The graph shows both alerting threshold. After experiencing 15% errors for 10 minutes, the short window average goes over the alerting threshold immediately, and the long window average goes over the threshold after 5 minutes, at which point the alert starts firing. The short window average drops below the threshold 5 minutes after the errors stop, at which point the alert stops firing. The long window average drops below the threshold 60 minutes after the errors stop.

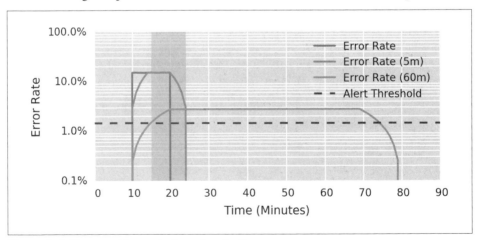

Figure 5-6. Short and long windows for alerting

For example, you can send a page-level alert when you exceed the 14.4x burn rate over both the previous one hour and the previous five minutes. This alert fires only once you've consumed 2% of the budget, but exhibits a better reset time by ceasing to fire five minutes later, rather than one hour later:

```
expr: (
        job:slo_errors_per_request:ratio_rate1h{job="myjob"} > (14.4*0.001)
      and
        job:slo_errors_per_request:ratio_rate5m{job="myjob"} > (14.4*0.001)
      )
    or
      (
        job:slo_errors_per_request:ratio_rate6h{job="myjob"} > (6*0.001)
      and
        job:slo_errors_per_request:ratio_rate30m{job="myjob"} > (6*0.001)
      )
severity: page

expr: (
        job:slo_errors_per_request:ratio_rate24h{job="myjob"} > (3*0.001)
      and
        job:slo_errors_per_request:ratio_rate2h{job="myjob"} > (3*0.001)
      )
    or
      (
        job:slo_errors_per_request:ratio_rate3d{job="myjob"} > 0.001
      and
        job:slo_errors_per_request:ratio_rate6h{job="myjob"} > 0.001
      )
severity: ticket
```

We recommend the parameters listed in Table 5-8 as the starting point for your SLO-based alerting configuration.

Table 5-8. Recommended parameters for a 99.9% SLO alerting configuration

Severity	Long window	Short window	Burn rate	Error budget consumed
Page	1 hour	5 minutes	14.4	2%
Page	6 hours	30 minutes	6	5%
Ticket	3 days	6 hours	1	10%

We have found that alerting based on multiple burn rates is a powerful way to implement SLO-based alerting.

Table 5-9 shows the benefits and limitations of using multiple burn rates and window sizes.

Table 5-9. Pros and cons of using multiple burn rates and window sizes

Pros	Cons
A flexible alerting framework that allows you to control the type of alert according to the severity of the incident and the requirements of the organization.	Lots of parameters to specify, which can make alerting rules hard to manage. For more on managing alerting rules, see "Alerting at Scale" on page 89.
Good precision, as with all fixed-budget portion alert approaches.	
Good recall, because of the three-day window.	

Low-Traffic Services and Error Budget Alerting

The multiwindow, multi-burn-rate approach just detailed works well when a sufficiently high rate of incoming requests provides a meaningful signal when an issue
arises. However, these approaches can cause problems for systems that receive a low
rate of requests. If a system has either a low number of users or natural low-traffic
periods (such as nights and weekends), you may need to alter your approach.

It's harder to automatically distinguish unimportant events in low-traffic services.
For example, if a system receives 10 requests per hour, then a single failed request
results in an hourly error rate of 10%. For a 99.9% SLO, this request constitutes a
1,000x burn rate and would page immediately, as it consumed 13.9% of the 30-day
error budget. This scenario allows for only seven failed requests in 30 days. Single
requests can fail for a large number of ephemeral and uninteresting reasons that
aren't necessarily cost-effective to solve in the same way as large systematic outages.

The best solution depends on the nature of the service: what is the impact[3] of a single
failed request? A high-availability target may be appropriate if failed requests are one-
off, high-value requests that aren't retried. It may make sense from a business perspective to investigate every single failed request. However, in this case, the alerting
system notifies you of an error too late.

We recommend a few key options to handle a low-traffic service:

- Generate artificial traffic to compensate for the lack of signal from real users.
- Combine smaller services into a larger service for monitoring purposes.
- Modify the product so that either:
    - It takes more requests to qualify a single incident as a failure.
    - The impact of a single failure is lower.

---

3 The section "What to Measure: Using SLIs" on page 20 recommends a style of SLI that scales according to the
impact on the user.

Generating Artificial Traffic

A system can synthesize user activity to check for potential errors and high-latency requests. In the absence of real users, your monitoring system can detect synthetic errors and requests, so your on-call engineers can respond to issues before they impact too many actual users.

Artificial traffic provides more signals to work with, and allows you to reuse your existing monitoring logic and SLO values. You may even already have most of the necessary traffic-generating components, such as black-box probers and integration tests.

Generating artificial load does have some downsides. Most services that warrant SRE support are complex, and have a large system control surface. Ideally, the system should be designed and built for monitoring using artificial traffic. Even for a non-trivial service, you can synthesize only a small portion of the total number of user request types. For a stateful service, the greater number of states exacerbates this problem.

Additionally, if an issue affects real users but doesn't affect artificial traffic, the successful artificial requests hide the real user signal, so you aren't notified that users see errors.

Combining Services

If multiple low-traffic services contribute to one overall function, combining their requests into a single higher-level group can detect significant events more precisely and with fewer false positives. For this approach to work, the services must be related in some way—you can combine microservices that form part of the same product, or multiple request types handled by the same binary.

A downside to combining services is that a complete failure of an individual service may not count as a significant event. You can increase the likelihood that a failure will affect the group as a whole by choosing services with a shared failure domain, such as a common backend database. You can still use longer-period alerts that eventually catch these 100% failures for individual services.

Making Service and Infrastructure Changes

Alerting on significant events aims to provide sufficient notice to mitigate problems before they exhaust the entire error budget. If you can't adjust the monitoring to be less sensitive to ephemeral events, and generating synthetic traffic is impractical, you might instead consider changing the service to reduce the user impact of a single failed request. For example, you might:

- Modify the client to retry, with exponential backoff and jitter.[4]
- Set up fallback paths that capture the request for eventual execution, which can take place on the server or on the client.

These changes are useful for high-traffic systems, but even more so for low-traffic systems: they allow for more failed events in the error budget, more signal from monitoring, and more time to respond to an incident before it becomes significant.

Lowering the SLO or Increasing the Window

You might also want to reconsider if the impact of a single failure on the error budget accurately reflects its impact on users. If a small number of errors causes you to lose error budget, do you really need to page an engineer to fix the issue immediately? If not, users would be equally happy with a lower SLO. With a lower SLO, an engineer is notified only of a larger sustained outage.

Once you have negotiated lowering the SLO with the service's stakeholders (for example, lowering the SLO from 99.9% to 99%), implementing the change is very simple: if you already have systems in place for reporting, monitoring, and alerting based upon an SLO threshold, simply add the new SLO value to the relevant systems.

Lowering the SLO does have a downside: it involves a product decision. Changing the SLO affects other aspects of the system, such as expectations around system behavior and when to enact the error budget policy. These other requirements may be more important to the product than avoiding some number of low-signal alerts.

In a similar manner, increasing the time window used for the alerting logic ensures alerts that trigger pages are more significant and worthy of attention.

In practice, we use some combination of the following methods to alert for low-traffic services:

- Generating fake traffic, when doing so is possible and can achieve good coverage
- Modifying clients so that ephemeral failures are less likely to cause user harm
- Aggregating smaller services that share some failure mode
- Setting SLO thresholds commensurate with the actual impact of a failed request

---

4 See "Overloads and Failure" (*http://bit.ly/2J2gqr0*) in *Site Reliability Engineering*.

Extreme Availability Goals

Services with an extremely low or an extremely high availability goal may require special consideration. For example, consider a service that has a 90% availability target. Table 5-8 says to page when 2% of the error budget in a single hour is consumed. Because a 100% outage consumes only 1.4% of the budget in that hour, this alert could never fire. If your error budgets are set over long time periods, you may need to tune your alerting parameters.

For services with an extremely high availability goal, the time to exhaustion for a 100% outage is extremely small. A 100% outage for a service with a target monthly availability of 99.999% would exhaust its budget in 26 seconds—which is smaller than the metric collection interval of many monitoring services, let alone the end-to-end time to generate an alert and pass it through notification systems like email and SMS. Even if the alert goes straight to an automated resolution system, the issue may entirely consume the error budget before you can mitigate it.

Receiving notifications that you have only 26 seconds of budget left isn't necessarily a bad strategy; it's just not useful for defending the SLO. The only way to defend this level of reliability is to design the system so that the chance of a 100% outage is extremely low. That way, you can fix issues before consuming the budget. For example, if you initially roll out that change to only 1% of your users, and burn your error budget at the same rate of 1%, you now have 43 minutes before you exhaust your error budget. See Chapter 16 for tactics on designing such a system.

Alerting at Scale

When you scale your service, make sure that your alerting strategy is likewise scalable. You might be tempted to specify custom alerting parameters for individual services. If your service comprises 100 microservices (or equivalently, a single service with 100 different request types), this scenario very quickly accumulates toil and cognitive load that does not scale.

In this case, we strongly advise against specifying the alert window and burn rate parameters independently for each service, because doing so quickly becomes overwhelming.[5] Once you decide on your alerting parameters, apply them to all your services.

One technique for managing a large number of SLOs is to group request types into buckets of approximately similar availability requirements. For example, for a service

---

5 With the exception of temporary changes to alerting parameters, which are necessary when you're fixing an ongoing outage and you don't need to receive notifications during that period.

with availability and latency SLOs, you can group its request types into the following buckets:

CRITICAL
> For request types that are the most important, such as a request when a user logs in to the service.

HIGH_FAST
> For requests with high availability and low latency requirements. These requests involve core interactive functionality, such as when a user clicks a button to see how much money their advertising inventory has made this month.

HIGH_SLOW
> For important but less latency-sensitive functionality, such as when a user clicks a button to generate a report of all advertising campaigns over the past few years, and does not expect the data to return instantly.

LOW
> For requests that must have some availability, but for which outages are mostly invisible to users—for example, polling handlers for account notifications that can fail for long periods of time with no user impact.

NO_SLO
> For functionality that is completely invisible to the user—for example, dark launches or alpha functionality that is explicitly outside of any SLO.

By grouping requests rather than placing unique availability and latency objectives on all request types, you can group requests into five buckets, like the example in Table 5-10.

Table 5-10. Request class buckets according to similar availability requirements and thresholds

Request class	Availability	Latency @ 90%[a]	Latency @ 99%
CRITICAL	99.99%	100 ms	200 ms
HIGH_FAST	99.9%	100 ms	200 ms
HIGH_SLOW	99.9%	1,000 ms	5,000 ms
LOW	99%	None	None
NO_SLO	None	None	None

[a] Ninety percent of requests are faster than this threshold (*http://bit.ly/2LgeYy1*).

These buckets provide sufficient fidelity for protecting user happiness, but entail less toil than a system that is more complicated and expensive to manage that *probably* maps more precisely to the user experience.

Conclusion

If you set SLOs that are meaningful, understood, and represented in metrics, you can configure alerting to notify an on-caller only when there are actionable, specific threats to the error budget.

The techniques for alerting on significant events range from alerting when your error rate goes above your SLO threshold to using multiple levels of burn rate and window sizes. In most cases, we believe that the multiwindow, multi-burn-rate alerting technique is the most appropriate approach to defending your application's SLOs.

We hope we have given you the context and tools required to make the right configuration decisions for your own application and organization.

CHAPTER 6

Eliminating Toil

By David Challoner, Joanna Wijntjes, David Huska,
Matthew Sartwell, Chris Coykendall, Chris Schrier,
John Looney, and Vivek Rau
with Betsy Beyer, Max Luebbe, Alex Perry, and Murali Suriar

Google SREs spend much of their time optimizing—squeezing every bit of performance from a system through project work and developer collaboration. But the scope of optimization isn't limited to compute resources: it's also important that SREs optimize how they spend their time. Primarily, we want to avoid performing tasks classified as *toil*. For a comprehensive discussion of toil, see Chapter 5 (*http://bit.ly/2Lg1TEN*) in *Site Reliability Engineering*. For the purposes of this chapter, we'll define toil as the repetitive, predictable, constant stream of tasks related to maintaining a service.

Toil is seemingly unavoidable for any team that manages a production service. System maintenance inevitably demands a certain amount of rollouts, upgrades, restarts, alert triaging, and so forth. These activities can quickly consume a team if left unchecked and unaccounted for. Google limits the time SRE teams spend on operational work (including both toil- and non-toil-intensive work) at 50% (for more context on why, see Chapter 5 (*http://bit.ly/2Lg1TEN*) in our first book). While this target may not be appropriate for your organization, there's still an advantage to placing an upper bound on toil, as identifying and quantifying toil is the first step toward optimizing your team's time.

What Is Toil?

Toil tends to fall on a spectrum measured by the following characteristics, which are described in our first book. Here, we provide a concrete example for each toil characteristic:

Manual
> When the *tmp* directory on a web server reaches 95% utilization, engineer Anne logs in to the server and scours the filesystem for extraneous log files to delete.

Repetitive
> A full *tmp* directory is unlikely to be a one-time event, so the task of fixing it is repetitive.

Automatable[1]
> If your team has remediation documents with content like "log in to X, execute this command, check the output, restart Y if you see...," these instructions are essentially pseudocode to someone with software development skills! In the *tmp* directory example, the solution has been partially automated. It would be even better to fully automate the problem detection and remediation by not requiring a human to run the script. Better still, submit a patch so that the software no longer breaks in this way.

Nontactical/reactive
> When you receive too many alerts along the lines of "disk full" and "server down," they distract engineers from higher-value engineering and potentially mask other, higher-severity alerts. As a result, the health of the service suffers.

Lacks enduring value
> Completing a task often brings a satisfying sense of accomplishment, but this repetitive satisfaction isn't a positive in the long run. For example, closing that alert-generated ticket ensured that the user queries continued to flow and HTTP requests continued to serve with status codes < 400, which is good. However, resolving the ticket today won't prevent the issue in the future, so the payback has a short duration.

Grows at least as fast as its source
> Many classes of operational work grow as fast as (or faster than) the size of the underlying infrastructure. For example, you can expect time spent performing

---

1 Whether something is automatable is the most subjective characteristic listed here; your perspective will evolve as you gain experience by automating away toil. A problem space that once seemed intractable (or too risky) will become feasible once you get comfortable with "letting the robots do the work."

hardware repairs to increase in lock-step fashion with the size of a server fleet. Physical repair work may unavoidably scale with the number of machines, but ancillary tasks (for example, making software/configuration changes) doesn't necessarily have to.

Sources of toil may not always meet all of these criteria, but remember that toil comes in many forms. In addition to the preceding traits, consider the effect a particular piece of work has on team morale. Do people enjoy doing a task and find it rewarding, or is it the type of work that's often neglected because it's viewed as boring or unrewarding?[2] Toil can slowly deflate team morale. Time spent working on toil is generally time not spent thinking critically or expressing creativity; reducing toil is an acknowledgment that an engineer's effort is better utilized in areas where human judgment and expression are possible.

Example: Manual Response to Toil

by John Looney, Production Engineering Manager at Facebook, and always an SRE at heart

It's not always clear that a certain chunk of work is toil. Sometimes, a "creative" solution—writing a workaround—is not the right call. Ideally, your organization should reward root-cause fixes over fixes that simply mask a problem.

My first assignment after joining Google (April 2005) was to log in to broken machines, investigate why they were broken, then fix them or send them to a hardware technician. This task seemed simple until I realized there were over 20,000 broken machines at any given time!

The first broken machine I investigated had a root filesystem that was completely full with gigabytes of nonsense logs from a Google-patched network driver. I found another thousand broken machines with the same problem. I shared my plan to address the issue with my teammate: I'd write a script to ssh into all broken machines and check if the root filesystem was full. If the filesystem was full, the script would truncate any logs larger than a megabyte in */var/log* and restart syslog.

My teammate's less-than-enthusiastic reaction to my plan gave me pause. He pointed out that it's better to fix root causes when possible. In the medium to long term, writing a script that masked the severity of the problem would waste time (by not fixing the *actual* problem) and potentially cause more problems later.

---

2 Some engineers do not mind working on toil for a prolonged period—not everyone's tolerance threshold for toil is the same. Over the longer term, toil causes career stagnation while promoting burnout-induced turnover. A certain level of toil is unavoidable, but we recommend reducing it where feasible—for the health of the team, the service, and individuals alike.

Analysis demonstrated that each server probably cost $1 per hour. According to my train of thought, shouldn't cost be the most important metric? I hadn't considered that if I fixed the symptom, there would be no incentive to fix the root cause: the kernel team's release test suite didn't check the volume of logs these machines produced.

The senior engineer directed me at the kernel source so I could find the offensive line of code and log a bug against the kernel team to improve their test suite. My objective cost/benefit analysis showing that the problem was costing Google $1,000 per hour convinced the devs to fix the problem with my patch.

My patch was turned into a new kernel release that evening, and the next day I rolled it out to the affected machines. The kernel team updated their test suite later the following week. Instead of the short-term endorphin hit of fixing those machines every morning, I now had the more cerebral pleasure of knowing that I'd fixed the problem properly.

Measuring Toil

How do you know how much of your operational work is toil? And once you've decided to take action to reduce toil, how do you know if your efforts were successful or justified? Many SRE teams answer these questions with a combination of experience and intuition. While such tactics might produce results, we can improve upon them.

Experience and intuition are not repeatable, objective, or transferable. Members of the same team or organization often arrive at different conclusions regarding the magnitude of engineering effort lost to toil, and therefore prioritize remediation efforts differently. Furthermore, toil reduction efforts can span quarters or even years (as demonstrated by some of the case studies in this chapter), during which time team priorities and personnel can change. To maintain focus and justify cost over the long term, you need an objective measure of progress. Usually, teams must choose a toil-reduction project from several candidates. An objective measure of toil allows your team to evaluate the severity of the problems and prioritize them to achieve maximum return on engineering investment.

Before beginning toil reduction projects, it's important to analyze cost versus benefit and to confirm that the time saved through eliminating toil will (at minimum) be proportional to the time invested in first developing and then maintaining an automated solution (Figure 6-1). Projects that look "unprofitable" from a simplistic comparison of hours saved versus hours invested might still be well worth undertaking because of the many indirect or intangible benefits of automation. Potential benefits could include:

- Growth in engineering project work over time, some of which will further reduce toil

- Increased team morale and decreased team attrition and burnout
- Less context switching for interrupts, which raises team productivity
- Increased process clarity and standardization
- Enhanced technical skills and career growth for team members
- Reduced training time
- Fewer outages attributable to human errors
- Improved security
- Shorter response times for user requests

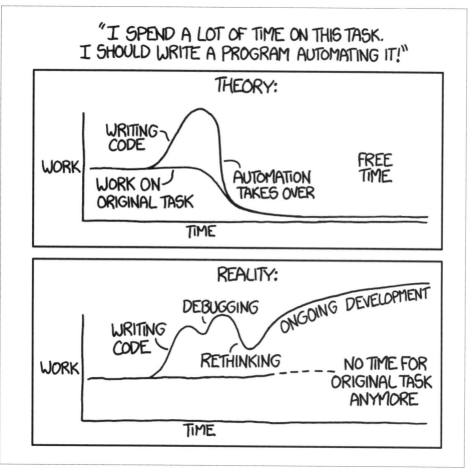

Figure 6-1. Estimate the amount of time you'll spend on toil reduction efforts, and make sure that the benefits outweigh the cost (source: xkcd.com/1319/)

So how do we recommend you measure toil?

1. Identify it. Chapter 5 (*http://bit.ly/2Lg1TEN*) of the first SRE book offers guidelines for identifying the toil in your operations. The people best positioned to identify toil depend upon your organization. Ideally, they will be stakeholders, including those who will perform the actual work.

2. Select an appropriate unit of measure that expresses the amount of *human* effort applied to this toil. Minutes and hours are a natural choice because they are objective and universally understood. Be sure to account for the cost of context switching. For efforts that are distributed or fragmented, a different well-understood bucket of human effort may be more appropriate. Some examples of units of measure include an applied patch, a completed ticket, a manual production change, a predictable email exchange, or a hardware operation. As long as the unit is objective, consistent, and well understood, it can serve as a measurement of toil.

3. Track these measurements continuously before, during, and after toil reduction efforts. Streamline the measurement process using tools or scripts so that collecting these measurements doesn't create additional toil!

Toil Taxonomy

Toil, like a crumbling bridge or a leaky dam, hides in the banal day to day. The categories in this section aren't exhaustive, but represent some common categories of toil. Many of these categories seem like "normal" engineering work, and they are. It's helpful to think of toil as a spectrum rather than a binary classification.

Business Processes

This is probably the most common source of toil. Maybe your team manages some computing resource—compute, storage, network, load balancers, databases, and so on—along with the hardware that supplies that resource. You deal with onboarding users, configuring and securing their machines, performing software updates, and adding and removing servers to moderate capacity. You also work to minimize cost or waste of that resource. Your team is the human interface to the machine, typically interacting with internal customers who file tickets for their needs. Your organization may even have multiple ticketing systems and work intake systems.

Ticket toil is a bit insidious because ticket-driven business processes usually accomplish their goal. Users get what they want, and because the toil is typically dispersed evenly across the team, the toil doesn't loudly and obviously call for remediation. Wherever a ticket-driven process exists, there's a chance that toil is quietly accumulating nearby. Even if you're not explicitly planning to automate a process, you can still perform process improvement work such as simplification and streamlining—the processes will be easier to automate later, and easier to manage in the meantime.

Production Interrupts

Interrupts are a general class of time-sensitive janitorial tasks that keep systems running. For example, you may need to fix an acute shortage of some resource (disk, memory, I/O) by manually freeing up disk space or restarting applications that are leaking memory. You may be filing requests to replace hard drives, "kicking" unresponsive systems, or manually tweaking capacity to meet current or expected loads. Generally, interrupts take attention away from more important work.

Release Shepherding

In many organizations, deployment tools automatically shepherd releases from development to production. Even with automation, thorough code coverage, code reviews, and numerous forms of automated testing, this process doesn't always go smoothly. Depending on the tooling and release cadence, release requests, rollbacks, emergency patches, and repetitive or manual configuration changes, releases may still generate toil.

Migrations

You may find yourself frequently migrating from one technology to another. You perform this work manually or with limited scripting because, hopefully, you're only going to move from X to Y once. Migrations come in many forms, but some examples include changes of data stores, cloud vendors, source code control systems, application libraries, and tooling.

If you approach a large-scale migration manually, the migration quite likely involves toil. You may be inclined to execute the migration manually because it's a one-time effort. While you might even be tempted to view it as "project work" rather than "toil," migration work can also meet many of the criteria of toil. Technically, modifying backup tooling for one database to work with another is software development, but this work is basically just refactoring code to replace one interface with another. This work is repetitive, and to a large extent, the business value of the backup tooling is the same as before.

Cost Engineering and Capacity Planning

Whether you own hardware or use an infrastructure provider (cloud), cost engineering and capacity planning usually entail some associated toil. For example:

- Ensuring a cost-effective baseline or burstable capability for future needs across resources like compute, memory, or IOPS (input/output operations per second). This may translate into purchase orders, AWS Reserved Instances, or Cloud/Infrastructure as a Service contract negotiation.

- Preparing for (and recovering from) critical high-traffic events like a product launch or holiday.

- Reviewing downstream and upstream service levels/limits.

- Optimizing workload against different footprint configurations. (Do you want to buy one big box, or four smaller boxes?)

- Optimizing applications against the billing specifics of proprietary cloud service offerings (DynamoDB for AWS or Cloud Datastore for GCP).

- Refactoring tooling to make better use of cheaper "spot" or "preemptable" resources.

- Dealing with oversubscribed resources, either upstream with your infrastructure provider or with your downstream customers.

Troubleshooting for Opaque Architectures

Distributed microservice architectures are now common, and as systems become more distributed, new failure modes arise. An organization may not have the resources to build sophisticated distributed tracing, high-fidelity monitoring, or detailed dashboards. Even if the business does have these tools, they might not work with all systems. Troubleshooting may even require logging in to individual systems and writing ad hoc log analytics queries with scripting tools.

Troubleshooting itself isn't inherently bad, but you should aim to focus your energy on novel failure modes—not the same type of failure every week caused by brittle system architecture. With each new critical upstream dependency of availability P, availability decreases by 1 − P due to the combined chance of failure. A four 9s service that adds nine critical four 9s dependencies is now a three 9s service.[3]

---

[3] In other words, if a service and its nine dependencies each have 99.99% availability, the aggregate availability of the service will be 0.9999^{10} = 99.9%. For further reading on how dependencies factor into service availability, see "The Calculus of Service Availability" (*http://queue.acm.org/detail.cfm?id=3096459*).

Toil Management Strategies

We've found that performing toil management is critical if you're operating a production system of any scale. Once you identify and quantify toil, you need a plan for eliminating it. These efforts may take weeks or quarters to accomplish, so it's important to have a solid overarching strategy.

Eliminating toil at its source is the optimal solution, but if doing so isn't possible, then you must handle the toil by other means. Before we dive into the specifics of two in-depth case studies, this section provides some general strategies to consider when you're planning a toil reduction effort. As you'll observe across the two stories, the nuances of toil vary from team to team (and from company to company), but regardless of specificity, some common tactics ring true for organizations of any size or flavor. Each of the following patterns is illustrated in a concrete way in at least one of the subsequent case studies.

Identify and Measure Toil

We recommend that you adopt a data-driven approach to identify and compare sources of toil, make objective remedial decisions, and quantify the time saved (return on investment) by toil reduction projects. If your team is experiencing toil overload, treat toil reduction as its own project. Google SRE teams often track toil in bugs and rank toil according to the cost to fix it and the time saved by doing so. See the section "Measuring Toil" on page 96 for techniques and guidance.

Engineer Toil Out of the System

The optimal strategy for handling toil is to eliminate it at the source. Before investing effort in managing the toil generated by your existing systems and processes, examine whether you can reduce or eliminate that toil by changing the system.

A team that runs a system in production has invaluable experience with how that system works. They know the quirks and tedious bits that cause the most amount of toil. An SRE team should apply this knowledge by working with product development teams to develop operationally friendly software that is not only less toilsome, but also more scalable, secure, and resilient.

Reject the Toil

A toil-laden team should make data-driven decisions about how best to spend their time and engineering effort. In our experience, while it may seem counterproductive, rejecting a toil-intensive task should be the first option you consider. For a given set of toil, analyze the cost of responding to the toil versus not doing so. Another tactic is to intentionally delay the toil so that tasks accumulate for batch or parallelized processing. Working with toil in larger aggregates reduces interrupts and helps you identify patterns of toil, which you can then target for elimination.

Use SLOs to Reduce Toil

As discussed in Chapter 2, services should have a documented service level objective (SLO) (*http://bit.ly/2LL02ch*). A well-defined SLO enables engineers to make informed decisions. For example, you might ignore certain operational tasks if doing so does not consume or exceed the service's error budget. An SLO that focuses on overall service health, rather than individual devices, is more flexible and sustainable as the service grows. See Chapter 2 for guidance on writing effective SLOs.

Start with Human-Backed Interfaces

If you have a particularly complex business problem with many edge cases or types of requests, consider a partially automated approach as an interim step toward full automation. In this approach, your service receives structured data—usually via a defined API—but engineers may still handle some of the resulting operations. Even if some manual effort remains, this "engineer behind the curtain" approach allows you to incrementally move toward full automation. Use customer input to progress toward a more uniform way of collecting this data; by decreasing free-form requests, you can move closer to handling all requests programmatically. This approach can save back and forth with customers (who now have clear indicators of the information you need) and save you from overengineering a big-bang solution before you've fully mapped and understood the domain.

Provide Self-Service Methods

Once you've defined your service offering via a typed interface (see "Start with Human-Backed Interfaces" on page 102), move to providing self-service methods for users. You can provide a web form, binary or script, API, or even just documentation that tells users how to issue pull requests to your service's configuration files. For example, rather than asking engineers to file a ticket to provision a new virtual machine for their development work, give them a simple web form or script that triggers the provisioning. Allow the script to gracefully degrade to a ticket for specialized requests or if a failure occurs.[4] Human-backed interfaces are a good start in the war against toil, but service owners should always aim to make their offerings self-service where possible.

---

4 Of course, you won't be able to handle some one-off cases via self-service ("you want a VM with *how* much RAM?"), but aim to cover the majority of use cases. Moving 80–90% of requests to self-service is still a huge reduction in workload!

Get Support from Management and Colleagues

In the short term, toil reduction projects reduce the staff available to address feature requests, performance improvements, and other operational tasks. But if the toil reduction is successful, in the long term the team will be healthier and happier, and have more time for engineering improvements.

It is important for everyone in the organization to agree that toil reduction is a worthwhile goal. Manager support is crucial in defending staff from new demands. Use objective metrics about toil to make the case for pushback.

Promote Toil Reduction as a Feature

To create strong business cases for toil reduction, look for opportunities to couple your strategy with other desirable features or business goals. If a complementary goal —for example, security, scalability, or reliability—is compelling to your customers, they'll be more willing to give up their current toil-generating systems for shiny new ones that aren't as toil intentive. Then, reducing toil is just a nice side effect of helping users!

Start Small and Then Improve

Don't try to design the perfect system that eliminates all toil. Automate a few high-priority items first, and then improve your solution using the time you gained by eliminating that toil, applying the lessons learned along the way. Pick clear metrics such as MTTR (Mean Time to Repair) to measure your success.

Increase Uniformity

At scale, a diverse production environment becomes exponentially harder to manage. Special devices require time-consuming and error-prone ongoing management and incident response. You can use the "pets versus cattle" approach[5] to add redundancy and enforce consistency in your environment. Choosing what to consider cattle depends on the needs and scale of an organization. It may be reasonable to evaluate network links, switches, machines, racks of machines, or even entire clusters as interchangeable units.

Shifting devices to a cattle philosophy may have a high initial cost, but can reduce the cost of maintenance, disaster recovery, and resource utilization in the medium to long term. Equipping multiple devices with the same interface implies that they have

---

5 In short, moving away from individual specialized devices toward a fleet of devices with a common interface. See "Case Study 1: Reducing Toil in the Datacenter with Automation" on page 107 for a detailed explanation of this analogy.

consistent configuration, are interchangeable, and require less maintenance. A consistent interface (to divert traffic, restore traffic, perform a shutdown, etc.) for a variety of devices allows for more flexible and scalable automation.

Google aligns business incentives to encourage engineering teams to unify across our ever-evolving toolkit of internal technologies and tools. Teams are free to choose their own approaches, but they have to own the toil generated by unsupported tools or legacy systems.

Assess Risk Within Automation

Automation can save countless hours in human labor, but in the wrong circumstances, it can also trigger outages. In general, defensive software is always a good idea; when automation wields admin-level powers, defensive software is crucial. Every action should be assessed for its safety before execution. This includes changes that might reduce serving capacity or redundancy. When you're implementing automation, we recommend the following practices:

- Handle user input defensively, even if that input is flowing from upstream systems—that is, be sure to validate the input carefully in context.
- Build in safeguards that are equivalent to the types of indirect alerts that a human operator might receive. Safeguards might be as simple as command timeouts, or might be more sophisticated checks of current system metrics or the number of current outages. For this reason, monitoring, alerting, and instrumentation systems should be consumable by both machine and human operators.
- Be aware that even read operations, naively implemented, can spike device load and trigger outages. As automation scales, these safety checks can eventually dominate workload.
- Minimize the impact of outages caused by incomplete safety checks of automation. Automation should default to human operators if it runs into an unsafe condition.

Automate Toil Response

Once you identify a piece of toil as automatable, it's worthwhile to consider how to best mirror the human workflow in software. You rarely want to literally transcribe a human workflow into a machine workflow. Also note that automation shouldn't eliminate human understanding of what's going wrong.

Once your process is thoroughly documented, try to break down the manual work into components that can be implemented separately and used to create a composable software library that other automation projects can reuse later. As the upcoming datacenter repair case study illustrates, automation often provides the opportunity to reevaluate and simplify human workflows.

Use Open Source and Third-Party Tools

Sometimes you don't have to do all of the work to reduce toil yourself. Many efforts like one-off migrations may not justify building their own bespoke tooling, but you're probably not the first organization to tread this path. Look for opportunities to use or extend third-party or open source libraries to reduce development costs, or at least to help you transition to partial automation.

Use Feedback to Improve

It's important to actively seek feedback from other people who interact with your tools, workflows, and automation. Your users will make different assumptions about your tools depending on their understanding of the underlying systems. The less familiar your users are with these systems, the more important it is to actively seek feedback from users. Leverage surveys, user experience (UX) studies, and other mechanisms to understand how your tools are used, and integrate this feedback to produce more effective automation in the future.

Human input is only one dimension of feedback you should consider. Also measure the effectiveness of automated tasks according to metrics like latency, error rate, rework rate, and human time saved (across all groups involved in the process). Ideally, find high-level measures you can compare before and after any automation or toil reduction efforts.

Legacy Systems

Most engineers with SRE-like responsibilities have encountered at least one legacy system in their work. These older systems often introduce problems with respect to user experience, security, reliability, or scalability. They tend to operate like a magical black box in that they "mostly work," but few people understand how they work. They're scary and expensive to modify, and keeping them running often requires a good deal of toilsome operational ritual.

The journey away from a legacy system usually follows this path:

1. **Avoidance:** There are many reasons to not tackle this problem head on: you may not have the resources to replace this system. You judge the cost and risk to your business as not worth the cost of a replacement. There may not be any substantially better solutions commercially available. Avoidance is effectively choosing to accept technical debt and to move away from SRE principles and toward system administration.

---

2. **Encapsulation/augmentation:** You can bring SREs on board to build a shell of abstracted APIs, automation, configuration management, monitoring, and testing around these legacy systems that will offload work from SAs. The legacy system remains brittle to change, but now you can at least reliably identify misbehavior and roll back when appropriate. This tactic is still avoidance, but is a bit like refinancing high-interest technical debt into low-interest technical debt. It's usually a stopgap measure to prepare for an incremental replacement.

3. **Replacement/refactoring:** Replacing a legacy system can require a vast amount of determination, patience, communication, and documentation. It's best undertaken incrementally. One approach is to define a common interface that sits in front of and abstracts a legacy system. This strategy helps you slowly and safely migrate users to alternatives (*http://bit.ly/2HbyKbw*) using release engineering techniques like canarying or blue-green deployments. Often, the "specification" of a legacy system is really defined only by its historical usage, so it's helpful to build production-sized data sets of historical expected inputs and outputs to build confidence that new systems aren't diverging from expected behavior (or are diverging in an expected way).

4. **Retirement/custodial ownership:** Eventually the majority of customers or functionality is migrated to one or more alternatives. To align business incentives, stragglers who haven't migrated can assume custodial ownership of remnants of the legacy system.

Case Studies

The following case studies illustrate the strategies for toil reduction just discussed. Each story describes an important area of Google's infrastructure that reached a point at which it could no longer scale sublinearly with human effort; over time, an increasing number of engineer hours resulted in smaller returns on that investment. Much of that effort you'll now recognize as toil. For each case study, we detail how the engineers identified, assessed, and mitigated that toil. We also discuss the results and the lessons we learned along the way.

In the first case study, Google's datacenter networking had a scaling problem: we had a massive number of Google-designed components and links to monitor, mitigate, and repair. We needed a strategy to minimize the toilsome nature of this work for datacenter technicians.

The second case study focuses on a team running their own "outlier" specialized hardware to support toil-intensive business processes that had become deeply entrenched within Google. This case study illustrates benefits of reevaluating and replacing operationally expensive business processes. It demonstrates that with a little persistence and perseverance, it's possible to move to alternatives even when constrained by the institutional inertia of a large organization.

Taken together, these case studies provide a concrete example of each toil reduction strategy covered earlier. Each case study begins with a list of relevant toil reduction strategies.

Case Study 1: Reducing Toil in the Datacenter with Automation

Toil reduction strategies highlighted in Case Study 1:

- Engineer toil out of the system
- Start small and then improve
- Increase uniformity
- Use SLOs to reduce toil
- Assess risk within automation
- Use feedback to improve
- Automate toil response

Background

This case study takes place in Google's datacenters. Similar to all datacenters, Google's machines are connected to switches, which are connected to routers. Traffic flows in and out from these routers via links that in turn connect to other routers on the internet. As Google's requirements for handling internet traffic grew, the number of machines required to serve that traffic increased dramatically. Our datacenters grew in scope and complexity as we figured out how to serve a large amount of traffic efficiently and economically. This growth changed the nature of datacenter manual repairs from occasional and interesting to frequent and rote—two signals of toil.

When Google first began running its own datacenters, each datacenter's network topology featured a small number of network devices that managed traffic to a large number of machines. A single network device failure could significantly impact network performance, but a relatively small team of engineers could handle troubleshooting the small number of devices. At this early stage, engineers debugged problems and shifted traffic away from failed components manually.

Our next-generation datacenter had significantly more machines and introduced software-defined networking (SDN) with a folded Clos topology (*http://bit.ly/ 2LfbMCG*), which greatly increased the number of switches. Figure 6-2 shows the complexity of traffic flow for a small datacenter Clos switch network. This proportionately larger number of devices meant that a larger number of components could now fail. While each individual failure had less impact on network performance than before, the sheer volume of issues began to overwhelm the engineering staff.

In addition to introducing a heavy load of new problems to debug, the complex layout was confusing to technicians: Which exact links needed to be checked? Which line card[6] did they need to replace? What was a Stage 2 switch, versus a Stage 1 or Stage 3 switch? Would shutting down a switch create problems for users?

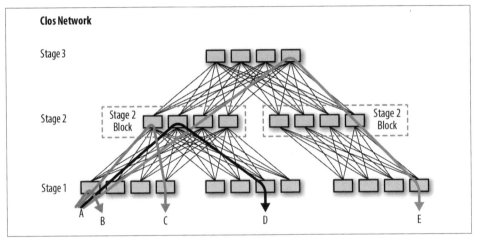

Figure 6-2. A small Clos network, which supports 480 machines attached below Stage 1

Repairing failed datacenter line cards was one obvious growing work backlog, so we targeted this task as our first stage of creating datacenter network repair automation. This case study describes how we introduced repair automation for our first generation of line cards (named Saturn). We then discuss the improvements we introduced with the next generation of line cards for Jupiter fabrics.

As shown in Figure 6-3, before the automation project, each fix in the datacenter line-card repair workflow required an engineer to do the following:

1. Check that it was safe to move traffic from the affected switch.
2. Shift traffic away from the failed device (a "drain" operation).

---

6 A line card is a modular component that usually provides multiple interfaces to the network. It is seated in the backplane of a chassis along with other line cards and components. Modular network switches consist of a chassis that includes a backplane, power entry modules, control card module, and one or more line cards. Each line card supports network connections either to machines or other line cards (in other switches). As with a USB network interface adapter, you can replace any line card without powering down the whole switch, provided the line card has been "drained," meaning that the other interfaces have been told to stop sending traffic to it.

---

3. Perform a reboot or repair (such as replacing a line card).

4. Shift traffic back to the device (an "undrain" operation).

This unvarying and repetitive work of draining, undraining, and repairing devices is a textbook example of toil. The repetitive nature of the work introduced problems of its own—for example, engineers might multitask by working on a line card while also debugging more challenging problems. As a result, the distracted engineer might accidentally introduce an unconfigured switch back to the network.

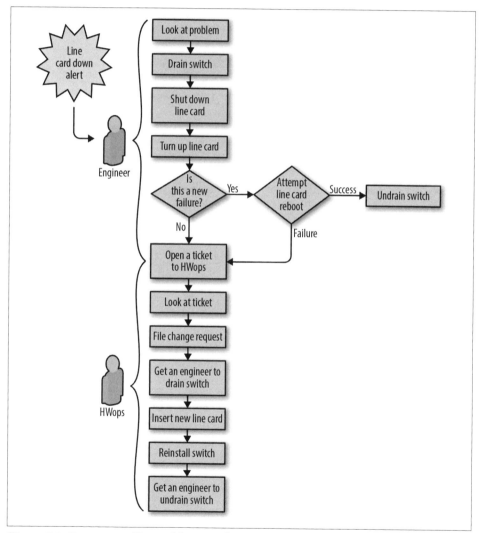

Figure 6-3. Datacenter (Saturn) line-card repair workflow before automation: all steps require manual work

Problem Statement

The datacenter repairs problem space had the following dimensions:

- We couldn't grow the team fast enough to keep up with the volume of failures, and we couldn't fix problems fast enough to prevent negative impact to the fabric.

- Performing the same steps repeatedly and frequently introduced too many human errors.

- Not all line-card failures had the same impact. We didn't have a way to prioritize more serious failures.

- Some failures were transient. We wanted the option to restart the line card or reinstall the switch as a first pass at repair. Ideally, we could then programmatically capture the problem if it happened again and flag the device for replacement.

- The new topology required us to manually assess the risk of isolating capacity before we could take action. Every manual risk assessment was an opportunity for human error that could result in an outage. Engineers and technicians on the floor didn't have a good way to gauge how many devices and links would be impacted by their planned repair.

What We Decided to Do

Instead of assigning every issue to an engineer for risk assessment, drain, undrain, and validation, we decided to create a framework for automation that, when coupled with an on-site technician where appropriate, could support these operations programmatically.

Design First Effort: Saturn Line-Card Repair

Our high-level goal was to build a system that would respond to problems detected on network devices, rather than relying on an engineer to triage and fix these problems. Instead of sending a "line card down" alert to an engineer, we wrote the software to request a drain (to remove traffic) and create a case for a technician. The new system had a few notable features:

- We leveraged existing tools where possible. As shown in Figure 6-3, our alerting could already detect problems on the fabric line cards; we repurposed that alerting to trigger an automated repair. The new workflow also repurposed our ticketing system to support network repairs.

- We built in automated risk assessment to prevent accidental isolation of devices during a drain and to trigger safety mechanisms where required. This eliminated a huge source of human errors.
- We adopted a strike policy that was tracked by software: the first failure (or strike) only rebooted the card and reinstalled the software. A second failure triggered card replacement and full return to the vendor.

Implementation

The new automated workflow (shown in Figure 6-4) proceeded as follows:

1. The problematic line card is detected and a symptom is added to a specific component in the database.

2. The repair service picks up the problem and enables repairs on the switch. The service performs a risk assessment to confirm that no capacity will be isolated by the operation, and then:

   a. Drains traffic from the entire switch.

   b. Shuts down the line card.

   c. If this is a first failure, reboots the card and undrains the switch, restoring service to the switch. At this point, the workflow is complete.

   d. If this is the second failure, the workflow proceeds to step 3.

3. The workflow manager detects the new case and sends it to a pool of repair cases for a technician to claim.

4. The technician claims the case, sees a red "stop" in the UI (indicating that the switch needs to be drained before repairs are started), and executes the repair in three steps:

   a. Initiates the chassis drain via a "Prep component" button in the technician UI.

   b. Waits for the red "stop" to clear, indicating that the drain is complete and the case is actionable.

   c. Replaces the card and closes the case.

5. The automated repair system brings the line card up again. After a pause to give the card time to initialize, the workflow manager triggers an operation to restore traffic to the switch and close the repair case.

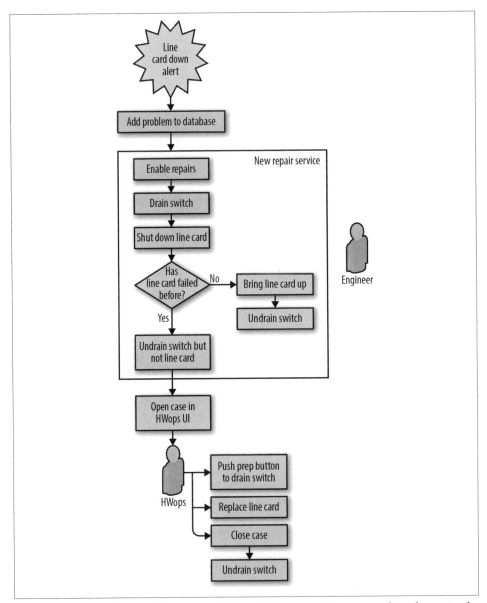

Figure 6-4. Saturn line-card repair workflow with automation: manual work required only to push a button and replace the line card

The new system freed the engineering team from a large volume of toilsome work, giving them more time to pursue productive projects elsewhere: working on Jupiter, the next-generation Clos topology.

Design Second Effort: Saturn Line-Card Repair Versus Jupiter Line-Card Repair

Capacity requirements in the datacenter continued to double almost every 12 months. As a result, our next-generation datacenter fabric, Jupiter, was more than six times larger than any previous Google fabric. The volume of problems was also six times larger. Jupiter presented scaling challenges for repair automation because thousands of fiber links and hundreds of line cards could fail in each layer. Fortunately, the increase in potential failure points was accompanied by far greater redundancy, which meant we could implement more ambitious automation. As shown in Figure 6-5, we preserved some of the general workflow from Saturn and added a few important modifications:

- After an automated drain/reboot cycle determined that we wanted to replace hardware, we sent the hardware to a technician. However, instead of requiring a technician to initiate the drain with the "Push prep button to drain switch," we automatically drained the entire switch when it failed.

- We added automation for installing and pushing the configuration that engages after component replacement.

- We enabled automation for verifying that the repair was successful before undraining the switch.

- We focused attention on recovering the switch without involving a technician unless absolutely necessary.

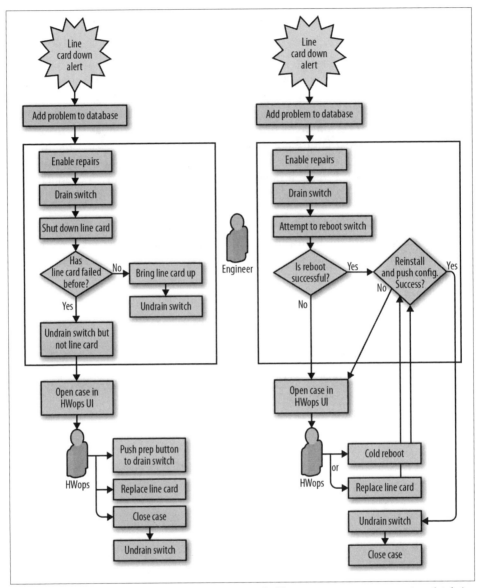

Figure 6-5. Saturn line-card down automation (left) versus Jupiter automation (right)

Implementation

We adopted a simple and uniform workflow for every line-card problem on Jupiter switches: declare the switch down, drain it, and begin a repair.

The automation carried out the following:

1. The problem switch-down is detected and a symptom is added to the database.
2. The repair service picks up the problem and enables repairs on the switch: drain the entire switch, and add a drain reason.
   a. If this is the second failure within six months, proceed to step 4.
   b. Otherwise, proceed to step 3.
3. Attempt (via two distinct methods) to power-cycle the switch.
   a. If the power-cycle is successful, run automated verification, then install and configure the switch. Remove the repair reason, clear the problem from the database, and undrain the switch.
   b. If preceding sanity-checking operations fail, send the case to a technician with an instruction message.
4. If this was the second failure, send the case directly to the technician, requesting new hardware. After the hardware change occurs, run automated verification and then install and configure the switch. Remove the repair reason, clear the problem from the database, and undrain the switch.

This new workflow management was a complete rewrite of the previous repair system. Again, we leveraged existing tools when possible:

- The operations for configuring new switches (install and verify) were the same operations we needed to verify that a switch that had been replaced.
- Deploying new fabrics quickly required the ability to BERT[7] and cable-audit[8] programmatically. Before restoring traffic, we reused that capability to automatically run test patterns on links that had fallen into repairs. These tests further improved performance by identifying faulty links.

The next logical improvement was to automate mitigation and repair of memory errors on Jupiter switch line cards. As shown in Figure 6-6, prior to automation, this workflow depended heavily on an engineer to determine if the failure was hardware- or software-related, and then to drain and reboot the switch or arrange a repair if appropriate.

---

7 Bit error rate test: check for unhealthy links before restoring service.

8 Check for miscabled ports.

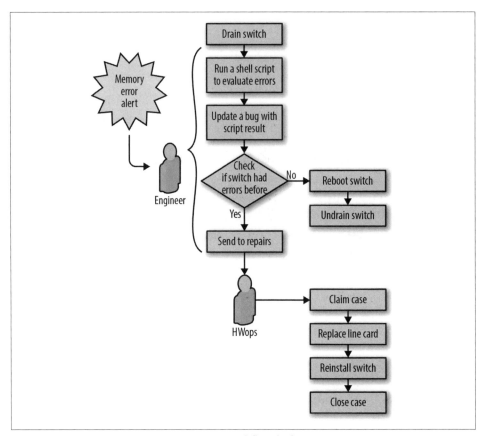

Figure 6-6. Jupiter memory error repair workflow before automation

Our automation simplified the repair workflow by no longer attempting to trouble-shoot memory errors (see "Sometimes imperfect automation is good enough" on page 119 for why this made sense). Instead, we treated memory errors the same way we handled failed line cards. To extend automation to memory errors, we simply had to add another symptom to a config file to make it act on the new problem type. Figure 6-7 depicts the automated workflow for memory errors.

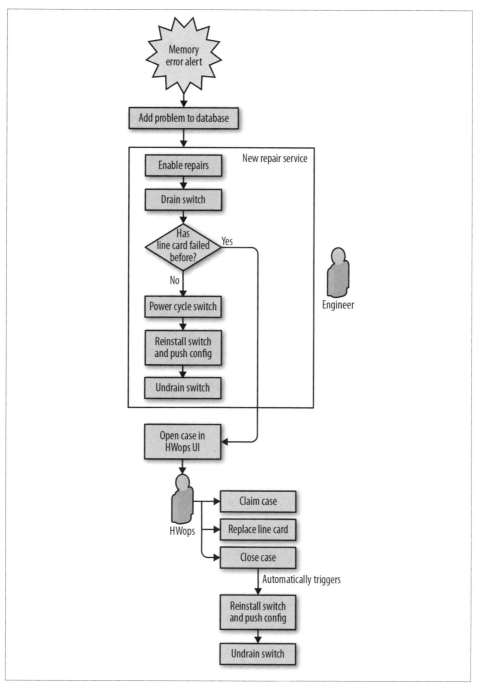

Figure 6-7. Jupiter memory error repair workflow with automation

Lessons Learned

During the several years we worked to automate network repair, we learned a lot of general lessons about how to effectively reduce toil.

UIs should not introduce overhead or complexity

For Saturn-based line cards, replacing a line card required draining the entire switch. Draining the entire switch early in the repair process meant losing the working capacity of all line cards on the switch while waiting for replacement parts and a technician. We introduced a button in the UI called "Prep component" that allowed a technician to drain traffic from the entire switch right before they were ready to replace the card, thereby eliminating unnecessary downtime for the rest of the switch (see "Push prep button to drain switch" in Figure 6-5).

This aspect of the UI and repair workflow introduced a number of unexpected problems:

- After pressing the button, the technician did not get feedback on drain progress but instead simply had to wait for permission to proceed.
- The button didn't reliably sync with the actual state of the switch. As a result, sometimes a drained switch did not get repaired, or a technician interrupted traffic by acting upon an undrained switch.
- Components that did not have automation enabled returned a generic "contact engineering" message when a problem arose. Newer technicians did not know the best way to reach someone who could help. Engineers who were contacted were not always immediately available.

In response to user reports and problems with regressions caused by the complexity of the feature, we designed future workflows to ensure the switch was safe and ready for repair before the technician arrived at the switch.

Don't rely on human expertise

We leaned too heavily on experienced datacenter technicians to identify errors in our system (for example, when the software indicated it was safe to proceed with repairs, but the switch was actually undrained). These technicians also had to perform several tasks manually, without being prompted by automation.

Experience is difficult to replicate. In one particularly high-impact episode, a technician decided to expedite the "press button and wait for results" experience by initiating concurrent drains on every line card waiting for repairs at the datacenter, resulting in network congestion and user-visible packet loss. Our software didn't anticipate and prevent this action because we didn't test the automation with new technicians.

Design reusable components

Where possible, avoid monolithic designs. Build complex automation workflows from separable components, each of which handles a distinct and well-defined task. We could easily reuse or adapt key components of our early Jupiter automation for each successive generation of fabric, and it was easier to add new features when we could build on automation that already existed. Successive variations on Jupiter-type fabrics could leverage work done in earlier iterations.

Don't overthink the problem

We overanalyzed the memory error problem for Jupiter line cards. In our attempts at precise diagnosis, we sought to distinguish software errors (fixable by reboots) from hardware errors (which required card replacement), and also to identify errors that impacted traffic versus errors that did not. We spent nearly three years (2012–2015) collecting data on over 650 discrete memory error problems before realizing this exercise was probably overkill, or at least shouldn't block our repair automation project.

Once we decided to act upon any error we detected, it was straightforward to use our existing repair automation to implement a simple policy of draining, rebooting, and reinstalling switches in response to memory errors. If the problem recurred, we concluded that the failure was likely hardware-based and requested component replacement. We gathered data over the course of a quarter and discovered that most of the errors were transient—most switches recovered after being rebooted and reinstalled. We didn't need additional data to perform the repair, so the three-year delay in implementing the automation was unnecessary.

Sometimes imperfect automation is good enough

While the ability to verify links with BERT before undraining them was handy, BERT tooling didn't support network management links. We added these links into the existing link repair automation with a check that allowed them to skip verification. We were comfortable bypassing verification because the links didn't carry customer traffic, and we could add this functionality later if verification turned out to be important.

Repair automation is not fire and forget

Automation can have a very long lifetime, so make sure to plan for project continuity as people leave and join the team. New engineers should be trained on legacy systems so they can fix bugs. Due to parts shortages for Jupiter fabrics, Saturn-based fabrics lived on long after the originally targeted end-of-life date, requiring us to introduce some improvements quite late in Saturn's overall lifespan.

Once adopted, automation may become entrenched for a long time, with positive and negative consequences. When possible, design your automation to evolve in a flexible way. Relying on inflexible automation makes systems brittle to change. Policy-based automation can help by clearly separating intent from a generic implementation engine, allowing automation to evolve more transparently.

Build in risk assessment and defense in depth

After building new tools for Jupiter that determined the risk of a drain operation before executing it, the complexity we encountered led us to introduce a secondary check for defense in depth. The second check established an upper limit for the number of impacted links, and another limit for impacted devices. If we exceeded either threshold, a tracking bug to request further investigation opened automatically. We tuned these limits over time to reduce false positives. While we originally considered this a temporary measure until the primary risk assessment stabilized, the secondary check has proven useful for identifying atypical repair rates due to power outages and software bugs (for one example, see "Automation: Enabling Failure at Scale" (*http://bit.ly/2LfMKDh*) in *Site Reliability Engineering*).

Get a failure budget and manager support

Repair automation can sometimes fail, especially when first introduced. Management support is crucial in preserving the project and empowering the team to persevere. We recommend establishing an error budget for antitoil automation. You should also explain to external stakeholders that automation is essential despite the risk of failures, and that it enables continuous improvement in reliability and efficiency.

Think holistically

Ultimately, the complexity of scenarios to be automated is the real hurdle to overcome. Reexamine the system before you work on automating it—can you simplify the system or workflow first?

Pay attention to all aspects of the workflow you are automating, not just the aspects that create toil for you personally. Conduct testing with the people directly involved in the work and actively seek their feedback and assistance. If they make mistakes, find out how your UI could be clearer, or what additional safety checks you need. Make sure your automation doesn't create new toil—for example, by opening unnecessary tickets that need human attention. Creating problems for other teams will increase resistance to future automation endeavors.

Case Study 2: Decommissioning Filer-Backed Home Directories

 Toil reduction strategies highlighted in Case Study 2:

- Consider decommissioning legacy systems
- Promote toil reduction as a feature
- Get support from management and colleagues
- Reject the toil
- Start with human-backed interfaces
- Provide self-service methods
- Start small and then improve
- Use feedback to improve

Background

In the early days of Google, the Corp Data Storage (CDS) SRE team provided home directories to all Googlers. Similar to Active Directory's Roaming Profiles, common in Enterprise IT, Googlers could use the same home directories across workstations and platforms. The CDS team also offered "Team Shares" for cross-team collaboration in a shared storage space. We provided home directories and Team Shares via a fleet of Netapp Storage Appliances over NFS/CIFS (or "filers"). This storage was operationally expensive but provided a much-needed service to Googlers.

Problem Statement

As years passed, these filer solutions were mostly deprecated by other, better, storage solutions: our version control systems (Piper[9]/Git-on-borg[10]), Google Drive, Google Team Drive, Google Cloud Storage, and an internal, shared, globally distributed file-system called x20. These alternatives were superior for a number of reasons:

---

9 Piper is Google's internal version control system. For more information, see Rachel Potvin and Josh Levenberg, "Why Google Stores Billions of Lines of Code in a Single Repository," *Communications of the ACM* 59, no. 7 (2016): 78–87, *http://bit.ly/2J4jgMi*.

10 Google also has scalable self-service Git hosting for code that doesn't live in Piper.

- NFS/CIFS protocols were never designed to operate over a WAN, so user experience rapidly degraded with even a few tens of milliseconds of latency. This created problems for remote workers or globally distributed teams, as the data could live only in one location.
- Compared to alternatives, these appliances were expensive to run and scale.
- It would have taken significant work to make NFS/CIFS protocols compatible with Google's Beyond Corp[11] network security model.

Most relevant to this chapter, home directories and Team Shares were toil-intensive. Many facets of storage provisioning were ticket-driven. Although these workflows were often partially scripted, they represented a sizable amount of the CDS team's toil. We spent a lot of time creating and configuring shares, modifying access, troubleshooting end user issues, and performing turnups and turndowns to manage capacity. CDS also managed the provisioning, racking, and cabling processes for this specialized hardware, in addition to their configuration, updates, and backups. Due to latency requirements, we often had to deploy in remote offices instead of Google datacenters—which sometimes required a team member to travel a substantial distance to manage a deployment.

What We Decided to Do

First, we gathered data: CDS created a tool called Moonwalk to analyze how employees used our services. We collected traditional business intelligence metrics like daily active users (DAU) and monthly active users (MAU), and asked questions like, "Which job families actually use their home directories?" and "Of the users who use filers every day, what kind of files do they access the most?" Moonwalk, combined with user surveys, validated that the business needs currently served by filers could be better served by alternative solutions that had lower operational overhead and cost. Another compelling business reason led us to move away from filers: if we could migrate most of our filer use cases to G Suite/GCP, then we could use the lessons we learned to improve these products, thereby enabling other large enterprises to migrate to G Suite/GCP.

No single alternative could meet all of the current filer use cases. However, by breaking the problem into smaller addressable components, we found that in aggregate, a handful of alternatives could cover all of our use cases. The alternative solutions were

---

11 Beyond Corp (*https://cloud.google.com/beyondcorp/*) is an initiative to move from a traditional perimeter-based security model to a cryptographic identity-based model. When a Google laptop connects to an internal Google service, the service verifies trust through a combination of a cryptographic certificate identifying the laptop, a second factor owned by the user (such as a USB security key), the client device config/state, and the user's credentials.

more specialized, but each provided a better user experience than a generalized filer-powered solution. For example:

x20[12]
> Was a great way for teams to globally share static artifacts like binaries

G Suite Team Drive (http://bit.ly/2soMbjQ)
> Worked well for office document collaboration, and was much more tolerant of user latency than NFS

Google's Colossus File System
> Allowed teams to share large data files more securely and scalably than NFS

Piper/Git-on-Borg
> Could better sync dotfiles (engineers' personalized tool preferences)

A new history-as-a-service tool
> Could host cross-workstation command-line history

As we catalogued use cases and found alternatives, the decommissioning plan took shape.

Design and Implementation

Moving away from filers was an ongoing, iterative, multiyear effort that entailed multiple internal projects:

Moira
> Home directory decommissioning

Tekmor
> Migrating the long tail of home directory users

Migra
> Team Share decommissioning

Azog
> Retiring home directory/share infrastructure and associated hardware

This case study focuses on the first project, Moira. The subsequent projects built upon what we learned from and created for Moira.

As shown in Figure 6-8, Moira consisted of four phases.

---

12 x20 is an internal globally shared, highly available filesystem with POSIX-like filesystem semantics.

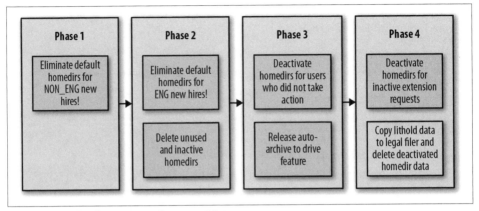

Figure 6-8. The four stages of Project Moira

The first step to retiring a legacy system is to stop or (often more realistically) to slow or discourage new adoption. It's much more painful to take something away from users than never offer it in the first place. Moonwalk data showed that nonengineering Googlers used their shared home directories the least, so our initial phase targeted these users. As the phases grew in scope, so did our confidence in the alternative storage solutions and our migration processes and tooling. Each phase of the project had an associated design document that examined the proposal along dimensions like security, scalability, testing, and launch. We also paid special attention to user experience, expectations, and communication. Our goal was making sure that users affected by each phase understood the reasons for the decommissioning project and the easiest way to archive or migrate their data.

Key Components

Moonwalk

While we had basic statistics about our users' shares (share sizes, for example), we needed to understand our users' workflows to help drive business decisions around the deprecation. We set up a system called Moonwalk to gather and report this information.

Moonwalk stored the data about who was accessing what files and when in BigQuery, which allowed us to create reports and perform ad hoc queries to understand our users better. Using BigQuery, we summarized access patterns across 2.5 billion files using 300 terabytes of disk space. This data was owned by 60,000 POSIX users in 400 disk volumes on 124 NAS appliances in 60 geographic sites around the world.

Moira Portal

Our large user base made managing the home directory decommissioning effort with a manual ticket-based process untenable. We needed to make the entire process—surveying users, communicating the reasons for the decommissioning project, and walking through either archiving their data or migrating to an alternative—as low-touch as possible. Our final requirements were:

- A landing page describing the project
- A continually updated FAQ
- The status and usage information associated with the current user's share
- Options to request, deactivate, archive, delete, extend, or reactivate a share

Our business logic became fairly complicated because we had to account for a number of user scenarios. For example, a user might leave Google, go on a temporary leave, or have data under a litigation hold. Figure 6-9 provides a sample design doc state diagram illustrating this complexity.

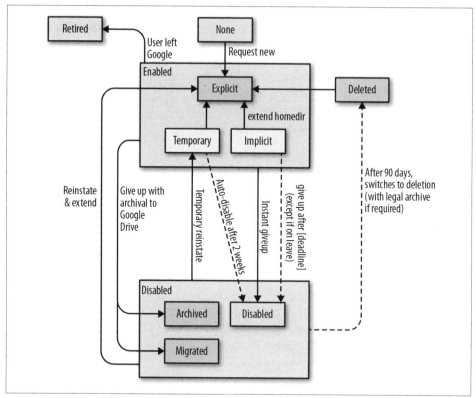

Figure 6-9. Business logic based upon user scenarios

The technology powering the portal was relatively simple. Written in Python with the Flask framework, it read and wrote to a Bigtable, and used a number of background jobs and schedulers to manage its work.

Archiving and migration automation

We needed a lot of ancillary tooling to glue the portal and configuration management together, and to query and communicate with users. We also needed to be sure we identified the right users for the right communications. False positives (erroneously reporting action required) or false negatives (failing to notify a user that you were taking something away) were both unacceptable, and errors here would mean extra work in the form of lost credibility and customer service.

We worked with alternative storage system owners to add features to their roadmaps. As a result, less mature alternatives became more suitable for filer use cases as the project progressed. We could also use and extend tooling from other teams. For example, we used another team's internally developed tool to migrate data from Google Cloud Storage to Google Drive as part of the Portal's auto-archiving functionality.

The effort required substantial software development over the life of the project. We built and iterated upon each component—the Moonwalk reporting pipeline, the portal, and the automation to better manage retiring and archiving shares—in response to the next phase's requirements and user feedback. We approached a feature-complete state only in phase three (almost two years in); and even then, we needed additional tooling to handle a "long tail" of around 800 users. This low and slow approach had definite benefits. It allowed us to:

- Maintain a lean team (averaging three CDS team members)
- Reduce the disruption to user workflows
- Limit toil for Techstop (Google's internal technical support organization)
- Build tools on an as-needed basis to avoid wasted engineering effort

As with all engineering decisions, there were tradeoffs: the project would be long-lived, so the team had to endure filer-related operational toil while engineering these solutions.

The program officially completed in 2016. We've reduced home directories from 65,000 to around 50 at the time of writing. (The current Azog Project aims to retire these last users and fully decommission the filer hardware.) Our users' experience has improved, and CDS has retired operationally expensive hardware and processes.

Lessons Learned

While no one alternative could replace the filer-backed storage that Googlers had used for 14+ years, we didn't necessarily need a wholesale replacement. By effectively moving up the stack from a generalized but limited filesystem-level solution to multiple application-specific solutions, we traded flexibility for improved scalability, latency tolerance, and security. The Moira team had to anticipate a variety of user journeys and consider alternatives in various stages of maturity. We had to manage expectations around these alternatives: in aggregate, they could provide a better user experience, but getting there wouldn't be painless. We learned the following lessons about effectively reducing toil along the way.

Challenge assumptions and retire expensive business processes

Business requirements drift and new solutions continuously emerge, so it's worthwhile to periodically question toil-intensive business processes. As we discussed in "Toil Management Strategies" on page 101, rejecting toil (deciding not to perform toilsome tasks) is often the simplest way to eliminate it, even though this approach isn't always quick or easy. Shore up your case with user analytics and business justifications beyond mere toil reduction. The primary business justification for filer decommissioning came down to the benefits of a Beyond Corp security model. So, while Moira was a great way to reduce the CDS team's toil, emphasizing the many security benefits of decommissioning filers made for a more compelling business case.

Build self-service interfaces

We built a custom portal for Moira (which was relatively expensive), but there are often easier alternatives. Many teams at Google manage and configure their services using version control, and process organizational requests in the form of pull requests (called *changelists*, or CLs). This approach requires little or no involvement from the service's team, but gives us the benefits of code review and continuous deployment processes to validate, test, and deploy internal service configuration changes.

Start with human-backed interfaces

At several points, the Moira team used an "engineer behind the curtain" approach that married automation with manual work by engineers. For example, share requests opened tracking bugs, which our automation updated as we processed the requests. The system also assigned end users bugs to remind them to address their shares. Tickets can serve as a quick and dirty GUI for automation: they keep a log of work, update stakeholders, and provide a simple human fallback mechanism if automation goes awry. In our case, if a user needed help with their migration or if automation couldn't process their request, the bug was automatically routed to a queue that SREs handled manually.

Melt snowflakes

Automation craves conformity. Moira's engineers chose to retool our automation to either handle share edge cases specifically, or to delete/modify nonconforming shares to match expectations of tooling. This allowed us to approach zero-touch automation for much of the migration processes.

 Fun Fact: At Google, this practice of changing reality to fit the code rather than the other way around is called "buying the gnome." This phrase references a legend about Froogle, a shopping search engine from the very early days of the company.

Early in Froogle's life, a serious search quality bug caused a search for [running shoes] to return a garden gnome (wearing running shoes) as a high-ranking result. After several unsuccessful attempts to fix the bug, someone noticed that the gnome was not a mass-produced item, but a single eBay listing with a Buy It Now option. They purchased the gnome (Figure 6-10).

Figure 6-10. The garden gnome that wouldn't go away

Employ organizational nudges

Look for ways to nudge new users to adopt better (and hopefully less toil-intensive) alternatives. In this vein, Moira required escalations for new share or quota requests and recognized users who retired their shares. It's also important to provide good documentation around service setup, best practices, and when to use your service. Google teams frequently employ codelabs or cookbooks that teach users how to set up and use their service for common use cases. As a result, most user onboarding doesn't require help from the team that owns the service.

Conclusion

At minimum, the amount of toil associated with running a production service grows linearly with its complexity and scale. Automation is often the gold standard of toil elimination, and can be combined with a number of other tactics. Even when toil isn't worth the effort of full automation, you can decrease engineering and operations workloads through strategies like partial automation or changing business processes.

The patterns and methods for eliminating toil described in this chapter can be generalized to work for a variety of other large-scale production services. Eliminating toil frees up engineering time to focus on the more enduring aspects of services, and allows teams to keep manual tasks at a minimum as the complexity and scale of modern service architectures continue to increase.

It's important to note that eliminating toil isn't always the best solution. As mentioned throughout this chapter, you should consider the measurable costs associated with identifying, designing, and implementing processes or automation solutions around toil. Once you identify toil, it's crucial to determine when toil reduction makes sense, using metrics, return on investment (ROI) analysis, risk assessment, and iterative development.

Toil usually starts small, and can rapidly grow to consume an entire team. SRE teams must be relentless in eliminating toil, because even if the task seems daunting, the benefits usually exceed the costs. Each of the projects we described required perseverance and dedication from its respective teams, who sometimes battled skepticism or institutional resistance, and who always faced competing high priorities. We hope these stories encourage you to identify your toil, quantify it, and then work toward eliminating it. Even if you can't invest in a big project today, you can start with a small proof of concept that can help change your team's willingness to deal with toil.

## CHAPTER 7

Simplicity

By John Lunney, Robert van Gent, and Scott Ritchie
with Diane Bates and Niall Richard Murphy

A complex system that works is invariably found to have evolved from a simple system that worked.

—Gall's Law (*http://bit.ly/2syRTi5*)

Simplicity is an important goal for SREs, as it strongly correlates with reliability: simple software breaks less often and is easier and faster to fix when it does break. Simple systems are easier to understand, easier to maintain, and easier to test.

For SREs, simplicity is an end-to-end goal: it should extend beyond the code itself to the system architecture and the tools and processes used to manage the software lifecycle. This chapter explores some examples that demonstrate how SREs can measure, think about, and encourage simplicity.

Measuring Complexity

Measuring the complexity of software systems is not an absolute science. There are a number of ways to measure software code complexity, most of which are quite objective.[1] Perhaps the best-known and most widely available standard is cyclomatic code complexity (*http://bit.ly/1nKIrVc*), which measures the number of distinct code paths through a specific set of statements. For example, a block of code with no loops or conditionals has a cyclomatic complexity number (CCN) of 1. The software community is actually quite good at measuring code complexity, and there are measurement

---

[1] If you're interested in learning more, read this recent review (*https://arxiv.org/abs/1608.01533*) of trends in software complexity, or read Horst Zuse, *Software Complexity: Measures and Methods* (Berlin: Walter de Gruyter, 1991).

tools for a number of integrated development environments (including Visual Studio, Eclipse, and IntelliJ). We're less adept at understanding whether the resulting measured complexity is necessary or accidental, how the complexity of one method might influence a larger system, and which approaches are best for refactoring.

On the other hand, formal methodologies for measuring system complexity are rare.[2] You might be tempted to try a CCN-type approach of counting the number of distinct entities (e.g., microservices) and possible communication paths between them. However, for most sizable systems, that number can grow hopelessly large very quickly.

Some more practical proxies for systems-level complexity include:

Training time
How long does it take a new team member to go on-call? Poor or missing documentation can be a significant source of subjective complexity.

Explanation time
How long does it take to explain a comprehensive high-level view of the service to a new team member (e.g., diagram the system architecture on a whiteboard and explain the functionality and dependencies of each component)?

Administrative diversity
How many ways are there to configure similar settings in different parts of the system? Is configuration stored in a centralized place, or in multiple locations?

Diversity of deployed configurations
How many unique configurations are deployed in production (including binaries, binary versions, flags, and environments)?

Age
How old is the system? Hyrum's Law (*http://www.hyrumslaw.com/*) states that over time, the users of an API depend on every aspect of its implementation, resulting in fragile and unpredictable behaviors.

While measuring complexity is occasionally worthwhile, it's difficult. However, there seems to be no serious opposition to the observations that:

- In general, complexity will increase in living software systems unless there is a countervailing effort.
- Providing that effort is a worthwhile thing to do.

---

2 Although there are examples of it—for example, "Automated Formal Reasoning about AWS Systems" (*http://bit.ly/2spRz6g*).

Simplicity Is End-to-End, and SREs Are Good for That

Generally, production systems are not designed in a holistic fashion; rather, they grow organically. They accumulate components and connections over time as teams add new features and launch new products. While a single change might be relatively simple, every change impacts the components around it. Therefore, overall complexity can quickly become overwhelming. For example, adding retries in one component might overload a database and destabilize the whole system, or make it harder to reason about the path a given query follows through the system.

Frequently, the cost of complexity does not directly affect the individual, team, or role that introduces it—in economic terms, complexity is an externality. Instead, complexity impacts those who continue to work in and around it. Thus, it is important to have a champion for end-to-end system simplicity.

SREs are a natural fit for this role because their work requires them to treat the system as a whole.[3] In addition to supporting their own services, SREs must also have insight into the systems their service interacts with. Google's product development teams often don't have visibility on production-wide issues, so they find it valuable to consult SREs for advice on the design and operation of their systems.

 Reader action: Before an engineer goes on-call for the first time, encourage them to draw (and redraw) system diagrams. Keep a canonical set of diagrams in your documentation: they're useful to new engineers and help more experienced engineers keep up with changes.

In our experience, product developers usually end up working in a narrow subsystem or component. As a result, they don't have a mental model for the overall system, and their teams don't create system-level architecture diagrams. These diagrams are useful because they help team members visualize system interactions and articulate issues using a common vocabulary. More often than not, we find the SRE team for the service draws the system-level architecture diagrams.

 Reader action: Ensure that an SRE reviews all major design docs, and that the team documents show how the new design affects the system architecture. If a design adds complexity, the SRE might be able to suggest alternatives that simplify the system.

---

3 As a result, SRE may be a useful investment for product development leads who wish to attack complexity as a proxy for technical debt, but find it hard to justify that work within the scope of their existing team.

Case Study 1: End-to-End API Simplicity

Background

In a previous role, one of the chapter authors worked at a startup that used a key/value bag data structure in its core libraries. RPCs (remote procedure calls) took a bag and returned a bag; actual parameters were stored as key/value pairs inside the bag. The core libraries supported common operations on bags, such as serialization, encryption, and logging. All of the core libraries and APIs were extremely simple and flexible—success, right?

Sadly, no: the clients of the libraries ended up paying a penalty for the abstract nature of the core APIs. The set of keys and values (and value types) needed to be carefully documented for each service, but usually weren't. In addition, maintaining backward/forward compatibility became difficult as parameters were added, removed, or changed over time.

Lessons learned

Structured data types like Google's Protocol Buffers (*http://bit.ly/1HhFC5L*) or Apache Thrift (*https://thrift.apache.org/*) might seem more complex than their abstract general-purpose alternatives, but they result in simpler end-to-end solutions because they force upfront design decisions and documentation.

Case Study 2: Project Lifecycle Complexity

When you review the tangled spaghetti of your existing system, it might be tempting to replace it wholesale with a new, clean, simple system that solves the same problem. Unfortunately, the cost of creating a new system while maintaining the current one might not be worthwhile.

Background

Borg (*http://bit.ly/2LgqcTd*) is Google's internal container management system. It runs huge numbers of Linux containers and has a wide variety of usage patterns: batch versus production, pipelines versus servers, and more. Over the years, Borg and its surrounding ecosystem grew as hardware changed, features were added, and its scale increased.

Omega (*http://bit.ly/2HdcFJo*) was intended to be a more principled, cleaner version of Borg that supported the same use cases. However, the planned switch from Borg to Omega had a few serious problems:

- Borg continued to evolve as Omega was developed, so Omega was always chasing a moving target.

- Early estimates of the difficulty of improving Borg proved overly pessimistic, while the expectations for Omega proved overly optimistic (in practice, the grass isn't always greener).

- We didn't fully appreciate how difficult it would be to migrate from Borg to Omega. Millions of lines of configuration code across thousands of services and many SRE teams meant that the migration would be extremely costly in terms of engineering and calendar time. During the migration period, which would likely take years, we'd have to support and maintain both systems.

What we decided to do

Eventually (*http://bit.ly/2Lf4FKm*), we fed some of the ideas that emerged while designing Omega back into Borg. We also used many of Omega's concepts to jump-start Kubernetes (*https://kubernetes.io/*), an open source container management system.

Lessons learned

When considering a rewrite, think about the full project lifecycle, including development toward a moving target, a full migration plan, and extra costs you might incur during the migration time window. Wide APIs with lots of users are very hard to migrate. Don't compare the expected result to your current system. Instead, compare the expected result to what your current system would look like if you invested the same effort in improving it. Sometimes a rewrite is the best way forward, but make sure you've weighed the costs and benefits and that you don't underestimate the costs.

Regaining Simplicity

Most simplification work consists of removing elements from a system. Sometimes simplification is direct (e.g., removing a dependency on an unused piece of data fetched from a remote system). Other times, simplification requires redesign. For example, two parts of a system might need access to the same remote data. Rather than fetch it twice, a simpler system might fetch the data once and forward the result.

Whatever the work, leadership must ensure that simplification efforts are celebrated and explicitly prioritized. Simplification is efficiency—instead of saving compute or network resources, it saves engineering time and cognitive load. Treat successful simplification projects just as you treat useful feature launches, and measure and celebrate code addition and removal equally.[4] For example, Google's intranet displays a "Zombie Code Slayer" badge for engineers that delete significant amounts of code.

Simplification is a feature. You need to prioritize and staff simplification projects and reserve time for SREs to work on them. If product developers and SREs do not see simplification projects as beneficial to their careers, they won't undertake these projects. Consider making simplicity an explicit goal for particularly complex systems or overloaded teams. Create a separate bucket of time to do this work. For example, reserve 10% of engineering project time for "simplicity" projects.[5]

 Reader action: Have engineers brainstorm known complexities in the system and discuss ideas to reduce them.

As a system grows in complexity, there is a temptation to split SRE teams, focusing each new team on smaller parts of the system. While this is sometimes necessary, the reduced scope of the new teams might lessen their motivation or ability to drive larger simplification projects. Consider designating a small rotating group of SREs who maintain working knowledge of the entire stack (likely with less depth), and can push for conformity and simplification across it.

As previously mentioned, the act of diagramming your system can help you identify deeper design problems that hinder your ability to understand the system and predict its behavior. For example, when diagramming your system, you might look for the following:

Amplification
    When a call returns an error or times out and is retried on several levels, it causes the total number of RPCs to multiply.

Cyclic dependencies
    When a component depends on itself (often indirectly), system integrity can be gravely compromised—in particular, a cold start of the whole system might become impossible.

---

4 As Dijkstra said (*http://bit.ly/2xwycxq*), "If we wish to count lines of code, we should not regard them as 'lines produced' but as 'lines spent.'"

5 Reserving some portion of time for simplicity projects (10%, for example) doesn't mean the team has a green light to introduce complexity with the other 90%. It just means you are setting aside some effort with the specific goal of simplification.

Case Study 3: Simplification of the Display Ads Spiderweb

Background

Google's Display Ads business has many related products, including some that originated from acquisitions (DoubleClick, AdMob, Invite Media, etc.). These products had to be adapted to work with Google infrastructure and existing products. For example, we wanted a website using DoubleClick for Publishers to be able to show ads chosen by Google's AdSense; similarly, we wanted bidders using DoubleClick Bid Manager to have access to the real-time auctions run on Google's Ad Exchange.

These independently developed products formed a system of interconnected back-ends that was difficult to reason about. Observing what happened to traffic as it passed through components was difficult, and provisioning the right amount of capacity for each piece was inconvenient and imprecise. At one point, we added tests to make sure we had removed all infinite loops in the query flow.

What we decided to do

Ads serving SREs were the natural drivers for standardization: while each component had a specific developer team, SREs were on-call for the entire stack. One of our first undertakings was to draft uniformity standards and work with developer teams to incrementally adopt them. These standards:

- Established a single way to copy large data sets
- Established a single way to perform external data lookups
- Provided common templates for monitoring, provisioning, and configuration

Before this initiative, separate programs provided frontend and auction functionality for each product. As shown in Figure 7-1, when an ad request might hit two targeting systems, we rewrote the request to meet the expectations of the second system. This required additional code and processing, and it also opened the possibility of undesirable loops.

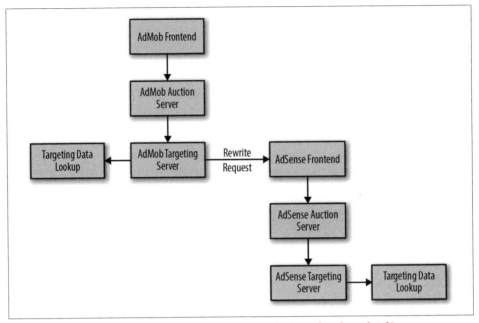

Figure 7-1. Previously, an ad request might hit both the AdMob and AdSense systems

To simplify the system, we added logic to common programs that satisfied all of our use cases, along with flags to guard the programs. Over time, we removed the flags and consolidated the functionality into fewer server backends.

Once the servers were unified, the auction server could talk to both targeting servers directly. As shown in Figure 7-2, when multiple targeting servers needed data lookups, the lookup needed to happen only once in the unified auction server.

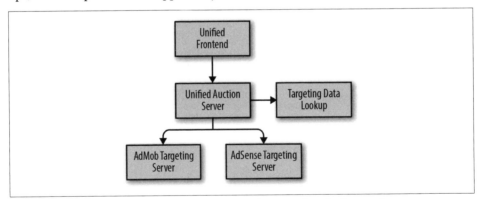

Figure 7-2. The unified auction server now performs a data lookup only once

Lessons learned

It's best to integrate an already running system into your own infrastructure incrementally.

Just as the presence of very similar functions in a single program represents a "code smell" that indicates deeper design problems, redundant lookups in a single request represent a "system smell."

When you create well-defined standards with buy-in from SRE and developers, you can provide a clear blueprint for removing complexity that managers are more likely to endorse and reward.

Case Study 4: Running Hundreds of Microservices on a Shared Platform

by Mike Curtis

Background

Over the past 15 years, Google has developed multiple successful product verticals (Search, Ads, and Gmail, to name a few) and produced a steady stream of new and refactored systems. Many of these systems have a dedicated SRE team and a corresponding domain-specific production stack that includes a bespoke development workflow, continuous integration and continuous delivery (CI/CD) software cycles, and monitoring. These unique production stacks incur significant overhead in terms of maintenance, development costs, and independent SRE engagement. They also make it harder to move services (or engineers!) between teams, or to add new services.

What we decided to do

A set of SRE teams in the social networking space worked to converge the production stacks for their services into a single managed microservices platform, managed by a single group of SREs. The shared platform is compliant with best practices, and it bundles and automatically configures many previously underused features that improve reliability and facilitate debugging. Regardless of their SRE engagement level, new services within the scope of the SRE team were required to use the common platform, and legacy services had to either migrate to the new platform or be phased out.

After its success in the social network space, the shared platform is gaining adoption with other SRE and non-SRE teams across Google.

Design

We used microservices so we could quickly update and deploy features—a single monolithic service changes slowly. Services are *managed*, not *hosted*: rather than removing control and responsibility from individual teams, we empower them to manage their services effectively themselves. We provide workflow tools that service teams can use to release, monitor, and more.

The tools we provide include a UI, API, and a command-line interface that SREs and developers use to interact with their stack. The tools make the developer experience feel unified, even when it involves many underlying systems.

Outcomes

The platform's high quality and feature set had an unexpected benefit: developer teams can run hundreds of services without any deep SRE engagement.

The common platform also changed the SRE-developer relationship. As a result, *tiered* SRE engagement is becoming common at Google. Tiered engagement includes a spectrum of SRE involvement, ranging from light consulting and design reviews to deep engagement (i.e., SREs share on-call duties).

Lessons learned

Shifting from sparse or ill-defined standards to a highly standardized platform is a long-term investment. Each step might feel incremental, but ultimately, these steps reduce overhead and make running services at scale possible.

It's important that developers see the value in such a transition. Aim for incremental productivity wins that are unlocked at each stage of development. Don't try to convince people to perform a huge refactor that pays off only at the very end.

Case Study 5: pDNS No Longer Depends on Itself

Background

When a client in Google production wants to look up the IP address for a service, it often uses a lookup service called Svelte. In the past, to find the IP address for Svelte, the client used a Google naming service called pDNS (Production DNS). The pDNS service is accessed through a load balancer, which looks up the IP addresses for the actual pDNS servers...using Svelte.

Problem statement

pDNS had a transitive dependency on itself, which was unintentionally introduced at some point and only later identified as a reliability concern. Lookups normally didn't run into issues because the pDNS service is replicated, and the data needed to break out of the dependency loop was always available somewhere in Google production. However, a cold start would have been impossible. In the words of one SRE, "We were like cave dwellers who could only light fires by running with a torch lit from the last campfire."

What we decided to do

We modified a low-level component in Google production to maintain a list of current IP addresses for nearby Svelte servers in local storage for all Google production machines. In addition to breaking the circular dependency described earlier, this change also eliminated an implicit dependency on pDNS for most other Google services.

To avoid similar issues, we also introduced a method for whitelisting the set of services allowed to communicate with pDNS, and slowly worked to reduce that set. As a result, each service lookup in production now has a simpler and more reliable path through the system.

Lessons learned

Be careful about your service's dependencies—use an explicit whitelist to prevent accidental additions. Also, be on the lookout for circular dependencies.

Conclusion

Simplicity is a natural goal for SREs because simple systems tend to be reliable and easy to run. It's not easy to quantitatively measure simplicity (or its inverse, complexity) for distributed systems, but there are reasonable proxies, and it's worth picking some and working to improve them.

Because of their end-to-end understanding of a system, SREs are in an excellent position to identify, prevent, and fix sources of complexity, whether they are found in software design, system architecture, configuration, deployment processes, or elsewhere. SREs should be involved in design discussions early on to provide their unique perspective about the costs and benefits of alternatives, with a particular eye toward simplicity. SREs can also proactively develop standards to homogenize production.

As an SRE, pushing for simplicity is an important part of your job description. We strongly recommend that SRE leadership empower SRE teams to push for simplicity, and to explicitly reward these efforts. Systems inevitably creep toward complexity as they evolve, so the fight for simplicity requires continuous attention and commitment—but it is very much worth pursuing.

Practices

Building upon the solid foundation of SRE principles covered in Part I, Part II dives deep into how to conduct SRE-related activities that Google has found important for operating at scale.

Some of these topics, such as data processing pipelines and managing load, won't apply to all organizations. Other topics, such as safely handling changes with configuration and canarying, on-call practices, and what to do when things go wrong, contain valuable lessons for any SRE team.

This part also introduces an important SRE skill—Non-Abstract Large System Design (NALSD)—and presents a detailed example of how to practice this design process.

As we move from SRE foundations to practices, we wanted to provide a bit more context on the relationship between operational duties and project work, and the engineering it takes to accomplish both strategically.

Defining Operational Work (Versus Project Work and Overhead)

Before we move from foundations to practices, we wanted to touch on the difference between operational and project work, and how these two types of work inform each other. The topic is an area of philosophical debate in the SRE community, so this interlude presents how we define the two types of work in the context of this book.

SRE practices apply software engineering solutions to operational problems. Because our SRE teams are responsible for the day-to-day functioning of the systems we support, our engineering work often focuses on tasks that might be operations elsewhere: we automate release processes instead of performing them manually; we implement sharding to make our services more reliable and less demanding of human attention; we utilize algorithmic approaches to capacity planning so that engineers don't have to perform error-prone manual calculations.

While engineering and operational work do inform each other, we can conceptualize the work any given SRE team performs as two separate categories, as shown in Figure II-1. Over the years, we've worked toward ways to maximize the efficiency and scalability of each bucket of work.

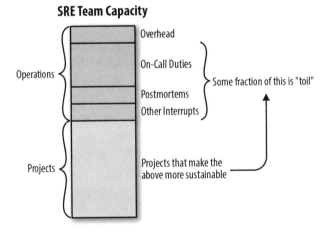

Figure II-1. The two categories of SRE work

We can break down operational work into four general categories:

- On-call work
- Customer requests (most commonly, tickets)
- Incident response
- Postmortems

Each of these categories receives its own detailed treatment in both our first book (Chapter 11 (*http://bit.ly/2JgUBU7*); Chapter 14 (*http://bit.ly/2J7G0qt*); Chapter 15 (*http://bit.ly/2J2Po2W*)) and this one (Chapter 6; Chapter 8; Chapter 9; Chapter 10). Here, we show how all four are interconnected, and why it's important to consider these types of work as closely related.

What types of work are not included in operational work? As shown in Figure II-1, project work is the other main bucket of SRE work. When a team's interrupt work is well managed, they have time for longer-term engineering work to achieve stability, reliability, and availability goals. This might include software engineering projects aimed at improving the reliability of a service, or systems engineering projects like safely rolling out a new feature to a globally replicated service.

Also shown in Figure II-1, *overhead* is the administrivia necessary to working at a company: meetings, training, responding to emails, tracking your accomplishments, filling out paperwork, and so on. Overhead isn't immediately important to the discussion at hand, but all team members spend time on it.

You might notice that we don't specifically call out documentation as a separate activity. This is because we believe that healthy documentation procedures embed themselves into all of your work. You don't need to think about documenting code, playbooks, and service features—or even making sure that tickets and bugs contain all of the information they should—as separate from your project or operational tasks. It's simply another facet of those tasks.

At Google, we specify that SREs should spend at least 50% of their time on project work; anything less makes for unsustainable engineering and burned-out, unhealthy teams. While every team and organization needs to find its own healthy balance, we've found that about one-third of time spent on operational tasks and two-thirds of time spent on project work is just about right (this ratio also informs an ideal on-call rotation size, where your engineers are only on-call one-third of the time).

We encourage teams to conduct periodic reviews to track whether you're striking the appropriate balance between types of work. At Google, we conduct regular Production Excellence (ProdEx) Reviews, which allow senior SRE leadership a view into the state of every SRE team using a clearly defined rubric. You'll need to determine the appropriate time intervals and rubric according to your own constraints and organizational maturity, but the key here is to generate metrics about team health that you can track over time.

Remember one caveat when finding your ideal balance: a team that spends too little of its time on operational tasks risks operational underload. In this situation, engineers might start to forget crucial aspects of the service they are responsible for. You can counter operational underload by taking more risks and moving faster—for example, shorten your release cycles, push more features per release, or perform more disaster recovery testing. If your team is perpetually underloaded, consider onboarding related services or handing back a service that no longer needs SRE support to the development team (for more discussion of team size, see Chapter 8).

The Relationship Between Operational Work and Project Work

While they are different classes of work, operational and project work aren't entirely separate concerns. In fact, the issues raised in the former should feed into the latter: SRE project work should be strategic initiatives that make the system more efficient, scalable, and reliable, and/or that reduce operational load and toil. As shown in Figure II-1, there should be a continuous feedback loop between the sources of operational load and the project work that systematically improves production. This longer-term work might involve moving to more robust storage systems, redesigning frameworks to reduce brittleness or maintenance load, or addressing systemic sources of outages and incidents. These initiatives are developed and implemented via *projects*, defined as temporary endeavors (with a clear beginning and end) that deliver a specified objective or deliverable.

## CHAPTER 8

On-Call

By Ollie Cook, Sara Smollett, Andrea Spadaccini,
Cara Donnelly, Jian Ma, and Garrett Plasky (Evernote)
with Stephen Thorne and Jessie Yang

Being on-call means being available during a set period of time, and being ready to respond to production incidents during that time with appropriate urgency. *Site Reliability Engineers* (SREs) are often required to take part in on-call rotations. During on-call shifts, SREs diagnose, mitigate, fix, or escalate incidents as needed. In addition, SREs are regularly responsible for nonurgent production duties.

At Google, being on-call is one of the defining characteristics of SRE. SRE teams mitigate incidents, repair production problems, and automate operational tasks. Since most of our SRE teams have not yet fully automated all their operational tasks, escalations need human points of contact—on-call engineers. Depending on how critical the supported systems are, or the state of development the systems are in, not all SRE teams may need to be on-call. In our experience, most SRE teams staff on-call shifts.

On-call is a large and complex topic, saddled with many constraints and a limited margin for trial and error. Chapter 11 (*http://bit.ly/2JgUBU7*) of our first book (*Site Reliability Engineering*), "Being On-Call," already explored this topic. This chapter addresses specific feedback and questions we received about that chapter. These include the following:

- "We are not Google; we're much smaller. We don't have as many people in the rotation, and we don't have sites in different time zones. What you described in your first book is irrelevant to me."

- "We have a mixture of developers and DevOps for on-call rotation. What's the best way to organize them? Split the responsibilities?"

- "Our on-call engineer gets paged about a hundred times in a typical 24-hour shift. A lot of pages get ignored, while the real problems are buried under the pile. Where should we start?"
- "We have a high turnover rate for on-call rotations. How do you address the knowledge gap within the team?"
- "We want to reorg our DevOps team into SRE.[1] What's the difference between SRE on-call, DevOps on-call, and developers on-call? Please be specific, because the DevOps team is very concerned about this."

We offer practical advice for these situations. Google is a large company with a mature SRE organization, but much of what we've learned over the years can be applied to any company or organization, regardless of size or maturity. Google has hundreds of on-call rotations across services of all sizes, and various on-call setups from simple to complicated. On-call is not exclusively an SRE function: many developer teams are directly on-call for their service. Each on-call setup meets the need of a particular service.

This chapter describes on-call setups both within Google and outside of Google. While your setup and situation will likely differ from our specific examples, the essential concepts we cover are widely applicable.

We then delve into the anatomy of pager load, explaining what causes pager load. We suggest strategies to optimize on-call setup and minimize that load.

Finally, we share two examples of practices inside Google: on-call flexibility and on-call team dynamics. These practices show that no matter how mathematically sound an on-call setup is, you cannot solely rely on logistics of the on-call setup. Incentives and human nature play an important role, and should also be taken into account.

Recap of "Being On-Call" Chapter of First SRE Book

Site Reliability Engineering, in "Being On-Call" (*http://bit.ly/2JgUBU7*), explains the principles behind on-call rotations at Google. This section discusses the main points of that chapter.

At Google, the overall goal of being on-call is to provide coverage for critical services, while making sure that we never achieve reliability at the expense of an on-call engineer's health. As a result, SRE teams strive for *balance*. SRE work should be a healthy mix of duties: on-call and project work. Specifying that SREs spend at least 50% of their time on project work means that teams have time to tackle the projects required

---

[1] Note that this example is often a red flag situation for organizations that aren't actually practicing DevOps, in which case, a name change won't fix more structural problems.

to strategically address any problems found in production. Team staffing must be adequate to ensure time for project work.

We target a maximum of two incidents per on-call shift,[2] to ensure adequate time for follow-up. If the pager load gets too high, corrective action is warranted. (We explore pager load later in this chapter.)

Psychological safety[3] is vital for effective on-call rotations. Since being on-call can be daunting and highly stressful, on-call engineers should be fully supported by a series of procedures and escalation paths to make their lives easier.

On-call usually implies some amount of out-of-hours work. We believe this work should be compensated. While different companies may choose to handle this in different ways, Google offers time-off-in-lieu or cash compensation, capped at some proportion of the overall salary. The compensation scheme provides an incentive for being part of on-call, and ensures that engineers do not take on too many on-call shifts for economic reasons.

Example On-Call Setups Within Google and Outside Google

This section describes real-world examples of on-call setups at Google and Evernote, a California company that develops a cross-platform app that helps individuals and teams create, assemble, and share information. For each company, we explore the reasoning behind on-call setups, general on-call philosophy, and on-call practices.

Google: Forming a New Team

Initial scenario

A few years ago, Sara, an SRE at Google Mountain View, started a new SRE team that needed to be on-call within three months. To put this in perspective, most SRE teams at Google do not expect new hires to be ready for on-call before three to nine months. The new Mountain View SRE team would support three Google Apps services that were previously supported by an SRE team in Kirkland, Washington (a two-hour flight from Mountain View). The Kirkland team had a sister SRE team in London, which would continue to support these services alongside the new Mountain View SRE team, and distributed product development teams.[4]

---

2 One "incident" is defined as one "problem," no matter how many alerts have been fired for the same "problem." One shift is 12 hours.

3 There is more on this topic in *Seeking SRE* (*https://oreil.ly/2kIawNe*) by David Blank-Edelman (O'Reilly).

4 SRE teams at Google are paired across time zones for service continuity.

The new Mountain View SRE team came together quickly, assembling seven people:

- Sara, an SRE tech lead
- Mike, an experienced SRE from another SRE team
- A transfer from a product development team who was new to SRE
- Four new hires ("Nooglers")

Even when a team is mature, going on-call for new services is always challenging, and the new Mountain View SRE team was a relatively junior team. Nonetheless, the new team was able to onboard the services without sacrificing service quality or project velocity. They made immediate improvements to the services, including lowering machine costs by 40%, and fully automating release rollouts with canarying and other safety checks. The new team also continued to deliver reliable services, targeting 99.98% availability, or roughly 26 minutes of downtime per quarter.

How did the new SRE team bootstrap themselves to accomplish so much? Through starter projects, mentoring, and training.

Training roadmap

Although the new SRE team didn't know much about their services, Sara and Mike were familiar with Google's production environment and SRE. As the four Nooglers completed company orientation, Sara and Mike compiled a checklist of two dozen focus areas for people to practice before going on-call, such as:

- Administering production jobs
- Understanding debugging info
- "Draining" traffic away from a cluster
- Rolling back a bad software push
- Blocking or rate-limiting unwanted traffic
- Bringing up additional serving capacity
- Using the monitoring systems (for alerting and dashboards)
- Describing the architecture, various components, and dependencies of the services

The Nooglers found some of this information on their own by researching existing documentation and *codelabs* (guided, hands-on coding tutorials) and gained understanding on relevant topics by working on their starter projects. When a team member learned about specific topics relevant to the Nooglers' starter projects, that person led a short, impromptu session to share that information with the rest of the team. Sara and Mike covered the remaining topics. The team also held lab sessions to perform common debugging and mitigation tasks to help everyone build muscle memory and gain confidence in their abilities.

In addition to the checklist, the new SRE team ran a series of "deep dives" to dig into their services. The team browsed monitoring consoles, identified running jobs, and tried debugging recent pages. Sara and Mike explained that an engineer *didn't* need years of expertise with each of the services to become reasonably proficient. They coached the team to explore a service from first principles, and encouraged Nooglers to become familiar with the services. They were open about the limits of their knowledge, and taught others when to ask for help.

Throughout the ramp-up, the new SRE team wasn't alone. Sara and Mike traveled to meet the other SRE teams and product developers and learn from them. The new SRE team met with the Kirkland and London teams by holding video conferences, exchanging email, and chatting over IRC. In addition, the team attended weekly production meetings, read daily on-call handoffs and postmortems, and browsed existing service documentation. A Kirkland SRE visited to give talks and answer questions. A London SRE put together a thorough set of disaster scenarios and ran them during Google's disaster recovery training week (see the section "Preparedness and Disaster Testing" (*http://bit.ly/2JiPfaV*) in *Site Reliability Engineering*, Chapter 33).

The team also practiced being on-call through "Wheel of Misfortune" training exercises (see the section "Disaster Role Playing" (*http://bit.ly/2Hb8ONg*) in *Site Reliability Engineering*, Chapter 28), where they role-played recent incidents to practice debugging production problems. During these sessions, all SREs were encouraged to offer suggestions on how to resolve mock production failures. After everyone ramped up, the team still held these sessions, rotating through each team member as the session leader. The team recorded these for future reference.

Before going on-call, the team reviewed precise guidelines about the responsibilities of on-call engineers. For example:

- At the start of each shift, the on-call engineer reads the handoff from the previous shift.

- The on-call engineer minimizes user impact first, then makes sure the issues are fully addressed.

- At the end of the shift, the on-call engineer sends a handoff email to the next engineer on-call.

The guidelines also specified when to escalate to others, and how to write postmortems for large incidents.

Finally, the team read and updated on-call *playbooks*. Playbooks contain high-level instructions on how to respond to automated alerts. They explain the severity and impact of the alert, and include debugging suggestions and possible actions to take to mitigate impact and fully resolve the alert. In SRE, whenever an alert is created, a corresponding playbook entry is usually created. These guides reduce stress, the mean time to repair (MTTR), and the risk of human error.

Maintaining Playbooks

Details in playbooks go out of date at the same rate as production environment changes. For daily releases, playbooks might need an update on any given day. Writing good documentation, like any form of communication, is hard. So how do you maintain playbooks?

Some SREs at Google advocate keeping playbook entries general so they change slowly. For example, they may have just one entry for all "RPC Errors High" alerts, for a trained on-call engineer to read, in conjunction with an architecture diagram for the currently alerting service. Other SREs advocate for step-by-step playbooks to reduce human variability and drive down MTTR. If your team has conflicting views about playbook content, the playbooks might get pulled in many directions.

This is a contentious topic. If you agree on nothing else, at least decide with your team what minimal, structured details your playbooks must have, and try to notice when your playbooks have accumulated a lot of information beyond these structured details. Pencil in a project to turn new, hard-won, production knowledge into automation or monitoring consoles. If your playbooks are a deterministic list of commands that the on-call engineer runs every time a particular alert fires, we recommend implementing automation.

After two months, Sara, Mike, and the SRE transfer shadowed the on-call shifts of the outgoing Kirkland SRE team. At three months, they became the primary on-call, with the Kirkland SREs as backup. That way, they could easily escalate to the Kirkland SREs if needed. Next, the Nooglers shadowed the more experienced, local SREs and joined the rotation.

Good documentation and the various strategies discussed earlier all helped the team form a solid foundation and ramp up quickly. Although on-call can be stressful, the teams' confidence grew enough to take action without second-guessing themselves. There was psychological safety in knowing that their responses were based on the team's collective knowledge, and that even when they escalated, the on-call engineers were still regarded as competent engineers.

Afterword

While the Mountain View SREs were ramping up, they learned that their experienced, sister SRE team in London would be moving on to a new project, and a new team was being formed in Zürich to support the services previously supported by the London SRE team. For this second transition, the same basic approach the Mountain View SREs used proved successful. The previous investment by Mountain View SREs in developing onboarding and training materials helped the new Zürich SRE team ramp up.

While the approach used by the Mountain View SREs made sense when a cohort of SREs were becoming a team, they needed a more lightweight approach when only one person joined the team at a given time. In anticipation of future turnover, the SREs created service architecture diagrams and formalized the basic training checklist into a series of exercises that could be completed semi-independently with minimal involvement from a mentor. These exercises included describing the storage layer, performing capacity increases, and reviewing how HTTP requests are routed.

Evernote: Finding Our Feet in the Cloud

Moving our on-prem infrastructure to the cloud

We didn't set out to reengineer our on-call process, but as with many things in life, necessity is the mother of invention. Prior to December 2016, Evernote ran only on on-prem datacenters, built to support our monolithic application. Our network and servers were designed with a specific architecture and data flow in mind. This, combined with a host of other constraints, meant we lacked the flexibility needed to support a horizontal architecture. Google Cloud Platform (GCP) provided a concrete solution to our problem. However, we still had one major hurdle to surmount: migrating all our production and supporting infrastructure to GCP. Fast-forward 70 days. Through a Herculean effort and many remarkable feats (for example, moving thousands of servers and 3.5 PB of data), we were happily settled in our new home. At this point, though, our job still wasn't done: how were we going to monitor, alert, and—most importantly—respond to issues in our new environment?

Adjusting our on-call policies and processes

The move to the cloud unleashed the potential for our infrastructure to grow rapidly, but our on-call policies and processes were not yet set up to handle such growth. Once the migration wrapped up, we set out to remedy the problem. In our previous physical datacenter, we built redundancy into nearly every component. This meant that while component failure was common given our size, generally no individual component was capable of negatively impacting users. The infrastructure was very stable because we controlled it—any small bump would inevitably be due to a failure somewhere in the system. Our alerting policies were structured with that in mind: a few dropped packets, resulting in a JDBC (Java Database Connectivity) connection exception, invariably meant that a VM (virtual machine) host was on the verge of failing, or that the control plane on one of our switches was on the fritz. Even before our first day in the cloud, we realized that this type of alert/response system was not tenable going forward. In a world of live migrations and network latency, we needed to take a much more holistic approach to monitoring.

Reframing paging events in terms of first principles, and writing these principles down as our explicit SLOs (service level objectives), helped give the team clarity regarding what was important to alert on and allowed us to trim the fat from our monitoring infrastructure. Our focus on higher-level indicators such as API responsiveness, rather than lower-level infrastructure such as InnoDB row lock waits in MySQL, meant we could focus more time on the real pain our users experience during an outage. For our team, this meant less time spent chasing transient problems. This translated into more sleep, effectiveness, and ultimately, job satisfaction.

Restructuring our monitoring and metrics

Our primary on-call rotation is staffed by a small but scrappy team of engineers who are responsible for our production infrastructure and a handful of other business systems (for example, staging and build pipeline infrastructure). We have a weekly, 24/7 schedule with a well-oiled handoff procedure, alongside a morning review of incidents at a daily stand-up. Our small team size and comparatively large scope of responsibility necessitates that we make every effort to keep the process burden light, and focus on closing the alert/triage/remediation/analysis loop as quickly as possible. One of the ways we achieve this is to keep our signal-to-noise ratio low by maintaining simple but effective alerting SLAs (service level agreements). We classify any event generated by our metrics or monitoring infrastructure into three categories:

P1: Deal with immediately

- Should be immediately actionable
- Pages the on-call
- Leads to event triage
- Is SLO-impacting

P2: Deal with the next business day

- Generally is not customer-facing, or is very limited in scope
- Sends an email to team and notifies event stream channel

P3: Event is informational only

- Information is gathered in dashboards, passive email, and the like
- Includes capacity planning–related information

Any P1 or P2 event has an incident ticket attached to it. The ticket is used for obvious tasks like event triage and tracking remediation actions, as well as for SLO impact, number of occurrences, and postmortem doc links, where applicable.

When an event pages (category P1), the on-call is tasked with assessing the impact to users. Incidents are triaged into severities from 1 to 3. For severity 1 (Sev 1) incidents, we maintain a finite set of criteria to make the escalation decision as straightforward as possible for the responder. Once the event is escalated, we assemble an incident team and begin our incident management process. The incident manager is paged, a scribe and communications lead is elected, and our communication channels open. After the incident is resolved, we conduct an automatic postmortem and share the results far and wide within the company. For events rating Sev 2 or Sev 3, the on-call responder handles the incident lifecycle, including an abbreviated postmortem for incident review.

One of the benefits of keeping our process lightweight is that we can explicitly free the on-call from any expectations of project work. This empowers and encourages the on-call to take immediate follow-up action, and also to identify any major gaps in tooling or process after completing the post-incident review. In this way, we achieve a constant cycle of improvement and flexibility during every on-call shift, keeping pace with the rapid rate of change in our environment. The goal is to make every on-call shift better than the last.

Tracking our performance over time

With the introduction of SLOs, we wanted to track performance over time, and share that information with stakeholders within the company. We implemented a monthly service review meeting, open to anyone who's interested, to review and discuss the previous month of the service. We have also used this forum to review our on-call burden as a barometer of team health, and discuss remediation actions when we exceed our pager budget. This forum has the dual purpose of spreading the importance of SLOs within the company and keeping the technical organization accountable for maintaining the health and wellness of our service and team.

Engaging with CRE

Expressing our objectives in terms of SLOs provides a basis for engaging with Google's Customer Reliability Engineering (CRE) team. After we discussed our SLOs with CRE to see if they were realistic and measurable, both teams decided CRE would be paged alongside our own engineers for SLO-impacting events. It can be difficult to pinpoint root causes that are hidden behind layers of cloud abstraction, so having a Googler at our side take the guesswork out of black-box event triaging was helpful. More importantly, this exercise further reduced our MTTR, which is ultimately what our users care about.

Sustaining a self-perpetuating cycle

Rather than spending all our time in the triage/root-cause analysis/postmortem cycle, we now have more time as a team to think about how we move the business forward. Specifically, this translates into projects such as improving our microservices platform and establishing production readiness criteria for our product development teams. The latter includes many of the principles we followed in restructuring our on-call, which is particularly helpful for teams in their first "carry the pager" rodeo. Thus, we perpetuate the cycle of improving on-call for everyone.

Practical Implementation Details

So far, we've discussed details about on-call setups, both within Google and outside of Google. But what about specific considerations of being on-call? The following sections discuss these implementation details in more depth:

- Pager load—what it is, how it works, and how to manage it
- How to factor flexibility into on-call scheduling to create a healthier work/life balance for SREs
- Strategies for improving team dynamics, both within a given SRE team, and with partner teams

Anatomy of Pager Load

Your pager is noisy and it's making your team unhappy. You've read through Chapter 31 (*http://bit.ly/2sqRwad*) in *Site Reliability Engineering*, and run regular production meetings, both with your team and the developer teams you support. Now everyone *knows* that your on-call engineers are unhappy. What next?

Pager load is the number of paging incidents that an on-call engineer receives over a typical shift length (such as per day or per week). An incident may involve more than one page. Here, we'll walk through the impact of various factors on pager load, and suggest techniques for minimizing future pager load.

Appropriate Response Times

Engineers shouldn't have to be at a computer and working on a problem within minutes of receiving a page unless there is a very good reason to do so. While a complete outage of a customer-facing, revenue-generating service typically requires an immediate response, you can deal with less severe issues (for example, failing backups) within a few hours.

We recommend checking your current paging setup to see if you actually *should* be paged for everything that currently triggers a page. You may be paging for issues that would be better served by automated repair (as it's generally better for a computer to fix a problem than requiring a human to fix it) or a ticket (if it's not actually high priority). Table 8-1 shows some sample events and appropriate responses.

Table 8-1. Examples of realistic response times

Incident description	Response time	SRE impact
Revenue-impacting network outage	5 minutes	SRE needs to be within arm's reach of a charged and authenticated laptop with network access at all times; cannot travel; must heavily coordinate with secondary at all times
Customer order batch processing system stuck	30 minutes	SRE can leave their home for a quick errand or short commute; secondary does not need to provide coverage during this time
Backups of a database for a pre-launch service are failing	Ticket (response during work hours)	None

Scenario: A team in overload

The (hypothetical) Connection SRE Team, responsible for frontend load balancing and terminating end-user connections, found itself in a position of high pager load. They had an established pager budget of two paging incidents per shift, but for the past year they had regularly been receiving five paging incidents per shift. Analysis revealed that fully one-third of shifts were exceeding their pager budget. Members of the team heroically responded to the daily onslaught of pages but couldn't keep up; there simply was not enough time in the day to find the root cause and properly fix the incoming issues. Some engineers left the team to join less operationally burdened teams. High-quality incident follow-up was rare, since on-call engineers only had time to mitigate immediate problems.

The team's horizon wasn't entirely bleak: they had a mature monitoring infrastructure that followed SRE best practices. Alerting thresholds were set to align with their SLO, and paging alerts were symptom-based in nature, meaning they fired only when customers were impacted. When senior management were approached with all of this information, they agreed that the team was in operational overload and reviewed the project plan to bring the team back to a healthy state.

In less positive news, over time the Connection team had taken ownership of software components from more than 10 developer teams and had hard dependencies on Google's customer-facing edge and backbone networks. The large number of inter-group relationships was complex and had quietly grown difficult to manage.

Despite the team following best practices in structuring their monitoring, many of the pages that they faced were outside their direct control. For example, a black-box probe may have failed due to congestion in the network, causing packet loss. The only action the team could take to mitigate congestion in the backbone was to escalate to the team directly responsible for that network.

On top of their operational burden, the team needed to deliver new features to the frontend systems, which would be used by all Google services. To make matters worse, their infrastructure was being migrated from a 10-year-old legacy framework and cluster management system to a better-supported replacement. The team's services were subject to an unprecedented rate of change, and the changes themselves caused a significant portion of the on-call load.

The team clearly needed to combat this excessive pager load using a variety of techniques. The technical program manager and the people manager of the team approached senior management with a project proposal, which senior management reviewed and approved. The team turned their full attention to reducing their pager load, and learned some valuable lessons along the way.

Pager load inputs

The first step in tackling high pager load is to determine what is causing it. Pager load is influenced by three main factors: bugs[5] in production, alerting, and human processes. Each of these factors has several inputs, some of which we discuss in more detail in this section.

For production:

- The number of existing bugs in production
- The introduction of new bugs into production
- The speed with which newly introduced bugs are identified
- The speed with which bugs are mitigated and removed from production

For alerting:

- The alerting thresholds that trigger a paging alert
- The introduction of new paging alerts
- The alignment of a service's SLO with the SLOs of the services upon which it depends

---

5 A "bug" in this context is any undesirable system behavior resulting from software or configuration error. Logic errors in code, incorrect configuration of a binary, incorrect capacity planning, misconfigured load balancers, or newly discovered vulnerabilities are all valid examples of "production bugs" that contribute to pager load.

For human processes:

- The rigor of fixes and follow-up on bugs
- The quality of data collected about paging alerts
- The attention paid to pager load trends
- Human-actuated changes to production

Preexisting bugs.   No system is perfect. There will always be bugs in production: in your own code, the software and libraries that you build upon, or the interfaces between them. The bugs may not be causing paging alerts right now, but they are definitely present. You can use a few techniques to identify or prevent bugs that haven't yet caused paging alerts:

- Ensure systems are as complicated as they need to be, and no more (see Chapter 7).
- Regularly update the software or libraries that your system is built upon to take advantage of bug fixes (however, see the next section about new bugs).
- Perform regular destructive testing or fuzzing (for example, using Netflix's Chaos Monkey (*https://github.com/Netflix/chaosmonkey*)).
- Perform regular load testing in addition to integration and unit testing.

New bugs.   Ideally, the SRE team and its partner developer teams should detect new bugs before they even make it into production. In reality, automated testing misses many bugs, which are then launched to production.

Software testing is a large topic well covered elsewhere (e.g., Martin Fowler on Testing (*https://martinfowler.com/tags/testing.html*)). However, software testing techniques are particularly useful in reducing the number of bugs that reach production, and the amount of time they remain in production:

- Improve testing over time. In particular, for each bug you discover in production, ask "How could we have detected this bug preproduction?" Make sure the necessary engineering follow-up occurs (see "Rigor of follow-up" on page 164).
- Don't ignore load testing, which is often treated as lower priority than functional testing. Many bugs manifest only under particular load conditions or with a particular mix of requests.
- Run staging (testing with production-like but synthetic traffic) in a production-like environment. We briefly discuss generating synthetic traffic in Chapter 5 of this book.
- Perform canarying (Chapter 16) in a production environment.

- Have a low tolerance to new bugs. Follow a "detect, roll back, fix, and roll forward" strategy rather than a "detect, continue to roll forward despite identifying the bug, fix, and roll forward again" strategy. (See "Mitigation delay" on page 162 for more details.)

This kind of rollback strategy requires predictable and frequent releases so that the cost of rolling back any one release is small. We discuss this and related topics in *Site Reliability Engineering*, in "Release Engineering" (*http://bit.ly/2xyT9aK*).

Some bugs may manifest only as the result of changing client behavior. For example:

- Bugs that manifest only under specific levels of load—for example, September back-to-school traffic, Black Friday, Cyber Monday, or that week of the year when Daylight Saving Time means Europe and North America are one hour closer, meaning more of your users are awake and online simultaneously.
- Bugs that manifest only with a particular mix of requests—for example, servers closer to Asia experiencing a more expensive traffic mix due to language encodings for Asian character sets.
- Bugs that manifest only when users exercise the system in unexpected ways—for example, Calendar being used by an airline reservation system! Therefore, it is important to expand your testing regimen to test behaviors that do not occur every day.

When a production system is plagued by several concurrent bugs, it's much more difficult to identify if a given page is for an *existing* or *new* bug. Minimizing the number of bugs in production not only reduces pager load, it also makes identifying and classifying new bugs easier. Therefore, it is critical to remove production bugs from your systems as quickly as possible. Prioritize fixing existing bugs above delivering new features; if this requires cross-team collaboration, see Chapter 18.

Architectural or procedural problems, such as automated health checking, self-healing, and load shedding, may need significant engineering work to resolve. Remember, for simplicity's sake we'll consider these problems "bugs," even if their size, their complexity, or the effort required to resolve them is significant.

Chapter 3 (*http://bit.ly/2so6uOc*) of *Site Reliability Engineering* describes how error budgets are a useful way to manage the rate at which new bugs are released to production. For example, when a service's SLO violations exceed a certain fraction of its total quarterly error budget—typically agreed in advance between the developer and SRE teams—new feature development and feature-related rollouts can be halted temporarily to focus on stabilizing the system and reducing the frequency of pages.

The Connection team from our example adopted a strict policy requiring every outage to have a tracking bug. This enabled the team's technical program manager to examine the root cause of their new bugs in aggregate. This data revealed that human error was the second most common cause of new bugs in production.

Because humans are error-prone, it's better if all changes made to production systems are made by automation informed by (human-developed) intent configuration. Before you make a change to production, automation can perform additional testing that humans cannot. The Connection team was making complex changes to production semimanually. Not surprisingly, the team's manual changes went wrong sometimes; the team introduced new bugs, which caused pages. Automated systems making the same changes would have determined that the changes were not safe before they entered production and became paging events. The technical program manager took this data to the team and convinced them to prioritize automation projects.

Identification delay. It's important to promptly identify the cause(s) of alerts because the longer it takes to identify the root cause of a page, the more opportunity it has to recur and page again. For example, given a page that manifests only under high load, say at daily peak, if the problematic code or configuration is not identified before the next daily peak, it is likely that the problem will happen again. There are several techniques you might use to reduce identification delays:

Use good alerts and consoles
> Ensure pages link to relevant monitoring consoles, and that consoles highlight where the system is operating out of specification. In the console, correlate black-box and white-box paging alerts together, and do the same with their associated graphs. Make sure playbooks are up to date with advice on responding to each type of alert. On-call engineers should update the playbook with fresh information when the corresponding page fires.

Practice emergency response
> Run "Wheel of Misfortune" exercises (*http://bit.ly/2JnX5Qp*) (described in *Site Reliability Engineering*) to share general and service-specific debugging techniques with your colleagues.

Perform small releases
> If you perform frequent, smaller releases instead of infrequent monolithic changes, correlating bugs with the corresponding change that introduced them is easier. Canarying releases, described in Chapter 16 gives a strong signal about whether a new bug is due to a new release.

Log changes
> Aggregating change information into a searchable timeline makes it simpler (and hopefully quicker) to correlate new bugs with the corresponding change that introduced them. Tools like the Slack plug-in for Jenkins (*http://bit.ly/2sAgzqJ*) can be helpful.

Ask for help

In *Site Reliability Engineering,* "Managing Incidents" (*http://bit.ly/2J7G0qt*), we talked about working together to manage large outages. The on-call engineer is never alone; encourage your team to feel safe when asking for help.

Mitigation delay. The longer it takes to mitigate a bug once it's identified, the more opportunity it has to recur and page again. Consider these techniques for reducing mitigation delays:

Roll back changes

- If the bug was introduced in a recent code or configuration rollout, promptly remove the bug from production with a rollback, if safe and appropriate (a rollback alone may be necessary but is not sufficient if the bug caused data corruption, for example). Remember that even a "quick fix" needs time to be tested, built, and rolled out. Testing is vital to making sure the quick fix actually fixes the bug, and that it doesn't introduce additional bugs or other unintended consequences. Generally, it is better to "roll back, fix, and roll forward" rather than "roll forward, fix, and roll forward again."

- If you aim for 99.99% availability, you have approximately 15 minutes of error budget per quarter. The build step of rolling forward may take much longer than 15 minutes, so rolling back impacts your users much less.

  (99.999% availability affords an error budget of 80 seconds per quarter. At this point, systems may need self-healing properties, which is out of scope for this chapter.)

- If at all possible, avoid changes that can't be rolled back, such as API-incompatible changes and lockstep releases.

Use feature isolation

- Design your system so that if feature X goes wrong, you can disable it via, for example, a feature flag without affecting feature Y. This strategy also improves release velocity, and makes disabling feature X a much simpler decision—you don't need to check that your product managers are comfortable with also disabling feature Y.

Drain requests away

- Drain requests (i.e., redirect customer requests) away from the elements of your system that exhibit the bug. For example, if the bug is the result of a code or config rollout, and you roll out to production gradually, you may have the opportunity to drain the elements of your infrastructure that have received the update. This allows you to mitigate the customer impact in seconds, rather than rolling back, which may take minutes or longer.

Alerting. Google SRE's maximum of two distinct incidents per 12-hour shift encourages us to be thoughtful and cautious about how we configure paging alerts and how we introduce new ones. *Site Reliability Engineering*, "Monitoring Distributed Systems" (*http://bit.ly/2KNCD9F*), describes Google's approach to defining the thresholds for paging alerts. Strictly observing these guidelines is critical to maintaining a healthy on-call rotation.

It is worth highlighting some key elements discussed in that chapter:

- All alerts should be immediately actionable. There should be an action we expect a human to take immediately after they receive the page that the system is unable to take itself. The signal-to-noise ratio should be high to ensure few false positives; a low signal-to-noise ratio raises the risk for on-call engineers to develop alert fatigue.

- If a team fully subscribes to SLO-based alerting, or paging only when error budget is burned (see the section "Black-Box Versus White-Box" (*http://bit.ly/2J4YrjR*) in *Site Reliability Engineering*), it is critical that all teams involved in developing and maintaining the service agree about the importance of meeting the SLO and prioritize their work accordingly.

- If a team fully subscribes to SLO-based and symptom-based alerting, relaxing alert thresholds is rarely an appropriate response to being paged.

- Just like new code, new alerts should be thoroughly and thoughtfully reviewed. Each alert should have a corresponding playbook entry.

Receiving a page creates a negative psychological impact. To minimize that impact, only introduce new paging alerts when you really need them. Anyone on the team can write a new alert, but the whole team reviews proposed alert additions and can suggest alternatives. Thoroughly test new alerts in production to vet false positives before they are upgraded to paging alerts. For example, you might email the alert's author when the alert fires, rather than paging the on-call engineer.

New alerts may find problems in production that you weren't aware of. After you address these production bugs, alerting will only page on *new* bugs, effectively functioning like regression tests.

Be sure to run the new alerts in test mode long enough to experience typical periodic production conditions, such as regular software rollouts, maintenance events by your Cloud provider, weekly load peaks, and so on. A week of testing is probably about right. However, this appropriate window depends on the alert and the system.

Finally, use the alert's trigger rate during the testing period to predict the expected consumption of your pager budget as a result of the new alert. Explicitly approve or disallow the new alert as a team. If introducing a new paging alert causes your service to exceed its paging budget, the stability of the system needs additional attention.

Rigor of follow-up. Aim to identify the root cause of every page. "Root causes" extend out of the machine and into the team's processes. Was an outage caused by a bug that would have been caught by a unit test? The root cause might not be a bug in the code, but rather a bug in the team's processes around code review.

If you know the root cause, you can fix and prevent it from ever bothering you or your colleagues again. If your team cannot figure out the root cause, add monitoring and/or logging that will help you find the root cause of the page the next time it occurs. If you don't have enough information to identify the bug, you can always do *something* to help debug the page further next time. You should rarely conclude that a page is triggered by "cause unknown." Remember that as an on-call engineer, you are never alone, so ask a colleague to review your findings and see if there's anything you missed. Typically, it's easiest to find the root cause of an alert soon after the alert has triggered and fresh evidence is available.

Explaining away a page as "transient," or taking no action because the system "fixed itself" or the bug inexplicably "went away," invites the bug to happen again and cause another page, which causes trouble for the next on-call engineer.

Simply fixing the immediate bug (or making a "point" fix) misses a golden opportunity to prevent similar alerts in the future. Use the paging alert as an chance to surface engineering work that improves the system and obviates an entire class of possible future bugs. Do this by filing a project bug in your team's production component, and advocate to prioritize its implementation by gathering data about how many individual bugs and pages this project would remove. If your proposal will take 3 working weeks or 120 working hours to implement, and a page costs on average 4 working hours to properly handle, there's a clear break-even point after 30 pages.

For example, imagine a situation where there are too many servers on the same failure domain, such as a switch in a datacenter, causing regular multiple simultaneous failures:

Point fix
> Rebalance your current footprint across more failure domains and stop there.

Systemic fix
> Use automation to ensure that this type of server, and all other similar servers, are always spread across sufficient failure domains, and that they rebalance automatically when necessary.

Monitoring (or prevention) fix
> Alert preemptively when the failure domain diversity is below the expected level, but not yet service-impacting. Ideally, the alert would be a ticket alert, not a page,

since it doesn't require an immediate response. The system is still serving happily, albeit at a lower level of redundancy.

To make sure you're thorough in your follow-up to paging alerts, consider the following questions:

- How can I prevent this specific bug from happening again?
- How can I prevent bugs like this from happening again, both for this system and other systems I'm responsible for?
- What tests could have prevented this bug from being released to production?
- What ticket alerts could have triggered action to prevent the bug from becoming critical before it paged?
- What informational alerts could have surfaced the bug on a console before it became critical?
- Have I maximized the impact of the fixes I'm making?

Of course, it's not enough for an on-call engineer to just file bugs related to the pages that occur on their shift. It's incredibly important that bugs identified by the SRE team are dealt with swiftly, to reduce the possibility of them recurring. Make sure resource planning for both the SRE and developer teams consider the effort required to respond to bugs.

We recommend reserving a fraction of SRE and developer team time for responding to production bugs as they arise. For example, a Google on-caller typically doesn't work on projects during their on-call shift. Instead, they work on bugs that improve the health of the system. Make sure that your team routinely prioritizes production bugs above other project work. SRE managers and tech leads should make sure that production bugs are promptly dealt with, and escalate to the developer team decision makers when necessary.

When a paging event is serious enough to warrant a postmortem, it's even more important to follow this methodology to catalog and track follow-up action items. (See Chapter 10 for more details.)

Data quality. Once you identify bugs in your system that caused pages, a number of questions naturally arise:

- How do you know which bug to fix first?
- How do you know which component in your system caused most of your pages?
- How do you determine what repetitive, manual action on-call engineers are taking to resolve the pages?
- How do you tell how many alerts with unidentified root causes remain?

- How do you tell which bugs are *truly*, not just anecdotally, the worst?

The answer is simple: collect data!

When building up your data collection processes, you might track and monitor the patterns in on-call load, but this effort doesn't scale. It's far more sustainable to file a placeholder bug for each paging alert in your bug tracking system (e.g., Jira, Issue-Tracker (*http://bit.ly/2syxEBq*)), and for the on-call engineer to create a link between the paging alerts from your monitoring system and the relevant bug in the bug tracking system, as and when they realize that each alert is symptomatic of a preexisting issue. You will end up with a list of as-yet-not-understood bugs in one column, and a list of all of the pages that each bug is believed to have caused in the next.

Once you have structured data about the causes of the pages, you can begin to analyze that data and produce reports. Those reports can answer questions such as:

- Which bugs cause the most pages? Ideally we'd roll back and fix bugs immediately, but sometimes, finding the root cause and deploying the fix takes a long time, and sometimes silencing key alerts isn't a reasonable option. For example, the aforementioned Connection SRE Team might experience ongoing network congestion that isn't immediately resolvable but still needs to be tracked. Collecting data on which production issues are causing the most pages and stress to the team supports data-driven conversations about prioritizing your engineering effort systematically.
- Which component of the system is the cause of most pages (payments gateway, authentication microservice, etc.)?
- When correlated with your other monitoring data, do particular pages correspond to other signals (peaks in request rate, number of concurrent customer sessions, number of signups, number of withdrawals, etc.)?

Tying structured data to bugs and the root causes of your pages has other benefits:

- You can automatically populate a list of existing bugs (that is, known issues), which may be useful for your support team.
- You can automatically prioritize fixing bugs based on the number of pages each bug causes.

The quality of the data you collect will determine the quality of the decisions either humans or automata can make. To ensure high-quality data, consider the following techniques:

- Define and document your team's policy and expectations on data collection for pages.

- Set up nonpaging alerts from the monitoring system to highlight where pages were not handled according to those expectations. Managers and tech leads should make sure that the expectations are met.

- Teammates should follow up with each other when handoffs don't adhere to expectations. Positive comments such as, "Maybe this could be related to bug 123," "I've filed a bug with your findings so we can follow up in more detail," or "This looks a lot like what happened on my shift last Wednesday: <link to page, bug>" powerfully reinforce the expected behaviors and ensure that you maximize opportunities for improvement. No one wants to be paged for the same issue that paged their teammate in the previous shift.

Vigilance.   All too often, teams fall into operational overload by a thousand cuts. To avoid boiling the frog (*http://bit.ly/2kFMYIL*), it is important to pay attention to the health of on-call engineers over time, and ensure that production health is consistently and continuously prioritized by both SRE and developer teams.

The following techniques can help a team keep a watchful eye on pager load:

- At production meetings (see the section "Communications: Production Meetings" (*http://bit.ly/2LNbtjs*) in *Site Reliability Engineering*, Chapter 31), regularly talk about trends in pager load based on the structured data collected. We've found a 21-day trailing average to be useful.

- Set up ticket alerts, possibly targeted at tech leads or managers, for when pager load crosses a "warning" threshold that your team agrees on beforehand.

- Hold regular meetings between the SRE team and developer team to discuss the current state of production and the outstanding production bugs that are paging SRE.

On-Call Flexibility

Shift Length

An on-call rotation that has to handle one or more pages per day must be structured in a sustainable way: we recommend limiting shift lengths to 12 hours. Shorter shifts are better for the mental health of your engineers. Team members run the risk of exhaustion when shifts run long, and when people are tired, they make mistakes. Most humans simply can't produce high-quality work if they're on-call continuously. Many countries have laws about maximum working hours, breaks, and working conditions.

While spreading on-call shifts across a team's daylight hours is ideal, a 12-hour shift system doesn't necessitate a globally distributed team. Being on-call overnight for 12 hours is preferable to being on-call for 24 hours or more. You can make 12-hour shifts work even in a single location. For example, instead of asking a single engineer to be on-call for 24 hours a day across an entire week-long shift, it would be better for two engineers to split a week of on-call, with one person on-call during the day and one on-call overnight.

In our experience, 24 hours of on-call duty without reprieve isn't a sustainable setup. While not ideal, occasional overnight 12-hour shifts at least ensure breaks for your engineers. Another option is to shorten shifts to last less than a week—something like 3 days on, 4 days off.

Scenario: A change in personal circumstances

Imagine you are a member of an on-call team for a large service that has a 24/7 follow-the-sun model split across two sites. The arrangement works well for you. While you're not thrilled about the possibility of a 6 a.m. page, you are happy with the work you and the team are doing to keep the operational load manageable while improving the reliability of the service.

All is well…until one day you realize that the on-call schedule and the demands of your personal life are starting to clash. There are many potential reasons why—for example, becoming a parent, needing to travel on short notice and take a leave from work, or illness.

You need your on-call duties to coexist with your new personal schedule.

Many teams and organizations face this challenge as they mature. People's needs change over time, and maintaining a healthy balance of diverse teammate backgrounds leads to an on-call rotation characterized by diverse needs. The key to keeping a healthy, fair, and equitable balance of on-call work and personal life is flexibility.

There are a number of ways that you can apply flexibility to on-call rotations to meet the needs of team members while still ensuring coverage for your services or products. It is impossible to write down a comprehensive, one-size-fits-all set of guidelines. We encourage embracing flexibility as a *principle* rather than simply adopting the examples listed here.

Automate on-call scheduling. As teams grow, accounting for scheduling constraints—vacation plans, distribution of on-call weekdays versus weekends, individual preferences, religious requirements, and so on—becomes increasingly difficult. You can't manage this task manually; it's hard to find any solution at all, much less a fair one.

"Fairness" doesn't mean a completely uniform distribution of each type of shift across team members. Different people have different needs and different preferences. Therefore, it's important for the team to share those preferences and try to meet them in an intelligent way. Team composition and preferences dictate whether your team prefers a uniform distribution, or a more customized way of meeting scheduling preferences.

Using an automated tool to schedule on-call shifts makes this task much easier. This tool should have a few basic characteristics:

- It should rearrange on-call shifts to accommodate the changing needs of team members.
- It should automatically rebalance on-call load in response to any changes.
- It should do its best to ensure fairness by factoring in personal preferences such as "no primary during weekends in April," as well as historical information such as recent on-call load per engineer.
- So that on-call engineers can plan around their on-call shifts, it must never change an already generated schedule.

Schedule generation can be either fully automated or scheduled by a human. Likewise, some teams prefer to have members explicitly sign off on the schedule, while others are comfortable with a fully automated process. You might opt to develop your own tool in-house if your needs are complex, but there are a number of commercial and open source software packages that can aid in automating on-call scheduling.

Plan for short-term swaps.   Requests for short-term changes in the on-call schedule happen frequently. No one can promise on Monday that they won't have the flu on Thursday. Or you might need to run an unforeseen urgent errand in the middle of your on-call shift.

You may also want to facilitate on-call swaps for nonurgent reasons—for example, to allow on-callers to attend sports training sessions. In this situation, team members can swap a subset of the on-call day (for example, half of Sunday). Nonurgent swaps are typically best-effort.

Teams with a strict pager response SLO need to take commute coverage into account. If your pager response SLO is 5 minutes, and your commute is 30 minutes, you need to make sure that someone else can respond to emergencies while you get to work.

To achieve these goals in flexibility, we recommend giving team members the ability to update the on-call rotation. Also, have a documented policy in place describing how swaps should work. Decentralization options range from a fully centralized policy, where only the manager can change the schedule, to a fully decentralized one, where any team member can change the policy independently. In our experience, instituting peer review of changes provides a good tradeoff between safety and flexibility.

Plan for long-term breaks.   Sometimes team members need to stop serving in the on-call rotation because of changes in personal circumstances or burnout. It's important that teams are structured to allow on-callers to temporarily leave the rotation.

Ideally, team size should allow for a (temporary) staff reduction without causing the rest of the team to suffer too much operational load. In our experience, you need a bare minimum of five people per site to sustain on-call in a multisite, 24/7 configuration, and eight people in a single-site, 24/7 configuration. Therefore, it is safe to assume each site will need one extra engineer as protection against staff reduction, bringing the minimum staffing to six engineers per site (multisite) or nine per site (single-site).

Plan for part-time work schedules.   Being on-call with part-time working schedules may seem incompatible, but we've found that on-call and part-time work arrangements *are* compatible if you take certain precautions. The following discussion assumes that if a member of your on-call rotation works part-time, they'll be unavailable for on-call shifts outside of their part-time working week.

There are two main models of part-time working:

- Working a reduced amount of full days per week—for example, four 8-hour days a week, instead of five
- Working a reduced amount of time each day—for example, 6 hours a day, instead of 8 hours a day

Both models are compatible with on-call work, but require different adjustments to on-call scheduling.

The first model easily coexists with on-call work, especially if the nonworking day(s) are constant over time. In response, you can adopt an on-call shift length of fewer than seven days a week (for example, Monday through Thursday, or Friday through Sunday) and configure the automated scheduler not to schedule the part-time engineer(s) to be on-call on the days they don't work.

The second model is possible in a couple ways:

- Split on-call hours with another engineer, so that no one is on-call when they are not supposed to be. For example, if an on-call engineer needs to work from 9 a.m. to 4 p.m., you can assign the first half of the shift (9 a.m. to 3 p.m.) to them. Rotate the second half (3 p.m. to 9 p.m.) within the team the same way you rotate other on-call shifts.

- The part-time engineer can work full hours on their on-call days, which may be feasible if the on-call shift is not too frequent.

As mentioned in Chapter 11 (*http://bit.ly/2JgUBU7*) of *Site Reliability Engineering*, Google SRE compensates support outside of regular hours with a reduced hourly rate of pay or time off, according to local labor law and regulations. Take a part-time engineer's reduced schedule into account when determining on-call compensation.

In order to maintain a proper balance between project time and on-call time, engineers working reduced hours should receive a proportionately smaller amount of on-call work. Larger teams absorb this additional on-call load more easily than smaller teams.

On-Call Team Dynamics

Our first book touched upon how stress factors like high pager load and time pressure can force on-call engineers to adopt decision strategies based on intuition and heuristics rather than reason and data (see the section "Feeling Safe" in Chapter 11 (*http://bit.ly/2JgUBU7*) of that book). Working from this discussion of team psychology, how do you go about building a team with positive dynamics? Consider an on-call team with the following set of hypothetical problems.

Scenario: A culture of "survive the week"

A company begins with a couple of founders and a handful of employees, all feature developers. Everyone knows everyone else, and everyone takes pagers.

The company grows bigger. On-call duty is limited to a smaller set of more experienced feature developers who know the system better.

The company grows even bigger. They add an ops role to tackle reliability. This team is responsible for production health, and the job role is focused on operations, not coding. The on-call becomes a joint rotation between feature developers and ops. Feature developers have the final say in maintaining the service, and ops input is limited to operational tasks. By this time, there are 30 engineers in the on-call rotation: 25 feature developers and 5 ops, all located at the same site.

The team is plagued by high pager volume. Despite following the recommendations described earlier in this chapter to minimize pager load, the team is suffering from low morale. Because the feature developers prioritize developing new features, on-call follow-up takes a long time to implement.

To make matters worse, the feature developers are concerned about their own subsystem's health. One feature developer insists on paging by error rate rather than error ratio for their mission-critical module, despite complaints from others on the team. These alerts are noisy, and return many false positives or unactionable pages.

Other members of the on-call rotation aren't especially bothered by the high pager volume. Sure, there are a lot of pages, but most of them don't take much time to resolve. As one on-call engineer puts it: "I take a quick look at the page subject and know they are duplicates. So I just ignore them."

Sound familiar?

Some Google teams experienced similar problems during their earlier days of maturity. If not handled carefully, these problems have the potential to tear the feature developer and ops teams apart and hinder on-call operation. There's no silver bullet to solve these problems, but we found a couple of approaches particularly helpful. While your methodology may differ, your overall goal should be the same: build positive team dynamics, and carefully avoid tailspin.

Proposal one: Empower your ops engineers.   You can remodel the operations organization according to the guidelines outlined in this book and *Site Reliability Engineering*, perhaps even including a change of name (SRE, or similar) to indicate the change of role. Simply retitling your ops organization is not a panacea, but it can be helpful in communicating an *actual* change in responsibilities away from the old ops-centric model. Make it clear to the team and the entire company that SREs own the site operation. This includes defining a shared roadmap for reliability, driving the full resolution of issues, maintaining monitoring rules, and so on. Feature developers are necessary collaborators but don't own these endeavors.

To return to our hypothetical team, this announcement ushered in the following operational changes:

- Action items are assigned only to the five DevOps engineers—who are now SREs. SREs work with subject experts—many of them feature developers—to accomplish these tasks. SREs take on the previously mentioned "error rate versus error ratio" debate by negotiating a change in alerting with the feature developers.

- SREs are encouraged to dive into the code to make the changes themselves, if possible. They send code reviews to the subject experts. This has the benefit of building a sense of ownership among SREs, as well as upgrading their skills and authority for future occasions.

With this arrangement, feature developers are explicit collaborators on reliability features, and SREs are given the responsibility to own and improve the site.

Proposal two: Improve team relations.   Another possible solution is to build stronger team bonds between team members. Google designates a "fun budget" specifically for organizing offsite activities to strengthen team bonds.

We've found that more robust team relationships create a spirit of increased understanding and collaboration among teammates. As a result, engineers are more likely to fix bugs, finish action items, and help out their colleagues. For example, say you turned off a nightly pipeline job, but forgot to turn off the monitoring that checked if the pipeline ran successfully. As a result, you accidentally page a colleague at 3 a.m. If you've spent a little time with that colleague, you'd feel much worse about what happened, and strive to be considerate by being more careful in the future. The mentality of "I protect my colleagues" translates to a more productive work atmosphere.

We've also found that making all members of the on-call rotation sit together, regardless of job title and function area, helps improve team relations tremendously. Encourage teams to eat lunch with each other. Don't underestimate the power of relatively straightforward changes like these. It plays directly into team dynamics.

Conclusion

SRE on-call is different than traditional ops roles. Rather than focusing solely on day-to-day operations, SRE fully owns the production environment, and seeks to better it through defining appropriate reliability thresholds, developing automation, and undertaking strategic engineering projects. On-call is critical for site operations, and handling it right is crucial to the company's bottom line.

On-call is a source of much tension, both individually and collectively. But if you've stared into the eyes of the monster long enough, there is wisdom to be found. This chapter illustrates some of the lessons about on-call that we learned the hard way; we hope that our experience can help others avoid or tackle similar issues.

If your on-call team is drowning in endless alerts, we recommend taking a step back to observe the situation from a higher level. Compare notes with other SRE and partner teams. Once you've gathered the necessary information, address the problems in a systematic way. Thoughtfully structuring on-call is time well spent for on-call engineers, on-call teams, and the whole company.

## CHAPTER 9

Incident Response

By Jennifer Mace, Jelena Oertel, Stephen Thorne,
and Arup Chakrabarti (PagerDuty)
with Jian Ma and Jessie Yang

Everyone wants their services to run smoothly all the time, but we live in an imperfect world in which outages *do* occur. What happens when a not-so-ordinary, urgent problem requires multiple individuals or teams to resolve it? You are suddenly faced with simultaneously managing the incident response and resolving the problem.

Resolving an incident means mitigating the impact and/or restoring the service to its previous condition. Managing an incident means coordinating the efforts of responding teams in an efficient manner and ensuring that communication flows both between the responders and to those interested in the incident's progress. Many tech companies, including Google, have adopted and adapted best practices for managing incidents from emergency response organizations, which have been using these practices for many years.

The basic premise of incident management is to respond to an incident in a structured way. Large-scale incidents can be confusing; a structure that teams agree on beforehand can reduce chaos. Formulating rules about how to communicate and coordinate your efforts *before* disaster strikes allows your team to concentrate on resolving an incident when it occurs. If your team has already practiced and familiarized themselves with communication and coordination, they don't need to worry about these factors during an incident.

Setting up an incident response process doesn't need to be a daunting task. There are a number of widely available resources that can provide some guidance, such as Managing Incidents (*http://bit.ly/2J7G0qt*) in the first SRE Book. The basic principles of incident response include the following:

- Maintain a clear line of command.
- Designate clearly defined roles.
- Keep a working record of debugging and mitigation as you go.
- Declare incidents early and often.

This chapter shows how incident management is set up at Google and PagerDuty, and gives examples of where we got this process right and where we didn't. The simple checklist in "Putting Best Practices into Practice" on page 191 can help you get started on creating your own incident response practice, if you don't already have one.

Incident Management at Google

Incident response provides a system for responding to and managing an incident. A framework and set of defined procedures allow a team to respond to an incident effectively and scale up their response. Google's incident response system is based on the Incident Command System (ICS) (*http://bit.ly/2Jcs6Dq*).

Incident Command System

ICS was established in 1968 by firefighters as a way to manage wildfires. This framework provides standardized ways to communicate and fill clearly specified roles during an incident. Based upon the success of the model, companies later adapted ICS to respond to computer and system failures. This chapter explores two such frameworks: PagerDuty's Incident Response process (*http://bit.ly/2JlldDs*) and Incident Management At Google (IMAG (*http://bit.ly/2J7G0qt*)).

Incident response frameworks have three common goals, also known as the "three Cs" (3Cs) of incident management:

- *Coordinate* response effort.
- *Communicate* between incident responders, within the organization, and to the outside world.
- Maintain *control* over the incident response.

When something goes wrong with incident response, the culprit is likely in one of these areas. Mastering the 3Cs is essential for effective incident response.

Main Roles in Incident Response

The main roles in incident response are the Incident Commander (IC), Communications Lead (CL), and Operations or Ops Lead (OL). IMAG organizes these roles into a hierarchy: the IC leads the incident response, and the CL and OL report to the IC.

When disaster strikes, the person who declares the incident typically steps into the IC role and directs the high-level state of the incident. The IC concentrates on the 3Cs and does the following:

- Commands and *coordinates* the incident response, delegating roles as needed. By default, the IC assumes all roles that have not been delegated yet.
- *Communicates* effectively.
- Stays in *control* of the incident response.
- Works with other responders to resolve the incident.

The IC may either hand off their role to someone else and assume the OL role, or assign the OL role to someone else. The OL works to respond to the incident by applying operational tools to mitigate or resolve the incident.

While the IC and OL work on mitigating and resolving the incident, the CL is the public face of the incident response team. The CL's main duties include providing periodic updates to the incident response team and stakeholders, and managing inquiries about the incident.

Both the CL and OL may lead a team of people to help manage their specific areas of incident response. These teams can expand or contract as needed. If the incident becomes small enough, the CL role can be subsumed back into the IC role.

Case Studies

The following four large-scale incidents illustrate how incident response works in practice. Three of these case studies are from Google, and the last is a case study from PagerDuty, which provides perspective on how other organizations use ICS-derived frameworks. The Google examples start with an incident that wasn't managed effectively, and progress to incidents that were managed well.

Case Study 1: Software Bug—The Lights Are On but No One's (Google) Home

This example shows how failing to declare an incident early on can leave a team without the tools to respond to an incident quickly and efficiently. While this incident was resolved without major calamity, early escalation would have produced a quicker, more organized response, and a better outcome.

Context

Google Home is a smart speaker and home assistant that responds to voice commands. The voice commands interact with Google Home's software, which is called Google Assistant.

Interacting with Google Home starts when a user says a *hotword*, a given phrase that triggers Google Assistant. Multiple users can use the same Google Home device by training the assistant to listen for a given hotword. The hotword model that identifies speakers is trained on the client, but the training data (i.e., the speaker recognition files) is stored on the server. The server handles bidirectional streaming of data. To handle overload during busy times, the server has a quota policy for Google Assistant. In order to protect servers from overly large request values, the quota limit is significantly higher than the baseline usage for Google Assistant on a given device.

A bug in Google Assistant version 1.88 caused speaker recognition files to be fetched 50 times more often than expected, exceeding this quota. Initially, Google Home users in the central United States experienced only small traffic losses. As the rollout increased progressively to all Google Home devices, however, users lost half of their requests during the weekend of June 3, 2017.

Incident

At 11:48 a.m. PST on Monday, May 22, Jasper, the developer on-call for Google Home, happened to be looking at the queries per second (QPS) graphs and noticed something strange: Google Assistant had been pinging training data every 30 minutes, instead of once per day as expected. He stopped the release of version 1.88, which had rolled out to 25% of users. He raised a bug—let's call it bug 12345—with Google's bug tracking system to explore why this was happening. On the bug, he noted that Google Assistant was pinging data 48 times a day, causing it to exceed its QPS capacity.

Another developer, Melinda, linked the issue to a previously reported bug, which we'll call bug 67890: any time an app refreshed the device authentication and enrollment state, the speech processor restarted. This bug was slated to be fixed after the version 1.88 release, so the team requested a temporary increase in quota for the model to mitigate the overload from extra queries.

The version 1.88 release was started again and continued to roll out, reaching 50% of users by Wednesday, May 31. Unfortunately, the team later learned that bug 67890, while responsible for some extra traffic, was not the actual root cause of the more frequent fetches that Jasper had noticed.

That same morning, customers started reporting an issue to Google's support team: any time someone said "OK Google" (or any other hotword to activate Google Home), the device responded with an error message. This issue prevented users from giving commands to Google Assistant. The team began to investigate what could be causing the errors that users reported. They suspected quota issues, so they requested another increase to the quota, which seemed to mitigate the problem.

Meanwhile, the team continued to investigate bug 12345 to see what was triggering the errors. Although the quota connection was established early in the debugging process, miscommunication between the client and server developers had led developers down the wrong path during troubleshooting, and the full solution remained out of reach.

The team also puzzled over why Google Assistant's traffic kept hitting quota limits. The client and server developers were confused by client-side errors that didn't seem to be triggered by any problems on the server side. The developers added logging to the next release to help the team understand the errors better, and hopefully make progress in resolving the incident.

By Thursday, June 1, users reported that the issue had been resolved. No new issues were reported, so the version 1.88 release continued to roll out. However, the root cause of the original issue had not yet been identified.

By early Saturday morning, June 3, the version 1.88 release rollout surpassed 50%. The rollout was happening on a weekend, when developers were not readily available. The team had not followed the best practice of performing rollouts only during business days to ensure developers are around in case something goes wrong.

When the version 1.88 release rollout reached 100% on Saturday, June 3, the client once more hit server limits for Google Assistant traffic. New reports from customers started coming in. Google employees reported that their Google Home devices were throwing errors. The Google Home support team received numerous customer phone calls, tweets, and Reddit posts about the issue, and Google Home's help forum displayed a growing thread (*http://bit.ly/2Jkbk8N*) discussing the issue. Despite all the user reports and feedback, the bug wasn't escalated to a higher priority.

On Sunday, June 4, as the number of customer reports continued to increase, the support team finally raised the bug priority to the highest level. The team did not declare an incident, but continued to troubleshoot the issue via "normal" methods, using the bug tracking system for communication. The on-call developer noticed error rates in one of the datacenter clusters and pinged SRE, asking them to drain it. At the same time, the team submitted another request for a quota increase. Afterward, an engineer on the developer team noticed the drain had pushed errors into other cells, which provided additional evidence of quota issues. At 3:33 p.m., the developer team manager increased the quota for Google Assistant once again, and the impact on users stopped. The incident was over. The team identified the root cause (see the previous "Context" section) shortly thereafter.

Review

Some aspects of incident handling went really well, while others had room for improvement.

First, the developers rallied on the weekend and provided valuable input to resolve the issue. This was both good and bad. While the team valued the time and effort these individuals contributed over the weekend, successful incident management shouldn't rely on heroic efforts of individuals. What if the developers had been unreachable? At the end of the day, Google supports a good work-life balance—engineers shouldn't be tapped during their free time to fix work-related problems. Instead, we should have conducted rollouts during business hours or organized an on-call rotation that provided paid coverage outside of business hours.

Next, the team worked to mitigate the issue. Google always aims to first stop the impact of an incident, and then find the root cause (unless the root cause just happens to be identified early on). Once the issue is mitigated, it's just as important to understand the root cause in order to prevent the issue from happening again. In this case, mitigation successfully stopped the impact on three separate occasions, but the team could only prevent the issue from recurring when they discovered the root cause. After the first mitigation, it would have been better to postpone the rollout until the root cause was fully determined, avoiding the major disruption that happened over the weekend.

Finally, the team did not declare an incident when problems first appeared. Our experience shows that managed incidents are resolved faster. Declaring an incident early ensures that:

- Miscommunication between the client and server developers is prevented.
- Root-cause identification and incident resolution occur sooner.
- Relevant teams are looped in earlier, making external communications faster and smoother.

Centralized communication is an important principle of the IMAG protocol. For example, when disaster strikes, SREs typically gather in a "war room." The war room can be a physical location like a conference room, or it can be virtual: teams might gather on an IRC channel or Hangout. The key here is to gather all the incident responders in one place and to communicate in real time to manage—and ultimately resolve—an incident.

Case Study 2: Service Fault—Cache Me If You Can

The following incident illustrates what happens when a team of experts tries to debug a system with so many interactions that no single person can grasp *all* the details. Sound familiar?

Context

Kubernetes is an open source container management system built collaboratively by many companies and individual contributors. Google Kubernetes Engine, or GKE, is a Google-managed system that creates, hosts, and runs Kubernetes clusters for users. This hosted version operates the control plane, while users upload and manage workloads in the way that suits them best.

When a user first creates a new cluster, GKE fetches and initializes the Docker images their cluster requires. Ideally, these components are fetched and built internally so we can validate them. But because Kubernetes is an open source system, new dependencies sometimes slip in through the cracks.

Incident

One Thursday at 6:41 a.m. PST, London's on-call SRE for GKE, Zara, was paged for CreateCluster prober failures across several zones. No new clusters were being successfully created. Zara checked the prober dashboard and saw that failures were above 60% for two zones. She verified this issue was affecting user attempts to create new clusters, though traffic to existing clusters was not affected. Zara followed GKE's documented procedure and declared an incident at 7:06 a.m.

Initially, four people were involved in the incident:

- Zara, who first noticed the problem, and was therefore the designated default Incident Commander
- Two of Zara's teammates
- Rohit, the customer support engineer paged by the incident procedure

Since Rohit was based in Zurich, Zara (the IC) opened a GKE Panic IRC channel where the team could debug together. While the other two SREs dug into monitoring and error messages, Zara explained the outage and its impact to Rohit. By 7:24 a.m., Rohit posted a notice to users that CreateCluster was failing in the Europe-West region. This was turning into a large incident.

Between 7 a.m. and 8:20 a.m., Zara, Rohit, and the others worked on troubleshooting the issue. They examined cluster startup logs, which revealed an error:

```
error: failed to run Kubelet: cannot create certificate signing request: Post
https://192.0.2.53/apis/certificates.k8s.io/v1beta1/certificatesigningrequests
```

They needed to determine which part of the certificate creation failed. The SREs investigated the network, resource availability, and the certificate signing process. All seemed to work fine separately. At 8:22 a.m., Zara posted a summary of the investigation to the incident management system, and looked for a developer who could help her.

Thankfully, GKE had a developer on-call who could be paged for emergencies. The developer, Victoria, joined the channel. She asked for a tracking bug and requested that the team escalate the issue to the infrastructure on-call team.

It was now 8:45 a.m. The first Seattle SRE, Il-Seong, arrived at the office, lightly caffeinated and ready for the day. Il-Seong was a senior SRE with many years of experience in incident response. When he was informed about the ongoing incident, he jumped in to help. First, Il-Seong checked the day's release against the timing of the alerts, and determined that the day's release did not cause the incident. He then started a working document[1] to collect notes. He suggested that Zara escalate the incident to the infrastructure, cloud networking, and compute engine teams to possibly eliminate those areas as root causes. As a result of Zara's escalation, additional people joined the incident response:

- The developer lead for GKE nodes
- Cloud Networking on-call
- Compute Engine on-call
- Herais, another Seattle SRE

At 9:10 a.m., the incident channel had a dozen participants. The incident was 2.5 hours old, with no root cause and no mitigation. Communication was becoming a challenge. Normally, on-call handover from London to Seattle occurred at 10 a.m., but Zara decided to hand over incident command to Il-Seong before 10 a.m., since he had more experience with IMAG.

As Incident Commander, Il-Seong set up a formal structure to address the incident. He then designated Zara as Ops Lead and Herais as Communications (Comms) Lead. Rohit remained the External Communications Lead. Herais immediately sent an "all hands on deck" email to several GKE lists, including all developer leads, and asked experts to join the incident response.

So far, the incident responders knew the following:

- Cluster creation failed where nodes attempted to register with the master.
- The error message indicated the certificate signing module as the culprit.
- All cluster creation in Europe was failing; all other continents were fine.
- No other GCP services in Europe were seeing network or quota problems.

---

1 When three or more people work on an incident, it's useful to start a collaborative document that lists working theories, eliminated causes, and useful debugging information, such as error logs and suspect graphs. The document preserves this information so it doesn't get lost in the conversation.

Thanks to the call for all hands on deck, Puanani, a GKE Security team member, joined the effort. She noticed the certificate signer was not starting. The certificate signer was trying to pull an image from DockerHub, and the image appeared to be corrupted. Victoria (the on-call GKE developer) ran Docker's `pull` command for the image in two geographic locations. It failed when it ran on a cluster in Europe and succeeded on a cluster in the US. This indicated that the European cluster was the problem. At 9:56 a.m., the team had identified a plausible root cause.

Because DockerHub was an external dependency, mitigation and root causing would be especially challenging. The first option for mitigation was for someone at Docker to quickly fix the image. The second option was to reconfigure the clusters to fetch the image from a different location, such as Google Container Registry (GCR), Google's secure image hosting system. All the other dependencies, including other references to the image, were located in GCR.

Il-Seong assigned owners to pursue both options. He then delegated a team to investigate fixing the broken cluster. Discussion became too dense for IRC, so detailed debugging moved to the shared document, and IRC became the hub for decision making.

For the second option, pushing a new configuration meant rebuilding binaries, which took about an hour. At 10:59 a.m., when the team was 90% done rebuilding, they discovered another location that was using the bad image fetch path. In response, they had to restart the build.

While the engineers on IRC worked on the two mitigation options, Tugay, an SRE, had an idea. Instead of rebuilding the configuration and pushing it out (a cumbersome and risky process), what if they intercepted Docker's `pull` requests and substituted the response from Docker with an internal cached image? GCR had a mirror for doing precisely this. Tugay reached out to contacts on GCR's SRE team, and they confirmed that the team could set `--registry-mirror=https://mirror.gcr.io` on the Docker configuration. Tugay started setting up this functionality and discovered that *the mirror was already in place!*

At 11:29 a.m., Tugay reported to IRC that these images were being pulled *from the GCR mirror, not DockerHub*. At 11:37 a.m., the Incident Commander paged GCR on-call. At 11:59 a.m., GCR on-call purged the corrupt image from their European storage layer. By 12:11 p.m., all European zones had fallen to 0% error.

The outage was over. All that remained was cleanup, and writing a truly epic postmortem.

CreateCluster had failed in Europe for 6 hours and 40 minutes before it was fixed. In IRC, 41 unique users appeared throughout the incident, and IRC logs stretched to 26,000 words. The effort spun up seven IMAG task forces at various times, and as many as four worked simultaneously at any given time. On-calls were summoned from six teams, not including those from the "all hands on deck" call. The postmortem contained 28 action items.

Review

The GKE CreateCluster outage was a large incident by anyone's standards. Let's explore what went well, and what could have been handled better.

What went well?   The team had several documented escalation paths and was familiar with incident response tactics. Zara, the GKE on-call, quickly verified that the impact was affecting actual customers. She then used an incident management system prepared beforehand to bring in Rohit, who communicated the outage to customers.

What could have been handled better?   The service itself had some areas of concern. Complexity and dependence on specialists were problematic. Logging was insufficient for diagnosis, and the team was distracted by the corruption on DockerHub, which was not the real issue.

At the beginning of the incident, the Incident Commander didn't put a formal incident response structure in place. While Zara assumed this role and moved the conversation to IRC, she could have been much more proactive in coordinating information and making decisions. As a result, a handful of first responders pursued their own investigations without coordination. Il-Seong put a formal incident response structure in place two hours after the first page.

Finally, the incident revealed a gap in GKE's disaster readiness: the service didn't have any early generic mitigations that would reduce user pain. *Generic mitigations* are actions that first responders take to alleviate pain, even before the root cause is fully understood. For example, responders could roll back a recent release when an outage is correlated with the release cycle, or reconfigure load balancers to avoid a region when errors are localized. It's important to note that generic mitigations are blunt instruments and may cause other disruptions to the service. However, while they may have broader impact than a precise solution, they can be put in place quickly to stop the bleeding while the team discovers and addresses the root cause.

Let's look at the timeline of this incident again to see where a generic mitigation might have been effective:

- **7 a.m. (Assessed impact).** Zara confirmed that users were affected by the outage.
- **9:56 a.m. (Found possible cause).** Puanani and Victoria identified a rogue image.
- **10:59 a.m. (Bespoke mitigation).** Several team members worked on rebuilding binaries to push a new configuration that would fetch images from a different location.

- **11:59 a.m. (Found root cause and fixed the issue).** Tugay and GCR on-call disabled GCR caching and purged a corrupt image from their European storage layer.

A generic mitigation after step 2 (found possible cause) would have been very useful here. If the responders had rolled back all images to a known good state once they discovered the issue's general location, the incident would have been mitigated by 10 a.m. To mitigate an incident, you don't have to fully understand the details—you only need to know the location of the root cause. Having the ability to mitigate an outage before its cause is fully understood is crucial for running robust services with high availability.

In this case, the responders would have benefited from some sort of tool that facilitated rollbacks. Mitigation tools do take engineering time to develop. The right time to create general-purpose mitigation tools is before an incident occurs, not when you are responding to an emergency. Browsing postmortems is a great way to discover mitigations and/or tools that would have been useful in retrospect, and build them into services so that you can better manage incidents in the future.

It's important to remember that first responders must *prioritize mitigation above all else*, or time to resolution suffers. Having a generic mitigation in place, such as rollback and drain, speeds recovery and leads to happier customers. Ultimately, customers do not care whether or not you fully understand what caused an outage. What they want is to stop receiving errors.

With mitigation as top priority, an active incident should be addressed as follows:

1. Assess the impact of the incident.
2. Mitigate the impact.
3. Perform a root-cause analysis of the incident.
4. After the incident is over, fix what caused the incident and write a postmortem.

Afterward, you can run incident response drills to exercise the vulnerabilities in the system, and engineers can work on projects to address these vulnerabilities.

Case Study 3: Power Outage—Lightning Never Strikes Twice... Until It Does

The previous examples showed what can go wrong when you don't have good incident response strategies in place. The next example illustrates an incident that was successfully managed. When you follow a well-defined and clear response protocol, you can handle even rare or unusual incidents with ease.

Context

Power grid events, such as lightning strikes, cause the power coming into a datacenter facility to vary wildly. Lightning strikes affecting the power grid are rare, but not unexpected. Google protects against sudden, unexpected power outages with backup generators and batteries, which are well tested and known to work in these scenarios.

Many of Google's servers have a large number of disks attached to them, with the disks located on a separate tray above or below the server. These trays have their own uninterruptible power supply (UPS) battery. When a power outage occurs, the backup generators activate but take a few minutes to start. During this period, the backup batteries attached to the servers and disk trays provide power until the backup generators are fully running, thereby preventing power grid events from impacting datacenter operation.

Incident

In mid-2015, lightning struck the power grid near a Google datacenter in Belgium four times within two minutes. The datacenter's backup generators activated to supply power to all the machines. While the backup generators were starting up, most of the servers ran on backup batteries for a few minutes.

The UPS batteries in the disk trays did not swap power usage to the backup batteries on the third and fourth lightning strikes because the strikes were too closely spaced. As a result, the disk trays lost power until the backup generators kicked in. The servers did not lose power, but were unable to access the disks that had power cycled.

Losing a large number of disk trays on persistent disk storage resulted in read and write errors for many virtual machine (VM) instances running on Google Compute Engine (GCE). The Persistent Disk SRE on-call was immediately notified of these errors. Once the Persistent Disk SRE team established the impact, a major incident was declared and announced to all affected parties. The Persistent Disk SRE on-call assumed the role of Incident Commander.

After an initial investigation and communication between stakeholders, we established that:

- Each machine that lost a disk tray because of the temporary power outage needed to be rebooted.
- While waiting for the reboot, some customer VMs had trouble reading and writing to their disks.
- Any host that had both a disk tray and customer VMs could not simply be "rebooted" without losing the customer VMs that hadn't been affected. Persistent Disk SRE asked GCE SRE to migrate unaffected VMs to other hosts.

The Persistent Disk SRE's primary on-call retained the IC role, since that team had the best visibility into customer impact.

Operations team members were tasked with the following objectives:

- Safely restore power to use grid power instead of backup generators.
- Restart all machines that were not hosting VMs.
- Coordinate between Persistent Disk SRE and GCE SRE to safely move VMs away from the affected machines before restarting them.

The first two objectives were clearly defined, well understood, and documented. The datacenter ops on-call immediately started working to safely restore power, providing regular status reports to the IC. Persistent Disk SRE had defined procedures for restarting all machines not hosting virtual machines. A team member began restarting those machines.

The third objective was more vague and wasn't covered by any existing procedures. The Incident Commander assigned a dedicated operations team member to coordinate with GCE SRE and Persistent Disk SRE. These teams collaborated to safely move VMs away from the affected machines so the affected machines could be rebooted. The IC closely monitored their progress and realized that this work called for new tools to be written quickly. The IC organized more engineers to report to the operations team so they could create the necessary tools.

The Communications Lead observed and asked questions about all incident-related activities, and was responsible for reporting accurate information to multiple audiences:

- Company leaders needed information about the extent of the problem, and assurance that the problem was being addressed.
- Teams with storage concerns needed to know when their storage would be fully available again.
- External customers needed to be proactively informed about the problem with their disks in this cloud region.
- Specific customers who had filed support tickets needed more information about the problems they were seeing, and advice on workarounds and timelines.

After we mitigated the initial customer impact, we needed to do some follow-up, such as:

- Diagnosing why the UPS used by the disk trays failed, and making sure that it doesn't happen again.
- Replacing the batteries in the datacenter that failed.

- Manually clearing "stuck" operations caused by losing so many storage systems simultaneously.

Post-incident analysis revealed that only a small number of writes—the writes pending on the machines that lost power during the incident—weren't ever written to disk. Since Persistent Disk snapshots and all Cloud Storage data are stored in multiple datacenters for redundancy, only 0.000001% of data from running GCE machines was lost, and only data from running instances was at risk.

Review

By declaring the incident early and organizing a response with clear leadership, a carefully managed group of people handled this complex incident effectively.

The Incident Commander delegated the normal problems of restoring power and rebooting servers to the appropriate Operations Lead. Engineers worked on fixing the issue and reported their progress back to the Operations Lead.

The more complex problem of meeting the needs of both GCE and Persistent Disk required coordinated decision making and interaction among multiple teams. The Incident Commander made sure to assign appropriate operations team members from both teams to the incident, and worked directly with them to drive toward a solution. The Incident Commander wisely focused on the most important aspect of the incident: addressing the needs of the impacted customers as quickly as possible.

Case Study 4: Incident Response at PagerDuty

by Arup Chakrabarti of PagerDuty

PagerDuty has developed and refined our internal incident response practices over the course of several years. Initially, we staffed a permanent, company-wide Incident Commander and dedicated specific engineers per service to take part in incident response. As PagerDuty grew to over 400 employees and dozens of engineering teams, our Incident Response processes also changed. Every few months, we take a hard look at our processes, and update them to reflect business needs. Nearly everything we have learned is documented at *https://response.pagerduty.com*. Our Incident Response processes are purposefully not static; they change and evolve just as our business does.

Major incident response at PagerDuty

Typically, small incidents require only a single on-call engineer to respond. When it comes to larger incidents, we place heavy emphasis on teamwork. An engineer shouldn't feel alone in high-stress and high-impact scenarios. We use the following techniques to help promote teamwork:

Participating in simulation exercises

One way we teach teamwork is by participating in Failure Friday (*http://bit.ly/ 2LP7JOE*). PagerDuty drew inspiration from Netflix's Simian Army (*http://bit.ly/ 2yukZU8*) to create this program. Originally, Failure Friday was a manual failure injection exercise aimed at learning more about the ways our systems could break. Today, we also use this weekly exercise to recreate common problems in production and incident response scenarios.

Before Failure Friday starts, we nominate an Incident Commander (typically, a person training to become an IC). They are expected to behave and act like a real IC while conducting failure injection exercises. Throughout the drill, subject-matter experts use the same processes and vernacular they would use during an actual incident. This practice both familiarizes new on-call engineers with incident response language and processes and provides more seasoned on-call engineers with a refresher.

Playing time-bound simulation games

While Failure Friday exercises go a long way toward training engineers on different roles and processes, they can't fully replicate the urgency of actual major incidents. We use simulation games with a time-bound urgency to capture that aspect of incident response.

"Keep Talking and Nobody Explodes" (*http://www.keeptalkinggame.com/*) is one game we've leveraged heavily. It requires players to work together to defuse bombs within time limits. The stressful and communication-intensive nature of the game forces players to cooperate and work together effectively.

Learning from previous incidents

Learning from previous incidents helps us respond better to major incidents in the future. To this end, we conduct and regularly review postmortems.

PagerDuty's postmortem process involves open meetings and thorough documentation. By making this information easily accessible and discoverable, we aim to reduce the resolution time of future incidents, or prevent a future incident from happening altogether.

We also record all of the phone calls involved in a major incident so we can learn from the real-time communication feed.

Let's look at a recent incident in which PagerDuty had to leverage our incident response process. The incident occurred on October 6, 2017, and lasted more than 10 hours, but had very minimal customer impact.

- **7:53 p.m.** A member of the PagerDuty SRE team was alerted that PagerDuty internal NTP servers were exhibiting clock drift. The on-call SRE validated that all automated recovery actions had been executed, and completed the mitigation steps in relevant runbooks. This work was documented in the SRE team's dedicated Slack channel.

- **8:20 p.m.** A member of PagerDuty Software Team A received an automated alert about clock drift errors in their services. Software Team A and the SRE team worked toward resolving the problem.

- **9:17 p.m.** A member of PagerDuty Software Team B received an automated alert about clock drift errors on their services. The engineer from Team B joined the Slack channel where the issue was already being triaged and debugged.

- **9:49 p.m.** The SRE on-call declared a major incident and alerted the Incident Commander on-call.

- **9:55 p.m.** The IC assembled the response team, which included every on-call engineer that had a service dependent on NTP, and PagerDuty's customer support on-call. The IC had the response team join the dedicated conference call and Slack channel.

For the next eight hours, the response team worked on addressing and mitigating the issue. When the procedures in our runbooks didn't resolve the issue, the response team started trying new recovery options in a methodical manner.

During this time, we rotated on-call engineers and the IC every four hours. Doing so encouraged engineers to get rest and brought new ideas into the response team.

- **5:33 a.m.** The on-call SRE made a configuration change to the NTP servers.

- **6:13 a.m.** The IC validated that all services had recovered with their respective on-call engineers. Once validation was complete, the IC shut off the conference call and Slack channel and declared the incident complete. Given the wide impact of the NTP service, a postmortem was warranted. Before closing out the incident, the IC assigned the postmortem analysis to the SRE team on-call for the service.

Tools used for incident response

Our Incident Response processes leverage three main tools:

PagerDuty
> We store all of our on-call information, service ownership, postmortems, incident metadata, and the like, in PagerDuty. This allows us to rapidly assemble the right team when something goes wrong.

Slack
> We maintain a dedicated channel (#incident-war-room) as a gathering place for all subject-matter experts and Incident Commanders. The channel is used mostly

as an information ledger for the scribe, who captures actions, owners, and time-stamps.

Conference calls
When asked to join any incident response, on-call engineers are required to dial in to a static conference call number. We prefer that all coordination decisions are made in the conference call, and that decision outcomes are recorded in Slack. We found this was the fastest way to make decisions. We also record every call to make sure that we can recreate any timeline in case the scribe misses important details.

While Slack and conference calls are our communication channels of choice, you should use the communication method that works best for your company and its engineers.

At PagerDuty, how we handle incident response relates directly to the success of the company. Rather than facing such events unprepared, we purposefully prepare for incidents by conducting simulation exercises, reviewing previous incidents, and choosing the right tools to help us be resilient to any major incident that may come our way.

Putting Best Practices into Practice

We've seen examples of incidents that were handled well, and some that were not. By the time a pager alerts you to a problem, it's too late to think about how to manage the incident. The time to start thinking about an incident management process is *before* an incident occurs. So how do you prepare and put theory into practice before disaster strikes? This section provides some recommendations.

Incident Response Training

We highly recommend training responders to organize an incident so they have a pattern to follow in a real emergency. Knowing how to organize an incident, having a common language to use throughout the incident, and sharing the same expectations reduce the chance of miscommunication.

The full Incident Command System approach may be more than you need, but you can develop a framework for handling incidents by selecting the parts of the incident management process that are important to your organization. For example:

- Let on-calls know they can delegate and escalate during an incident.
- Encourage a mitigation-first response.
- Define Incident Commander, Communications Lead, and Operations Lead roles.

You can adapt and summarize your incident response framework, and create a slide deck to present to new team members. We've learned that people are more receptive to incident response training when they can connect the theory of incident response to actual scenarios and concrete actions. Therefore, be sure to include hands-on exercises and share what happened in past incidents, analyzing what went well and what didn't go so well. You might also consider using external agencies that specialize in incident response classes and training.

Prepare Beforehand

In addition to incident response training, it helps to prepare for an incident beforehand. Use the following tips and strategies to be better prepared.

Decide on a communication channel

Decide and agree on a communication channel (Slack, a phone bridge, IRC, HipChat, etc.) beforehand—no Incident Commander wants to make this decision during an incident. Practice using it so there are no surprises. If possible, pick a communications channel the team is already familiar with so that everyone on the team feels comfortable using it.

Keep your audience informed

Unless you acknowledge that an incident is happening and actively being addressed, people will automatically assume nothing is being done to resolve the issue. Similarly, if you forget to call off the response once the issue has been mitigated or resolved, people will assume the incident is ongoing. You can preempt this dynamic by keeping your audience informed throughout the incident with regular status updates. Having a prepared list of contacts (see the next tip) saves valuable time and ensures you don't miss anyone.

Think ahead about how you'll draft, review, approve, and release public blog posts or press releases. At Google, teams seek guidance from the PR team. Also, prepare two or three ready-to-use templates for sharing information, making sure the on-call knows how to send them. No one wants to write these announcements under extreme stress with no guidelines. The templates make sharing information with the public easy and minimally stressful.

Prepare a list of contacts

Having a list of people to email or page prepared beforehand saves critical time and effort. In "Case Study 2: Service Fault—Cache Me If You Can" on page 180, the Comms Lead made an "all hands on deck" call by sending an email to several GKE lists that were prepared beforehand.

Establish criteria for an incident

Sometimes it's clear that a paging issue is truly an incident. Other times, it's not so clear. It's helpful to have an established list of criteria for determining if an issue is indeed an incident. A team can come up with a solid list of criteria by looking at past outages, taking known high-risk areas into consideration.

In summary, it's important to establish common ground for coordination and communication when responding to incidents. Decide on ways to communicate the incident, who your audience is, and who is responsible for what during an incident. These guidelines are easy to set up and have high impact on shortening the resolution time of an incident.

Drills

The final step in the incident management process is practicing your incident management skills. By practicing during less critical situations, your team develops good habits and patterns of behavior for when lightning strikes—figuratively and literally. After introducing the theory of incident response through training, practice ensures that your incident response skills stay fresh.

There are several ways to conduct incident management drills. Google runs company-wide resilience testing (called Disaster Recovery Testing, or DiRT; see Kripa Krishnan's article "Weathering the Unexpected"[2]), in which we create a controlled emergency that doesn't actually impact customers. Teams respond to the controlled emergency as if it were a real emergency. Afterward, the teams review the emergency response procedures and discuss what happened. Accepting failure as a means of learning, finding value in gaps identified, and getting our leadership on board were key to successfully establishing the DiRT program at Google. On a smaller scale, we practice responding to specific incidents using exercises like Wheel of Misfortune (see "Disaster Role Playing" (*http://bit.ly/2Hb8ONg*) in *Site Reliability Engineering*).

You can also practice incident response by intentionally treating minor problems as major ones requiring a large-scale response. This lets your team practice with the procedures and tools in a real-world situation with lower stakes.

Drills are a friendly way of trying out new incident response skills. Anyone on your team who could get swept into incident response—SREs, developers, and even customer support and marketing partners—should feel comfortable with these tactics.

---

2 Kripa Krishan, "Weathering the Unexpected," *Communications of the ACM* 10, no. 9 (2012), *https://queue.acm.org/detail.cfm?id=2371516*.

To stage a drill, you can invent an outage and allow your team to respond to the incident. You can also create outages from postmortems, which contain plenty of ideas for incident management drills. Use real tools as much as possible to manage the incident. Consider breaking your test environment so the team can perform real troubleshooting using existing tools.

All these drills are far more useful if they're run periodically. You can make drills impactful by following up each exercise with a report detailing what went well, what didn't go well, and how things could have been handled better. The most valuable part of running a drill is examining their outcomes, which can reveal a lot about any gaps in incident management. Once you know what they are, you can work toward closing them.

Conclusion

Be prepared for when disaster strikes. If your team practices and refreshes your incident response procedures regularly, you won't panic when the inevitable outage occurs.

The circle of people you need to collaborate with during an incident expands with the size of the incident. When you're working with people you don't know, procedures help create the structure you need to quickly move toward a resolution. We strongly recommend establishing these procedures ahead of time when the world is *not* on fire. Regularly review and iterate on your incident management plans and playbooks.

The Incident Command System is a simple concept that is easily understood. It scales up or down according to the size of the company and the incident. Although it's simple to understand, it isn't easy to implement, especially in the middle of an incident when panic suddenly overtakes you. Staying calm and following the response structure during an emergency takes practice, and practice builds "muscle memory." This gives you the confidence you'll need for a real emergency.

We strongly recommend carving out some time in your team's busy schedule to practice incident management on a regular basis. Secure support from leadership for dedicated practice time, and make sure they understand how incident response works in case you need to involve them in a real incident. Disaster preparedness can shave off valuable minutes or hours from response time and gives you a competitive edge. No company gets it right all the time—learn from your mistakes, move on, and do better the next time.

## CHAPTER 10

Postmortem Culture: Learning from Failure

By Daniel Rogers, Murali Suriar, Sue Lueder,
Pranjal Deo, and Divya Sudhakar
with Gary O'Connor and Dave Rensin

Our experience shows that a truly blameless postmortem culture results in more reliable systems—which is why we believe this practice is important to creating and maintaining a successful SRE organization.

Introducing postmortems into an organization is as much a cultural change as it is a technical one. Making such a shift can seem daunting. The key takeaway from this chapter is that making this change is possible, and needn't seem like an insurmountable challenge. Don't emerge from an incident hoping that your systems will eventually remedy themselves. You can start small by introducing a very basic postmortem procedure, and then reflect and tune your process to best suit your organization—as with many things, there is no one size that fits all.

When written well, acted upon, and widely shared, postmortems can be a very effective tool for driving positive organizational change and preventing repeat outages. To illustrate the principles of good postmortem writing, this chapter presents a case study of an actual outage that happened at Google. An example of a poorly written postmortem highlights the reasons why "bad" postmortem practices are damaging to an organization that's trying to create a healthy postmortem culture. We then compare the bad postmortem with the actual postmortem that was written after the incident, highlighting the principles and best practices of a high-quality postmortem.

The second part of this chapter shares what we've learned about creating incentives for nurturing of a robust postmortem culture and how to recognize (and remedy) the early signs that the culture is breaking down.

Finally, we provide tools and templates that you can use to bootstrap a postmortem culture.

For a comprehensive discussion on blameless postmortem philosophy, see Chapter 15 (*http://bit.ly/2J2Po2W*) in our first book, *Site Reliability Engineering*.

Case Study

This case study features a routine rack decommission that led to an increase in service latency for our users. A bug in our maintenance automation, combined with insufficient rate limits, caused thousands of servers carrying production traffic to simultaneously go offline.

While the majority of Google's servers are located in our proprietary datacenters, we also have racks of proxy/cache machines in colocation facilities (or "colos"). Racks in colos that contain our proxy machines are called *satellites*. Because satellites undergo regular maintenance and upgrades, a number of satellite racks are being installed or decommissioned at any point in time. At Google, these maintenance processes are largely automated.

The decommission process overwrites the full content of all drives in the rack using a process we call *diskerase*. Once a machine is sent to diskerase, the data it once stored is no longer retrievable. The steps for a typical rack decommission are as follows:

```
# Get all active machines in "satellite"
machines = GetMachines(satellite)

# Send all candidate machines matching "filter" to decom
SendToDecom(candidates=GetAllSatelliteMachines(),
            filter=machines)
```

Our case study begins with a satellite rack that was marked for decommissioning. The diskerase step of the decommission process finished successfully, but the automation responsible for the remainder of the machine decommission failed. To debug the failure, we retried the decommission process. The second decommission ran as follows:

```
# Get all active machines in "satellite"
machines = GetMachines(satellite)

# "machines" is an empty list, because the decom flow has already run.
# API bug: an empty list is treated as "no filter", rather than "act on no
# machines"

# Send all candidate machines matching "filter" to decom
SendToDecom(candidates=GetAllSatelliteMachines(),
            filter=machines)

# Send all machines in "candidates" to diskerase.
```

Within minutes, the disks of all satellite machines, globally, were erased. The machines were rendered inert and could no longer accept connections from users, so subsequent user connections were routed directly to our datacenters. As a result, users experienced a slight increase in latency. Thanks to good capacity planning, very few of our users noticed the issue during the two days it took us to reinstall machines in the affected colo racks. Following the incident, we spent several weeks auditing and adding more sanity checks to our automation to make our decommission workflow idempotent.

Three years after this outage, we experienced a similar incident: a number of satellites were drained, resulting in increased user latency. The action items implemented from the original postmortem dramatically reduced the blast radius and rate of the second incident.

Suppose you were the person responsible for writing the postmortem for this case study. What would you want to know, and what actions would you propose to prevent this outage from happening again?

Let's start with a not-so-great postmortem for this incident.

Bad Postmortem

Postmortem: All Satellite Machines Sent to Diskerase

2014-August-11

Owner:	maxone@, logantwo@, sydneythree@, dylanfour@
Shared with:	satellite-infra-team@
Status:	Final
Incident date:	2014-August-11
Published:	2014-December-30

Executive Summary

Impact:	All Satellite machines are sent to diskerase, which practically wiped out Google Edge.
Root cause:	dylanfour@ ignored the automation setup and ran the cluster turnup logic manually, which triggered an existing bug.

Problem Summary

Duration of problem:	40min
Product(s) affected:	satellite-infra-team

% of product affected:	All satellite clusters.
User impact:	All queries that normally go to satellites were served from the core instead, causing increased latency.
Revenue impact:	Some ads were not served due to the lost queries. Exact revenue impact unknown at this time.
Detection:	Monitoring alert.
Resolution:	Diverting traffic to core followed by manual repair of edge clusters.

Background (optional)

Impact

User impact

All queries that normally go to satellites were instead served from the core, causing increased latency to user traffic.

Revenue impact

Some ads were not served due to the lost queries.

Root Causes and Trigger

Cluster turnup/turndown automation is not meant to be idempotent. The tool has safeguards to ensure that certain steps cannot be run more than once. Unfortunately, there is nothing to stop someone from running the code manually as many times as they want. None of the documentation mentioned this gotcha. As a result, most team members think it's okay to run the process multiple times if it doesn't work.

This is exactly what happened during a routine decommissioning of a rack. The rack was being replaced with a new Iota-based satellite. dylanfour@ completely ignored the fact that the turnup had already executed once and was stuck in the first attempt. Due to careless ignorance, they triggered a bad interaction that assigned all the satellite machines to the diskerase team.

Recovery Efforts

Lessons Learned

Things that went well

- Alerting caught the issue immediately.
- Incident management went well.

Things that went poorly

- The team (especially maxone@, logantwo@) never wrote any documentation to tell SREs not to run the automation multiple times, which is ridiculous.
- On-call did not act soon enough to prevent most satellite machines from being erased. This is not the first time that on-call failed to react in time.

Where we got lucky

- Core was able to serve all the traffic that normally would have gone to the Edge. I can't believe we survived this one!!!

Action Items

Action item	Type	Priority	Owner	Tracking bug
Make automation better.	mitigate	P2	logantwo@	
Improve paging and alerting.	detect	P2		
sydneythree@ needs to learn proper cross-site handoff protocol so nobody has to work on duplicate issues.	mitigate	P2		BUG6789
Train humans not to run unsafe commands.	prevent	P2		

Glossary

Why Is This Postmortem Bad?

The example "bad" postmortem contains a number of common failure modes that we try to avoid. The following sections explain how to improve upon this postmortem.

Missing context

From the outset, our example postmortem introduces terminology that's specific to traffic serving (e.g., "satellites") and lower layers of machine management automation at Google (e.g., "diskerase"). If you need to provide additional context as part of the postmortem, use the Background and/or Glossary sections (which can link to longer documents). In this case, both sections were blank.

If you don't properly contextualize content when writing a postmortem, the document might be misunderstood or even ignored. It's important to remember that your audience extends beyond the immediate team.

Key details omitted

Multiple sections contain high-level summaries but lacked important details. For example:

Problem summary
> For outages affecting multiple services, you should present numbers to give a consistent representation of impact. The only numerical data our example provides is the duration of the problem. We don't have enough details to estimate the size or impact of the outage. Even if there is no concrete data, a well-informed estimate is better than no data at all. After all, if you don't know how to measure it, then you can't know it's fixed!

Root causes and trigger
> Identifying the root causes and trigger is one of the most important reasons to write a postmortem. Our example contains a small paragraph that describes the root causes and trigger, but it doesn't explore the lower-level details of the issue.

Recovery efforts
> A postmortem acts as the record of an incident for its readers. A good postmortem will let readers know what happened, how the issue was mitigated, and how users were impacted. The answers to many of these questions are typically found in the Recovery Efforts section, which was left empty in our example.

If an outage merits a postmortem, you should also take the time to accurately capture and document the necessary details. The reader should get a complete view of the outage and, more importantly, learn something new.

Key action item characteristics missing

The Action Items (AIs) section of our example is missing the core aspects of an actionable plan to prevent recurrence. For example:

- The action items are mostly mitigative. To minimize the likelihood of the outage recurring, you should include some preventative action items and fixes. The one "preventative" action item suggests we "make humans less error-prone." In general, trying to change human behavior is less reliable than changing automated systems and processes. (Or as Dan Milstein once quipped (*http://bit.ly/2syrmBF*): "Let's plan for a future where we're all as stupid as we are today.")

- All of the action items have been tagged with an equal priority. There's no way to determine which action to tackle first.

- The first two action items in the list use ambiguous phrases like "Improve" and "Make better." These terms are vague and open to interpretation. Using unclear language makes it difficult to measure and understand success criteria.

- Only one action item was assigned a tracking bug. Without a formal tracking process, action items from postmortems are often forgotten, resulting in outages.

 In the words of Ben Treynor Sloss, Google's VP for 24/7 Operations: "To our users, a postmortem without subsequent action is indistinguishable from no postmortem. Therefore, all postmortems which follow a user-affecting outage must have at least one P[01] bug associated with them. I personally review exceptions. There are very few exceptions."

Counterproductive finger pointing

Every postmortem has the potential to lapse into a blameful narrative. Let's take a look at some examples:

Things that went poorly
The entire team is blamed for the outage, while two members (maxone@ and logantwo@) are specifically called out.

Action items
The last item in the list targets sydneythree@ for succumbing to pressure and mismanaging the cross-site handoff.

Root causes and trigger
dylanfour@ is held solely responsible for the outage.

It may seem like a good idea to highlight individuals in a postmortem. Instead, this practice leads team members to become risk-averse because they're afraid of being publicly shamed. They may be motivated to cover up facts critical to understanding and preventing recurrence.

Animated language

A postmortem is a factual artifact that should be free from personal judgments and subjective language. It should consider multiple perspectives and be respectful of others. Our example postmortem contains multiple examples of undesirable language:

Root causes and trigger
Superfluous language (e.g., "careless ignorance")

Things that went poorly
Animated text (e.g., "which is ridiculous")

Where we got lucky
An exclamation of disbelief (e.g., "I can't believe we survived this one!!!")

Animated language and dramatic descriptions of events distract from the key message and erode psychological safety. Instead, provide verifiable data to justify the severity of a statement.

Missing ownership

Declaring official ownership results in accountability, which leads to action. Our example postmortem contains several examples of missing ownership:

- The postmortem lists four owners. Ideally, an owner is a single point of contact who is responsible for the postmortem, follow-up, and completion.
- The Action Items section has little or no ownership for its entries. Actions items without clear owners are less likely to be resolved.

It's better to have a single owner and multiple collaborators.

Limited audience

Our example postmortem was shared only among members of the team. By default, the document should have been accessible to everyone at the company. We recommend proactively sharing your postmortem as widely as possible—perhaps even with your customers. The value of a postmortem is proportional to the learning it creates. The more people that can learn from past incidents, the less likely they are to be repeated. A thoughtful and honest postmortem is also a key tool in restoring shaken trust.

As your experience and comfort grows, you will also likely expand your "audience" to nonhumans. Mature postmortem cultures often add machine-readable tags (and other metadata) to enable downstream analytics.

Delayed publication

Our example postmortem was published four months after the incident. In the interim, had the incident recurred (which in reality, did happen), team members likely would have forgotten key details that a timely postmortem would have captured.

Good Postmortem

 This is an actual postmortem. In some cases, we fictionalized names of individuals and teams. We also replaced actual values with placeholders to protect sensitive capacity information. In the postmortems that you create for your internal consumption, you should absolutely include specific numbers!

Postmortem: All Satellite Machines Sent to Diskerase

2014-August-11

Owner:	Postmortem: maxone@, logantwo@ Datacenter Automation: sydneythree@ Network: dylanfour@ Server Management: finfive@
Shared with:	*all_engineering_employees@google.com*
Status:	Final
Incident date:	Mon, August 11, 2014, 17:10 to 17:50 PST8PDT
Published:	Fri, August 15, 2014

Executive Summary

Impact:	Frontend queries dropped Some ads were not served There was a latency increase for all services normally served from satellite for nearly two days
Root cause:	A bug in turndown automation caused all satellite machines, instead of just one rack of satellite machines, to be sent to diskerase. This resulted in all satellite machines entering the decom workflow, which wiped their disks. The result was a global satellite frontend outage.

Problem Summary

Duration of problem:	Main outage: Mon, August 11, 17:10 to 17:50 PST8PDT Reconstruction work and residual pains through Wed, August 13, 07:46 PST8PDT, then the incident was closed.
Product(s) affected:	Frontend Infrastructure, specifically all satellite locations.
% of product affected:	Global—all traffic normally served from satellites (typically 60% of global queries).

User impact:	[Value redacted] frontend queries dropped over a period of 40 minutes ([value redacted] QPS averaged over the period, [value redacted] % of global traffic). Latency increase for all services normally served from satellite for nearly two days.
Revenue impact:	The exact revenue impact unknown at this time.
Detection:	Blackbox alerting: traffic-team was paged with "satellite a12bcd34 failing too many HTTP requests" for ~every satellite in the world.
Resolution:	The outage itself was rapidly mitigated by moving all of Google's frontend traffic to core clusters, at the cost of additional latency for user traffic.

Background (optional)

If you're unfamiliar with frontend traffic serving and the lower layers of serving automation at Google, read the glossary before you continue.

Impact

User impact

- [Value redacted] frontend queries dropped over a period of [value redacted] minutes. [Value redacted] QPS averaged over the period, [value redacted] % of global traffic. Our monitoring suggests a much larger crater; however, the data was unreliable as it ceased monitoring satellites that were still serving, thinking they were turned down. The appendix describes how the above numbers were estimated.

- There was a latency increase for all services normally served from satellite for nearly two days:
    — [Value redacted] ms RTT spikes for countries near core clusters
    — Up to+[value redacted] ms for locations relying more heavily on satellites (e.g., Australia, New Zealand, India)

Revenue impact

Some ads were not served due to the lost queries. The exact revenue impact is unknown at this time:

- Display and video: The data has very wide error bars due to day-on-day fluctuations, but we estimate between [value redacted] % and [value redacted] % of revenue loss on the day of the outage.

- Search: [Value redacted] % to [value redacted] % loss between 17:00 to 18:00, again with wide error bars.

Team impact

- The Traffic team spent ~48 hours with all hands on deck rebuilding satellites.
- NST had a higher-than-normal interrupt/pager load because they needed to traffic-engineer overloaded peering links.
- Some services may have seen increased responses served at their frontends due to reduced cache hit rate in the GFEs.
  — For example, see this thread [link] about [cache-dependent service].
  — [Cache-dependent service] saw their cache hit rate at the GFEs drop from [value redacted] % to [value redacted] % before slowly recovering.

Incident document

[The link to our incident tracking document has been redacted.]

Root Causes and Trigger

A longstanding input validation bug in the Traffic Admin server was triggered by the manual reexecution of a workflow to decommission the `a12bcd34` satellite. The bug removed the machine constraint on the decom action, sending all satellite machines to decommission.

From there, datacenter automation executed the decom workflow, wiping the hard drives of the majority of satellite machines before this action could be stopped.

The Traffic Admin server provides a `ReleaseSatelliteMachines` RPC. This handler initiates satellite decommission using three MDB API calls:

- Look up the rack name associated with the edge node (e.g., `a12bcd34` -> <rack name>).
- Look up the machine names associated with the rack (<rack> -> <machine 1>, <machine 2>, etc.).
- Reassign those machines to diskerase, which indirectly triggers the decommission workflow.

This procedure is not idempotent, due to a known behavior of the MDB API combined with a missing safety check. If a satellite node was previously successfully sent to decom, step 2 above returns an empty list, which is interpreted in step 3 as the absence of a constraint on a machine hostname.

This dangerous behavior has been around for a while, but was hidden by the workflow that invokes the unsafe operation: the workflow step invoking the RPC is marked "run once," meaning that the workflow engine will not reexecute the RPC once it has succeeded.

However, "run once" semantics don't apply across multiple instances of a workflow. When the Cluster Turnup team manually started another run of the workflow for `a12bcd34`, this action triggered the `admin_server` bug.

Timeline/Recovery Efforts

[The link to our Timeline log has been elided for book publication. In a real postmortem, this information would always be included.]

Lessons Learned

Things that went well

- Evacuating the edge. GFEs in core are explicitly capacity-planned to allow this to happen, as is the production backbone (aside from peering links; see the Outage list in the next section). This edge evacuation allowed the Traffic team to mitigate promptly without fear.
- Automatic mitigation of catastrophic satellite failure. Cover routes automatically pull traffic from failing satellites back to core clusters, and satellites drain themselves when abnormal churn is detected.
- Satellite decom/diskerase worked very effectively and rapidly, albeit as a confused deputy (*http://bit.ly/2syHumz*).
- The outage triggered a quick IMAG response via OMG and the tool proved useful for ongoing incident tracking. The cross-team response was excellent, and OMG further helped keep everyone talking to each other.

Things that went poorly

Outage

- The Traffic Admin server lacked the appropriate sanity checks on the commands it sent to MDB. All commands should be idempotent, or at least fail-safe on repeat invocations.
- MDB did not object to the missing hostname constraint in the ownership change request.
- The decom workflow doesn't cross-check decom requests with other data sources (e.g., planned rack decoms). As a result, there were no objections to the request to trash (many) geographically diverse machines.
- The decom workflow is not rate-limited. Once the machines entered decom, disk erase and other decom steps proceeded at maximum speed.
- Some peering links between Google and the world were overloaded as a result of the egress traffic shifting to different locations when satellites stopped serving, and their queries were instead served from core. This resulted in short bursts of

congestion to select peers until satellites were restored, and mitigation work by NST to match.

Recovery

- Reinstalls of satellite machines were slow and unreliable. Reinstallations use TFTP to transmit data, which works poorly when transmitting to satellites at the end of high-latency links.
- The Autoreplacer infrastructure was not able to handle the simultaneous setup of [value redacted] of GFEs at the time of the outage. Matching the velocity of automated setups required the labor of many SREs working in parallel performing manual setups. The factors below contributed to the initial slowness of the automation:
  - Overly strict SSH timeouts prevented reliable Autoreplacer operation on very remote satellites.
  - A slow kernel upgrade process was executed regardless of whether the machine already had the correct version.
  - A concurrency regression in Autoreplacer prevented running more than two machine setup tasks per worker machine.
  - Confusion about the behavior of the Autoreplacer wasted time and effort.
- The monitoring configuration delta safety checks (25% change) did not trigger when 23% of the targets were removed, but did trigger when the same contents (29% of what remained) were readded. This caused a 30-minute delay in reenabling monitoring of the satellites.
- "The installer" has limited staffing. As a result, making changes is difficult and slow.
- Use of superuser powers to claw machines back from diskerase left a lot of zombie state, causing ongoing cleanup pain.

Where we got lucky

- GFEs in core clusters are managed very differently from satellite GFEs. As a result, they were not affected by the decom rampage.
- Similarly, YouTube's CDN is run as a distinct piece of infrastructure, so YouTube video serving was not affected. Had this failed, the outage would have been much more severe and prolonged.

Action Items

Due to the wide-reaching nature of this incident, we split action items into five themes:

1. Prevention/risk education
2. Emergency response
3. Monitoring/alerting
4. Satellite/edge provisioning
5. Cleanup/miscellaneous

Table 10-1. Prevention/risk education

Action items	Type	Priority	Owner	Tracking bug
Audit all systems capable of turning live servers into paperweights (i.e., not just repairs and diskerase workflow).	investigate	P1	sydneythree@	BUG1234
File bugs to track implementation of bad input rejection to all systems identified in BUG1234.	prevent	P1	sydneythree@	BUG1235
Disallow any single operation from affecting servers spanning namespace/class boundaries.	mitigate	P1	maxone@	BUG1236
Traffic admin server needs a safety check to not operate on more than [value redacted] number of nodes.	mitigate	P1	dylanfour@	BUG1237
Traffic admin server should ask <safety check service> to approve destructive work.	prevent	P0	logantwo@	BUG1238
MDB should reject operations that do not provide values for an expected-present constraint.	prevent	P0	louseven@	BUG1239

Table 10-2. Emergency response

Action items	Type	Priority	Owner	Tracking bug
Ensure that serving from core does not overload egress network links.	repair	P2	rileysix@	BUG1240
Ensure decom workflow problems are noted under [the link to our emergency stop doc has been redacted] and [the link to our escalations contact page has been redacted].	mitigate	P2	logantwo@	BUG1241
Add a big-red-button[a] disable approach to decom workflows.	mitigate	P0	maxone@	BUG1242

[a] A general term for a shut-down switch (e.g., an emergency power-off button) to be used in catastrophic circumstances to avert further damage.

Table 10-3. Monitoring/alerting

Action items	Type	Priority	Owner	Tracking bug
Monitoring target safety checks should not allow you to push a change that cannot be rolled back.	mitigate	P2	dylanfour@	BUG1243
Add an alert when more than [value redacted] % of our machines have been taken away from us. Machines were taken from satellites at 16:38 while the world started paging only at around 17:10.	detect	P1	rileysix@	BUG1244

Table 10-4. Satellite/edge provisioning

Action items	Type	Priority	Owner	Tracking bug
Use iPXE to use HTTPS to make reinstalls more reliable/ faster.	mitigate	P2	dylanfour@	BUG1245

Table 10-5. Cleanup/miscellaneous

Action items	Type	Priority	Owner	Tracking bug
Review MDB-related code in our tools and bring the admin server backup to unwedge turnups/turndowns.	repair	P2	rileysix@	BUG1246
Schedule DiRT tests:	mitigate	P2	louseven@	BUG1247

- Bring back satellite after diskerase.
- Do the same for YouTube CDN.

Glossary

Admin server

An RPC server that enables automation to execute privileged operations for frontend serving infrastructure. The automation server is most visibly involved in the implementation of PCRs and cluster turnups/turndowns.

Autoreplacer

A system that moves non-Borgified servers from machine to machine. It's used to keep services running in the face of machine failures, and also to support fork-lifts and colo reconfigs.

Borg

A cluster management system designed to manage tasks and machine resources on a massive scale. Borg owns all of the machines in a Borg cell, and assigns tasks to machines that have resources available.

Decom

An abbreviation of *decommissioning*. Decom of equipment is a process that is relevant to many operational teams.

Diskerase

A process (and associated hardware/software systems) to securely wipe production hard drives before they leave Google datacenters. Diskerase is a step in the decom workflow.

GFE (Google Front End)

The server that the outside world connects to for (almost) all Google services.

IMAG (Incident Management at Google)

A program that establishes a standard, consistent way to handle all types of incidents—from system outages to natural disasters—and organize an effective response.

MDB (Machine Database)

A system that stores all sorts of information about the state of Google machine inventory.

OMG (Outage Management at Google)

An incident management dashboard/tool that serves as a central place for tracking and managing all ongoing incidents at Google.

Satellites

Small, inexpensive racks of machine that serve only nonvideo, frontend traffic from the edge of Google's network. Almost none of the traditional production cluster infrastructure is available for satellites. Satellites are distinct from the CDN that serves YouTube video content from the edge of Google's network, and from other places on the wider internet. YouTube CDN was not affected by this incident.

Appendix

Why is `ReleaseSatelliteMachines` *not idempotent?*

[The response to this question has been elided.]

What happened after the Admin Server assigned all satellites to the diskerase-team?

[The response to this question has been elided.]

What was the true QPS (http://bit.ly/2JksYtc) loss during the outage?

[The response to this question has been elided.]

IRC logs

[The IRC logs have been elided.]

Graphs

Faster latency statistics—what have satellites ever done for us?

Empirically from this outage, satellites shave [value redacted] ms latency off many locations near core clusters, and up to [value redacted] ms off locations further from our backbone:

[The explanation of the graphs has been elided.]

Core vs. Edge serving load

A nice illustration of the reconstruction effort. Being able to once again serve 50% of traffic from the edge took about 36 hours, and returning to the normal traffic balance took an additional 12 hours (see Figure 10-1 and Figure 10-2).

Peering strain from traffic shifts

[Graph elided.]

The graph shows packet loss aggregated by network region. There were a few short spikes during the event itself, but the majority of the loss occurred as various regions entered peak with little/no satellite coverage.

Person vs. Machine, the GFE edition

[Graph explanation of human vs. automated machine setup rates elided.]

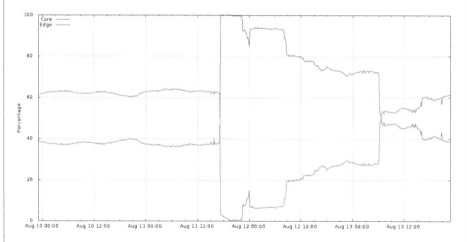

Figure 10-1. Core vs. Edge QPS breakdown

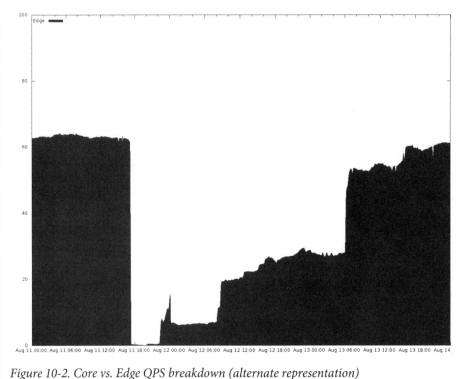

Figure 10-2. Core vs. Edge QPS breakdown (alternate representation)

Why Is This Postmortem Better?

This postmortem exemplifies several good writing practices.

Clarity

The postmortem is well organized and explains key terms in sufficient detail. For example:

Glossary
> A well-written glossary makes the postmortem accessible and comprehensible to a broad audience.

Action items
> This was a large incident with many action items. Grouping action items by theme makes it easier to assign owners and priorities.

Quantifiable metrics
> The postmortem presents useful data on the incident, such as cache hit ratios, traffic levels, and duration of the impact. Relevant sections of the data are presented with links back to the original sources. This data transparency removes ambiguity and provides context for the reader.

Concrete action items

A postmortem with no action items is ineffective. These action items have a few notable characteristics:

Ownership
> All action items have both an owner and a tracking number.

Prioritization
> All action items are assigned a priority level.

Measurability
> The action items have a verifiable end state (e.g., "Add an alert when more than X% of our machines have been taken away from us").

Preventative action
> Each action item "theme" has Prevent/Mitigate action items that help avoid outage recurrence (for example, "Disallow any single operation from affecting servers spanning namespace/class boundaries").

Blamelessness

The authors focused on the gaps in system design that permitted undesirable failure modes. For example:

Things that went poorly
> No individual or team is blamed for the incident.

Root cause and trigger
> Focuses on "what" went wrong, not "who" caused the incident.

Action items
> Are aimed at improving the system instead of improving people.

Depth

Rather than only investigating the proximate area of the system failure, the postmortem explores the impact and system flaws across multiple teams. Specifically:

Impact
> This section contains lots of details from various perspectives, making it balanced and objective.

Root cause and trigger
> This section performs a deep dive on the incident and arrives at a root cause and trigger.

Data-driven conclusions
> All of the conclusions presented are based on facts and data. Any data used to arrive at a conclusion is linked from the document.

Additional resources
> These present further useful information in the form of graphs. Graphs are explained to give context to readers who aren't familiar with the system.

Promptness

The postmortem was written and circulated less than a week after the incident was closed. A prompt postmortem tends to be more accurate because information is fresh in the contributors' minds. The people who were affected by the outage are waiting for an explanation and some demonstration that you have things under control. The longer you wait, the more they will fill the gap with the products of their imagination. That seldom works in your favor!

Conciseness

The incident was a global one, impacting multiple systems. As a result, the postmortem recorded and subsequently parsed a lot of data. Lengthy data sources, such as chat transcripts and system logs, were abstracted, with the unedited versions linked from the main document. Overall, the postmortem strikes a balance between verbosity and readability.

Organizational Incentives

Ideally, senior leadership should support and encourage effective postmortems. This section describes how an organization can incentivize a healthy postmortem culture. We highlight warning signs that the culture is failing and offer some solutions. We also provide tools and templates to streamline and automate the postmortem process.

Model and Enforce Blameless Behavior

To properly support postmortem culture, engineering leaders should consistently exemplify blameless behavior and encourage blamelessness in every aspect of postmortem discussion. You can use a few concrete strategies to enforce blameless behavior in an organization.

Use blameless language

Blameful language stifles collaboration between teams. Consider the following scenario:

> Sandy missed a service Foo training and wasn't sure how to run a particular update command. The delay ultimately prolonged an outage.
>
> SRE Jesse [to Sandy's manager]: "You're the manager; why aren't you making sure that everyone finishes the training?"

The exchange includes a leading question that will instantly put the recipient on the defensive. A more balanced response would be:

> SRE Jesse [to Sandy's manager]: "Reading the postmortem, I see that the on-caller missed an important training that would have allowed them to resolve the outage more quickly. Maybe team members should be required to complete this training before joining the on-call rotation? Or we could remind them that if they get stuck to please quickly escalate. After all, escalation is not a sin—especially if it helps lower customer pain! Long term, we shouldn't really rely so much on training, as it's easy to forget in the heat of the moment."

Include all incident participants in postmortem authoring

It can be easy to overlook key contributing factors to an outage when the postmortem is written in isolation or by a single team.

Gather feedback

A clear review process and communication plan for postmortems can help prevent blameful language and perspectives from propagating within an organization. For a suggested structured review process, see the section "Postmortem checklist" on page 221.

Reward Postmortem Outcomes

When well written, acted upon, and widely shared, postmortems are an effective vehicle for driving positive organizational change and preventing repeat outages. Consider the following strategies to incentivize postmortem culture.

Reward action item closeout

If you reward engineers for writing postmortems, but not for closing the associated action items, you risk an unvirtuous cycle of unclosed postmortems. Ensure that incentives are balanced between writing the postmortem and successfully implementing its action plan.

Reward positive organizational change

You can incentivize widespread implementation of postmortem lessons by presenting postmortems as an opportunity to expand impact across an organization. Reward this level of impact with peer bonuses, positive performance reviews, promotion, and the like.

Highlight improved reliability

Over time, an effective postmortem culture leads to fewer outages and more reliable systems. As a result, teams can focus on feature velocity instead of infrastructure patching. It's intrinsically motivating to highlight these improvements in reports, presentations, and performance reviews.

Hold up postmortem owners as leaders

Celebrating postmortems through emails or meetings, or by giving the authors an opportunity to present lessons learned to an audience, can appeal to individuals that appreciate public accolades. Setting up the owner as an "expert" on a type of failure and its avoidance can be rewarding for many engineers who seek peer acknowledgment. For example, you might hear someone say, "Talk to Sara, she's an expert now. She just coauthored a postmortem where she figured out how to fix that gap!"

Gamification

Some individuals are incentivized by a sense of accomplishment and progress toward a larger goal, such as fixing system weaknesses and increasing reliability. For these individuals, a scoreboard or burndown of postmortem action items can be an incentive. At Google, we hold "FixIt" weeks twice a year. SREs who close the most postmortem action items receive small tokens of appreciation and (of course) bragging rights. Figure 10-3 shows an example of a postmortem leaderboard.

Figure 10-3. Postmortem leaderboard

Share Postmortems Openly

In order to maintain a healthy postmortem culture within an organization, it's important to share postmortems as widely as possible. Implementing even one of the following tactics can help.

Share announcements across the organization

Announce the availability of the postmortem draft on your internal communication channels, email, Slack, and the like. If you have a regular company all-hands, make it a practice to share a recent postmortem of interest.

Conduct cross-team reviews

Conduct cross-team reviews of postmortems. In these reviews, a team walks though their incident while other teams ask questions and learn vicariously. At Google, several offices have informal Postmortem Reading Clubs that are open to all employees.

In addition, a cross-functional group of developers, SREs, and organizational leaders reviews the overall postmortem process. These folks meet monthly to review the effectiveness of the postmortem process and template.

Hold training exercises

Use the Wheel of Misfortune (*http://bit.ly/2JiOazR*) when training new engineers: a cast of engineers reenacts a previous postmortem, assuming roles laid out in the postmortem. The original Incident Commander attends to help make the experience as "real" as possible.

Report incidents and outages weekly

Create a weekly outage report containing the incidents and outages from the past seven days. Share the report with as wide an audience as possible. From the weekly outages, compile and share a periodic greatest hits report.

Respond to Postmortem Culture Failures

The breakdown of postmortem culture may not always be obvious. The following are some common failure patterns and recommended solutions.

Avoiding association

Disengaging from the postmortem process is a sign that postmortem culture at an organization is failing. For example, suppose SRE Director Parker overhears the following conversation:

> SWE Sam: Wow, did you hear about that huge blow-up?
>
> SWE Riley: Yeah, it was terrible. They'll have to write a postmortem now.
>
> SWE Sam: Oh no! I'm so glad I'm not involved with that.
>
> SWE Riley: Yeah, I really wouldn't want to be in the meeting where that one is discussed.

Ensuring that high-visibility postmortems are reviewed for blameful prose can help prevent this kind of avoidance. In addition, sharing high-quality examples and discussing how those involved were rewarded can help reengage individuals.

Failing to reinforce the culture

Responding when a senior executive uses blameful language can be challenging. Consider the following statement made by senior leadership at a meeting about an outage:

> VP Ash: I know we are supposed to be blameless, but this is a safe space. Someone must have known beforehand this was a bad idea, so why didn't you listen to that person?

Mitigate the damage by moving the narrative in a more constructive direction. For example:

> SRE Dana: Hmmm, I'm sure everyone had the best intent, so to keep it blameless, maybe we ask generically if there were any warning signs we could have heeded, and why we might have dismissed them.

Individuals act in good faith and make decisions based on the best information available. Investigating the source of misleading information is much more beneficial to the organization than assigning blame. (If you have encountered Agile principles, this should be familiar to you (*http://bit.ly/2sthid8*).)

Lacking time to write postmortems

Quality postmortems take time to write. When a team is overloaded with other tasks, the quality of postmortems suffers. Subpar postmortems with incomplete action items make a recurrence far more likely. Postmortems are letters you write to future team members: it's very important to keep a consistent quality bar, lest you accidentally teach future teammates a bad lesson. Prioritize postmortem work, track the postmortem completion and review, and allow teams adequate time to implement the associated action plan. The tooling we discuss in the section "Tools and Templates" on page 220 can help with these activities.

Repeating incidents

If teams are experiencing failures that mirror previous incidents, it's time to dig deeper. Consider asking questions like:

- Are action items taking too long to close?
- Is feature velocity trumping reliability fixes?
- Are the right action items being captured in the first place?
- Is the faulty service overdue for a refactor?
- Are people putting Band-Aids on a more serious problem?

If you uncovered a systemic process or technical problem, it's time to take a step back and consider the overall service health. Bring the postmortem collaborators from each similar incident together to discuss the best course of action to prevent repeats.

Tools and Templates

A set of tools and templates can bootstrap a postmortem culture by making writing postmortems and managing the associated data easier. There are a number of resources from Google and other companies that you can leverage in this space.

Postmortem Templates

Templates make it easier to write complete postmortems and share them across an organization. Using a standard format makes postmortems more accessible for readers outside the domain. You can customize the template to fit your needs. For example, it may be useful to capture team-specific metadata like hardware make/model for a datacenter team, or Android versions affected for a mobile team. You can then add customizations as the team matures and performs more sophisticated postmortems.

Google's template

Google has shared a version of our postmortem template in Google Docs format at *http://g.co/SiteReliabilityWorkbookMaterials*. Internally, we primarily use Docs to write postmortems because it facilitates collaboration via shared editing rights and comments. Some of our internal tools prepopulate this template with metadata to make the postmortem easier to write. We leverage Google Apps Script (*https://devel opers.google.com/apps-script/*) to automate parts of the authoring, and capture a lot of the data into specific sections and tables to make it easier for our postmortem repository to parse out data for analysis.

Other industry templates

Several other companies and individuals have shared their postmortem templates:

- Pager Duty (*http://bit.ly/2J6FaP7*)
- An adaptation of the original Google Site Reliability Engineering book template (*http://bit.ly/2kIhFNC*)
- A list of four templates hosted on GitHub (*http://bit.ly/2svJA7R*)
- GitHub user Julian Dunn (*http://bit.ly/2LcOzRy*)
- Server Fault (*http://bit.ly/2spHl5P*)

Postmortem Tooling

As of this writing, Google's postmortem management tooling is not available for external use (check our blog (*https://cloudplatform.googleblog.com/*) for the latest updates). We can, however, explain how our tools facilitate postmortem culture.

Postmortem creation

Our incident management tooling collects and stores a lot of useful data about an incident and pushes that data automatically into the postmortem. Examples of data we push includes:

- Incident Commander and other roles
- Detailed incident timeline and IRC logs
- Services affected and root-cause services
- Incident severity
- Incident detection mechanisms

Postmortem checklist

To help authors ensure a postmortem is properly completed, we provide a postmortem checklist that walks the owner through key steps. Here are just a few example checks on the list:

- Perform a complete assessment of incident impact.
- Conduct sufficiently detailed root-cause analysis to drive action item planning.
- Ensure action items are vetted and approved by the technical leads of the service.
- Share the postmortem with the wider organization.

The full checklist is available at *http://g.co/SiteReliabilityWorkbookMaterials*.

Postmortem storage

We store postmortems in a tool called Requiem so it's easy for any Googler to find them. Our incident management tool automatically pushes all postmortems to Requiem, and anyone in the organization can post their postmortem for all to see. We have thousands of postmortems stored, dating back to 2009. Requiem parses out metadata from individual postmortems and makes it available for searching, analysis, and reporting.

Postmortem follow-up

Our postmortems are stored in Requiem's database. Any resulting action items are filed as bugs in our centralized bug tracking system. Consequently, we can monitor the closure of action items from each postmortem. With this level of tracking, we can ensure that action items don't slip through the cracks, leading to increasingly unstable services. Figure 10-4 shows a mockup of postmortem action item monitoring enabled by our tooling.

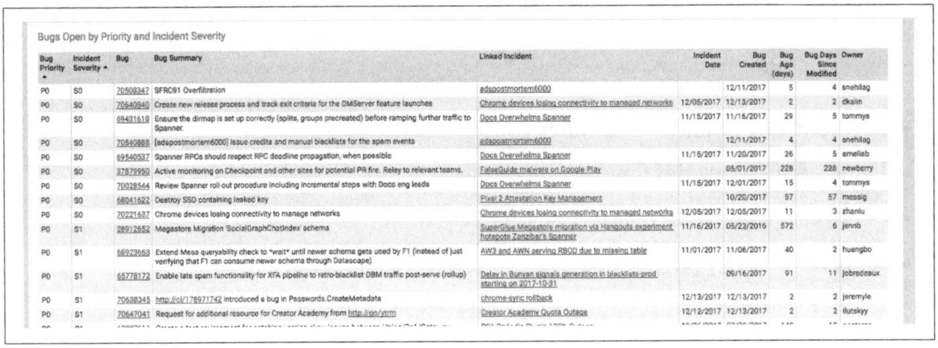

Bugs Open by Priority and Incident Severity

Bug Priority	Incident Severity	Bug	Bug Summary	Linked Incident	Incident Date	Bug Created	Bug Age (days)	Bug Days Since Modified	Owner
P0	S0	70508347	SFRC91 Overfiltration	adspostmortem6000		12/11/2017	5	4	snehilag
P0	S0	70640840	Create new release process and track exit criteria for the DMServer feature launches	Chrome devices losing connectivity to managed networks	12/05/2017	12/13/2017	2	2	dkalin
P0	S0	69431618	Ensure the dirmap is set up correctly (splits, groups precreated) before ramping further traffic to Spanner.	Docs Overwhelms Spanner	11/15/2017	11/16/2017	29	5	tommys
P0	S0	70540888	[adspostmortem6000] Issue credits and manual blacklists for the spam events	adspostmortem6000		12/11/2017	4	4	snehilag
P0	S0	69540537	Spanner RPCs should respect RPC deadline propagation, when possible	Docs Overwhelms Spanner	11/15/2017	11/20/2017	26	5	ameliab
P0	S0	37879950	Active monitoring on Checkpoint and other sites for potential PR fire. Relay to relevant teams.	FalseGuide malware on Google Play		05/01/2017	228	228	newberry
P0	S0	70028544	Review Spanner roll-out procedure including incremental steps with Docs eng leads	Docs Overwhelms Spanner	11/15/2017	12/01/2017	15	4	tommys
P0	S0	68041622	Destroy SSD containing leaked key	Pixel 2 Attestation Key Management		10/20/2017	57	57	messig
P0	S0	70221637	Chrome devices losing connectivity to manage networks	Chrome devices losing connectivity to managed networks	12/05/2017	12/05/2017	11	3	zhanlu
P0	S1	28912652	Megastore Migration 'SocialGraphChatIndex' schema	SuperGlue Megastore migration via Hangouts experiment hotspots Zanzibar's Spanner	11/16/2017	05/23/2016	572	6	jennb
P0	S1	68923663	Extend Mesa queryability check to *wait* until newer schema gets used by F1 (instead of just verifying that F1 can consume newer schema through Datascape)	AW3 and AWN serving RBOD due to missing table	11/01/2017	11/06/2017	40	2	huangbo
P0	S1	65778172	Enable late spam functionality for XFA pipeline to retro-blacklist DBM traffic post-serve (rollup)	Delay in Bunyan signals generation in blacklists-prod starting on 2017-10-31		09/16/2017	91	11	jobredeaux
P0	S1	70638345	http://cl/178971742 introduced a bug in Passwords.CreateMetadata	chrome-sync rollback	12/13/2017	12/13/2017	2	2	jeremyle
P0	S1	70647041	Request for additional resource for Creator Academy from http://go/ytrm	Creator Academy Quota Outage	12/12/2017	12/13/2017	2	2	ilutskyy

Figure 10-4. Postmortem action item monitoring

Postmortem analysis

Our postmortem management tool stores its information in a database for analysis. Teams can use the data to write reports about their postmortem trends and identify their most vulnerable systems. This helps us uncover underlying sources of instability or incident management dysfunctions that may otherwise go unnoticed. For example, Figure 10-5 shows charts that were built with our analysis tooling. These charts show us trends like how many postmortems we have per month per organization, incident mean duration, time to detect, time to resolve, and blast radius.

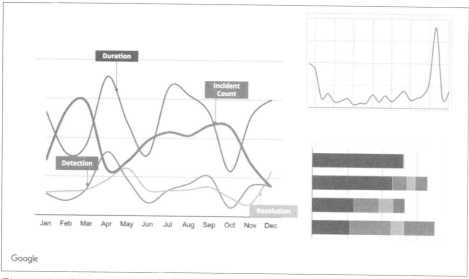

Figure 10-5. Postmortem analysis

Other industry tools

Here are some third-party tools that can help you create, organize, and analyze postmortems:

- Pager Duty Postmortems (*http://bit.ly/2xvrCqK*)
- Morgue by Etsy (*https://github.com/etsy/morgue*)
- VictorOps (*http://bit.ly/2J87dcR*)

Although it's impossible to fully automate every step of writing postmortems, we've found that postmortem templates and tooling make the process run more smoothly. These tools free up time, allowing authors to focus on the critical aspects of the post-mortem, such as root-cause analysis and action item planning.

Conclusion

Ongoing investment in cultivating a postmortem culture pays dividends in the form of fewer outages, a better overall experience for users, and more trust from the people that depend on you. Consistent application of these practices results in better system design, less downtime, and more effective and happier engineers. If the worst does happen and an incident recurs, you will suffer less damage and recover faster and have even more data to continue reinforcing production.

## CHAPTER 11

Managing Load

By Cooper Bethea, Gráinne Sheerin, Jennifer Mace, and Ruth King
with Gary Luo and Gary O'Connor

No service is 100% available 100% of the time: clients can be inconsiderate, demand can grow fifty-fold, a service might crash in response to a traffic spike, or an anchor might pull up a transatlantic cable. There are people who depend upon your service, and as service owners, we care about our users. When faced with these chains of outage triggers, how can we make our infrastructure as adaptive and reliable as possible?

This chapter describes Google's approach to traffic management with the hope that you can use these best practices to improve the efficiency, reliability, and availability of your services. Over the years, we have discovered that there's no single solution for equalizing and stabilizing network load. Instead, we use a combination of tools, technologies, and strategies that work in harmony to help keep our services reliable.

Before we dive in to this chapter, we recommend reading the philosophies discussed in Chapters 19 ("Load Balancing at the Frontend" (*http://bit.ly/2LQ6TRQ*)) and 20 ("Load Balancing in the Datacenter" (*http://bit.ly/2J4faDU*)) of our first SRE book.

Google Cloud Load Balancing

These days, most companies don't develop and maintain their own global load balancing solutions, instead opting to use load balancing services from a larger public cloud provider. We'll discuss Google Cloud Load Balancer (GCLB) as a concrete example of large-scale load balancing, but nearly all of the best practices we describe also apply to other cloud providers' load balancers.

Google has spent the past 18 years building infrastructure to make our services fast and reliable. Today we use these systems to serve YouTube, Maps, Gmail, Search, and many other products and services. GCLB is our publicly consumable global load balancing solution, and is the externalization of one of our internally developed global load balancing systems.

This section describes the components of GCLB and how they work together to serve user requests. We trace a typical user request from its creation to delivery at its destination. The Niantic Pokémon GO case study provides a concrete implementation of GCLB in the real world.

Chapter 19 (*http://bit.ly/2LQ6TRQ*) of our first SRE book described how DNS-based load balancing is the simplest and most effective way to balance load before the user's connection even starts. We also discussed an endemic problem of this approach: it relies on client cooperation to properly expire and refetch DNS records. For this reason, GCLB does not use DNS load balancing.

Instead, we use *anycast*, a method for sending clients to the closest cluster without relying on DNS geolocation. Google's global load balancer knows where the clients are located and directs packets to the closest web service, providing low latency to users while using a single virtual IP (VIP) (*http://bit.ly/2kFchKX*). Using a single VIP means we can increase the time to live (TTL) of our DNS records, which further reduces latency.

Anycast

Anycast is a network addressing and routing methodology. It routes datagrams from a single sender to the topologically nearest node in a group of potential receivers, which are all identified by the same destination IP address. Google announces IPs via Border Gateway Protocol (BGP) (*http://bit.ly/2J5GyBi*) from multiple points in our network. We rely on the BGP routing mesh to deliver packets from a user to the closest frontend location that can terminate a transmission control protocol (TCP) session. This deployment eliminates the problems of unicast IP proliferation and finding the closest frontend for a user. Two main issues remain:

- Too many nearby users can overwhelm a frontend site.
- BGP route calculation might reset connections.

Consider an ISP that frequently recalculates its BGP routes such that one of its users prefers either of two frontend sites. Each time the BGP route "flaps," all in-progress TCP streams are reset as the unfortunate user's packets are directed to a new frontend with no TCP session state. To address these problems, we have leveraged our connection-level load balancer, Maglev (described shortly), to cohere TCP streams even when routes flap. We refer to this technique as *stabilized anycast*.

Stabilized anycast

As shown in Figure 11-1, Google implements stabilized anycast using Maglev, our custom load balancer. To stabilize anycast, we provide each Maglev machine with a way to map client IPs to the closest Google frontend site. Sometimes Maglev processes a packet destined for an anycast VIP for a client that is closer to another frontend site. In this case, Maglev forwards that packet to another Maglev on a machine located at the closest frontend site for delivery. The Maglev machines at the closest frontend site then simply treat the packet as they would any other packet, and route it to a local backend.

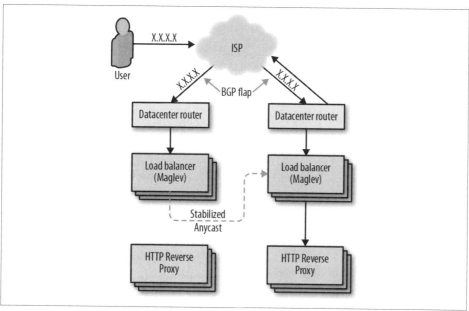

Figure 11-1. Stabilized anycast

Maglev

Maglev (*http://bit.ly/2LcdhBw*), shown in Figure 11-2, is Google's custom distributed packet-level load balancer. An integral part of our cloud architecture, Maglev machines manage incoming traffic to a cluster. They provide stateful TCP-level load balancing across our frontend servers. Maglev differs from other traditional hardware load balancers in a few key ways:

- All packets destined for a given IP address can be evenly spread across a pool of Maglev machines via Equal-Cost Multi-Path (ECMP) forwarding (*http://bit.ly/2H9vYDr*). This enables us to boost Maglev capacity by simply adding servers to a pool. Spreading packets evenly also enables Maglev redundancy to be modeled as $N + 1$, enhancing availability and reliability over traditional load balancing systems (which typically rely on active/passive pairs to give $1 + 1$ redundancy).

- Maglev is a Google custom solution. We control the system end-to-end, which allows us to experiment and iterate quickly.

- Maglev runs on commodity hardware in our datacenters, which greatly simplifies deployment.

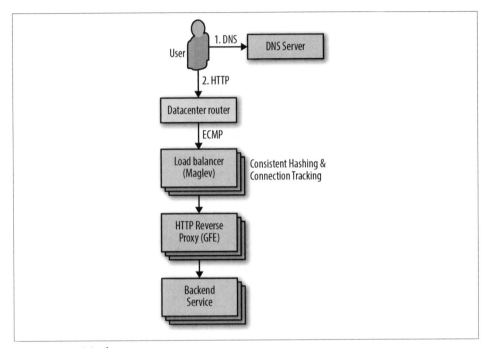

Figure 11-2. Maglev

Maglev packet delivery uses *consistent hashing* and *connection tracking*. These techniques coalesce TCP streams at our HTTP reverse proxies (also known as *Google Front Ends*, or *GFEs*), which terminate TCP sessions. Consistent hashing and connection tracking are key to Maglev's ability to scale by packet rather than by number of connections. When a router receives a packet destined for a VIP hosted by Maglev, the router forwards the packet to any Maglev machine in the cluster through ECMP. When a Maglev receives a packet, it computes the packet's 5-tuple hash[1] and looks up the hash value in its connection tracking table, which contains routing results for recent connections. If Maglev finds a match and the selected backend service is still

---

1 5-tuple includes the following: source address, destination address, source port, destination port, and the transport protocol type.

healthy, it reuses the connection. Otherwise, Maglev falls back to consistent hashing to choose a backend. The combination of these techniques eliminates the need to share connection state among individual Maglev machines.

Global Software Load Balancer

GSLB is Google's Global Software Load Balancer. It allows us to balance live user traffic between clusters so that we can match user demand to available service capacity, and so we can handle service failures in a way that's transparent to users. As shown in Figure 11-3, GSLB controls both the distribution of connections to GFEs and the distribution of requests to backend services. GSLB allows us to serve users from backends and GFEs running in different clusters. In addition to load balancing between frontends and backends, GSLB understands the health of backend services and can automatically drain traffic away from failed clusters.

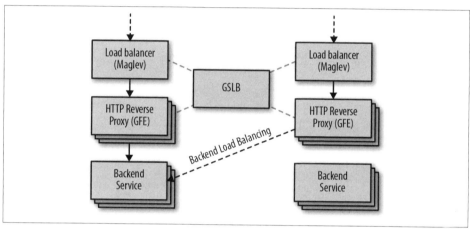

Figure 11-3. GSLB

Google Front End

As shown in Figure 11-4, the GFE sits between the outside world and various Google services (web search, image search, Gmail, etc.) and is frequently the first Google server a client HTTP(S) request encounters. The GFE terminates the client's TCP and SSL sessions and inspects the HTTP header and URL path to determine which backend service should handle the request. Once the GFE decides where to send the request, it reencrypts the data and forwards the request. For more information on how this encryption process works, see our whitepaper "Encryption in Transit in Google Cloud" (*http://bit.ly/2snyORO*).

The GFE is also responsible for health-checking its backends. If a backend server returns a *negative acknowledgment* ("NACKs" the request) or times out health checks, GFEs stop sending traffic to the failed backend. We use this signal to update

GFE backends without impacting uptime. By putting GFE backends into a mode in which they fail health checks while continuing to respond to in-flight requests, we can gracefully remove GFE backends from service without disrupting any user requests. We call this "lame duck" mode and we discuss it in more detail in Chapter 20 (*http://bit.ly/2J4faDU*) of the first SRE book.

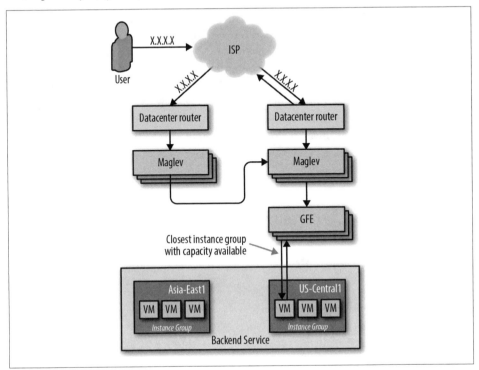

Figure 11-4. GFE

The GFEs also maintain persistent sessions to all their recently active backends so that a connection is ready to use as soon as a request arrives. This strategy helps reduce latency for our users, particularly in scenarios when we use SSL to secure the connection between GFE and the backend.

GCLB: Low Latency

Our network provisioning strategy aims to reduce end-user latency to our services. Because negotiating a secure connection via HTTPS requires two network round trips between client and server, it's particularly important that we minimize the latency of this leg of the request time. To this end, we extended the edge of our network to host Maglev and GFE. These components terminate SSL as close to the user as possible, then forward requests to backend services deeper within our network over long-lived encrypted connections.

We built GCLB atop this combined Maglev/GFE-augmented edge network. When customers create a load balancer, we provision an anycast VIP and program Maglev to load-balance it globally across GFEs at the edge of our network. GFE's role is to terminate SSL, accept and buffer HTTP requests, forward those requests to the customer's backend services, and then proxy the responses back to users. GSLB provides the glue between each layer: it enables Maglev to find the nearest GFE location with available capacity, and enables GFE to route requests to the nearest VM instance group with available capacity.

GCLB: High Availability

In the interest of providing high availability to our customers, GCLB offers an availability SLA[2] of 99.99%. In addition, GCLB provides support tools that enable our customers to improve and manage the availability of their own applications. It's useful to think of the load balancing system as a sort of traffic manager. During normal operation, GCLB routes traffic to the nearest backend with available capacity. When one instance of your service fails, GCLB detects the failure on your behalf and routes traffic to healthy instances.

Canarying and gradual rollouts help GCLB maintain high availability. Canarying is one of our standard release procedures. As described in Chapter 16 this process involves deploying a new application to a very small number of servers, then gradually increasing traffic and carefully observing system behavior to verify that there are no regressions. This practice reduces the impact of any regressions by catching them early in the canary phase. If the new version crashes or otherwise fails health checks, the load balancer routes around it. If you detect a nonfatal regression, you can administratively remove the instance group from the load balancer without touching the main version of the application.

Case Study 1: Pokémon GO on GCLB

Niantic launched Pokémon GO in the summer of 2016. It was the first new Pokémon game in years, the first official Pokémon smartphone game, and Niantic's first project in concert with a major entertainment company. The game was a runaway hit and more popular than anyone expected—that summer you'd regularly see players gathering to duel around landmarks that were Pokémon Gyms in the virtual world.

Pokémon GO's success greatly exceeded the expectations of the Niantic engineering team. Prior to launch, they load-tested their software stack to process up to 5x their most optimistic traffic estimates. The actual launch requests per second (RPS) rate

---

2 See the Google Cloud Platform blog post "SLOs, SLIs, SLAs, Oh My—CRE Life Lessons" (*http://bit.ly/2LL02ch*) for an explanation of the difference between SLOs and SLAs.

was nearly 50x that estimate—enough to present a scaling challenge for nearly any software stack. To further complicate the matter, the world of Pokémon GO is highly interactive and globally shared among its users. All players in a given area see the same view of the game world and interact with each other inside that world. This requires that the game produce and distribute near-real-time updates to a state shared by all participants.

Scaling the game to 50x more users required a truly impressive effort from the Niantic engineering team. In addition, many engineers across Google provided their assistance in scaling the service for a successful launch. Within two days of migrating to GCLB, the Pokemon GO app became the single largest GCLB service, easily on par with the other top 10 GCLB services.

As shown in Figure 11-5, when it launched, Pokémon GO used Google's regional Network Load Balancer (NLB) (*http://bit.ly/2J87EUx*) to load-balance ingress traffic across a Kubernetes (*http://bit.ly/2vgpMsX*) cluster. Each cluster contained pods of Nginx (*https://www.nginx.com/*) instances, which served as Layer 7 reverse proxies that terminated SSL, buffered HTTP requests, and performed routing and load balancing across pods of application server backends.

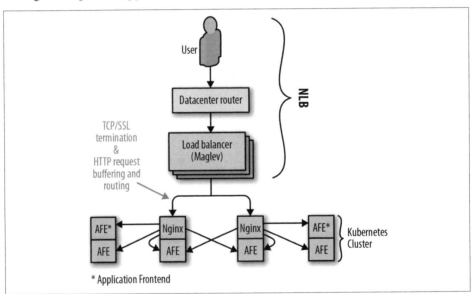

Figure 11-5. Pokémon GO (pre-GCLB)

NLB is responsible for load balancing at the IP layer, so a service that uses NLB effectively becomes a backend of Maglev. In this case, relying on NLB had the following implications for Niantic:

- The Nginx backends were responsible for terminating SSL for clients, which required two round trips from a client device to Niantic's frontend proxies.

- The need to buffer HTTP requests from clients led to resource exhaustion on the proxy tier, particularly when clients were only able to send bytes slowly.

- Low-level network attacks such as SYN flood (*http://bit.ly/2J7NKgw*) could not be effectively ameliorated by a packet-level proxy.

In order to scale appropriately, Niantic needed a high-level proxy operating on a large edge network. This solution wasn't possible with NLB.

Migrating to GCLB

A large SYN flood attack made migrating Pokémon GO to GCLB a priority. This migration was a joint effort between Niantic and the Google Customer Reliability Engineering (CRE) and SRE teams. The initial transition took place during a traffic trough and, at the time, was unremarkable. However, unforeseen problems emerged for both Niantic and Google as traffic ramped up to peak. Both Google and Niantic discovered that the true client demand for Pokémon GO traffic was 200% higher than previously observed. The Niantic frontend proxies received so many requests that they weren't able to keep pace with all inbound connections. Any connection refused in this way wasn't surfaced in the monitoring for inbound requests. The backends never had a chance.

This traffic surge caused a classic cascading failure scenario. Numerous backing services for the API—Cloud Datastore, Pokémon GO backends and API servers, and the load balancing system itself—exceeded the capacity available to Niantic's cloud project. The overload caused Niantic's backends to become extremely slow (rather than refuse requests), manifesting as requests timing out to the load balancing layer. Under this circumstance, the load balancer retried GET requests, adding to the system load. The combination of extremely high request volume and added retries stressed the SSL client code in the GFE at an unprecedented level, as it tried to reconnect to unresponsive backends. This induced a severe performance regression in GFE such that GCLB's worldwide capacity was effectively reduced by 50%.

As backends failed, the Pokémon GO app attempted to retry failed requests on behalf of users. At the time, the app's retry strategy was a single immediate retry, followed by constant backoff. As the outage continued, the service sometimes returned a large number of quick errors—for example, when a shared backend restarted. These error responses served to effectively synchronize client retries, producing a "thundering herd" problem, in which many client requests were issued at essentially the same time. As shown in Figure 11-6, these synchronized request spikes ramped up enormously to 20× the previous global RPS peak.

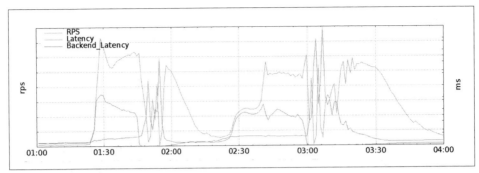

Figure 11-6. Traffic spikes caused by synchronous client retries

Resolving the issue

These request spikes, combined with the GFE capacity regression, resulted in queuing and high latency for all GCLB services. Google's on-call Traffic SREs acted to reduce collateral damage to other GCLB users by doing the following:

1. Isolating GFEs that could serve Pokémon GO traffic from the main pool of load balancers.

2. Enlarging the isolated Pokémon GO pool until it could handle peak traffic despite the performance regression. This action moved the capacity bottleneck from GFE to the Niantic stack, where servers were still timing out, particularly when client retries started to synchronize and spike.

3. With Niantic's blessing, Traffic SRE implemented administrative overrides to limit the rate of traffic the load balancers would accept on behalf of Pokémon GO. This strategy contained client demand enough to allow Niantic to reestablish normal operation and commence scaling upward.

Figure 11-7 shows the final network configuration.

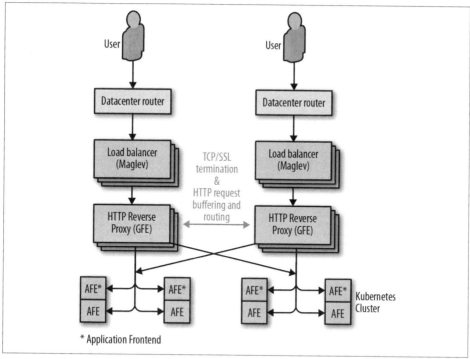

Figure 11-7. Pokémon GO GCLB

Future-proofing

In the wake of this incident, Google and Niantic both made significant changes to their systems. Niantic introduced jitter and truncated exponential backoff[3] to their clients, which curbed the massive synchronized retry spikes experienced during cascading failure. Google learned to consider GFE backends as a potentially significant source of load, and instituted qualification and load testing practices to detect GFE performance degradation caused by slow or otherwise misbehaving backends. Finally, both companies realized they should measure load as close to the client as possible. Had Niantic and Google CRE been able to accurately predict client RPS demand, we would have preemptively scaled up the resources allocated to Niantic even more than we did before conducting the switch to GCLB.

---

3 For more information on this topic, see Chapter 22 (*http://bit.ly/2Hbpl3z*) of the first SRE book.

Autoscaling

Tools like GCLB can help you balance load efficiently across your fleet, making your service more stable and reliable. Sometimes you simply don't have enough resources reserved to manage your existing traffic. You can use autoscaling (*http://bit.ly/2xBvgzu*) to scale your fleet strategically. Whether you increase the resources per machine (vertical scaling) or increase the total number of machines in the pool (horizontal scaling), autoscaling is a powerful tool and, when used correctly, can enhance your service availability and utilization. Conversely, if misconfigured or misused, autoscaling can negatively impact your service. This section describes some best practices, common failure modes, and current limitations of autoscaling.

Handling Unhealthy Machines

Autoscaling normally averages utilization over all instances regardless of their state, and assumes that instances are homogeneous in terms of request processing efficiency. Autoscaling runs into problems when machines are not serving (known as *unhealthy instances*) but are still counted toward the utilization average. In this scenario, autoscaling simply won't occur. A variety of issues can trigger this failure mode, including:

- Instances taking a long time to get ready to serve (e.g., when loading a binary or warming up)
- Instances stuck in a nonserving state (i.e., zombies)

We can improve this situation using a variety of tactics. You can make the following improvements in combination or individually:

Load balancing
> Autoscale using a capacity metric as observed by the load balancer. This will automatically discount unhealthy instances from the average.

Wait for new instances to stabilize before collecting metrics
> You can configure autoscaler to collect information about new instances only once new instances become healthy (GCE refers to this period of inactivity as a *cool-down period*).

Autoscale and autoheal
> Autohealing monitors your instances and attempts to restart them if they are unhealthy. Typically, you configure your autohealer to monitor a health metric exposed by your instances. If autohealer detects that an instance is down or unhealthy, it will attempt a restart. When configuring your autohealer, it's

important to ensure you leave sufficient time for your instances to become healthy after a restart.

Using a mix of these solutions, you can optimize horizontal autoscaling to keep track only of healthy machines. Remember that when running your service, autoscaler will continuously adjust the size of your fleet. Creating new instances is never instant.

Working with Stateful Systems

A stateful system sends all requests in a user session consistently to the same backend server. If these pathways are overburdened, adding more instances (i.e., horizontal scaling) won't help. Intelligent, task-level routing that spreads the load around (e.g., using consistent hashing[4]) is a better strategy for stateful systems.

Vertical autoscaling can be useful in stateful systems. When used in combination with task-level balancing to even out load on your system, vertical autoscaling can help absorb short-term hotspots. Use this strategy with caution: because vertical autoscaling is typically uniform across all instances, your low-traffic instances may grow unnecessarily large.

Configuring Conservatively

Using autoscaling to scale up is more important and less risky than using it to scale down since a failure to scale up can result in overload and dropped traffic. By design, most autoscaler implementations are intentionally more sensitive to jumps in traffic than to drops in traffic. When scaling up, autoscalers are inclined to add extra serving capacity quickly. When scaling down, they are more cautious and wait longer for their scaling condition to hold true before slowly reducing resources.

The load spikes you can absorb increase as your service moves further away from a bottleneck. We recommend configuring your autoscaler to keep your service far from key system bottlenecks (such as CPU). Autoscaler also needs adequate time to react, particularly when new instances cannot turn up and serve instantly. We recommend that user-facing services reserve enough spare capacity for both overload protection and redundancy.[5]

---

4 See *Site Reliability Engineering*, Chapter 19 (*http://bit.ly/2LQ6TRQ*).

5 For more info about redundancy in capacity planning, see *Site Reliability Engineering*, Appendix B (*http://bit.ly/2syqM76*).

Setting Constraints

Autoscaler is a powerful tool; if misconfigured, it can scale out of control. You might inadvertently trigger serious consequences by introducing a bug or changing a setting. For example, consider the following scenarios:

- You configured autoscaling to scale based on CPU utilization. You release a new version of your system, which contains a bug causing the server to consume CPU without doing any work. Autoscaler reacts by upsizing this job again and again until all available quota (*http://bit.ly/2sqo0RO*) is wasted.

- Nothing has changed in your service, but a dependency is failing. This failure causes all requests to get stuck on your servers and never finish, consuming resources all the while. Autoscaler will scale up the jobs, causing more and more traffic to get stuck. The increased load on your failing dependency can prevent the dependency from recovering.

It's useful to constrain the work that your autoscaler is allowed to perform. Set a minimum and maximum bound for scaling, making sure that you have enough quota to scale to the set limits. Doing so prevents you from depleting your quota and helps with capacity planning.

Including Kill Switches and Manual Overrides

It's a good idea to have a kill switch in case something goes wrong with your autoscaling. Make sure your on-call engineers understand how to disable autoscaling and how to manually scale if necessary. Your autoscaling kill switch functionality should be easy, obvious, fast, and well documented.

Avoiding Overloading Backends

A correctly configured autoscaler will scale up in response to an increase in traffic. An increase in traffic will have consequences down the stack. Backend services, such as databases, need to absorb any additional load your servers might create. Therefore, it's a good idea to perform a detailed dependency analysis on your backend services before deploying your autoscaler, particularly as some services may scale more linearly than others. Ensure your backends have enough extra capacity to serve increased traffic and are able to degrade gracefully when overloaded. Use the data from your analysis to inform the limits of your autoscaler configuration.

Service deployments commonly run a variety of microservices that share quota. If a microservice scales up in response to a traffic spike, it might use most of the quota. If increased traffic on a single microservice means increased traffic on other microservices, there will be no available quota for the remaining microservices to grow. In this scenario, a dependency analysis can help guide you toward preemptively implementing limited scaling. Alternatively, you can implement separate quotas per microservice (which may entail splitting your service into separate projects).

Avoiding Traffic Imbalance

Some autoscalers (e.g., AWS EC2, GCP) can balance instances across regional groups of instances (RMiGs (*http://bit.ly/2J7NNJe*)). In addition to regular autoscaling, these autoscalers run a separate job that constantly attempts to even out the size of each zone across the region. Rebalancing traffic in this way avoids having one large zone. If the system you're using allocates quota per zone, this strategy evens out your quota usage. In addition, autoscaling across regions provides more diversity for failure domains.

Combining Strategies to Manage Load

If your system becomes sufficiently complex, you may need to use more than one kind of load management. For example, you might run several managed instance groups that scale with load but are cloned across multiple regions for capacity; therefore, you also need to balance traffic between regions. In this case, your system needs to use both *load balancing* and *load-based autoscaling*.

Or maybe you run a website across three colocated facilities around the world. You'd like to serve locally for latency, but since it takes weeks to deploy more machines, overflow capacity needs to spill over to other locations. If your site gets popular on social media and suddenly experiences a five-fold increase in traffic, you'd prefer to serve what requests you can. Therefore, you implement load shedding to drop excess traffic. In this case, your system needs to use both *load balancing* and *load shedding*.

Or perhaps your data processing pipeline lives in a Kubernetes cluster in one cloud region. When data processing slows significantly, it provisions more pods to handle the work. However, when data comes in so fast that reading it causes you to run out of memory, or slows down garbage collection, your pods may need to shed that load temporarily or permanently. In this case, your system needs to use both *load-based autoscaling* and *load shedding* techniques.

Load balancing, load shedding, and autoscaling are all systems designed for the same goal: to equalize and stabilize the system load. Since the three systems are often implemented, installed, and configured separately, they seem independent. However, as shown in Figure 11-8, they're not entirely independent. The following case study illustrates how these systems can interact.

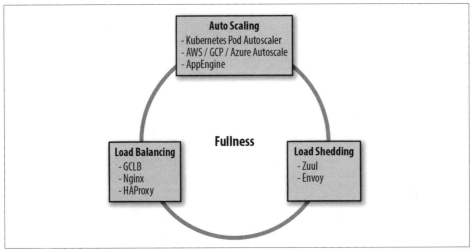

Figure 11-8. A full traffic management system

Case Study 2: When Load Shedding Attacks

Imagine a fictional company, Dressy, that sells dresses online via an app. As this is a traffic-driven service, the development team at Dressy deployed their app across three regions. This deployment allows their app to respond quickly to user requests and weather single-zone failures—or so they thought.

The customer service team at Dressy starts receiving complaints that customers can't access the app. Dressy's development teams investigate and notice a problem: their load balancing is inexplicably drawing all user traffic into region A, even though that region is full-to-overflowing and both B and C are empty (and equally large). The timeline of events (see Figure 11-9) is as follows:

1. At the beginning of the day, the traffic graphs showed all three clusters steady at 90 RPS.

2. At 10:46 a.m., traffic started to rise in all three regions as eager shoppers began hunting for bargains.

3. At 11:00 a.m., region A reached 120 RPS just before regions B and C.

4. At 11:10 a.m., region A continued to grow to 400 RPS, while B and C dipped to 40 RPS.

5. The load balancer settled at this state.

6. The majority of requests hitting region A were returning 503 errors.

7. Users whose requests hit this cluster started to complain.

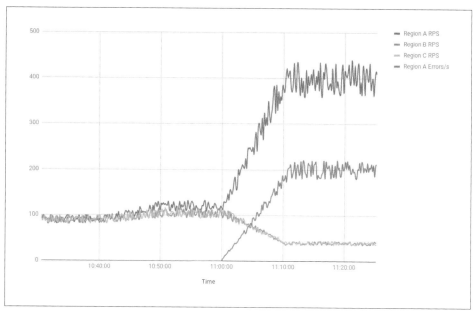

Figure 11-9. Regional traffic

If the development team had consulted their load balancer's fullness graphs, they would have seen something very strange. The load balancer was utilization-aware: it was reading CPU utilization from Dressy's containers and using this information to estimate fullness. As far as it could tell, per-request CPU utilization was 10 times lower in region A than either B or C. The load balancer determined that all regions were equally loaded, and its job was done.

What was happening?

Earlier in the week, to protect against cascading overload, the team enabled load shedding. Whenever CPU utilization reached a certain threshold, a server would return an error for any new requests it received rather than attempting to process them. On this particular day, region A reached this threshold slightly ahead of the other regions. Each server began rejecting 10% of requests it received, then 20% of requests, then 50%. During this time frame, CPU usage remained constant.

As far as the load balancer system was concerned, each successive dropped request was a reduction in the per-request CPU cost. Region A was far more efficient than regions B and C. It was serving 240 RPS at 80% CPU (the shedding cap), while B and C were managing only 120 RPS. Logically, it decided to send more requests to A.

What went wrong?

In brief, the load balancer didn't know that the "efficient" requests were errors because the load shedding and load balancing systems weren't communicating. Each system was added and enabled separately, likely by different engineers. No one had examined them as one unified load management system.

Lessons learned

To effectively manage system load, we need to be deliberate—both in the configuration of our individual load management tools and in the management of their interactions. For example, in the Dressy case study, adding error handling to the load balancer logic would have fixed the problem. Let's say each "error" request counts as 120% CPU utilization (any number over 100 will work). Now region A looks overloaded. Requests will spread to B and C, and the system will equalize.

You can use similar logic to extrapolate this example to any combination of load management tactics. When adopting a new load management tool, carefully examine how it interacts with other tools your system is already using and instrument their intersection. Add monitoring to detect feedback loops. Make sure your emergency shutdown triggers can be coordinated across your load management systems, and consider adding automatic shutdown triggers if these systems are behaving wildly out of control. If you don't take appropriate precautions up front, you'll likely have to do so in the wake of a postmortem.

It is easy to say "take precautions." More specifically, here are some precautions you might consider, depending on the kind of load management you deploy:

Load balancing
> Load balancing minimizes latency by routing to the location closest to the user. Autoscaling can work together with load balancing to increase the size of locations close to the user and then route more traffic there, creating a positive feedback loop.
>
> If demand is primarily closest to one location, that location will grow in size until all serving capacity is in one spot. If this location goes down, the remaining locations will become overloaded and traffic may be dropped. Scaling these locations up will not be instant. You can avoid this situation by setting a minimum number of instances per location to keep spare capacity for failover.

Load shedding
> It's a good idea to set your thresholds such that your system autoscales before load shedding kicks in. Otherwise, your system might start shedding traffic it could have served had it scaled up first.

Managing load with RPC

Handling the right requests is important for efficiency: you don't want to auto-scale up to serve requests that won't benefit users, or shed load unnecessarily because you're processing unimportant requests. When using both autoscaling and load shedding, it's important that you set deadlines on your RPC requests.

Processes hold resources for all in-flight requests, and release those resources when the requests are completed. In the absence of a specific deadline, the system will hold resources for all in-progress requests, up to the maximum possible limit. By default, this deadline is a very large number (which depends on the language implementation—some language APIs work in terms of a fixed point in time, and others with a duration of time). This behavior causes clients, and ultimately users, to experience higher latency. The service is also at risk of running out of resources (like memory) and crashing.

To handle this scenario gracefully, we recommend that the server terminates requests that take too long, and that clients cancel requests that are no longer useful to them. For example, a server shouldn't start an expensive search operation if the client already returned an error to the user. To set behavior expectations for a service, you could simply provide a comment in the API's *.proto* file to suggest a default deadline. Also, set deliberate deadlines for the client (for examples, see our blog post "gRPC and Deadlines" (*http://bit.ly/2xwpwXL*)).

Conclusion

In Google's experience, there are no perfect traffic management configurations. Autoscaling is a powerful tool, but it's easy to get wrong. Unless carefully configured, autoscaling can result in disastrous consequences—for example, potentially catastrophic feedback cycles between load balancing, load shedding, and autoscaling when these tools are configured in isolation. As the Pokémon GO case study illustrates, traffic management works best when it's based upon a holistic view of the interactions between systems.

Time and time again, we've seen that no amount of load shedding, autoscaling, or throttling will save our services when they all fail in sync. For example, in the Pokémon GO case study, we had a "thundering herd" of synchronized client retries combined with load balancers that waited for unresponsive backend servers. To fail your services gracefully, you need to plan ahead to mitigate potential problems. Your mitigation strategy might involve setting flags, changing default behaviors, enabling expensive logging, or exposing the current value of parameters the traffic management system uses for decisions.

We hope the strategies and insights provided in this chapter can help you manage traffic for your own services and keep your users happy.

## CHAPTER 12

Introducing Non-Abstract Large System Design

By Salim Virji, James Youngman, Henry Robertson,
Stephen Thorne, Dave Rensin, and Zoltan Egyed
with Richard Bondi

With responsibilities that span production operations and product engineering, SRE is in a unique position to align business case requirements and operational costs. Product engineering teams may not be aware of the maintenance cost of systems they design, especially if that product team is building a single component that factors into a greater production ecosystem.

Based on Google's experience developing systems, we consider reliability to be the most critical feature of any production system. We find that deferring reliability issues during design is akin to accepting fewer features at higher costs. By following an iterative style of system design and implementation, we arrive at robust and scalable designs with low operational costs. We call this style *Non-Abstract Large System Design (NALSD)*.

What Is NALSD?

This chapter presents a NALSD approach: we begin with the problem statement, gather requirements, and iterate through designs that become increasingly sophisticated until we reach a viable solution. Ultimately, we arrive at a system that defends against many failure modes and satisfies both the initial requirements and additional details that emerged as we iterated.

NALSD describes a skill critical to SRE: the ability to assess, design, and evaluate large systems. Practically, NALSD combines elements of capacity planning, component isolation, and graceful system degradation that are crucial to highly available production systems. Google SREs are expected to be able to start resource planning with a basic whiteboard diagram of a system, think through the various scaling and failure domains, and focus their design into a concrete proposal for resources. Because these systems change over time, it's vitally important that an SRE is able to analyze and evaluate the key aspects of the system design.

Why "Non-Abstract"?

All systems will eventually have to run on real computers in real datacenters using real networks. Google has learned (the hard way) that the people designing distributed systems need to develop and continuously exercise the muscle of turning a whiteboard design into concrete estimates of resources at multiple steps in the process. Without this rigor, it's too tempting to create systems that don't quite translate in the real world.

This extra bit of work up front typically leads to fewer last-minute system design changes to account for some unforeseen physical constraint.

Please note that while we drive these exercises to discrete results (e.g., number of machines), examples of sound reasoning and assumption making are more important than any final values. Early assumptions heavily influence calculation results, and making perfect assumptions isn't a requirement for NALSD. The value of this exercise is in combining many imperfect-but-*reasonable* results into a better understanding of the design.

AdWords Example

The Google AdWords service displays text advertisements on Google Web Search. The *click-through rate* (CTR) metric tells advertisers how well their ads are performing. CTR is the ratio of times the ad is clicked versus the number of times the ad is shown.

This AdWords example aims to design a system capable of measuring and reporting an accurate CTR for every AdWords ad. The data we need to calculate CTR is recorded in logs of the search and ad serving systems. These logs record the ads that are shown for each search query and the ads that are clicked, respectively.

Design Process

Google uses an iterative approach to design systems that meet our goals. Each iteration defines a potential design and examines its strengths and weaknesses. This analysis either feeds into the next iteration or indicates when the design is good enough to recommend.

In broad strokes, the NALSD process has two phases, each with two to three questions.

In the basic design phase, we try to invent a design that *works in principle*. We ask two questions:

Is it possible?
> Is the design even possible? If we didn't have to worry about enough RAM, CPU, network bandwidth, and so on, what would we design to satisfy the requirements?

Can we do better?
> For any such design, we ask, "Can we do better?" For example, can we make the system meaningfully faster, smaller, more efficient? If the design solves the problem in $O(N)$ time (*http://bit.ly/2LPpixO*), can we solve it more quickly—say, $O(\ln(N))$?

In the next phase, we *try to scale up* our basic design—for example, by dramatically increasing a requirement. We ask three questions:

Is it feasible?
> Is it possible to scale this design, given constraints on money, hardware, and so on? If necessary, what distributed design would satisfy the requirements?

Is it resilient?
> Can the design fail gracefully? What happens when this component fails? How does the system work when an entire datacenter fails?

Can we do better?

While we generally cover these phases and questions in this approximate order, in practice, we bounce around between the questions and phases. For example, during the basic design phase, we often have growth and scaling in the back of our minds.

Then we iterate. One design may successfully pass most of the phases, only to flounder later. When that happens, we start again, modifying or replacing components. The final design is the end of a story of twists and turns.

With these concepts in mind, let's walk through the iterative NALSD process.

Initial Requirements

Each advertiser may have multiple advertisements. Each ad is keyed by `ad_id` and is associated with a list of search terms selected by the advertiser.

When displaying a dashboard to an advertiser, we need to know the following for each ad and search term:

- How often this search term triggered this ad to be shown
- How many times the ad was clicked by someone who saw the ad

With this information, we can calculate the CTR: the number of clicks divided by the number of impressions.

We know our advertisers care about two things: that the dashboard displays quickly, and that the data is recent. Therefore, when iterating on the design, we will consider our requirements in terms of SLOs (see Chapter 2 for more details):

- 99.9% of dashboard queries complete in < 1 second.
- 99.9% of the time, the CTR data displayed is less than 5 minutes old.

These SLOs provide a reasonable goal that we should be able to consistently meet. They also provide an error budget (see Chapter 4 (*http://bit.ly/2szBKsK*) in *Site Reliability Engineering*), which we will compare our solution against in each iteration of the design.

We aim to create a system that can meet our SLOs and also support millions of advertisers who want to see their CTRs on a dashboard. For transaction rates, let's assume 500,000 search queries per second and 10,000 ad clicks per second.

One Machine

The simplest starting point is to consider running our entire application on a single computer.

For every web search query, we log:

time
: The time the query occurred

query_id
: A unique query identifier (query ID)

search_term
: The query content

ad_id
: The ad IDs of all the AdWords advertisements shown for the search

Together, this information forms the *query log*. Every time a user clicks an ad, we log the time of the click, the query ID, and the ad ID in the *click log*.

You may be wondering why we don't simply add the search_term to the click log to reduce complexity. In the arbitrarily reduced scope of our example, this could be feasible. However, in practice, CTR is actually only one of many insights calculated from these logs. Click logs are derived from URLs, which have inherent size limitations, making the separate query log a more scalable solution. Instead of proving this point by adding extra CTR-like requirements to the exercise, we will simply acknowledge this assumption and move forward.

Displaying a dashboard requires the data from both logs. We need to be able to show that we can achieve our SLO of displaying fresh data on the dashboard in under a second. Achieving this SLO requires that the speed of calculating a CTR remains constant as the system handles large amounts of clicks and queries.

To meet our SLO of displaying our dashboard in under one second, we need quick lookups of the number of clicked and shown query_ids per search_term for a given ad_id. We can extract the breakdown of *shown* query_ids per search_term and ad_id from the query log. A CTR dashboard needs all records from both the query log and the click log for the ad_ids.

If we have more than a few advertisers, scanning through the query log and the click log to generate the dashboard will be very inefficient. Therefore, our design calls for our one machine to create an appropriate data structure to allow fast CTR calculations as it receives the logs. On a single machine, using an SQL database with indexes on query_id and search_term should be able to provide answers in under a second. By joining these logs on query_id and grouping by search_term, we can report the CTR for each search.

Calculations

We need to calculate how many resources we need to parse all these logs. To determine our scaling limits, we need to make some assumptions, starting with the size of the query log:

time
: 64-bit integer, 8 bytes

query_id
: 64-bit integer, 8 bytes

ad_id
: Three 64-bit integers, 8 bytes

search_term
: A long string, up to 500 bytes

Other metadata
: 500–1,000 bytes of information, such as which machine served the ads, which language the search was in, and how many results the search term returned

To make sure we don't prematurely hit a limit, we aggressively round up to treat each query log entry as 2 KB. Click log volume should be considerably smaller than query log volume: because the average CTR is 2% (10,000 clicks / 500,000 queries), the click log will have 2% as many records as the query log. Remember that we chose big numbers to illustrate that these principles scale to arbitrarily large implementations. These estimations seem large because they're supposed to be.

Finally, we can use scientific notation to limit errors caused by arithmetic on inconsistent units. The volume of query logs generated in a 24-hour period will be:

$$(5 \times 10^5 \text{ queries/sec}) \times (8.64 \times 10^4 \text{ seconds/day}) \times (2 \times 10^3 \text{ bytes}) = 86.4 \text{ TB/day}$$

Because we receive 2% as many clicks as queries, and we know that our database indexes will add some reasonable amount of overhead, we can round our 86.4 TB/day up to 100 TB of space required to store one day's worth of log data.

With an aggregate storage requirement of ~100 TB, we have some new assumptions to make. Does this design still work with a single machine? While it is possible to attach 100 TB of disks to a single machine, we'll likely be limited by the machine's ability to read from and write to disk.

For example, a common 4 TB HDD might be able to sustain 200 input/output operations per second (IOPS). If every log entry can be stored and indexed in an average of one disk write per log entry, we see that IOPS is a limiting factor for our query logs:

$$(5 \times 10^5 \text{ queries/sec}) / (200 \text{ IOPS/disk}) = 2.5 \times 10^3 \text{ disks or 2,500 disks}$$

Even if we can batch our queries in a 10:1 ratio to limit the operations, in a best-case scenario we'd need several hundred HDDs. Considering that query log writes are only one component of the design's IO requirements, we need to use a solution that handles high IOPS better than traditional HDDs.

For simplicity's sake, we'll move straight to evaluating RAM and skip the evaluation of other storage media, such as solid state disk (SSD). A single machine can't handle a 100 TB footprint entirely in RAM: assuming we have a standard machine footprint of 16 cores, 64 GB RAM, and 1 Gbps network throughput available, we'll need:

$$(100 \text{ TB}) / (64 \text{ GB RAM/machine}) = 1,563 \text{ machines}$$

Evaluation

Ignoring our calculations for a moment and imagining we could fit this design in a single machine, would we actually want to? If we test our design by asking *what happens when this component fails*, we identify a long list of single points of failure (e.g.,

CPU, memory, storage, power, network, cooling). Can we reasonably support our SLOs if one of these components fails? Almost certainly not—even a simple power cycle would significantly impact our users.

Returning to our calculations, our one-machine design once again looks unfeasible, but this step hasn't been a waste of time. We've discovered valuable information about how to *reason* about the constraints of the system and its initial requirements. We need to evolve our design to use more than one machine.

Distributed System

The search_terms we need are in the query log, and the ad_ids are in the click log. Now that we know we'll need multiple machines, what's the best design to join them?

MapReduce

We can process and join the logs with a MapReduce (*http://bit.ly/2kELxue*). We can periodically grab the accumulated query logs and click logs, and the MapReduce will produce a data set organized by ad_id that displays the number of clicks each search_term received.

MapReduce works as a batch processor: its inputs are a large data set, and it can use many machines to process that data via workers and produce a result. Once all machines have processed their data, their output can be combined—the MapReduce can directly create summaries of every CTR for every AdWords ad and search term. We can use this data to create the dashboards we need.

Evaluation. MapReduce is a widely used model of computation that we are confident will scale horizontally. No matter how big our query log and click log inputs are, adding more machines will always allow the process to complete successfully without running out of disk space or RAM.

Unfortunately, this type of batch process can't meet our SLO of joined log availability within 5 minutes of logs being received. To serve results within 5 minutes, we'd need to run MapReduce jobs in small batches—just a few minutes of logs at a time.

The arbitrary and nonoverlapping nature of the batches makes small batches impractical. If a logged query is in batch 1, and its click is in batch 2, the click and query will never be joined. While MapReduce handles self-contained batches well, it's not optimized for this kind of problem. At this point, we could try to figure out potential workarounds using MapReduce. For simplicity's sake, however, we'll move on to examine another solution.

LogJoiner

The number of ads that users click is significantly smaller than the number of ads served. Intuitively, we need to focus on scaling the larger of the two: query logs. We do this by introducing a new distributed system component.

Rather than looking for the `query_id` in small batches, as in our MapReduce design, what if we created a store of all queries that we can look up by `query_id` on demand? We'll call it the *QueryStore*. It holds the full content of the query logs, keyed by `query_id`. To avoid repetition, we'll assume that our calculations from the one-machine design will apply to the QueryStore and we'll limit the review of QueryStore to what we've already covered. For a deeper discussion on how a component like this might work, we recommend reading about Bigtable.[1]

Because click logs also have the `query_id`, the scale of our processing loop is now much smaller: it only needs to loop over the click logs and pull in the specific queries referenced. We'll call this component the *LogJoiner*.

LogJoiner takes a continuous stream of data from the click logs, joins it with the data in QueryStore, and then stores that information, organized by `ad_id`. Once the queries that were clicked on are stored and indexed by `ad_id`, we have half the data required to generate the CTR dashboard. We will call this the *ClickMap*, because it maps from `ad_id` to the clicks.

If we don't find a query for a click (there may be a slowdown in receiving the query logs), we put it aside for some time and retry, up to a time limit. If we can't find a query for it by that time limit, we discard that click.

The CTR dashboard needs two components for each `ad_id` and `search_term` pair: the number of impressions, and the number of ads clicked on. ClickMap needs a partner to hold the queries, organized by `ad_id`. We'll call this *QueryMap*. QueryMap is directly fed all the data from the query log, and also indexes entries by `ad_id`.

Figure 12-1 depicts how data flows through the system.

The LogJoiner design introduces several new components: LogJoiner, QueryStore, ClickMap, and QueryMap. We need to make sure these components can scale.

---

1 Fay Chang et al., "Bigtable: A Distributed Storage System for Structured Data," *ACM Transactions on Computer Systems (TOCS)* 26, no. 2 (2008), *http://bit.ly/2J22BZv*.

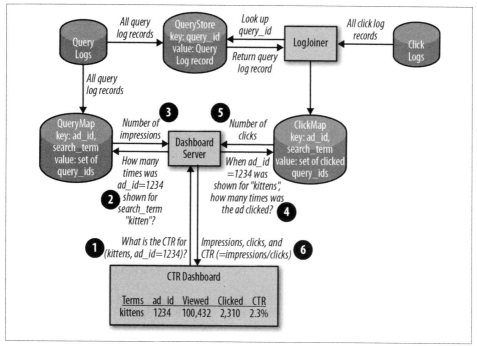

Figure 12-1. Basic LogJoiner design; the click data is processed and stored so the dashboard can retrieve it

Calculations. From the calculations we performed in previous iterations, we know the QueryStore will be around 100 TB of data for a day of logs. We can delete data that's too old to be of value.

The LogJoiner should process clicks as they come in and retrieve the corresponding query logs from the QueryStore.

The amount of network throughput LogJoiner needs to process the logs is based on how many clicks per second we have in our logs, multiplied by the 2 KB record size:

$$(10^4 \text{ clicks/sec}) \times (2 \times 10^3 \text{ bytes}) = 2 \times 10^7 = 20 \text{ MB/sec} = 160 \text{ Mbps}$$

The QueryStore lookups incur additional network usage. For each click log record, we look up the `query_id` and return a full log record:

- $(10^4 \text{ clicks/sec}) \times (8 \text{ bytes}) = 8 \times 10^4 = 80 \text{ KB/sec} = 640 \text{ Kbps}$
- $(10^4 \text{ clicks/sec}) \, ^\star \, (2 \times 10^3 \text{ bytes}) = 2 \times 10^7 = 20 \text{ MB/sec} = 160 \text{ Mbps}$

LogJoiner will also send results to ClickMap. We need to store the `query_id`, `ad_id`, and `time`. `search_term`. `time` and `query_id` are both 64-bit integers, so that data will be less than 1 KB:

$$(10^4 \text{ clicks/sec}) \times (10^3 \text{ bytes}) = 10^7 = 10 \text{ MB/sec} = 80 \text{ Mbps}$$

An aggregate of ~400 Mbps is a manageable rate of data transfer for our machines.

The ClickMap has to store the `time` and the `query_id` for each click, but does not need any additional metadata. We'll ignore `ad_id` and `search_term` because they are a small linear factor (e.g., number of advertisers × number of ads × 8 bytes). Even 10 million advertisers with 10 ads each is only ~800 MB. A day's worth of ClickMap is:

$$(10^4 \text{ clicks/sec}) \times (8.64 \times 10^4 \text{ seconds/day}) \times (8 \text{ bytes} + 8 \text{ bytes}) = 1.4 \times 10^{10} =$$
14 GB/day for ClickMap

We'll round ClickMap up to 20 GB/day to account for any overhead and our `ad_ids`.

As we fill out the QueryMap, we need to store the `query_id` for each ad that is shown. Our storage need increases because there are potentially three `ad_ids` that could be clicked on for each search query, so we'll need to record the `query_id` in up to three entries:

$$3 \times (5 \times 10^5 \text{ queries/sec}) \times (8.64 \times 10^4 \text{ seconds/day}) \times (8 \text{ bytes} + 8 \text{ bytes}) =$$
$2 \times 10^{12} = 2 \text{ TB/day for QueryMap}$

2 TB is small enough to be hosted on a single machine using HDDs, but we know from our one-machine iteration that the individual small writes are too frequent to store on a hard drive. While we could calculate the impact of using higher IOPS drives (e.g., SSD), our exercise is focused on demonstrating that the system can scale to an arbitrarily large size. In this case, we need to design around a single machine's IO limitations. Therefore, the next step in scaling the design is to *shard* the inputs and outputs: to divide the incoming query logs and click logs into multiple streams.

Sharded LogJoiner

Our goal in this iteration is to run multiple LogJoiner instances, each on a different shard of the data.[2] To this end, we need to think about several factors:

---

2 This section is based on Rajagopal Ananthanarayanan et al., "Photon: Fault-tolerant and Scalable Joining of Continuous Data Streams," in SIGMOD '13: *Proceedings of the 2013 ACM SIGMOD International Conference on Management of Data* (New York: ACM, 2013), *http://bit.ly/2Jse3Ns*.

Data management

> To join the query logs and click logs, we must match each click log record with its corresponding query log record on the query_id. The design should prevent network and disk throughput from constraining our design as we scale.

Reliability

> We know a machine can fail at any time. When a machine running LogJoiner fails, how do we make sure we don't lose the work that was in progress?

Efficiency

> Can we scale up without being wasteful? We need to use the minimum resources that meet our data management and reliability concerns.

Our LogJoiner design showed that we can join our query logs and click logs, but the resulting volume of data is very large. If we divide the work into shards based on query_id, we can run multiple LogJoiners in parallel.

Provided a reasonable number of LogJoiner instances, if we distribute the logs evenly, each instance receives only a trickle of information over the network. As the flow of clicks increases, we scale horizontally by adding more LogJoiner instances, instead of scaling vertically by using more CPU and RAM.

As shown in Figure 12-2, so that the LogJoiners receive the right messages, we introduce a component called a *log sharder*, which will direct each log entry to the correct destination. For every record, our click log sharders do the following:

1. Hash the record's query_id.

2. Modulo the result with N (the number of shards) and add 1 to arrive at a number between 1 and N.

3. Send the record to the shard number in step 2.

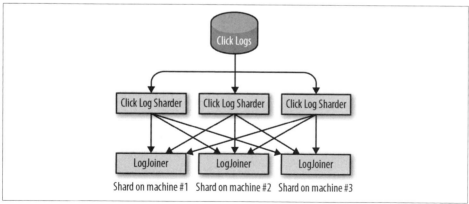

Figure 12-2. How should sharding work?

Now each LogJoiner will get a consistent subset of the incoming logs broken up by query_id, instead of the full click log.

The QueryMap needs to be sharded as well. We know that it will take many hard drives to sustain the IOPS required of QueryMap, and that the size of one day's QueryMap (2 TB) is too large for our 64 GB machines to store in RAM. However, instead of sharding by query_id like the LogJoiner, we will shard on ad_id. The ad_id is known before any read or write, so using the same hashing approach as the LogJoiner and CTR dashboard will provide a consistent view of the data.

To keep implementations consistent, we can reuse the same log sharder design for the ClickMap as the QueryMap, since the ClickMap is smaller than the QueryMap.

Now that we know our system will scale, we can move on to address the system's reliability. Our design must be resilient to LogJoiner failures. If a LogJoiner fails after receiving log messages but before joining them, all its work must be redone. This delays the arrival of accurate data to the dashboard, which will affect our SLO.

If our log sharder process sends duplicate log entries to two shards, the system can continue to perform at full speed and process accurate results even when a LogJoiner fails (likely because the machine it is on fails).

By replicating the work in this way, we reduce (but do not eliminate) the chance of losing those joined logs. Two shards might break at the same time and lose the joined logs. By distributing the workload to ensure no duplicate shards land on the same machine, we can mitigate much of that risk. If two machines fail concurrently and we lose both copies of the shard, the system's error budget (see Chapter 4 (*http://bit.ly/ 2szBKsK*) from the first SRE book) can cover the remaining risk. When a disaster *does* occur, we can reprocess the logs. The dashboard will show only data that's a bit older than 5 minutes for a brief window of time.

Figure 12-3 shows our design for a shard and its replica, where the LogJoiner, ClickMap, and QueryMap are built on both shards.

From the joined logs, we can construct a ClickMap on each of the LogJoiner machines. To display our user dashboards, all ClickMaps need to be combined and queried.

Evaluation. Hosting the sharded components in one datacenter creates a single point of failure: if either the right unlucky pair of machines or the datacenter is disconnected, we lose all the ClickMap work, and user dashboards stop working entirely! We need to evolve our design to use more than one datacenter.

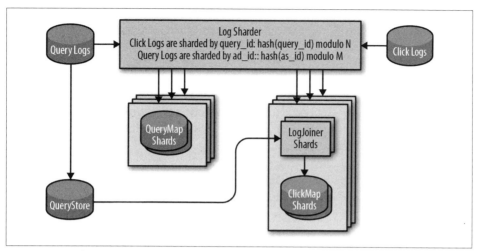

Figure 12-3. Sharding of logs with same query_id to duplicate shards

Multidatacenter

Duplicating data across datacenters in different geographic locations allows our serving infrastructure to withstand catastrophic failures. If one datacenter is down (e.g., because of a multiday power or network outage), we can fail over to another datacenter. For failover to work, ClickMap data must be available in all datacenters where the system is deployed.

Is such a ClickMap even possible? We don't want to multiply our compute requirements by the number of datacenters, but how can we efficiently synchronize work between sites to ensure sufficient replication without creating unnecessary duplication?

We've just described an example of the well-known consensus (*http://bit.ly/2J2erD7*) problem in distributed systems engineering. There are a number of complex algorithms for solving this problem, but the basic idea is:

1. Make three or five replicas of the service you want to share (like ClickMap).

2. Have the replicas use a consensus algorithm such as Paxos (*http://bit.ly/1X2NFew*) to ensure that we can reliably store the state of the calculations if a datacenter-sized failure occurs.

3. Implement at least one network round-trip time between the participating nodes to accept a write operation. This requirement places a limit on the sequential throughput for the system. We can still parallelize some of the writes to the distributed consensus-based map.

Following the steps just listed, the multidatacenter design now seems workable in principle. Will it also work in practice? What types of resources do we need, and how many of them do we need?

Calculations. The latency of executing the Paxos algorithm with fault-isolated datacenters means that each operation needs roughly 25 milliseconds to complete. This latency assumption is based upon datacenters at least a few hundred kilometers apart. Therefore, in terms of sequential processes, we can only perform one operation per 25 milliseconds or 40 operations per second. If we need to perform sequential processes 10^4 times per second (click logs), we need at least 250 processes per datacenter, sharded by ad_id, for the Paxos operations. In practice, we'd want to add more processes to increase parallelism—to handle accumulated backlog after any downtime or traffic spikes.

Building on our previous calculations for ClickMap and QueryMap, and using the estimate of 40 sequential operations per second, how many new machines do we need for our multidatacenter design?

Because our sharded LogJoiner design introduces a replica for each log record, we've doubled the number of transactions per second to create the ClickMap and Query-Map: 20,000 clicks/second and 1,000,000 queries/second.

We can calculate the minimum number of processes, or *tasks*, required by dividing the total queries per second by our maximum operations per second:

$(1.02 \times 10^6$ queries/sec$) / (40$ operations/sec$) = 25,500$ tasks

The amount of memory for each task (two copies of 2 TB QueryMap):

$(4 \times 10^{12}$ bytes$) / (25,500$ tasks$) = 157$ MB/task

Tasks per machine:

$(6.4 \times 10^{10}$ bytes$) / (1.57 \times 10^8$ bytes$) = 408$ tasks/machine

We know we can fit many tasks on a single machine, but we need to ensure that we won't be bottlenecked by IO. The total network throughput for ClickMap and Query-Map (using a high estimate of 2 KB per entry):

$(1.02 \times 10^6$ queries/sec$) \times (2 \times 10^3$ bytes$) = 2.04$ GB/sec $= 16$ Gbps

Throughput per task:

16 Gbps / 25,500 tasks = 80 KB/sec = 640 Kbps/task

Throughput per machine:

408 tasks × 640 Kbps/task = 256 Mbps

Our combination of 157 MB memory and 640 Kbps per task is manageable. We need approximately 4 TB of RAM in each datacenter to host the sharded ClickMap and QueryMap. If we have 64 GB of RAM per machine, we can serve the data from just 64 machines, and will use only 25% of each machine's network bandwidth.

Evaluation. Now that we've designed a multidatacenter system, let's review if the dataflow makes sense.

Figure 12-4 shows the entire system design. You can see how each search query and ad click is communicated to the servers, and how the logs are collected and pushed into each component.

We can check this system against our requirements:

10,000 ad clicks per second
    The LogJoiner can scale horizontally to process all log clicks, and store the result in the ClickMap.

500,000 search queries per second
    The QueryStore and QueryMap have been designed to handle storing a full day of data at this rate.

99.9% of dashboard queries complete in < 1 second
    The CTR dashboard fetches data from QueryMap and ClickMap, which are keyed by ad_id, making this transaction fast and simple.

99.9% of the time, the CTR data displayed is less than 5 minutes old
    Each component is designed to scale horizontally, meaning that if the pipeline is too slow, adding more machines will decrease the end-to-end pipeline latency.

We believe this system architecture scales to meet our requirements for throughput, performance, and reliability.

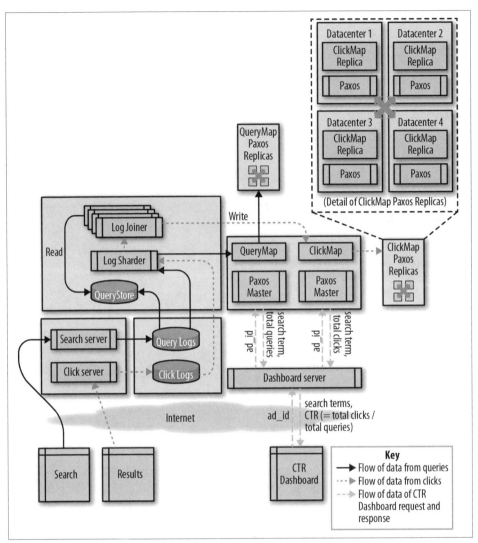

Figure 12-4. Multidatacenter design

Conclusion

NALSD describes the iterative process of system design that Google uses for production systems. By breaking down software into logical components and placing these components into a production ecosystem with reliable infrastructure, we arrive at systems that provide reasonable and appropriate targets for data consistency, system availability, and resource efficiency. The practice of NALSD allows us to improve our design without starting anew for each iteration. While various design iterations presented in this chapter satisfied our original problem statement, each iteration revealed new requirements, which we could meet by extending our previous work.

Throughout this process, we separated software components based on how we expected the system to grow. This strategy allowed us to scale different parts of the system independently and removed dependencies on single pieces of hardware or single instances of software, thereby producing a more reliable system.

Throughout the design process, we continued to improve upon each iteration by asking the four key NALSD questions:

Is it possible?
    Can we build it without "magic"?

Can we do better?
    Is it as simple as we can reasonably make it?

Is it feasible?
    Does it fit within our practical constraints (budget, time, etc.)?

Is it resilient?
    Will it survive occasional but inevitable disruptions?

NALSD is a learned skill. As with any skill, you need to practice it regularly to maintain your proficiency. Google's experience has shown that the ability to reason from an abstract requirement to a concrete approximation of resources is critical to building healthy and long-lived systems.

## CHAPTER 13

Data Processing Pipelines

By Rita Sodt and Igor Maravić (Spotify)
with Gary Luo, Gary O'Connor, and Kate Ward

Data processing is a complex field that's constantly evolving to meet the demands of larger data sets, intensive data transformations, and a desire for fast, reliable, and inexpensive results. The current landscape features data sets that are generated and collected from a variety of sources—from mobile usage statistics to integrated sensor networks to web application logs, and more. Data processing pipelines can turn these often unbounded, unordered, global-scale data sets into structured, indexed storage that can help inform crucial business decisions or unlock new product features. In addition to providing insight into system and user behavior, data processing is often business-critical. Delayed or incorrect data in your pipeline can manifest in user-facing issues that are expensive, labor-intensive, and time-consuming to fix.

This chapter starts by using product examples to examine some common types of applications of big data processing pipelines. We then explore how to identify pipeline requirements and design patterns, and enumerate some best practices of managing data processing pipelines throughout the development lifecycle. We cover tradeoffs you can make to optimize your pipeline and techniques for measuring the important signals of pipeline health. For a service to remain healthy and reliable once it's deployed, SREs (as well as developers) should be able to navigate all of these tasks. Ideally, SREs should be involved in this work from its early stages: Google's SRE teams regularly consult with teams developing a data processing pipeline to ensure that the pipeline can be easily released, modified, and run without causing issues for customers.

Finally, the Spotify case study provides an overview of their event delivery processing pipeline, which uses a combination of in-house, Google Cloud, and other third-party solutions to manage a complex, business-critical data processing pipeline. Whether you own a pipeline directly, or own another service that depends on the data that a pipeline produces, we hope you can use the information in this chapter to help make your pipelines (and services) more reliable.

For a comprehensive discussion of Google's philosophies on data processing pipelines, see Chapter 25 (*http://bit.ly/2JiPeDI*) of our first SRE book.

Pipeline Applications

There is a wide variety of pipeline applications, each with its own strengths and use cases. A pipeline can involve multiple stages; each stage is a separate process with dependencies on other stages. One pipeline might contain multiple stages, which are abstracted away with a high-level specification. An example of this is in Cloud Dataflow: a user writes the business logic with a relatively high-level API, and the pipeline technology (*http://bit.ly/2LRmU9P*) itself translates this data into a series of steps or stages where one's output is the input of another. To give you an idea of the breadth of pipeline applications, next we describe several pipeline applications and their recommended uses. We use two example companies with different pipeline and implementation requirements to demonstrate different ways of meeting their respective data needs. These examples illustrate how your specific use case defines your project goals, and how you can use these goals to make an informed decision on what data pipeline works best for you.

Event Processing/Data Transformation to Order or Structure Data

The Extract Transform Load (ETL) model is a common paradigm in data processing: data is extracted from a source, transformed, and possibly denormalized, and then "reloaded" into a specialized format. In more modern applications, this might look like a cognitive process: data acquisition from some kind of sensor (live or playback) and a selection and marshalling phase, followed by "training" of a specialized data structure (like a machine learning network).

ETL pipelines work in a similar way. Data is extracted from a single (or multiple) sources, transformed, and then loaded (or written) into another data source. The transformation phase can serve a variety of use cases, such as:

- Making changes to the data format to add or remove a field
- Aggregating computing functions across data sources
- Applying an index to the data so it has better characteristics for serving jobs that consume the data

Typically, an ETL pipeline prepares your data for further analysis or serving. When used correctly, ETL pipelines can perform complex data manipulations and ultimately increase the efficiency of your system. Some examples of ETL pipelines include:

- Preprocessing steps for machine learning or business intelligence use cases
- Computations, such as counting how many times a given event type occurs within a specific time interval
- Calculating and preparing billing reports
- Indexing pipelines like the ones that power Google's web search

Data Analytics

Business intelligence refers to technologies, tools, and practices for collecting, integrating, analyzing, and presenting large volumes of information to enable better decision making.[1] Whether you have a retail product, a mobile game, or Internet of Things–connected sensors (*http://bit.ly/2HboyQc*), aggregating data across multiple users or devices can help you identify where things are broken or working well.

To illustrate the data analytics use case, let's examine a fictional company and their recently launched mobile and web game, *Shave the Yak*. The owners want to know how their users interact with the game, both on their mobile devices and on the web. As a first step, they produce a data analytics report of the game that processes data about player events. The company's business leaders have requested monthly reports on the most used features of the game so they can plan new feature development and perform market analysis. The mobile and web analytics for the game are stored in Google Cloud BigQuery (*https://cloud.google.com/bigquery/*) tables that are updated three times a day by Google Analytics (*http://bit.ly/2JmC8oT*). The team set up a job that runs whenever new data is added to these tables. On completion, the job makes an entry in the company's daily aggregate table.

Machine Learning

Machine learning (ML) applications are used for a variety of purposes, like helping predict cancer, classifying spam, and personalizing product recommendations for users. Typically, an ML system has the following stages:

1 See Umeshwar Dayal et al., "Data Integration Flows for Business Intelligence," in *Proceedings of the 12th International Conference on Extending Database Technology: Advances in Database Technology* (New York: ACM, 2000), 1–11.

1. Data features and their labels (*http://bit.ly/2J8ZbQX*) are extracted from a larger data set.

2. An ML algorithm trains a model on the extracted features.

3. The model is evaluated on a test set of data.

4. The model is made available (served) to other services.

5. Other systems make decisions using the responses served by the model.

To demonstrate an ML pipeline in action, let's consider an example of a fictional company, Dressy, that sells dresses online. The company wants to increase their revenue by offering targeted recommendations to their users. When a new product is uploaded to the site, Dressy wants their system to start incorporating that product into user recommendations within 12 hours. Ultimately, Dressy would like to present users with near-real-time recommendations as they interact with the site and rate dresses. As a first step in their recommender system, Dressy investigates the following approaches:

Collaborative
    Show products that are similar to each other.

Clustering
    Show products that have been liked by a similar user.

Content-based
    Show products that are similar to other products that the user has viewed or liked.

As an online shop, Dressy has a data set of user profile information and reviews, so they opt to use a clustering filter. New products that are uploaded to their system don't have structured data or consistent labels (e.g., some vendors may include extra information about color, size, and features of the dress using different categories and formats). Consequently, they need to implement a pipeline to preprocess the data into a format compatible with TensorFlow (*https://www.tensorflow.org/*) that joins both the product information and user profile data. The ML system includes pipelines to preprocess data from multiple sources needed to train the model. Using the training data, Dressy's development team creates a TensorFlow model to serve the appropriate recommendations to customers. Figure 13-1 shows the full ML solution. We detail each step afterward.

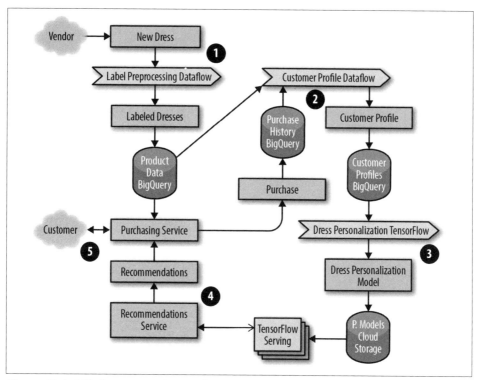

Figure 13-1. ML data processing pipeline

1. The development team elects to use a streaming dataflow pipeline, Google Cloud Dataflow, to preprocess the data into a format of labeled dresses by sending images to an image classification service that returns a list of characteristics.

2. The team preprocesses data from multiple sources that will be used to train a model that returns the top five most similar dresses. Their workflow generates an ML model from the dress product data and purchase history from customer profiles stored in BigQuery.

3. They choose to use a streaming Dataflow pipeline to preprocess the data into a format of customer personalization profiles. These profiles are used as input to train a TensorFlow model. The trained TensorFlow model binary is stored in a Google Cloud Storage (GCS) bucket (*https://cloud.google.com/storage/*). Before being promoted to production, the team ensures the model passes accuracy checks when evaluated against a test set of the preprocessed data used for model evaluation.

4. A service provides the recommendations for a given customer, which the web and mobile frontends use. The team uses TensorFlow with the Cloud ML online prediction service (*https://cloud.google.com/ml-engine/*).

5. A customer-facing, frontend service for making purchases serves the user data based on the up-to-date dress recommendations from the prediction service.

Dressy has noticed that occasionally a new model doesn't get published for over 24 hours, and the recommendations trigger intermittent errors. This is a common issue when a new model is deployed for the first time; however, there are some simple steps you can take to resolve this problem. If you start to notice that decisions, classifications, or recommendations either aren't being surfaced or are stale or incorrect, ask yourself:

- Is data stuck coming into the pipeline before it can be preprocessed to train the model?
- Do we have a poor ML model caused by a software bug? Is there a lot of spam? Are the features used to train the model poorly chosen?
- Has a new version of the ML model been recently generated, or is a stale version of the model running in production?

Luckily, Dressy has a set of tools to monitor and detect an issue before their customers experience any problems. If and when an outage occurs, these tools can help them to quickly repair or roll back any offending code. For more details on implementing monitoring and alerting, see Chapter 4.

Pipeline Best Practices

The following pipeline best practices apply to pipelines that are run as a service (i.e., pipelines that are responsible for correctly processing data in a timely manner for consumption by other systems). Multiple steps are required to properly deploy a pipeline as a service. These steps range from defining and measuring your customer needs with an SLO, to gracefully responding to degradations and failures, to writing documentation and creating a development lifecycle that catches issues before they reach production.

Define and Measure Service Level Objectives

It's important to automatically detect when your pipeline is unhealthy and if you are failing to meet your customer's needs. Receiving notifications when you're in danger of exceeding your error budget (for more details on error budget, see Chapter 2) helps to minimize customer impact. At the same time, it's important to strike a comfortable balance between reliability and feature launches—your customers care about both. The remainder of this section provides examples of pipeline SLOs and how to maintain them.

Data freshness

Most pipeline data freshness SLOs are in one of the following formats:

- X% of data processed in Y [seconds, days, minutes].
- The oldest data is no older than Y [seconds, days, minutes].
- The pipeline job has completed successfully within Y [seconds, days, minutes].

For example, the *Shave the Yak* mobile game could choose to target an SLO requiring 99% of all user actions that impact the user score to be reflected in the scoreboard within 30 minutes.

Data correctness

Creating SLOs for data correctness ensures that you are alerted about potential data errors in your pipeline. For example, a correctness error in a billing pipeline could result in customers being charged too much or too little. A correctness target can be difficult to measure, especially if there is no predefined correct output. If you don't have access to such data, you can generate it. For example, use test accounts to calculate the expected output. Once you have this "golden data," you can compare expected and actual output. From there, you can create monitoring for errors/discrepancies and implement threshold-based alerting as test data flows through a real production system.

Another data correctness SLO involves backward-looking analysis. For example, you might set a target that no more than 0.1% of your invoices are incorrect per quarter. You might set another SLO target for the number of hours/days that bad data or errors are served from the pipeline output data. The notion of data correctness varies by product and application.

Data isolation/load balancing

Sometimes you will have segments of data that are higher in priority or that require more resources to process. If you promise a tighter SLO on high-priority data, it's important to know that this data will be processed before lower-priority data if your resources become constrained. The implementation of this support varies from pipeline to pipeline, but often manifests as different queues in task-based systems or different jobs. Pipeline workers can be configured to take the highest available priority task. There could be multiple pipeline applications or pipeline worker jobs running with different configurations of resources—such as memory, CPU, or network tiers (*https://cloud.google.com/network-tiers*)—and work that fails to succeed on lower provisioned workers could be retried on higher provisioned ones. In times of resource or system constraints, when it's impossible to process all data quickly, this separation allows you to preferentially process higher-priority items over lower ones.

End-to-end measurement

If your pipeline has a series of stages, it can be tempting to measure a per-stage or per-component SLO. However, measuring SLOs in this fashion doesn't capture your customer's experience or the end-to-end health of your system. For example, imagine you have an event-based pipeline such as Google Analytics. The end-to-end SLO includes log input collection and any number of pipeline steps that happen before data reaches the serving state. You could monitor each stage individually and offer an SLO on each one, but customers only care about the SLO for the sum of all stages. If you're measuring SLOs for each stage, you would be forced to tighten your per-component alerting, which could result in more alerts that don't model the user experience.

Additionally, if you measure data correctness only per stage, you could miss end-to-end data corruption bugs. For example, each stage in your pipeline could report that all is well, but one stage introduces a field that it expects a downstream job to process. This upstream stage assumes that the extra data has been processed and used to serve requests to users. A downstream job doesn't expect the additional field, so it drops the data. Both jobs think they are correct, but the user doesn't see the data.

Plan for Dependency Failure

Once you define your SLO, it's good practice to confirm that you aren't overdepending on the SLOs/SLAs of other products that fail to meet their commitments. Many products, such as Google Cloud Platform, list their SLA promises (*https:// cloud.google.com/terms/sla*) on their sites. Once you identify any third-party dependencies, at a minimum, design for the largest failure accounted for in their advertised SLAs. For example, when defining an SLO, the owner of a pipeline that reads or writes data to Cloud Storage would ensure that the uptimes and guarantees advertised (*https://cloud.google.com/storage/sla*) are appropriate. If the single-region uptime guarantee was less than required by the pipeline to meet its SLO on data processing time, the pipeline owner may choose to replicate the data across regions to get the higher availability.

When a service provider's infrastructure breaks its SLAs, the result can negatively impact dependent pipelines. If your pipeline depends on more strict guarantees than the service provider advertises, your service could fail even if the service provider remains within their SLA. Sometimes, realistically planning for dependency failure can mean accepting a lower level of reliability and offering a looser SLA to your customers.[2]

---

2 For more details about factoring dependencies into your service's reliability, see Ben Treynor et al., "The Calculus of Service Availability," *ACM Queue* 15, no. 2 (2017), *https://queue.acm.org/detail.cfm?id=3096459*.

At Google, to encourage pipeline development with dependency failure in mind, we stage planned outages. For example, many pipelines at Google depend on the availability of the datacenter where they run. Our Disaster Recovery Testing (DiRT) frequently targets these systems, simulating a regional outage. When a regional outage occurs, pipelines that have planned for failure automatically fail over to another region. Other pipelines are delayed until the operator of the failed pipeline is alerted by their monitoring and manually fails over. Successful manual failover assumes that the pipeline can obtain enough resources to bring up a production stack in another region. In a best-case scenario, an unsuccessful manual failover prolongs an outage. In a worst-case scenario, processing jobs may have continued processing stale data, which introduces out-of-date or incorrect data in any downstream pipelines. Recovery tactics from an incident like this vary depending on your setup. For example, if correct data was overwritten with incorrect data, you may have to restore data from a previous backup version and reprocess any missing data.

In summary, it's good practice to prepare for the day when the systems you depend on are unavailable. Even the best products will fail and experience outages. Regularly practice disaster recovery scenarios to ensure your systems are resilient to common and uncommon failures. Assess your dependencies and automate your system responses as much as possible.

Create and Maintain Pipeline Documentation

When well written and maintained, system documentation can help engineers visualize the data pipeline and its dependencies, understand complex system tasks, and potentially shorten downtime in an outage. We recommend three categories of documentation for your pipeline.

System diagrams

System diagrams, similar to Figure 13-2, can help on-call engineers quickly find potential failure points. At Google, we encourage teams to draw system diagrams that show each component (both pipeline applications and data stores), and the transformations that happen at each step. Each of the components and transformations shown in your diagram can get stuck, causing data to stop flowing through the system. Each component can also introduce a software or application configuration bug that impacts data correctness.

A system diagram should contain quick links to other monitoring and debugging information at different pipeline stages. Ideally, these links should pull from live monitoring information, displaying the current status of each stage (e.g., waiting for dependent job to finish/processing/complete). Displaying historical runtime information can also indicate if a pipeline stage is taking longer than expected. This delay can foreshadow performance degradation or an outage.

Finally, even in complex systems, a system diagram makes it easier for developers to analyze data dependencies they should be aware of during feature launches.

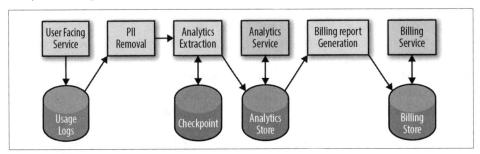

Figure 13-2. Pipeline system diagram (PII = personally identifiable information)

Process documentation

It's important to document how to perform common tasks, such as releasing a new version of a pipeline or introducing a change to the data format. Ideally, you should also document less common (often manual) tasks, such as initial service turnup or final service turndown in a new region. Once your tasks are documented, investigate the possibility of automating away any manual work. If the tasks and system are automated, consider generating your documentation directly from the source so you can keep both in sync.

Playbook entries

Each alert condition in your system should have a corresponding playbook entry that describes the steps to recovery. At Google, we find it useful to link this documentation in any alert messages sent to on-call engineers. Playbook entries are discussed in more detail in Chapter 11 of our first book (*http://bit.ly/2JgUBU7*).

Map Your Development Lifecycle

As shown in Figure 13-3, the development lifecycle of a pipeline (or a change to a pipeline) isn't too different from the development lifecycle of other systems. This section follows a typical release flow through each stage of the pipeline development lifecycle.

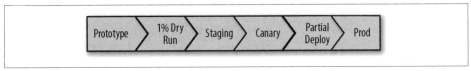

Figure 13-3. Pipeline development lifecycle with release workflow

Prototyping

The first phase of development involves prototyping your pipeline and verifying semantics. Prototyping ensures that you can express the business logic necessary to execute your pipeline. You may discover that one programming language allows you to better express your business logic, or that a particular language more easily integrates with your existing libraries. A particular programming model may suit your specific use case (e.g., Dataflow versus MapReduce, batch versus streaming). For an example of a completed programming model comparison, see our blog post "Dataflow/Beam & Spark: A Programming Model Comparison" (*http://bit.ly/2Jj0VdA*). If you are adding a feature to an existing pipeline, we recommend adding your code and running unit tests in the prototype stage.

Testing with a 1% dry run

Once you have completed your prototype, it's helpful to run a small setup on the full stack using production data. For example, run your pipeline using an experimental set, or a 1% dry run of production data in a nonproduction environment. Gradually scale up, tracking your pipeline performance to ensure you don't encounter any bottlenecks. When your product has launched to customers, run performance tests. These tests are an integral development step that helps prevent outages caused by new feature rollouts.

Staging

Before deploying to production, it's useful to run your system in a preproduction (or staging) environment. The data in your staging environment should be as close to actual production data as possible. We recommend keeping a full copy of production data or at least a representative subset. Unit tests won't catch all pipeline issues, so it's important to let the data flow through the system end-to-end to catch integration issues.

Integration tests can also identify errors. Using both unit and integration tests, run an A/B comparison of your newly generated data to previously generated known good data. For example, check your previous release for expected or unexpected differences before certifying the release and marking it ready to move to production.

Canarying

Pipeline testing and verification requires more time and care than stateless jobs—the data is persisted and the transformations are often complex. If something goes wrong in your production release, it's important to catch the issue early so you can limit the impact. Canarying your pipeline can help! Canarying is a process whereby you partially deploy your service (in this case, the pipeline application) and monitor the results. For a more detailed discussion of canarying, see Chapter 16. Canarying is tied to the entire pipeline rather than a single process. During a canary phase, you may choose to process the same real production data as the live pipeline but skip writes to production storage; techniques such as two-phase mutation can help (see the section "Idempotent and Two-Phase Mutations" on page 279). Often, you'll have to wait for the complete cycle of processing to finish before you can discover any customer-impacting issues. After your dry run (or two-phase mutation), compare the results of your canary pipeline with your live pipeline to confirm their health and check for data differences.

Sometimes it is possible to progress through the canary by gradually updating tasks of a job or by updating first in one region and then another, but this is not always possible with pipelines. Pipelines that use replicated data, such as Dataproc[3] and Dataflow,[4] support regional endpoints[5] and prevent this kind of canary progression—you can't reload one cell in isolation from another. If you run a multihomed pipeline, it may not be possible to deploy to a single region (or a percentage of servers) like you might with a serving job. Instead, perform a rollout for a small percentage of data first, or as described earlier, roll out in dry-run mode first.

During verification of your canary or preproduction environment, it is important to assess the health of your pipeline. Usually, you can use the same metrics you use to track your SLOs. Verifying your canary is a task that lends itself well to automation.

Performing a partial deployment

In addition to canarying your changes, you may also want to perform a partial deployment, particularly if there is a major feature launch or change that could impact system performance and resource usage. It can be difficult to predict the impact of these kinds of launches without first testing your changes on a subset of real traffic. You can implement a partial deployment as a flag or configuration option in your pipeline that accepts an allowed subset of data. Consider first processing your new features on one or two accounts, then gradually ramping up the amount of data (e.g., ~1%, ~10%, ~50%, and finally, 100% of your sample data).

---

3 Cloud Dataproc (*https://cloud.google.com/dataproc/*) is a fully managed cloud service for running Apache Spark and Apache Hadoop clusters.

4 Cloud Dataflow (*https://cloud.google.com/dataflow/*) is a fully managed cloud service for transforming data in stream and batch modes, with equal reliability and expressiveness.

5 Regional endpoints (*https://cloud.google.com/dataflow/docs/concepts/regional-endpoints*) control workers, and store and handle metadata for a Cloud Dataflow job.

There are a number of ways your partial deployment can go wrong: the input data might be incorrect or delayed, your data processing might have a bug, or your final storage might have an error. Any of these issues can result in an outage. Avoid promoting a corrupt set of data to your low-latency frontends. Aim to catch these types of issues as early as possible, before they reach your users.

Deploying to production

Once you have fully promoted your new pipeline binaries and/or config to production, you should be reasonably confident that you've vetted any potential issues (and if an issue does occur, that your monitoring will alert you). If your deployment goes wrong, be able to quickly restore from a known good state (e.g., roll back the binaries) and mark any potentially broken data as bad (e.g., replace the bad data with data from a previous backup version, make sure no jobs read the affected data, and/or reprocess the data if necessary).

Reduce Hotspotting and Workload Patterns

Hotspotting happens when a resource becomes overloaded from excessive access, resulting in an operation failure. Pipelines are susceptible to workload patterns—both through reads and writes—that can cause delays in isolated regions of data. Some common examples of hotspotting include:

- Errors thrown because multiple pipeline workers are accessing a single serving task, causing overload.
- CPU exhaustion due to concurrent access to a piece of data that is available on only one machine. Often, the internals of your data storage have a lowest level of granularity that may become unavailable if accessed heavily (e.g., a Spanner tablet (*http://bit.ly/2J9fnSj*) can become overloaded due to a problematic section of data even though most of the data storage is fine).
- Latency due to row-level lock contention in a database.
- Latency due to concurrent access to a hard drive, which exceeds the physical ability of the drive head to move fast enough to quickly locate the data. In this case, consider using solid state drives.
- A large work unit that requires many resources.

Hotspotting can be isolated to a subset of data. To combat hotspotting, you can also block fine-grained data such as individual records. If that data is blocked, the rest of the pipeline can progress. Typically, your infrastructure can provide this functionality. If a chunk of processing work is consuming a disproportionate amount of resources, the pipeline framework can dynamically rebalance by breaking the work into smaller pieces. To be safe, it's still best to build an emergency shutdown into your client logic to allow you to stop processing and isolate fine-grained chunks of processing work characterized by large resource usage or errors. For example, you should be able to quickly set a flag or push a config that allows you to skip input data that matches a certain pattern or problematic user.

Other strategies to reduce hotspotting include:

- Restructuring your data or access patterns to spread the load evenly
- Reducing the load (e.g., statically allocate some or all of your data)
- Reducing lock granularity to avoid data lock contention

Implement Autoscaling and Resource Planning

Spikes in workload are common and can lead to service outages if you're unprepared for them. Autoscaling can help you handle these spikes. By using autoscaling, you don't have to provision for peak load 100% of the time (for more details on autoscaling, see Chapter 11). Constantly running the number of workers required for peak capacity is an expensive and inefficient use of resources. Autoscaling turns down idle workers so you won't pay for resources you don't need. This strategy is particularly important for streaming pipelines and workloads that are variable. Batch pipelines may run simultaneously and will consume as many resources as are available.

Predicting the future growth of your system and allocating capacity accordingly ensures that your service won't run out of resources. It's also important to weigh the cost of resources against the engineering effort needed to make the pipeline more efficient. When conducting resource planning with an estimate of future growth, keep in mind that costs may not be isolated to just running your pipeline job. You may also be paying the data storage and network bandwidth costs for replicating data across regions or cross-region writes and reads. Additionally, some data store systems are more expensive than others. Even though unit storage costs are low, these costs can quickly add up for very large data sets or expensive data access patterns that use a lot of computing resources on the storage servers. It's good practice to help drive down costs by periodically examining your data set and pruning unused content.

Although the effectiveness of a series of pipeline stages should be measured according to its end-to-end SLO, the pipeline efficiency and resource usage should be measured at each individual stage. For example, imagine that you have many jobs using BigQuery and notice a significant increase in BigQuery resource usage after a release. If you can quickly determine which jobs are responsible, you can focus your engineering effort on those jobs to drive down costs.

Adhere to Access Control and Security Policies

Data flows through your system and is often persisted along the way. When managing any persisted data, we recommend you adhere to the following privacy, security, and data integrity principles:

- Avoid storing personally identifiable information (PII) in temporary storage. If you're required to store PII temporarily, make sure the data is properly encrypted.

- Restrict access to the data. Grant each pipeline stage only the minimal access it needs to read the output data from the previous stage.

- Put time to live (TTL) limits on logs and PII.

Consider a BigQuery instance that is tied to a GCP project whose access permissions can be managed with Google Cloud Identity and Access Management (e.g., the Dressy example described earlier). Creating different projects and instances per function allows more fine-grained scoping to restrict access. Tables can have a master project and cross-create views among client projects to allow them controlled access. For example, Dressy has restricted access to tables containing sensitive customer information for jobs from specific project roles.

Plan Escalation Paths

It is important to design your pipeline to be resilient so that a system failure (like a machine or zonal outage) never triggers an SLO violation page. By the time you get paged, you need to manually intervene because all automated measures have been exhausted. If you have well-defined SLOs and reliable metrics and alert detection, you'll be alerted before your customers notice or report issues. When an SLO is violated, it's important to respond quickly and send proactive communication to your customers.

Pipeline Requirements and Design

Today's market provides many pipeline technology and framework options, and it can be overwhelming to identify which one best suits your use case. Some platforms provide fully managed pipelines. Others give you more flexibility but require more hands-on management. In SRE, we often take a significant amount of time during the design phase to assess which technology is the best fit. We compare and contrast the various design options based on user needs, product requirements, and system constraints. This section discusses tools you can use to both assess your pipeline technology options and make improvements to existing pipelines.

What Features Do You Need?

Table 13-1 provides a list of features we recommend you optimize for when managing a data processing pipeline. Some of these features may already be present in your existing pipeline technology (e.g., via managed pipeline platforms, client application logic, or operational tools). Your application may not need some of these features—for example, you don't need "exactly once" semantics if your work units are idempotent and can be performed more than once for the same result.

Table 13-1. Recommended data pipeline features

Pipeline item	Feature
Latency	Use an API that supports streaming, batch, or both. Streaming processing is generally better than batch processing at supporting lower-latency applications. If you choose batch but might at some point want streaming, an API that is interchangeable may reduce the migration cost later.
Data correctness	Exactly-once semantics globally. You can require that data is processed (at most) once to get correct results. Two-phase mutations. Windowing functions for event processing and aggregations. You may want fixed time, session, or sliding windows to divide data (since data is not always processed in the order in which it's received). You may also want in-order guarantees. Black-box monitoring. The ability to control the flow of multiple jobs or stages of your pipeline. This control should allow you to gate a job until another completes so the job does not process incomplete data.
High availability	Multihoming. Autoscaling.
Mean Time to Resolve (MTTR) incidents in data processing	Tie your code changes to a release, which allows for fast rollbacks. Have tested data backup and restore procedures in place. In the event of an outage, ensure that you can easily drain a region from serving or processing. Have useful alert messages, dashboards, and logs for debugging. In particular, your monitoring should be quick to identify the reason(s) why a pipeline is delayed and/or why data is corrupt. Use data checkpointing to help recover faster when a pipeline is interrupted.
Mean Time to Detect (MTTD) outages	Ensure you have SLO monitoring in place. Monitoring out-of-SLO alerts allows you to detect issues that impact your customers. Alerting on the symptom (versus the cause) (*http://bit.ly/2J5tPum*) reduces monitoring gaps.
Development lifecycle to prevent errors from reaching production	We recommend running any changes in a canary environment before deploying to production. This strategy lowers the possibility of a change impacting SLOs in production.
Inspect and predict resource usage or cost	Create (or use an existing) resource accounting dashboard. Be sure to include resources like storage and network. Create a metric that allows you to correlate or predict growth.

Pipeline item	Feature
Ease of development	Support a language that best fits your use case. Often pipeline technologies limit your options to one or two languages.
	Use a simple API for defining data transformations and expressing your pipeline logic. Consider the tradeoff between simplicity and flexibility.
	Reuse base libraries, metrics, and reporting. When you're creating a new pipeline, reusable resources allow you to focus development on any new business logic.
Ease of operation	Use existing automation and operational tools as much as possible. Doing so reduces operational costs, as you don't need to maintain your own tools.
	Automate as many operational tasks as possible.
	Larger tasks that are performed infrequently may include a chain of dependencies and prerequisites that can be too numerous or complex for a human to assess in a timely manner (e.g., moving your data and pipeline stack from region A to region B, then turning down region A). To ease a transition like this, consider investing in automation. Perhaps introduce some pipeline health checks on the pipeline stack in region B before putting it into production.

Idempotent and Two-Phase Mutations

Pipelines can process large amounts of data. When a pipeline fails, some data must be reprocessed. You can use the *idempotent mutations* design pattern to prevent storing duplicate or incorrect data. An idempotent (*http://bit.ly/2xyQqhP*) mutation is a type of mutation that can be applied multiple times with the same result. Implementing this design pattern allows separate executions of a pipeline with the same input data to always produce the same result.

When testing or canarying a pipeline, you need to know if your applied mutations are acceptable to the pipeline owner according to the expected output. The *two-phase mutation* design pattern can help here. Typically, the data is read from a source and transformed, and then a mutation is applied. With two-phase mutation, the mutations themselves are stored in a temporary location. A separate verification step (or pipeline) can run against these potential mutations to validate them for correctness. A follow-up pipeline step applies the verified mutations only after the mutations pass validation. Figure 13-4 shows an example of two-phase mutation.

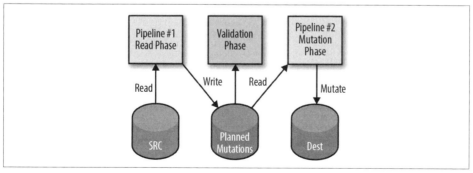

Figure 13-4. Two-phase mutation

Checkpointing

Typically, pipelines are long-running processes that analyze or mutate large amounts of data. Without special consideration, pipelines that are terminated early will lose their state, requiring the entire pipeline to be executed again. This is especially true for pipelines that create AI models, as each iteration of the model calculation relies on previous calculations. *Checkpointing* is a technique that enables long-running processes like pipelines to periodically save partial state to storage so that they can resume the process later.

While checkpointing is often used for the failure case, it's also useful when a job needs to be preempted or rescheduled (e.g., to change CPU or RAM limits). The job can be cleanly shut down, and upon rescheduling, it's able to detect which work units have already been processed. Checkpointing has the added advantage of enabling a pipeline to skip potentially expensive reads or computations because it already knows the work is done.

Code Patterns

Some common code patterns can make your pipelines more efficient to manage and reduce the effort required to make changes or updates.

Reusing code

If you operate multiple similar pipelines and want to implement a new monitoring capability or metric, you have to instrument each separate system. This common workflow isn't difficult if you use the right strategy. Implementing reusable code libraries allows you to add a metric for monitoring in one place and share it across multiple pipelines or stages. Shared libraries allow you to:

- Gain insight across all data pipelines in a standard way.
- Reuse other data analytics systems for each pipeline (e.g., a traffic report that works for all of your pipelines).
- Alert on the same metric for multiple jobs, such as a generic data freshness alert.

Using the microservice approach to creating pipelines

When using microservices, it's important to have a service perform a single task and do it well. It's easier to operate a group of microservices that use the same core libraries, varying only in their business logic, than it is to operate many custom services. A similar pattern can apply to pipelines. Instead of creating one monolithic pipeline application, create smaller pipelines that you can release and monitor separately. In doing so, you will get the same benefits as you get from a microservices architecture.

Pipeline Production Readiness

As discussed in Chapter 18, a PRR (Production Readiness Review) is the process that Google SRE teams use to onboard a new service. In the same spirit, we use a *pipeline maturity matrix* when consulting on the choice or design of a pipeline technology.

Pipeline maturity matrix

The matrix in Table 13-2 measures five key characteristics (but you can extend the matrix to measure other characteristics you wish to optimize or standardize for):

- Failure tolerance
- Scalability
- Monitoring and debugging
- Transparency and ease of implementation
- Unit and integration testing

The maturity matrix represents the collective knowledge of many pipeline experts at Google. These individuals are responsible for running pipelines across multiple Google products and productionizing the associated systems.

Each characteristic is measured on a scale of 1 to 5, where 1 represents "Chaotic" (unplanned, ad hoc, risky, fully manual) and 5 represents "Continuous improvement." To score your system, read the descriptions for each characteristic below, and select the best matching milestone. If more than one milestone applies, use the score in the middle (i.e., 2 or 4). A completed scoresheet will give you a clear picture of where your system needs improvement.

We recommend that you spend the time to make improvements in any weak areas identified by the matrix. Instrumenting monitoring, alerting, and other tooling recommended by the matrix can be time-intensive. When making improvements, you can start by looking for existing products or open source tools that fit your needs instead of creating your own. At Google, we encourage teams to use existing pipeline technologies or tools that provide out-of-the-box pipeline support and features. The more tools and processes that can be reused, the better.

Table 13-2. Pipeline maturity matrix, with example milestones for beginning, medium, and advanced maturity

	1. Chaotic	3. Functional	5. Continuous improvement
Failure tolerance			
Failover	No support for failover	Some support for work unit retries (even if manual)	Multihomed with automatic failover
Global work scheduling	No support for global work scheduling, multihoming, or failover	Support for hot/hot/hot processing (process same work in all three regions so if any region is unavailable, there is at least one still running)	Support for effective warm/warm/warm processing (distribute work in all three regions and store work centrally to deal with any region loss)
Failed task management	No support for failed work units	—	Automatic retries for failed work units Automatic quarantine of bad work units
Scalability			
Automatic scaling of available worker pool	No autoscaling; manual intervention required	Autoscaling works with the use of additional manual tools	Built-in automatic autoscaling support with no requirement for configuration inside a third-party tool
Automatic dynamic resharding to effect balanced load across the pool	Work units are fixed with no ability to make changes	Supports manual resharding of work, or resharding can be achieved automatically with additional code	Built-in support for dynamic subsharding to balance work across the available worker pool
Load shedding/task prioritization	No work unit prioritization exists	Some capability for work unit prioritization	An easy-to-use feature for work unit prioritization exists Built-in support for load shedding Workers understand preemption notification, after which a worker will clean up (finish work/mitigate)
Monitoring and debugging			
Debugging tools and capabilities	No logs; no way to identify or track failed work units	There is a solution to identify a failed work unit and extract associated logs	There is a solution that allows a user to access logs for the time at which the work unit failed; this data is retrieved directly from the failed work unit There is a solution to automatically quarantine and replay a failed work unit

	1. Chaotic	3. Functional	5. Continuous improvement
Dashboards and visualizations	No dashboards or visualization solutions that support the display of pipeline information	There is an easy-to-configure dashboard showing the following information: • Number of work units in various stages of completion • Latency and aging information for each stage	A fine-grained visualization of the entire execution map for a pipeline A visualization for delays up to each stage A visualization and rationale for throttling and pushback Information about limiting factors due to resource usage Information about the distribution of internal state worker machines (e.g., stack graph) Information about how many work units are failing, stuck, or slow Historical run statistics are presented and preserved

Ease of implementation and transparency

	1. Chaotic	3. Functional	5. Continuous improvement
Discoverability	No feature for discoverability (a list of the pipelines that are running and their status)	Some support for discoverability; manual setup might be required, or not all pipelines are discoverable	Built-in support for automatic discoverability; a global data registry service that allows the listing of configured pipelines
Code	Significant setup cost for using the technology	Some reusable components available	Base frameworks are available and require minimum code The pipeline can be configured in machine-readable format Zero config Libraries with semantics similar to other pipeline solutions that are most heavily used in related teams
Documentation and best practices	Sparse or outdated documentation	Minimal setup documentation for each component	Comprehensive and up-to-date documentation Training examples for new users

Unit and integration testing

	1. Chaotic	3. Functional	5. Continuous improvement
Unit testing framework	No support or unit testing framework	Tests take a long time to run and frequently time out Too many resource requirements No code coverage support Easy to switch data sources to test a resource	Runs with sanitizers (*https://github.com/google/sanitizers*) (ASAN, TSAN, etc.) The build dependency graph is as small as possible Code coverage support Provides debugging info and results No external dependencies Built-in test data generation library

	1. Chaotic	3. Functional	5. Continuous improvement
Ease of configuration (this has direct relevance to the scalability aspect of the pipeline)	Test configuration is not supported or requires a significant amount of time to learn, in addition to learning about the pipeline itself—for example, testing uses a different programming language and a different API than the pipeline	The first integration test requires significant setup, but subsequent tests are either a copy/paste or an extension to the first with minimal overrides —for example, a test data generator could be minimally tweaked to support collecting test data for many different pipeline applications	Decoupling from production configuration, while not preventing reuse; easier to define integration test configuration and reuse relevant parts of prod configuration
Support for integration testing frameworks (this describes how well a pipeline should interact and support various integration testing methodologies, which are not necessarily part of the pipeline itself)	Using Cloud or third-party open source tools for diffing, monitoring, integration testing, and so on, can be difficult to implement and/or resource-intensive; requires in-house tools or tools do not exist	Minimal documentation and examples of integration testing tools and methodologies used in conjunction with the pipeline Large amount of time required even for data sets with minimal input Difficult to trigger on-demand execution for testing scenarios Difficult to separate production from nonproduction concerns (e.g., all event logs go to production logging service)	Built-in support for scaled-down input data Support for diffing of output data (e.g., persisting output test data) Configurable monitoring for test run validation Ample documentation and examples of integration tests built for the pipeline

Pipeline Failures: Prevention and Response

A pipeline can fail for many reasons, but the most common culprits are data delay and data corruption. When an outage occurs, finding and repairing the issue quickly will greatly reduce its impact. At Google, when an outage or SLO violation occurs, we track metrics for MTTD and MTTR. Tracking these metrics indicates how effective we are at detecting and repairing an issue. In the postmortem that follows any outage at Google, we analyze the cause of the outage to elicit any patterns and address sources of operational toil.

This section describes some common failure modes, methods to effectively respond to pipeline failures, and strategies to help you prevent future pipeline failures.

Potential Failure Modes

Delayed data

A pipeline can fail if its input or output is delayed. Without the proper precautions, a downstream job may start running even though it doesn't have the necessary data. Stale data is almost always better than incorrect data. If your pipeline processes incomplete or corrupt data, errors will propagate downstream. Restoring or reprocessing bad data takes time and can prolong an outage. Instead, if your pipeline stalls, waits for data, and then resumes once the data becomes available, the data remains high quality. Creating data dependencies that are respected by all stages is important.

Depending on the type of pipeline, the impact of delayed data can range from stale application data to stalled pipelines. In batch processing pipelines, each stage waits for its predecessor to finish before it begins. Streaming systems are more flexible: using event-time processing, such as Dataflow, a downstream stage can start a portion of work as soon as the corresponding upstream portion completes, rather than waiting for all portions to complete.

When an outage of this nature occurs, you will likely need to notify any dependent services. If the outage is user-visible, you may also have to notify your customers. When you're debugging pipeline outages, it's helpful to see the progress of current and past pipeline runs, and to have direct links to log files and a diagram of the flow of data. It's also useful to be able to trace a unit of work through the system while analyzing its counters and statistics.

Corrupt data

If undetected, corrupt pipeline data (input and/or output) can cause user-facing issues. You can circumvent many user-facing issues by having tests that identify corrupt data in place, and using logic that alerts you to potential corruption. For example, pipeline systems can implement blocking policies and abuse/spam detection to automatically or manually filter out bad sources of data.

Corrupt data can have many causes: software bugs, data incompatibility, unavailable regions, configuration bugs, and so on. There are two main steps involved in fixing corrupt data:

1. Mitigate the impact by preventing further corrupt data from entering the system.
2. Restore your data from a previously known good version, or reprocess to repair the data.

If a single region is serving corrupt data, you may need to drain your serving jobs and/or data processing from that region. If a software or configuration bug is at fault, you may need to quickly roll back the relevant binary. Often, data corruption can cause windows of data that are incorrect and need to be reprocessed once the underlying issue has been fixed, such as fixing a software bug in a pipeline binary. To reduce the cost of reprocessing, consider selective reprocessing—read in and process only the user or account information impacted by the data corruption. Alternatively, you could persist some intermediate data that can serve as a checkpoint to avoid reprocessing a pipeline from end to end.

If the output of your pipeline is corrupt, downstream jobs may propagate the corrupt data or serving jobs may serve incorrect data. Even with the best testing, development, and release practices in place, a software or configuration bug can introduce data corruption. We recommend that you plan for this eventuality and have the ability to quickly reprocess and restore your data. Recovering from this kind of data corruption is labor-intensive and difficult to automate.

Potential Causes

Pipeline dependencies

When you're trying to determine the cause of an outage, it's useful to investigate pipeline dependencies, such as storage, network systems, or other services. These dependencies may be throttling your requests/traffic or, if they are out of resources, refusing any new data. The rate of input/output can slow for a variety of reasons:

- The output sink or storage could be refusing writes of a piece of data.
- There could be a particular hotspot data range that cannot complete.
- There might be a storage bug.

Some pipeline dependency issues won't resolve themselves. It's important to file a ticket or bug, and to allow for enough time to add more resources or address traffic patterns. Implementing load balancing and dropping low-priority data may help mitigate the impact.

Pipeline application or configuration

A pipeline failure could be the result of a bottleneck, a bug in your pipeline jobs, or a bug in the configurations themselves (e.g., CPU-intensive processing, performance regression, out-of-memory failures, abusive data prone to hotspotting, or configs that point to the incorrect input/output locations). Depending on the cause, there are several possible solutions:

- Roll back the binary/config, cherry-pick a fix, or repair any permission issues.
- Consider restructuring the data that's causing the issue.

Application or configuration errors can introduce data incorrectness or lead to delayed data. These kinds of errors are the most common causes of outages. We recommend spending time on pipeline development and ensuring that new binaries and configurations perform well in a nonproduction environment before they are fully deployed.

Unexpected resource growth

A sudden and unplanned jump in system load may cause a pipeline to fail. You may need additional unplanned resources to keep your service running. Automatic scaling of your application jobs can help meet the demand of new load, but you should also be aware that an increased pipeline load can also put a strain on downstream dependencies—you may also need to plan for more storage and/or network resources.

Good resource planning and accurate growth prediction can help in these cases, but such predictions may not always be correct. We recommend becoming familiar with the process of requesting additional emergency resources. Depending on the nature of your pipeline's deployment and the quantity of resources required, the time needed to acquire these resources can be substantial. Therefore, we recommend preparing interim solutions to keep your service up and running—for example, prioritize different classes of data through your pipeline.

Region-level outage

A regional outage is bad for all pipelines, but singly homed pipelines are particularly vulnerable. If your pipeline runs in a single region that suddenly becomes unavailable, the pipeline will stop until the region comes back up. If you have multihomed pipelines with automatic failover, your response may be as simple as draining processing or serving from an affected region until the outage is over. When a region is down, data can become stranded or delayed, resulting in incorrect output from your pipeline. As a result, the correctness of the data output from any dependent jobs or services may be compromised.

Case Study: Spotify

by Igor Maravić

Spotify is the leading music streaming company in the world. Every day, tens of millions of people use Spotify to listen to their favorite songs, share music with their friends, and discover new artists.

This case study describes our event delivery system, which is responsible for reliably collecting instrumentation data generated from Spotify applications. The data produced by this system helps us to better understand our end users and to provide them with the right music at the right time.

In this case study, a "customer" refers to the development teams within Spotify that use data from the event delivery system. "End user" refers to individuals that use the Spotify service to listen to music.

Event Delivery

We refer to end-user interactions as *events*. Every time a user listens to a song, clicks an ad, or follows a playlist, we record an event. Spotify captures and publishes hundreds of billions of events (of multiple types) to our servers daily. These events have many uses at Spotify, from A/B test analysis to showing play counts to powering personalized discovery playlists. Most importantly, we pay royalties to artists based on delivered events.[6] It's imperative that we have a reliable means of event storage and delivery.

Before we can process event data, that data needs to be collected and delivered to persistent storage. We use an event delivery system to reliably collect and persist all published events. The event delivery system is one of the core pillars of our data infrastructure, as almost all of our data processing depends—either directly or indirectly—on the data it delivers.

All delivered events are partitioned by type and publishing time. As shown in Figure 13-5, events published during any given hour are grouped together and stored in a designated directory, called a *delivered hourly bucket*. These buckets are then grouped into event-type directories. This partitioning scheme simplifies data access control, ownership, retention, and consumption at Spotify.

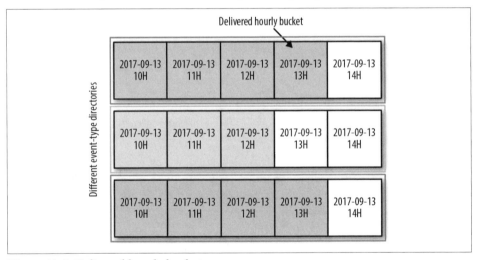

Figure 13-5. Delivered hourly buckets

---

6 Delivered events are events that have been delivered to persistent storage and are exposed in such a way that they can be consumed by customers of the event delivery system (e.g., data jobs).

Hourly buckets are the only interface our data jobs have with the event delivery system. As a result, we measure performance and define SLOs for our event delivery system based on how well we deliver hourly buckets per event type.

Event Delivery System Design and Architecture

Our hourly buckets reside on Google Cloud Storage (GCS). Early in the design process, we decided to decouple data collection from data delivery within the system. To achieve this, we used a globally distributed persistent queue, Google Cloud Pub/Sub (*https://cloud.google.com/pubsub/*), as an intermediate layer. Once decoupled, data collection and delivery act as independent failure domains, which limits the impact of any production issues and results in a more resilient system. Figure 13-6 depicts the architecture of our event delivery system.

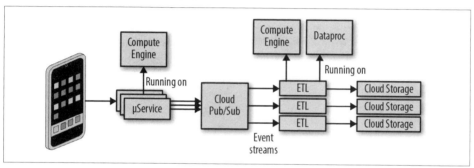

Figure 13-6. Event delivery system architecture

Data collection

Produced events[7] are grouped by event types. Each event type describes a user action in the Spotify application. For example, one event type could refer to a user subscribing to a playlist, while another event type could refer to a user starting playback of a song. To ensure that separate event types don't impact each other, the system has full event type isolation. Individual events from different event types are published to their allocated topics (*http://bit.ly/2HcNruH*) in Google Cloud Pub/Sub. Publishing is performed by our microservices, which run both in Spotify datacenters and on Google Compute Engine (GCE) (*http://bit.ly/2szT2Ga*). In order to be delivered, each published event stream is handled by a dedicated instance of an ETL process.

---

7 Produced events are both the events that have been delivered and the events that are currently flowing through the event delivery system.

Extract Transform Load

The ETL process is responsible for delivering published events to the correct hourly buckets on GCS. The ETL process has three steps/components:

1. A dedicated microservice consumes events from the event stream.

2. Another microservice assigns events to their hourly partitions.

3. A batch data job running on Dataproc deduplicates events from their hourly partitions and persists them to their final location on GCS.

Each ETL component has a single responsibility, which makes the components easier to develop, test, and operate.

Data delivery

Event type delivery is dynamically enabled or disabled directly by our customers (other engineering teams at Spotify). Delivery is controlled via simple configuration. In the configuration, customers define which event types should be delivered. As delivery of each event type is turned on or off, a microservice dynamically acquires and releases the Google GCE resources on which the ETL runs. The following code shows an example event type that a customer can enable/disable:

```
events:
    -CollectionUpdate
    -AddedToCollection
    -RemovedFromCollection
```

When a customer enables delivery of a new event type, we don't know in advance what quantity of resources are required to guarantee the delivery. Consequently, manually determining necessary resources is very expensive. To achieve optimal resource utilization for delivery of different event types, we use GCE Autoscaler (*http://bit.ly/2kGlZN7*).

Event Delivery System Operation

Defining and communicating SLOs for our event delivery system helps in three ways:

Design and development
> When developing our systems, having clear SLOs in place gives us goals to work toward. These goals help us make pragmatic design choices and optimize our systems for simplicity.

Identify performance issues
> Once our systems are deployed in production, SLOs help us to identify which parts of the system aren't performing well and where we need to focus our efforts.

Set customer expectations

SLOs allow us to manage our customer expectations and avoid unnecessary support requests. When the limits of our system are clear to our customers, they are empowered to decide how to design, build, and operate their own systems that depend on our data.

We provide our customers with three SLO types for our event delivery system: timeliness, completeness, and skewness (discussed next). These SLOs are based on hourly data buckets provided by GCS. To be as objective as possible and to avoid bloating event delivery with features that have nothing to do with it, we measure all SLOs using independent external systems (e.g., Datamon, a data visualization tool explained in the next section).

Timeliness

Our timeliness SLO is defined as the maximum delay of delivering an hourly bucket of data. Delivery delay is calculated as the time difference between when the bucket was delivered and the earliest theoretical time the bucket could have been closed. Figure 13-7 provides an example of this delivery delay. The diagram shows the buckets for hours 12, 13, and 14. If the bucket for hour 13 was closed at 14:53, we would say the closing delay was 53 minutes.

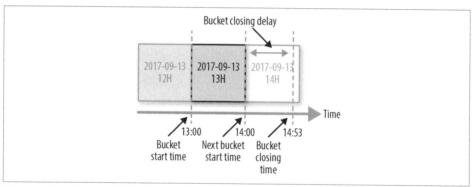

Figure 13-7. Event time partitioning

Timeliness of data delivery is the metric we use to evaluate the performance of our data pipelines. To measure and visualize timeliness, we use a tool called Datamon, our internal data monitoring tool that was built around the notion of hourly buckets. Figure 13-8 shows a typical Datamon UI. Each green rectangle (in grayscale, the vast majority of the rectangles) represents an on-time hourly bucket. Gray rectangles (clustered here on the righthand side) indicate buckets that have not been delivered, while red rectangles (3 dark rectangles on the very top row) indicate buckets that weren't delivered within the required SLO. Days when all hours were successfully delivered are shown as a single green rectangle.

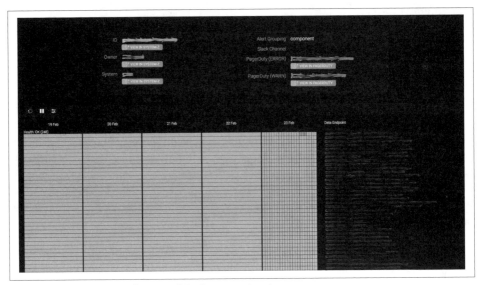

Figure 13-8. Datamon for Spotify's data monitoring system

Downstream data jobs can't start their processing until the hourly buckets on which they depend are delivered. Each data job periodically checks the delivery status of its dependencies before processing the data. Any delay in delivery affects the timeliness of downstream jobs. Our customers care deeply about having data delivered in a timely fashion. To help us prioritize delivery of events during an incident, our event delivery system's timeliness SLO is split into three priority tiers: high, normal, and low. Our customers configure to the appropriate tier for their event type.

Skewness

We define our skewness SLO as the maximal percentage of data that can be misplaced on a daily basis. Skewness (and completeness) are concepts specific to our event delivery system and are not present in our other data pipelines. Defining an SLO for these concepts was a key requirement when we were designing our event delivery system, as it processes (among other event types) finance-bearing events. For all other events, best-effort delivery is good enough and we don't expose a corresponding SLO. Whether or not an event is finance-bearing is determined by customer configuration.

To determine when an hourly bucket should be delivered, our event delivery system uses heuristics. By definition, heuristics aren't always completely correct. As a result, undelivered events from previously delivered buckets might be delivered to an incorrect future hourly bucket. This misplaced event is referred to as a *skew*. A skew can negatively impact jobs, since they might first underreport and then overreport values for some time periods. Figure 13-9 shows an example of skewed data delivery.

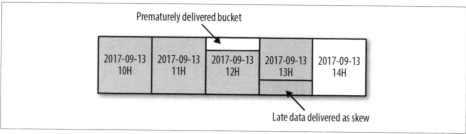

Figure 13-9. Delivery of skewed data

Completeness

Events can be lost in a distributed system in many ways—for example, a new release of our software may contain a bug, a cloud service may go down, or a developer might accidentally delete some persisted events. To ensure we are alerted about data loss, we measure completeness. We define completeness as the percentage of events that are delivered after they are successfully published to the system.

We report on skewness and completeness daily. To measure these values, we use an internal auditing system that compares the counts for all published and delivered events. Any mismatch is reported, and we take appropriate action.

In order to have timeliness, skewness, and completeness SLO guarantees, we assign events to our hourly buckets at the time they were received at our servers, not when they were produced on the clients. If our users are in offline mode, produced events can be buffered for up to 30 days on the clients before being published. Additionally, users can modify the system time on their device, which can result in inaccurately timestamped events. For these reasons, we use the timestamp from Spotify servers.

We don't provide any SLOs regarding the data quality or accuracy of events delivered via our event delivery system. We observed that in a majority of cases, quality depends on the content of each event, which is populated by the business logic of our customers. To allow our system to scale with the number of customers, we keep it focused exclusively on delivering data. In this regard, we use the analogy that event delivery should behave like a postal service: your mail should be delivered on time, intact, and unopened. We leave the responsibility of providing quality SLOs to our internal teams that own the business logic and therefore understand the contents of the data.

Customer Integration and Support

Many Spotify teams interact with the event delivery system daily. To encourage adoption and decrease the learning curve, we took the following steps to simplify user interaction with the event delivery system:

Event delivery as a fully managed service

We wanted to avoid exposing the complexity of the system to our customers, allowing them to focus on the specific problems they're trying to solve. We strived to hide any system complexities behind a well-defined and easy-to-understand API.

Limited functionality

To keep our APIs simple, we support only a limited set of functionalities. Events can be published only in a specific in-house format, and can be delivered only to hourly buckets with a single serialization format. These simple APIs cover the majority of our use cases.

Delivery of each event needs to be explicitly enabled

When a customer enables delivery of an event, they define whether the event is financial-bearing and its associated timeliness requirements. Furthermore, event ownership needs to be explicitly defined as part of the enabling process. We strongly believe that holding our internal teams accountable for events they produce results in higher data quality. Explicit ownership of the events also gives us a clear channel of communication during incidents.

Documentation

No matter how simple interacting with the system is, good documentation is required to provide a good customer experience. Subpar and stale documentation is a common problem in fast-paced companies like Spotify. To address this, we treat our documentation like any other software product: all support requests that come to our team are treated either as issues with our documentation or as issues in the actual product. Most support requests are related to the system's public APIs. Some examples of questions we try to answer when writing our documentation include:

- How is the delivery of an event type enabled?
- Where is the data delivered?
- How is the data partitioned?
- What are our SLOs?
- What kind of support should our customers expect during incidents?

Our goal is to minimize the amount of support requests we receive as our customer base grows.

System monitoring

Monitoring our SLOs provides high-level insights into the general health of the system. Our reliable catch-all monitoring solution ensures we always get alerted when something goes wrong. The main problem with using an SLO violation as criteria for monitoring is that we get alerted *after* our customers have been affected. To avoid this, we need sufficient operational monitoring of our system to resolve or mitigate issues before an SLO is broken.

We monitor the various components of our system separately, starting with basic system metrics, then building to more complex ones. For example, we monitor CPU usage as a signal for instance health. CPU usage is not always the most critical resource, but it works well as a basic signal.

Sometimes system monitoring is insufficient when we're trying to understand and fix production issues. To supplement our monitoring data, we also maintain application logs. These logs contain important information related to the operation and health of the component they describe. We take great care to ensure we gather only the correct amount of logging data, as it's easy for irrelevant logs to drown useful ones. For example, a bad logging implementation might log all the incoming requests for a high-volume component that deals with incoming requests. Assuming that most of the requests are similar, logging every request doesn't add much value. Additionally, when too many requests are logged, it becomes difficult to find other log entries, disk fills up faster, and the overall performance of our service starts to degrade. A better approach is to either rate-limit the amount of logged requests, or to log only interesting requests (like the ones that result in unhandled exceptions).

Debugging components in production by reading through application logs is challenging, and should be a last resort.

Capacity planning

Reliable round-the-clock operation of the event delivery system requires the correct amount of allocated resources, especially since the components are deployed into a single GCP project and they share a common quota pool. We use capacity planning to determine how many resources each system component needs.

For the majority of our system components, capacity planning is based on CPU usage. We provision each component to have 50% of CPU usage during peak hours. This provision acts as a safety margin that allows our system to handle unexpected bursts of traffic. When Spotify ran its own datacenters, we provided each component with static resources. This led to a waste of resources during off-peak hours and an inability to handle large bursts in traffic. To improve resource utilization, we use GCE Autoscaler for some of our stateless components.

We had some growing pains in the early days of implementing Autoscaler; under certain conditions, Autoscaler can cause failures. For example, we use CPU usage as a metric to perform autoscaling. Autoscaler itself depends on a strong correlation between CPU usage and the amount of work performed by each component instance. If the relationship is broken—either through the addition of CPU-hungry daemons to each component instance or due to component instances extensively burning CPU without doing any work—Autoscaler will start far too many instances.

When Autoscaler is presented with constantly increasing CPU usage that has no correlation with the amount of work performed, it will scale indefinitely until it uses all of the resources it can find. To prevent Autoscaler from using up all of our quota, we implemented some workarounds:

- We limit the maximum number of instances Autoscaler can use.
- We heavily restrict the CPU usage of all daemons running on an instance.
- We aggressively throttle a component's CPU usage as soon as we detect that no useful work is being done.

Even when using Autoscaler, we need to conduct capacity planning. We need to ensure that we have enough quota, and that the maximum number of instances Autoscaler can use is set high enough to serve traffic during peaks, but low enough to limit the impact of "runaway" autoscaling.

Development process

To ship new features and improvements swiftly, we developed the event delivery system (shown in Figure 13-10) following the continuous integration (*http://bit.ly/2J9F19p*) and continuous delivery (*http://bit.ly/2snAaey*) (CI/CD) process. According to this process, valid, proven, or reviewed system changes are deployed as soon as they're made. Having sufficient test coverage is a prerequisite for each change to be successfully deployed without negatively impacting our SLOs.

We write tests following a "testing pyramid" philosophy (*http://bit.ly/2kEMSRM*). This means that for each of our components, we have plenty of unit tests that focus on components' inner workings—in addition to a smaller number of integration tests that focus on components' public API. At the highest level of the testing pyramid, we have a system-wide, end-to-end test. In this end-to-end test, all components are treated as black boxes so the system in the test environment resembles the one in production as much as possible.

After initial development, every change goes through a peer review. As a part of the review process, all tests are executed on a shared CI/CD server, and the results are presented to the developers. Changes can be merged only after the reviewers approve the change and all the tests have successfully passed. As soon as the change is merged, the deployment process is triggered.

The event delivery system is a critical component in Spotify's infrastructure. If it stopped delivering data, all data processing in Spotify would stall. For this reason, we decided to take a more conservative approach to deployments and deploy each change in stages. We require a manual approval before a deployment can move from one stage to another.

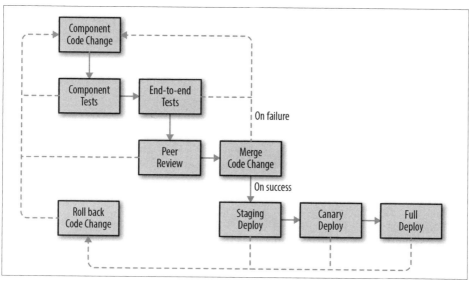

Figure 13-10. Development process

During the first deployment stage, the change is deployed to the staging environment. This low-risk staging system doesn't handle production traffic. For testing purposes, a representative fraction of production traffic is mirrored in the staging system, which is a replica of the system running in production. At the second deployment stage, the change is deployed to a small subset of production instances, or canaries. We perform a full production deployment only after we ensure that everything went well, both in staging and canaries (see Chapter 16).

Incident handling

When dealing with an incident, our first priority is to mitigate the damage and return the system to a stable previous state. To avoid making the situation worse, we refrain from deploying any major changes to our components during an incident. The exception to this rule is if we conclude that the incident was caused by recently deployed new code. In such cases, we immediately roll the system back to a previous working version.

Today, the most common operational failures we encounter are caused either by a system malfunction (e.g., we introduce a software bug or a performance regression) or a failure with an external service on which we depend (e.g., an update to a service API isn't backward-compatible or a service breaks its SLO). We use many battle-tested Google Cloud and internal Spotify services, like Cloud Pub/Sub and Helios (*https://github.com/spotify/helios*), to speed up development of our system and to reduce our operational load. In the event of an incident caused by an external service, we have a dedicated on-call team[8] who provides support. One drawback of using external services is that we can't do much to mitigate the problem ourselves. Furthermore, communicating the issue to a third party takes valuable time during an incident. Nevertheless, we believe that the ability to delegate responsibility is worth the occasional feeling of powerlessness.

Unexpected system behavior under heavy load is another common source of operational failure. Testing services under exact production conditions is impossible, so it's hard to predict all of the edge cases that can happen. It can also be difficult to emulate the load our components face in production. Heavy load in combination with unforeseen edge cases can lead to interesting failure scenarios, such as the Autoscaler example described earlier in "Capacity planning" on page 295.

Operational system failures can cause our SLOs to break. If our data freshness SLO is broken, no customer action is expected; customers must simply wait for their data to arrive. However, if our skewness or completeness SLOs are breached, we might need to involve customers, as data quality is compromised. When we detect either completeness or skewness issues, the impacted events require reprocessing to be delivered correctly:

- To deal with incompleteness, events need to be redelivered from the last checkpoint known to be good.
- To deal with excessive skewness, already delivered events are reshuffled and assigned to their correct hourly buckets.

Both redelivery and reshuffling of events are done manually. After the delivered events are modified, we strongly advise our customers to reprocess them to produce data of sufficient quality.

Summary

Spotify's event delivery system has evolved over the years. Because previous iterations were far less reliable, our engineers were paged every few nights. We spent the majority of our development sprints on incident remediations and postmortems. When designing the current incarnation, we focused on building a modularized system that does one core thing well: deliver events. Additionally, we wanted to provide event delivery as a product to the rest of Spotify. To achieve this, we needed to define and meet SLOs so that we could set clear expectations for our customers.

---

8 The external service provider guarantees SLAs and has its own on-call team to ensure the product is meeting these SLAs.

We employ a range of strategies to keep the service up and running—from well-documented on-call procedures to using well-proven external services (such as Google Cloud Pub/Sub). Furthermore, a single team is responsible for the development and operation of the system throughout its entire lifecycle. This development structure allows us to use the team experience we gain from maintaining the system to continually improve it.

As a result of these efforts, we now have a reliable system that allows us to focus our time on meeting more ambitious completeness, skewness, and timeliness SLOs. This results in better usability and a better overall customer experience.

Conclusion

Applying SRE best practices to pipelines can help you make smart design choices and develop automation tools so that pipelines are easy to operate, scale more effectively, and are more reliable. Spotify's event delivery system is an example of a pipeline built and operated with core SRE principles in mind, using a variety of technologies—from in-house, Google Cloud, and third parties—chosen to meet the customer's need for timely data processing. Without proper care for operational best practices, pipelines may be more prone to failure and require a lot of manual work, especially during periods of growth, migrations, feature launches, or cleanup after outages. As with any complex system design, it is important to know your requirements and the SLOs you have chosen to keep, assess the available technology, and document the design and how to perform common tasks.

## CHAPTER 14

Configuration Design and Best Practices

By Štěpán Davidovič
with Niall Richard Murphy, Christophe Kalt, and Betsy Beyer

Configuring systems is a common SRE task everywhere. It can be a tiring and frustratingly detailed activity, particularly if the engineer isn't deeply familiar with the system they're configuring or the configuration hasn't been designed with clarity and usability in mind. Most commonly, you perform configuration in one of two scenarios: during initial setup when you have plenty of time, or during an emergency reconfiguration when you need to handle an incident.

This chapter examines configuration from the perspective of someone who designs and maintains an infrastructure system. It describes our experiences and strategies for designing configuration in a safe and sustainable way.

What Is Configuration?

When we deploy software systems, we do not think of them as fixed and never-changing. Ever-evolving business needs, infrastructure requirements, and other factors mean that systems are constantly in flux. When we need to change system behavior quickly, and the change process requires an expensive, lengthy rebuild and redeployment process, a code change won't suffice. Instead, configuration—which we can loosely define as a human-computer interface for modifying system behavior—provides a low-overhead way to change system functionality. SREs take advantage of this on a regular basis, when deploying systems and tuning their performance, as well as during incident response.

We can reason about systems as having three key components:

- The software
- The data set that the system works with
- The system configuration

While we can intuitively identify each of these components, they are often far from clearly separated. For example, many systems use programming languages for configuration, or at least have the capability to reference programming languages. Examples include Apache and modules, such as mod_lua (*http://bit.ly/2HcOqen*) and its request hooks, or the window manager XMonad and its Haskell-based configuration (*http://bit.ly/2JlpXJg*). Similarly, data sets might contain code, such as stored SQL procedures, which can amount to complex applications.

A good configuration interface allows quick, confident, and testable configuration changes. When users don't have a straightforward way to update configuration, mistakes are more likely. Users experience increased cognitive load and a significant learning curve.

Configuration and Reliability

Because our systems are ultimately managed by humans, humans are responsible for configuration. The quality of the human-computer interface of a system's configuration impacts an organization's ability to run that system reliably. The impact of a well-crafted (or poorly crafted) configuration interface is similar to the impact of code quality on system maintainability over time.

However, configuration tends to differ meaningfully from code in several aspects. Changing a system's capabilities via code is typically a lengthy and involved process, involving small incremental changes, code reviews, and testing. In contrast, changing a single configuration option can have dramatic changes on functionality—for example, one bad firewall configuration rule may lock you out of your own system. Unlike code, configuration often lives in an untested (or even untestable) environment.

System configuration changes may need to be made under significant pressure. During an incident, a configuration system that can be simply and safely adjusted is essential. Consider the interface design of early airplanes: confusing controls and indicators led to accidents. Research at the time showed that operator failures were frequent, regardless of pilot skill or experience.[1] The link between usability and reliability translates to computing systems. Consider what happens if we swap a control stick and dial indicators for *.conf* files and monitoring graphs.

---

1 Kim Vicente, *The Human Factor* (New York: Routledge, 2006), 71–6.

Separating Philosophy and Mechanics

We usually discuss configuration when designing new software or assembling a new system out of existing software components. How will we configure it? How will the configuration load? We'll separate the overarching topic of configuration into two parts: configuration philosophy and configuration mechanics.

Configuration philosophy pertains to aspects of configuration that are completely independent of the chosen language and other mechanics. Our discussion of philosophy encompasses how to structure the configuration, how to achieve the correct level of abstraction, and how to support diverging use cases seamlessly.

Our discussion of mechanics covers topics like language design, deployment strategies, and interactions with other systems. This chapter focuses less on mechanics, partly because topics like language choice are already being discussed across the industry. Additionally, because a given organization may already have strong outside requirements like preexisting configuration infrastructure, configuration mechanics aren't easily generalizable. The following chapter on Jsonnet gives a practical example of configuration mechanics—in particular, language design—in existing software.

Discussing philosophy and mechanics separately allows us to reason more clearly about configuration. In practice, implementation details like configuration language (be it XML or Lua) don't matter if configuration requires a huge amount of user input that's difficult to understand. Conversely, even the simplest configuration inputs can cause problems if they must be entered into a very cumbersome interface. Consider the (very) old Linux kernel configuration process: configuration updates had to be made through a command-line terminal that required a sequence of commands to set each parameter. To make even the simplest correction, users had to start the configuration process from scratch.[2]

Configuration Philosophy

This section discusses aspects of configuration that are completely independent of implementation, so these topics generalize across all implementations.

In the following philosophy, our ideal configuration is no configuration at all. In this ideal world, the system automatically recognizes the correct configuration based on deployment, workload, or pieces of configuration that already existed when the new system was deployed. Of course, for many systems, this ideal is unlikely to be attaina-

---

2 While clearly a hyperbole, a Reddit thread about the worst volume control interface (*http://bit.ly/2J6JA8F*) can provide insight into the difference between good and bad mechanics of answering the same question, "What should the volume be?"

ble in practice. However, it highlights the desirable direction of configuration: away from a large number of tunables and toward simplicity.

Historically, mission-critical systems offered a large amount of controls (which amount to system configuration), but also required significant human operator training. Consider the complex array of operator controls in the NASA spacecraft control center in Figure 14-1. In modern computer systems, such training is no longer feasible for the majority of the industry.

Figure 14-1. Control panel in the NASA spacecraft control center, illustrating possibly very complex configuration

While this ideal reduces the amount of control we can exercise over a system, it decreases both the surface area for error and cognitive load on the operator. As the complexity of systems grows, operator cognitive load becomes increasingly important.

When we've applied these principles in practical systems at Google, they typically resulted in easy, broad adoption and low cost for internal user support.

Configuration Asks Users Questions

Regardless of what you're configuring and how you're configuring it, the human-computer interaction ultimately boils down to an interface that asks users questions, requesting inputs on how the system should operate. This model of conceptualization holds true regardless of whether users are editing XML files or using a configuration GUI wizard.

In modern software systems, we can approach this model from two different perspectives:

Infrastructure-centric view
> It's useful to offer as many configuration knobs as possible. Doing so enables users to tune the system to their exact needs. The more knobs, the better, because the system can be tuned to perfection.

User-centric view
> Configuration asks questions about infrastructure that the user must answer before they can get back to working on their actual business goal. The fewer knobs, the better, because answering configuration questions is a chore.

Driven by our initial philosophy of minimizing user inputs, we favor the user-centric view.

The implications of this software design decision extend beyond configuration. Focusing configuration on the user means that your software needs to be designed with a particular set of use cases for your key audience. This requires user research. In contrast, an infrastructure-centric approach means that your software effectively provides base infrastructure, but turning it into a practical system requires considerable configuration from the user. These models are not in strict conflict, but attempting to reconcile them can be quite difficult. Perhaps counterintuitively, limited configuration options can lead to better adoption than extremely versatile software—onboarding effort is substantially lower because the software mostly works "out of the box."

Systems that begin from an infrastructure-centric view may move toward a more user-centric focus as the system matures, by removing some configuration knobs via various means (some of which are discussed in subsequent sections).

Questions Should Be Close to User Goals

As we follow the philosophy of user-centric configuration, we want to make sure users can easily relate to the questions we ask. We can think of the nature of user inputs on a spectrum: on one end, the user describes their needs in their own terms (fewer configuration options); on the other end, the user describes exactly how the system should implement their needs (more configuration options).

Let's use making tea as an analogy to configuring a system. With fewer configuration options, a user can ask for "hot green tea" and get roughly what they want. On the opposite end of the spectrum, a user can specify the whole process: water volume, boiling temperature, tea brand and flavor, steeping time, tea cup type, and tea volume in the cup. Using more configuration options might be closer to perfection, but the effort required to adhere to such detail might cost more than the marginal benefit of a near-perfect drink.

This analogy is helpful both to the users and the developers who work on the configuration system. When a user specifies exact steps, the system needs to follow them. But when the user instead describes their high-level goals, the system can evolve over time and improve how it implements these goals. A good upfront understanding of user goals for the system is a necessary first step here.

For a practical illustration of how this spectrum plays out, consider job scheduling. Imagine you have a one-off analytical process to run. Systems like Kubernetes (*https://kubernetes.io/*) or Mesos (*http://mesos.apache.org/*) enable you to meet your *actual* goal of running analysis, without burdening you with minute details like deciding which physical machine(s) your analytical process should run on.

Mandatory and Optional Questions

A given configuration setup might contain two types of questions: mandatory and optional. Mandatory questions must be answered for the configuration to provide any functionality at all. One example might be who to charge for an operation. Optional questions don't dictate core functionality, but answering them can improve the quality of the function—for example, setting a number of worker processes.

In order to remain user-centric and easy to adopt, your system should minimize the number of mandatory configuration questions. This is not an easy task, but it's important. While one might argue that adding one or two small steps incurs little cost, the life of an engineer is often an endless chain of individually small steps. The principled reduction of these small steps can dramatically improve productivity.

An initial set of mandatory questions often includes the questions you thought about when designing the system. The easiest path to reduce mandatory questions is to convert them to optional questions, which means providing default answers that apply safely and effectively to most, if not all, users. For example, instead of requiring the user to define whether an execution should be dry-run or not, we can simply do dry-run by default.

While this default value is often a static, hardcoded value, it doesn't have to be. It can be dynamically determined based on other properties of the system. Taking advantage of dynamic determination can further simplify your configuration.

For context, consider the following examples of dynamic defaults. A computationally intensive system might typically decide how many computation threads to deploy via a configuration control. Its dynamic default deploys as many threads as the system (or container) has execution cores. In this case, a single static default isn't useful. Dynamic default means we don't need to ask the user to determine the right number of threads for the system to deploy on a given platform. Similarly, a Java binary deployed alone in a container could automatically adjust its heap limits depending on memory available in the container. These two examples of dynamic defaults reflect common deployments. If you need to restrict resource usage, it's useful to be able to override dynamic defaults in the configuration.

The implemented dynamic defaults might not work out for everyone. Over time, users might prefer different approaches and ask for greater control over the dynamic defaults. If a significant portion of configuration users report problems with dynamic defaults, it's likely that your decision logic no longer matches the requirements of your current user base. Consider implementing broad improvements that enable your dynamic defaults to run without requiring additional configuration knobs. If only a small fraction of users are unhappy, they may be better off manually setting configuration options. Implementing more complexity in the system creates more work for users (e.g., increased cognitive load to read documentation).

When choosing default answers for optional questions, regardless of whether you opt for static or dynamic defaults, think carefully about the impact of your choice. Experience shows that most users will use the default, so this is both a chance and a responsibility. You can subtly nudge people in the right direction, but designating the wrong default will do a lot of harm. For example, consider configuration defaults and their impact outside of computer science. Countries where the default for organ donors is opt-in (and individuals can opt out if they're so inclined) have dramatically greater ratios of organ donors (*http://bit.ly/2kEGp9c*) than countries with an opt-out default.[3] Simply selecting a specific default has a profound impact on medical options throughout the entire system.

Some optional questions start without a clear use case. You may want to remove these questions altogether. A large number of optional questions might confuse the user, so you should add configuration knobs only when motivated by a real need. Finally, if your configuration language happens to use the concept of inheritance, it is useful to be able to revert to the default value for any optional question in the leaf configurations.

---

3 Full text: *http://www.dangoldstein.com/papers/DefaultsScience.pdf.*

Escaping Simplicity

Thus far, we've discussed reducing the configuration of a system to its simplest form. However, the configuration system may need to account for power users as well. To return to our tea analogy, what if we really need to steep the tea for a particular duration?

One strategy to accommodate power users is to find the lowest common denominator of what regular users and power users require, and settle on that level of complexity as the default. The downside is that this decision impacts everyone; even the simplest use cases now need to be considered in low-level terms.

By thinking about configuration in terms of optional overrides of default behavior, the user configures "green tea," and then adds "steep the tea for five minutes." In this model, the default configuration is still high-level and close to the user's goals, but the user can fine-tune low-level aspects. This approach is not novel. We can draw parallels to high-level programming languages like C++ or Java, which enable programmers to include machine (or VM) instructions in code otherwise written in the high-level language. In some consumer software, we see screens with advanced options that can offer more fine-grained control than the typical view.

It's useful to think about optimizing for the sum of hours spent configuring across the organization. Consider not only the act of configuration itself, but also the decision paralysis users might experience when presented with many options, the time it takes to correct the configuration after taking a wrong turn, the slower rate of change due to lower confidence, and more. When you are considering configuration design alternatives, the option that accomplishes a complex configuration in fewer but significantly harder steps may be preferable if it makes supporting the most common use cases significantly easier.

If you find that more than a small subset of your users need a complex configuration, you may have incorrectly identified the common use cases. If so, revisit the initial product assumptions for your system and conduct additional user research.

Mechanics of Configuration

Our discussion up to this point has covered configuration philosophy. This section shifts focus to the mechanics of how a user interacts with the configuration.

Separate Configuration and Resulting Data

Which language to store the configuration in is an inevitable question. You could choose to have pure data like in an INI, YAML, or XML file. Alternatively, the configuration could be stored in a higher-level language that allows for much more flexible configuration.

Fundamentally, all questions the user is asked boil down to static information. This may include obviously static answers to questions like "How many threads should be used?" But even "What function should be used for every request?" is just a static reference to a function.

To answer the age-old question of whether configuration is code or data, our experience has shown that having *both* code and data, but separating the two, is optimal. The system infrastructure should operate on plain static data, which can be in formats like Protocol Buffers (*http://bit.ly/1HhFC5L*), YAML (*http://yaml.org/*), or JSON (*https://www.json.org/*). This choice does not imply that the user needs to actually interact with pure data. Users can interact with a higher-level interface that generates this data. This data format can, however, be used by APIs that allow further stacking of systems and automation.

This high-level interface can be almost anything. It can be a high-level language like Python-based Domain-Specific Language (DSL), Lua, or purpose-built languages, such as Jsonnet (which we will discuss in more detail in Chapter 15). We can think of such an interface as a compilation, similar to how we treat C++ code.[4] The high-level interface might also be no language at all, with the configuration ingested by a web UI.

Starting with a configuration UI that's deliberately separated from its static data representation means the system has flexibility for deployment. Various organizations may have different cultural norms or product requirements (such as using specific languages within the company or needing to externalize configuration to end users), and a system this versatile can be adapted to support diverse configuration requirements. Such a system can also effortlessly support multiple languages.[5] See Figure 14-2.

This separation can be completely invisible to the user. The user's common path may be to edit files in the configuration language while everything else happens behind the scenes. For example, once the user submits changes to the system, the newly stored configuration is automatically compiled into raw data.[6]

---

4 Jsonnet is used to compile into Kubernetes YAML, providing a real-world illustration for this parallel. See *http://ksonnet.heptio.com/*.

5 This can be useful when an organization performs migrations to new technologies, integrates acquisitions, or focuses on shared infrastructure but otherwise has divergent development and system management practices.

6 There are various practical ways to automate compiling a new configuration into raw data. For example, if you store your configuration in a version control system, a post-commit hook can facilitate this. Alternatively, a periodic update process can perform this, at the cost of some delay.

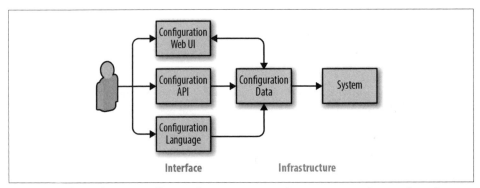

Figure 14-2. Configuration flow with a separate configuration interface and configuration data infrastructure. Note the web UI typically also displays the current configuration, making the relationship bidirectional.

Once the static configuration data is obtained, it can also be used in data analysis. For instance, if the generated configuration data is in JSON format, it can be loaded into PostgreSQL and analyzed with database queries (*http://bit.ly/2szj3W3*). As the infrastructure owner, you can then quickly and easily query for which configuration parameters are being used and by whom. This query is useful for identifying features you can remove or measuring the impact of a buggy option.

When consuming the final configuration data, you will find it useful to also store metadata about how the configuration was ingested. For example, if you know the data came from a configuration file in Jsonnet or you have the full path to the original before it was compiled into data, you can track down the configuration authors.

It is also acceptable for the configuration language to be static data. For example, both your infrastructure and interface might use plain JSON. However, avoid tight coupling between the data format you use as the interface and the data format you use internally. For example, you may use a data structure internally that contains the data structure consumed from configuration. The internal data structure might also contain completely implementation-specific data that never needs to be surfaced outside of the system.

Importance of Tooling

Tooling can make the difference between a chaotic nightmare and a sustainable and scalable system, but it is often overlooked when configuration systems are designed. This section discusses the key tools that should be available for an optimal configuration system.

Semantic validation

While most languages offer syntax validation out of the box, don't overlook semantic validation. Even if your configuration is syntactically valid, is it likely to do useful things? Or did the user reference a nonexistent directory (due to a typo), or need a thousand times more RAM than they actually have (because units aren't what the user expected)?

Validating that the configuration is semantically meaningful, to the maximum extent possible, can help prevent outages and decrease operational costs. For every possible misconfiguration, we should ask ourselves if we could prevent it at the moment the user commits the configuration, rather than after changes are submitted.

Configuration syntax

While it's key to ensure that configuration accomplishes what the user wants, it is also important to remove mechanical obstacles. From a syntax perspective, the configuration language should offer the following:

Syntax highlighting in editors (used within the company)
    Often, you've already solved this by reusing an existing language. However, domain-specific languages may have additional "syntactic sugar" that can benefit from specialized highlighting.

Linter
    Use a linter to identify common inconsistencies in language use. Pylint (*https://www.pylint.org/*) is one popular language example.

Automatic syntax formatter
    Built-in standardization minimizes relatively unimportant discussions about formatting and decreases cognitive load as contributors switch projects. Standard formatting may also allow for easier automatic editing, which is helpful in systems used broadly within a large organization. Examples of autoformatters in existing languages include clang-format[7] and autopep8 (*http://bit.ly/2LdJFDL*).

These tools enable users to write and edit configuration with confidence that their syntax is correct.[8] Incorrect indentation in whitespace-oriented configs can have potentially great consequences—some of which standard formatting can prevent.

---

7 Although C++ is unlikely to be used for configuration, clang-format (*http://bit.ly/2swrrG0*) nicely demonstrates that even a language more complex than most languages used for configuration can in fact be fully autoformatted.

8 In very large organizations, it is also useful to be able to annotate pieces of a broadly reused configuration that has been deprecated. When a replacement is available, automatic rewriting tools facilitate centralized changes, helping to avoid legacy issues.

Ownership and Change Tracking

Because configuration can potentially impact critical systems of companies and institutions, it's important to ensure good user isolation, and to understand what changes happened in the system. As mentioned in Chapter 10, an effective postmortem culture avoids blaming individuals. However, it's helpful both during an incident and while you're conducting a postmortem to know who changed a configuration, and to understand how the configuration change impacted the system. This holds true whether the incident is due to an accident or a malicious actor.

Each configuration snippet for the system should have a clear owner. For example, if you use configuration files, their directories might be owned by a single production group. If files in a directory can only have one owner, it's much easier to track who makes changes.

Versioning configuration, regardless of how it is performed, allows you to go back in time to see what the configuration looked like at any given point in time. Checking configuration files into a versioning system, such as Subversion or Git, is a common practice nowadays, but this practice is equally important for configuration ingested by web UI or remote APIs. You may also wish to have tighter coupling between the configuration and the software being configured. By doing so, you can avoid inadvertently configuring features that are either not yet available or no longer supported in the software.

On a related note, it is useful (and sometimes required) to log both changes to the configuration and the resulting application to the system. The simple act of committing a new version of a configuration does not always mean that the configuration is directly applied (more on that later). When a system configuration change is suspected as the culprit during an incident response, it is useful to be able to quickly determine the full set of configuration edits that went into the change. This enables confident rollbacks, and the ability to notify parties whose configurations were impacted.

Safe Configuration Change Application

As discussed earlier, configuration is an easy way to make large changes to system functionality, but it is often not unit-tested or even easily testable. Since we want to avoid reliability incidents, we should inspect what the safe application of a configuration change means.

For a configuration change to be safe, it must have three main properties:

- The ability to be deployed gradually, avoiding an all-or-nothing change
- The ability to roll back the change if it proves dangerous

- Automatic rollback (or at a minimum, the ability to stop progress) if the change leads to loss of operator control

When deploying a new configuration, it is important to avoid a global all-at-once push. Instead, push the new configuration out gradually—doing so allows you to detect issues and abort a problematic push before causing a 100% outage. This is one reason why tools such as Kubernetes use a rolling update strategy for updating software or configuration instead of updating every pod all at once. (See Chapter 16 for related discussions.)

The ability to roll back is important for decreasing incident duration. Rolling back the offending configuration can mitigate an outage much more quickly than attempting to patch it with a temporary fix—there is inherently lower confidence that a patch will improve things.

 In order to be able to roll forward and roll back configuration, it must be hermetic. Configuration that requires external resources that can change outside of its hermetic environment can be very hard to roll back. For example, configuration stored in a version control system that references data on a network filesystem is not hermetic.

Last but not least, the system should be especially careful when handling changes that might lead to sudden loss of operator control. On desktop systems, screen resolution changes often prompt a countdown and reset if a user does not confirm changes. This is because an incorrect monitor setting might prevent the user from reverting the change. Similarly, it is common for system admins to accidentally firewall themselves out of the system that they are currently setting up.

These principles are not unique to configuration and apply to other methods of changing deployed systems, such as upgrading binaries or pushing new data sets.

Conclusion

Trivial configuration changes can impact a production system in dramatic ways, so we need to deliberately design configuration to mitigate these risks. Configuration design carries aspects of both API and UI design and should be purposeful—not just a side effect of system implementation. Separating configuration into philosophy and mechanics helps us gain clarity as we design internal systems, and enables us to scope discussion correctly.

Applying these recommendations takes time and diligence. For an example of how we've applied these principles in practice, see the ACM Queue article on Canary Analysis Service (*http://bit.ly/2xyjq9f*). When designing this practical internal system, we spent about a month trying to reduce mandatory questions and finding good answers for optional questions. Our efforts created a simple configuration system. Because it was easy to use, it was widely adopted internally. We've seen little need for user support—since users can easily understand the system, they can make changes with confidence. Of course, we have not eliminated misconfigurations and user support entirely, nor do we ever expect to.

## CHAPTER 15

Configuration Specifics

By Dave Cunningham and Misha Brukman
with Christophe Kalt and Betsy Beyer

Managing production systems is one of the many ways SREs provide value to an organization. The task of configuring and running applications in production requires insight into how those systems are put together and how they work. When things go wrong, the on-call engineer needs to know exactly where the configurations are and how to change them. This responsibility can become a burden if a team or organization hasn't invested in addressing configuration-related toil.

This book covers the subject of toil at length (see Chapter 6). If your SRE team is burdened with a lot of configuration-related toil, we hope that implementing some of the ideas presented in this chapter will help you reclaim some of the time you spend making configuration changes.

Configuration-Induced Toil

At the start of a project's lifecycle, configuration is usually relatively lightweight and straightforward. You might have a few files in a *data-only* format like INI (*http://bit.ly/2HbuBo2*), JSON (*http://json.org*), YAML (*http://yaml.org*), or XML. Managing these files requires little toil. As the number of applications, servers, and variations increases over time, configuration can become very complex and verbose. For example, you might have originally "changed a setting" by editing one configuration file, but now you have to update configuration files in multiple locations. Reading such configuration is also hard, as important differences are hidden in a sea of irrelevant duplicated details. We can characterize this configuration-related toil as *replication toil*: the mundane task of managing configuration replicated across a system. This kind of toil isn't limited to large organizations and huge systems—it's especially common to microservice architectures with many independently configured components.

Engineers often respond to replication toil by building automation or a configuration framework. They aim to remove duplication in the config system, and to make configuration easier to understand and maintain. Reusing techniques from software engineering, this approach often makes use of a "configuration language." Google SRE has created a number of configuration languages with the aim of reducing toil for our largest and most complex production systems.

Unfortunately, this tactic doesn't necessarily eliminate configuration toil. Freed from an overwhelming number of individual configs, the project (and its config corpus) grows with renewed energy. Inevitably, you run up against *complexity toil*: the challenging and frustrating task of dealing with the emergent and sometimes undesirable behaviors of complex automation. This kind of toil typically materializes in larger organizations (10+ engineers) and compounds with growth. The earlier you can tackle complexity toil, the better; the size and complexity of configuration will only grow over time.

Reducing Configuration-Induced Toil

If your project is riddled with configuration-related toil, you have a few basic strategies for improving the situation.

In rare cases, and if your application is custom-built, you might opt to remove the configuration altogether. The application may be naturally better than a configuration language at handling certain aspects of configuration: it might make sense for the application to assign defaults because it has access to information about the machine, or to vary some values dynamically because it can scale according to load.

If removing configuration is not an option, and *replication toil* is becoming a problem, consider automation to reduce the duplication in your configuration corpus. You might integrate a new configuration language, or you might need to improve or replace your existing configuration setup.[1] The next section, "Critical Properties and Pitfalls of Configuration Systems" on page 317, provides some guidance on choosing or designing that system.

If you go the route of setting up a new configuration framework, you'll need to integrate the configuration language with the application that needs to be configured. "Integrating an Existing Application: Kubernetes" on page 322 uses Kubernetes as an example of an existing application to be integrated, and "Integrating Custom Applications (In-House Software)" on page 326 gives some more general advice. These sections walk through some examples using Jsonnet (which we chose as a representative configuration language for illustration purposes).

---

[1] Note that you may be able to write software to convert your old configuration language to the new language; however, if your original source language is nonstandard or broken, this isn't a viable option.

Once you have a configuration system in place to help with replication toil—whether you're already committed to your existing solution, or you choose to implement a new configuration language—the best practices in "Effectively Operating a Configuration System" on page 329, "When to Evaluate Configuration" on page 331, and "Guarding Against Abusive Configuration" on page 333 should be helpful in optimizing your setup, no matter which language you're using. Adopting those processes and tools can help minimize complexity toil.

Critical Properties and Pitfalls of Configuration Systems

Chapter 14 outlined some critical properties of any configuration system. In addition to generic ideal requirements like lightweightness, ease of learning, simplicity, and expressive power, an efficient configuration system must:

- Support configuration health, engineer confidence, and productivity via *tooling* for managing the config files (linters, debuggers, formatters, IDE integration, etc.).

- Provide *hermetic* evaluation of configuration for rollbacks and general replayability.

- *Separate config and data* to allow for easy analysis of the config and a range of configuration interfaces.

It is not widely understood that these properties are critical, and arriving at our current understanding was indeed a journey. During this journey, Google invented several configuration systems that lacked these critical properties. We were not alone, either. Despite the great variety of popular configuration systems, it is difficult to find one that does not fall foul of at least one of the following pitfalls.

Pitfall 1: Failing to Recognize Configuration as a Programming Language Problem

If you're not intentionally designing a language, then it's highly unlikely the "language" you'll end up with is a good one.

While configuration languages describe data rather than behavior, they still have the other characteristics of programming languages. If our configuration strategy starts with the objective of using a data-only format, programming language features tend to creep through the back door. Rather than remaining a *data-only* language, the format becomes an esoteric and complex *programming* language.

For example, some systems add a count attribute to the schema of a virtual machine (VM) being provisioned. This attribute is not a property of the VM itself, but instead indicates that you want more than one of them. While useful, this is a feature of a programming language, not a data format, because it requires an external evaluator or interpreter. A classical programming language approach would use logic outside the artifact, such as a for loop or list comprehension, to generate more VMs as required.

Another example is a configuration language that accrues string interpolation rules (*http://bit.ly/2LQyXnZ*) instead of supporting general expressions. The strings appear to be "just data," although they can actually contain complex code, including data structure operations, checksums, base64 encoding, and so on.

The popular YAML + Jinja solution also has drawbacks. Simple pure-data formats such as XML, JSON, YAML, and text-formatted protocol buffers are excellent choices for pure-data use cases. Likewise, textual templating engines such as Jinja2 or Go templates are excellent for HTML templating. But when combined in a configuration language, they become difficult for both humans and tools to maintain and analyze. In all of these cases, this pitfall leaves us with a complex esoteric "language" that isn't suited to tooling.

Pitfall 2: Designing Accidental or Ad Hoc Language Features

SREs typically feel configuration usability problems when operating systems at scale. A new language won't have good tooling support (IDE support, good linters), and developing custom tooling is painful if the language has undocumented or esoteric semantics.

Adding ad hoc programming language features to a simple config format over time might create a feature-complete solution, but ad hoc languages are more complex and usually have less expressive power than their formally designed equivalents. They also risk developing gotchas and idiosyncrasies because their authors couldn't consider the interaction between features ahead of time.

Instead of hoping your configuration system won't grow complex enough to need simple programming constructs, it's better to consider these requirements at the initial design phase.

Pitfall 3: Building Too Much Domain-Specific Optimization

The smaller the user base is for a new domain-specific solution, the longer you have to wait to accumulate enough users to justify building tooling. Engineers are unwilling to spend time understanding the language properly because it has little applicability outside this domain. Learning resources like Stack Overflow (*https://stackoverflow.com/*) are less likely to be available.

Pitfall 4: Interleaving "Configuration Evaluation" with "Side Effects"

Side effects include either making changes to external systems, or consulting out-of-band data sources (DNS, VM IDs, latest build versions) during configuration runs.

Systems that allow these side effects *violate hermeticity,* and also prevent the *separation of config from data.* In an extreme case, it is impossible to debug your config without spending money by reserving cloud resources. In order to allow separation of config and data, first evaluate the config, then make the resulting data available to the user to analyze, and only then allow for side effects.

Pitfall 5: Using an Existing General-Purpose Scripting Language Like Python, Ruby, or Lua

This seems like a trivial way to avoid the first four pitfalls, but implementations that use a general-purpose scripting language are heavyweight and/or need intrusive sandboxing to ensure hermeticity. Since general-purpose languages can access the local system, security considerations may also call for sandboxing.

Additionally, we can't assume that the people maintaining configuration will be familiar with all of these languages.

The desire to avoid these pitfalls led to the development of reusable domain-specific languages (DSLs) for configuration, such as HOCON (*http://bit.ly/2xyUPRT*), Flabbergast (*http://bit.ly/2kIuDec*), Dhall (*http://bit.ly/2J9Bx6E*), and Jsonnet (*http://jsonnet.org*). We recommend using an existing DSL for configuration. Even if a DSL seems too powerful for your needs, you may need the additional functionality at some point, and you can always restrict the functionality of the language using an in-house style guide.

A Very Quick Introduction to Jsonnet

Jsonnet is a hermetic open source DSL that can be used as a library or command-line tool to provide configuration for any application. It is used widely both inside and outside Google.[2]

The language is designed to be familiar to programmers: it uses Python-like syntax, object orientation, and functional constructs. It is an extension of JSON, meaning that a JSON file is simply a Jsonnet program that outputs itself. Jsonnet is more permissive with quotes and commas than JSON, and supports comments. More importantly, it adds computational constructs.

---

2 While fields from computational biology to video games use Jsonnet, the most enthusiastic adopters are from the Kubernetes community. Box.com uses Jsonnet to describe the workloads that run on their Kubernetes-based internal infrastructure platform. Databricks and Bitnami also use the language extensively.

While you don't need to be particularly familiar with Jsonnet syntax to follow the rest of this chapter, spending just a few moments reading the online tutorial (*http://bit.ly/2xIUZWX*) can help orient you.

 There is no dominant configuration language at Google or among our reader base, but we needed to choose *some* language that allows us to provide examples. This chapter uses Jsonnet to show practical examples of the recommendations we provide in Chapter 14.

If you aren't already committed to a particular configuration language and want to use Jsonnet, you can directly apply the examples in this chapter. In all cases, we've done our best to make it as easy as possible for you to abstract the underlying lesson from the code examples.

Additionally, some of the examples explore concepts (like Turing completeness) that you might expect to find in a programming book. We have taken great care to dive only as deep as required to explain a subtlety that has actually bitten us in production. In most complex systems—and certainly with respect to configurations—the failures are at the edges.

Integrating a Configuration Language

This section uses Jsonnet to discuss how to integrate a configuration language with the application you need to configure, but the same techniques also transfer to other configuration languages.

Generating Config in Specific Formats

A configuration language might natively output in the correct format. For example, Jsonnet outputs JSON, which is compatible with many applications. JSON is also sufficient for consumers of languages that extend JSON, such as JavaScript, YAML, or HashiCorp's Configuration Language (*https://github.com/hashicorp/hcl*). If this is your situation, you don't need to perform any further integration work.

For other configuration formats that are not natively supported:

1. You need to find a way to represent configuration data within the configuration language. Usually, this is not hard because configuration values like maps, lists, strings, and other primitive values are generic and available in all languages.

2. Once this data is represented in the config language, you can use the constructs of that language to reduce duplication (and thus, toil).

3. You need to write (or reuse) a serialization function for the necessary output format. For example, the Jsonnet standard library has functions for outputting INI and XML from its internal JSON-like representation. If configuration data resists representation within the configuration language (for example, a Bash script), you can use basic string templating techniques as a last resort. You can find practical examples at *http://bit.ly/2La0zDe*.

Driving Multiple Applications

Once you can drive arbitrary existing applications from the config language, you might be able to target several applications from the same config. If your applications use different config formats, you'll need to perform some conversion work. Once you're able to generate configuration in the necessary formats, you can easily unify, synchronize, and eliminate repetition across your entire config corpus. Given the prevalence of JSON and JSON-based formats, you may not even have to generate different formats—for example, this is true if you use a deployment architecture that uses GCP Deployment Manager (*http://bit.ly/2JkMq9f*), AWS Cloud Formation (*https://amzn.to/2kFPkHF*), or Terraform (*https://www.terraform.io/*) for base infrastructure, plus Kubernetes for containers.

At this point, you can:

- Output an Nginx web server configuration and a Terraform firewall configuration from a single Jsonnet evaluation that defines the port only once.
- Configure your monitoring dashboards, retention policies, and alert notification pipelines from the same files.
- Manage the performance tradeoff between VM startup scripts and disk image-building scripts by moving initialization commands from one list to another.

After you unite disparate configs in one place, you have many opportunities to refine and abstract the config. Configs can even be nested—for example, a Cassandra config (*https://cassandra.apache.org/*) may be embedded inside the Deployment Manager config of its base infrastructure or inside a Kubernetes ConfigMap. A good configuration language can handle any awkward string quoting and generally make this operation natural and simple.

To make it easy to write many different files for various applications, Jsonnet has a mode that expects config execution to yield a single JSON object that maps filenames to file content (formatted as needed). You can simulate this facility in other configuration languages by emitting a map from string to string and using a postprocessing step or wrapper script to write the files.

Integrating an Existing Application: Kubernetes

Kubernetes makes for an interesting case study for a couple of reasons:

- Jobs running on Kubernetes need to be configured, and their configuration can become complex.

- Kubernetes does not come with a bundled configuration language (not even an ad hoc one, thankfully).

Kubernetes users with minimally complex objects simply use YAML. Users with larger infrastructure extend their Kubernetes workflow with languages like Jsonnet to provide the abstraction facilities needed at that scale.

What Kubernetes Provides

Kubernetes is an open source system for orchestrating containerized workloads on a cluster of machines. Its API allows you to manage the containers themselves and many important details, such as communication between containers, communication in/out of the cluster, load balancing, storage, progressive rollout, and autoscaling. Each item of configuration is represented with a JSON object that can be managed via an API endpoint. The command-line tool kubectl lets you read these objects from disk and send them to the API.

On disk, the JSON objects are actually encoded as YAML streams.[3] YAML is easily readable and converts easily to JSON via commonly available libraries. The out-of-the-box user experience involves writing YAML files that represent Kubernetes objects and running kubectl to deploy them to a cluster.

To learn about best practices for configuring Kubernetes, see the Kubernetes documentation on that topic (*http://bit.ly/2J4kqr5*).

Example Kubernetes Config

YAML, the user interface to Kubernetes configuration, provides some simple features like comments, and has a concise syntax that most people prefer to raw JSON. However, YAML falls short when it comes to abstraction: it only provides anchors,[4] which are rarely useful in practice and are not supported by Kubernetes.

---

3 A YAML stream is a file that contains many YAML documents separated by "---".

4 YAML Specification §6.9.2.

Suppose you want to replicate a Kubernetes object four times with different name-spaces, labels, and other minor variations. Following the best practices of immutable infrastructure, you store the config of all four variants, duplicating the other identical aspects of the configuration. The following code snippet presents one variant (for the sake of brevity, we omit the other three files):

```
# example1.yaml
apiVersion: v1
kind: Service
metadata:
  labels:
    app: guestbook
    tier: frontend
  name: frontend
  namespace: prod
spec:
  externalTrafficPolicy: Cluster
  ports:
  - port: 80
    protocol: TCP
    targetPort: 80
  selector:
    app: guestbook
    tier: frontend
  sessionAffinity: None
  type: NodePort
```

The variants are hard to read and maintain because the important differences are obscured.

Integrating the Configuration Language

As discussed in "Configuration-Induced Toil" on page 315, managing a large number of YAML files can take a significant amount of time. A configuration language can help simplify this task. The most straightforward approach is to emit a single Kubernetes object from each execution of Jsonnet, then pipe the resulting JSON directly into kubectl, which processes the JSON as if it's YAML. Alternatively, you could emit a YAML stream (a sequence of such objects[5]) or a single kubectl list object, or have Jsonnet emit multiple files from the same config. For further discussion, see the Jsonnet website (*http://bit.ly/2snCIcC*).

Developers should be aware that in general, YAML allows you to write configs that are not expressible in JSON (and therefore, can't be generated by Jsonnet). YAML configs can contain exceptional IEEE floating-point values like NaN, or objects with nonstring fields like arrays, other objects, or null. In practice, these features are very

---

5 In the YAML specification, *objects* are known as *documents*.

rarely used, and Kubernetes doesn't allow them because the config must be JSON-encoded when sent to the API.

The following snippet shows what our example Kubernetes configuration would look like in Jsonnet:

```
// templates.libsonnet
{
  MyTemplate:: {
    local service = self,
    tier:: error 'Needs tier',
    apiVersion: 'v1',
    kind: 'Service',

    local selector_labels = { app: 'guestbook', tier: service.tier },

    metadata: {
      labels: selector_labels,
      name: 'guestbook-' + service.tier,
      namespace: 'default',
    },

    spec: {
      externalTrafficPolicy: 'Cluster',
      ports: [{
        port: 80,
        protocol: 'TCP',
        targetPort: 80,
      }],
      selector: selector_labels,
      sessionAffinity: 'None',
      type: 'NodePort',
    },
  },
}

// example1.jsonnet
local templates = import 'templates.libsonnet';

templates.MyTemplate {
  tier: 'frontend',
}

// example2.jsonnet
local templates = import 'templates.libsonnet';

templates.MyTemplate {
  tier: 'backend',
  metadata+: {
    namespace: 'prod',
  },
}
```

```
// example3.jsonnet
local templates = import 'templates.libsonnet';

templates.MyTemplate {
  tier: 'frontend',
  metadata+: {
    namespace: 'prod',
    labels+: { foo: 'bar' },
  },
}
```

```
// example4.jsonnet
local templates = import 'templates.libsonnet';

templates.MyTemplate {
  tier: 'backend',
}
```

Note the following:

- We express all four variants by instantiating an abstract template four times, but you could also use functional abstractions.

- While we use a separate Jsonnet file for each instance, you might also consolidate them in a single file.

- In the abstract template, the namespace defaults to `default` and the tier must be overridden.

- At first glance, the Jsonnet is slightly more verbose, but reduces toil as the number of template instantiations grows.

Within `MyTemplate`, the `local` keyword defines a variable `service`, which is initialized to `self` (a reference to the closest enclosing object). This allows you to refer to the object from within nested objects, where `self` is redefined.

The `tier` field has two colons (rather than the regular JSON single colon) and is hidden (not output) in the generated JSON. Otherwise, Kubernetes will reject `tier` as an unrecognized field. Hidden fields can still be overridden and referenced—in this case, as `service.tier`.

The template cannot be used by itself because referencing `service.tier` triggers the `error` construct, which raises a runtime error with the given text. To avoid the error, each instance of the template overrides the `tier` field with some other expression. In other words, this pattern expresses something similar to a pure virtual/abstract method.

Using functions for abstraction means that config can only be parameterized. In contrast, templates allow you to override any field from the parent. As described in

Chapter 14, while simplicity should be fundamental to your design, the ability to escape simplicity is important. Template overrides provide a useful escape hatch to change specific details that might normally be considered too low-level. For example:

```
templates.MyTemplate {
  tier: 'frontend',
  spec+: {
    sessionAffinity: 'ClientIP',
  },
}
```

Here's a typical workflow to convert an existing template to Jsonnet:

1. Convert one of the YAML variants to JSON.

2. Run the resulting JSON through the Jsonnet formatter.

3. Manually add Jsonnet constructs to abstract and instantiate the code (as shown in the example).

The example showed how to remove duplication while retaining certain fields that were different. Using a configuration language becomes more compelling as differences become more subtle (e.g., strings are slightly different) or challenging to express (e.g., configuration has structural differences like additional elements in arrays, or the same difference applied across all elements of an array).

In general, abstracting commonalities across different configurations promotes separation of concerns and has the same benefits as modularity in programming languages. You can take advantage of abstraction capabilities for a number of different use cases:

- A single team might need to create multiple versions of their configuration that are *almost* (but not quite) the same—for example, when managing deployments across varied environments (prod/stage/dev/test), tuning deployments on different architectures, or adjusting capacity in different geographies.

- An organization might have an infrastructure team that maintains reusable components—API serving frameworks, cache servers, or MapReduces—that are used by the application teams. For each component, the infrastructure team can maintain a template that defines the Kubernetes objects needed to run that component at scale. Each application team can instantiate that template to add the particulars of their application.

Integrating Custom Applications (In-House Software)

If your infrastructure utilizes any custom applications (i.e., software developed in-house, as opposed to off-the-shelf solutions), then you can design those applications to coexist with a reusable configuration language. The suggestions in this section should improve the overall user configuration experience when you are writing config files or interacting with the generated config data (e.g., for debugging purposes, or when integrating with other tools). They should also simplify the application's design and separate configuration from data.

Your broad strategy for approaching custom applications should be to:

- Let the config language handle what it's designed for: the language aspect of the problem.
- Let your application handle all other functionality.

The following best practices include examples that use Jsonnet, but the same recommendations apply to other languages:

- Consume a single pure data file, and let the config language split the config into files using imports. This means the config language implementation only has to emit (and the application only has to consume) a single file. Also, since applications can combine files in different ways, this strategy explicitly and clearly delineates how the files are combined to form the application configuration.
- Represent collections of named entities using objects, where the field contains the object name and the value contains the rest of the entity. Avoid using an array of objects where each element has a name field.

  Bad JSON:

  ```
  [
    { "name": "cat", ... },
    { "name": "dog", ... }
  ]
  ```

  Good JSON:

  ```
  {
    "cat": { ... },
    "dog": { ... }
  }
  ```

  This strategy makes the collection (and individual animals) easier to extend, and you can reference entities by name (e.g., `animals.cat`) instead of referencing brittle indexes (e.g., `animals[0]`).

- Avoid grouping entities by type at the top level. Structure the JSON so that logically related configuration is grouped in the same subtree. This allows abstraction (at the config language level) to follow functional boundaries.

Bad JSON:

```
{
  "pots": { "pot1": { ... }, "pot2": { ... } },
  "lids": { "lid1": { ... }, "lid2": { ... } }
}
```

Good JSON:

```
{
  "pot_assembly1": { "pot": { ... }, "lid": { ... } },
  "pot_assembly2": { "pot": { ... }, "lid": { ... } }
}
```

At the config language level, this strategy enables abstractions like the following:

```
local kitchen = import 'kitchen.libsonnet';
{
  pot_assembly1: kitchen.CrockPot,
  pot_assembly2: kitchen.SaucePan { pot+: { color: 'red' } },
}
```

- Generally keep the data representation design simple:

  — Avoid embedding language features in the data representation (as mentioned in "Pitfall 1: Failing to Recognize Configuration as a Programming Language Problem" on page 317). These types of abstractions will be underpowered and only create confusion, since they force users to decide whether to use the abstraction features in the data representation or in the configuration language.

  — Don't worry about overly verbose data representation. Solutions to reduce verbosity introduce complexity, and the problem can be managed in the configuration language.

  — Avoid interpreting custom string interpolation syntax, such as conditionals or placeholder references in strings, in your application. Sometimes interpretation is unavoidable—for example, when you need to describe actions that are performed after the pure data version of the config is generated (alerts, handlers, etc.). But otherwise, let the config language do as much of the language-level work as possible.

As mentioned earlier, if you *can* remove configuration altogether, doing so is always your best option. Although the configuration language can hide the complexity of the underlying model by using templates with default values, the generated config data is not completely hidden—it may be processed by tools, inspected by humans, or loaded into config databases. For the same reason, don't rely on the configuration language to fix inconsistent naming, plurals, or mistakes in the underlying model— fix them in the model itself. If you can't fix inconsistencies in the model, it is better to live with them at the language level to avoid even more inconsistency.

In our experience, configuration changes tend to dominate outage root causes over time in a system (see our list of top causes of outages in Appendix C). Validating your config changes is a key step to maintaining reliability. We recommend validating the generated config data immediately after configuration execution. Syntactic validation alone (i.e., checking whether JSON is parsable) won't find many bugs. After generic schema validation, check properties that are specific to your application's domain—for example, whether required fields are present, referenced filenames exist, and provided values are within allowed ranges.

You can validate Jsonnet's JSON with JSONschema (*http://json-schema.org/*). For applications using protocol buffers (*http://bit.ly/2szjO1l*), you can easily generate the canonical JSON form of these buffers from Jsonnet, and the protocol buffer implementation will validate during deserialization.

No matter how you decide to validate, do not ignore unrecognized field names, as they may indicate a typo at the configuration language level. Jsonnet can mask fields that should not be output using the `::` syntax. It's also a good idea to perform the same validation in a precommit hook.

Effectively Operating a Configuration System

When implementing "configuration as code" in any language, we recommend following the discipline and processes that aid software engineering generally.

Versioning

Configuration languages usually trigger engineers to write libraries of templates and utility functions. Often, one team maintains these libraries, but many other teams may consume them. When you need to make a breaking change to the library, you have two choices:

- Commit a global update of all client code, refactoring the code so that it still works (this may not be organizationally possible).

- Version the library so that different consumers can use different versions and migrate independently. Consumers who opt to use deprecated versions won't get the benefits of the new versions and will incur technical debt—someday, they will have to refactor their code to use the new library.

Most languages, including Jsonnet, do not provide any specific support for versioning; instead, you can easily use directories. For a practical example in Jsonnet, see the ksonnet-lib repository (*http://bit.ly/2snzCW0*), where the version is the first component of the imported path:

```
local k = import 'ksonnet.beta.2/k.libsonnet';
```

Source Control

Chapter 14 advocates keeping a historical record of config changes (including who made them) and ensuring that rollbacks are easy and reliable. Checking configuration into source control brings all these capabilities, plus the ability to code review config changes.

Tooling

Consider how you will enforce style and lint your configurations, and investigate if there's an editor plug-in that integrates these tools into your workflow. Your goals here are to maintain a consistent style across all authors, to improve readability, and to detect errors. Some editors support post-write hooks that can run formatters and other external tools for you. You can also use precommit hooks to run the same tools to ensure checked-in config is high quality.

Testing

We recommend implementing unit tests for upstream template libraries. Make sure the libraries generate the expected concrete configuration when instantiated in various ways. Similarly, libraries of functions should include unit tests so they can be maintained with confidence.

In Jsonnet, you can write tests as Jsonnet files that:

1. Import the library to be tested.

2. Exercise the library.

3. Use either the `assert` statement or the standard library `assertEqual` function to validate its output. The latter presents any mismatching values in its error messages.

The following example tests the `joinName` function and `MyTemplate`:

```
// utils_test.jsonnet
local utils = import 'utils.libsonnet';

std.assertEqual(utils.joinName(['foo', 'bar']), 'foo-bar') &&
std.assertEqual(utils.MyTemplate { tier: 'frontend' }, { ... })
```

For larger test suites, you can take advantage of a more comprehensive unit test framework developed by Jsonnet community members (*http://bit.ly/2xzbOTZ*). You can use this framework to define and run suites of tests in a structured manner—for example, to report the set of all failing tests instead of aborting execution at the first failing assertion.

When to Evaluate Configuration

Our critical properties include *hermeticity*; that is, configuration languages must generate the same config data regardless of where or when they execute. As described in Chapter 14 a system can be hard or impossible to roll back if it depends on resources that can change outside of its hermetic environment. Generally, hermeticism means that Jsonnet code is always interchangeable with the expanded JSON it represents. Accordingly, you can generate JSON from Jsonnet at any time between when the Jsonnet is updated and when you need the JSON—even each time you need the JSON.

We recommend storing configuration in version control. Then your earliest opportunity to validate the config is before check-in. At the other extreme, an application can evaluate the config when it needs the JSON data. As a middle-of-the-road option, you can evaluate at build time. Each of these options has various tradeoffs, and you should optimize according to the specifics of your use case.

Very Early: Checking in the JSON

You can generate JSON from the Jsonnet code before checking both in to version control. The typical workflow is as follows:

1. Modify the Jsonnet files.
2. Run the Jsonnet command-line tool (perhaps wrapped in a script) to regenerate JSON files.
3. Use a precommit hook to ensure that the Jsonnet code and JSON output are always consistent.
4. Package everything into a pull request for a code review.

Pros

- The reviewer can sanity-check the concrete changes—for example, a refactoring should not affect the generated JSON at all.
- You can inspect line annotations by multiple authors across different versions at both the generated and abstracted level. This is useful for auditing changes.
- You don't need to run Jsonnet at runtime, which can help to limit complexity, binary size, and/or risk exposure.

Cons

- The generated JSON is not necessarily readable—for example, if it embeds long strings.
- The JSON may not be suitable for checking into version control for other reasons —for example, if it's too large or contains secrets.
- Merge conflicts may arise if many concurrent edits to separate Jsonnet files converge to a single JSON file.

Middle of the Road: Evaluate at Build Time

You can avoid checking JSON into source control by running the Jsonnet command-line utility at build time and embedding the generated JSON into the release artifact (e.g., as a tarball). The application code simply reads the JSON file from disk at initialization time. If you're using Bazel, you can easily achieve this using the Jsonnet Bazel rules (*http://bit.ly/2xz0QxH*). At Google, we commonly favor this approach because of the pros listed next.

Pros

- You have the ability to control runtime complexity, binary size, and risk exposure without having to rebuild the JSON files in each pull request.
- There's no risk of desynchronization between originating Jsonnet code and resulting JSON.

Cons

- The build is more complex.
- It's harder to evaluate the concrete change during code review.

Late: Evaluate at Runtime

Linking the Jsonnet library allows the application itself to interpret the config at any time, yielding an in-memory representation of the generated JSON config.

Pros

- It's simpler, as you don't need a prior evaluation.
- You gain the ability to evaluate Jsonnet code provided by the user during execution.

Cons

- Any linked library increases the footprint and risk exposure.
- Configuration bugs may be discovered at runtime, which is too late.
- If the Jsonnet code is untrusted, you must take special care. (We discuss why in "Guarding Against Abusive Configuration" on page 333.)

To follow our running example, when should you run Jsonnet if you're generating Kubernetes objects?

The answer depends on your implementation. If you're building something like ksonnet (a client-side command-line tool that runs Jsonnet code from the local file-system), the easiest solution is to link the Jsonnet library into the tool and evaluate the Jsonnet in process. Doing so is safe because code runs on the author's own machine.

Box.com's infrastructure uses Git hooks to push configuration changes to produc-tion. To avoid executing Jsonnet on the server, the Git hooks act on generated JSON that's kept in the repository. For a deployment management daemon like Helm or Spinnaker, your only choice is to evaluate the Jsonnet on the server at runtime (with the caveats described in the next section).

Guarding Against Abusive Configuration

Unlike long-running services, configuration execution should quickly terminate with the resulting config. Unfortunately, due to bugs or deliberate attacks, configuration may take an arbitrary amount of CPU time or memory. To illustrate why, consider the following nonterminating Jsonnet program:

```
local f(x) = f(x + 1); f(0)
```

A program that uses unbounded memory is similar:

```
local f(x) = f(x + [1]); f([])
```

You can write equivalent examples using objects instead of functions, or in other configuration languages.

You might try to avoid overconsuming resources by restricting the language so that it is no longer Turing complete (*http://bit.ly/2J4jgfi*). However, enforcing that all configurations terminate doesn't necessarily prevent overconsuming resources. It's easy to write a program that consumes enough time or memory to be practically non-terminating. For example:

```
local f(x) = if x == 0 then [] else [f(x - 1), f(x - 1)]; f(100)
```

In fact, such programs exist (*http://bit.ly/2szYkl5*) even with simple config formats like XML and YAML.

In practice, the risk of these scenarios depends on the situation. On the less problematic side, suppose a command-line tool uses Jsonnet to build Kubernetes objects and then deploys those objects. In this case, the Jsonnet code is trusted: accidents that produce nontermination are rare, and you can use Ctrl-C to mitigate them. Accidental memory exhaustion is extremely unlikely. At the other extreme, with a service like Helm or Spinnaker, which accepts arbitrary config code from an end user and evaluates it in a request handler, you must be very careful to avoid DOS attacks that might tie up request handlers or exhaust memory.

If you evaluate untrusted Jsonnet code in a request handler, you can avoid such attacks by sandboxing the Jsonnet execution. One easy strategy is to use a separate process and ulimit (or its non-UNIX equivalent). Typically, you need to fork to the command-line executable instead of linking the Jsonnet library. As a result, programs that do not complete within given resources fail safely and inform the end user. For additional defense against C++ memory exploits, you can use the native Go implementation of Jsonnet.

Conclusion

Whether you use Jsonnet, adopt another configuration language, or develop your own, we hope that you can apply these best practices to manage the complexity and operational load required to configure your production system with confidence.

At a minimum, the critical properties of a configuration language are good *tooling*, *hermetic* configurations, and *separation of configuration and data*.

Your system may not be complex enough to need a configuration language. Transitioning to a domain-specific language like Jsonnet is a strategy to consider when your complexity increases. Doing so will allow you to provide a consistent and well-structured interface, and will free up your SRE team's time to work on other important projects.

## CHAPTER 16

Canarying Releases

By Alec Warner and Štěpán Davidovič
with Alex Hidalgo, Betsy Beyer, Kyle Smith, and Matt Duftler

Release engineering is a term we use to describe all the processes and artifacts related to getting code from a repository into a running production system. Automating releases can help avoid many of the traditional pitfalls associated with release engineering: the toil of repetitive and manual tasks, the inconsistency of a nonautomated process, the inability of knowing the exact state of a rollout, and the difficulty of rolling back. The automation of release engineering has been well covered in other literature—for example, books on continuous integration and continuous delivery (CI/CD).[1]

We define *canarying* as a partial and time-limited deployment of a change in a service and its evaluation. This evaluation helps us decide whether or not to proceed with the rollout. The part of the service that receives the change is "the canary," and the remainder of the service is "the control." The logic underpinning this approach is that usually the canary deployment is performed on a *much* smaller subset of production, or affects a much smaller subset of the user base than the control portion. Canarying is effectively an A/B testing process.

We'll first cover the basics of release engineering and the benefits of automating releases to establish a shared vocabulary.

---

1 The authors of this chapter are fans of Jez Humble and David Farley's book *Continuous Delivery: Reliable Software Releases Through Build, Test, and Deployment Automation* (Boston: Pearson, 2011).

Release Engineering Principles

The basic principles of release engineering are as follows:

Reproducible builds
> The build system should be able to take the build inputs (source code, assets, and so on) and produce repeatable artifacts. The code built from the same inputs last week should produce the same output this week.

Automated builds
> Once code is checked in, automation should produce build artifacts and upload them to a storage system.

Automated tests
> Once the automated build system builds artifacts, a test suite of some kind should ensure they function.

Automated deployments
> Deployments should be performed by computers, not humans.

Small deployments
> Build artifacts should contain small, self-contained changes.

These principles provide specific benefits to operators:

- Reducing operational load on engineers by removing manual and repetitive tasks.
- Enforcing peer review and version control, since automation is generally code-based.
- Establishing consistent, repeatable, automated processes, resulting in fewer mistakes.
- Enabling monitoring of the release pipeline, allowing for measurement and continuous improvement by addressing questions like:
  - How long does it take a release to reach production?
  - How often are releases successful? A successful release is a release made available to customers with no severe defects or SLO violations.
  - What changes can be made to catch defects as early in the pipeline as possible?
  - Which steps can be parallelized or further optimized?

CI/CD coupled with release automation can deliver continuous improvements to the development cycle, as shown in Figure 16-1. When releases are automated, you can release more often. For software with a nontrivial rate of change, releasing more often means fewer changes are bundled in any given release artifact. Smaller, self-contained release artifacts make it cheaper and easier to roll back any given release artifact in the event of a bug. Quicker release cadences mean that bug fixes reach users faster.

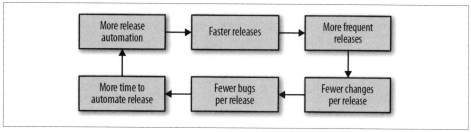

Figure 16-1. The virtuous cycle of CI/CD

Balancing Release Velocity and Reliability

Release velocity (hereafter called "shipping") and reliability are often treated as opposing goals. The business wants to ship new features and product improvements as quickly as possible with 100% reliability! While that goal is not achievable (as 100% is never the right target for reliability; see Chapter 2), it is possible to ship as quickly as possible while meeting specific reliability goals for a given product.

The first step toward this goal is understanding the impact of shipping on software reliability. In Google's experience, a majority of incidents are triggered by binary or configuration pushes (see Appendix C). Many kinds of software changes can result in a system failure—for example, changes in the behavior of an underlying component, changes in the behavior of a dependency (such as an API), or a change in configuration like DNS.

Despite the risk inherent in making changes to software, these changes—bug fixes, security patches, and new features—are necessary for the business to succeed. Instead of advocating against change, you can use the concept of SLOs and error budgets to measure the impact of releases on your reliability. Your goal should be to ship software as quickly as possible while meeting the reliability targets your users expect. The following section discusses how you can use a canary process to achieve these goals.

Separating Components That Change at Different Rates

Your services are composed of multiple components with different rates of change: binaries or code, environments such as JVM, kernel/OS, libraries, service config or flags, feature/experiment config, and user config. If you have only one way to deploy changes, actually allowing these components to change independently may be difficult.

Feature flag or experiment frameworks like Gertrude (*http://bit.ly/2H9ofW9*), Feature (*http://bit.ly/2LNpu0B*), and PlanOut (*http://bit.ly/2kIx3JO*) allow you to separate feature launches from binary releases. If a binary release includes multiple features, you can enable them one at a time by changing the experiment configuration. That way, you don't have to batch all of these changes into one big change or perform an individual release for each feature. More importantly, if only some of the new features don't behave as expected, you can selectively disable those features until the next build/release cycle can deploy a new binary.

You can apply the principles of feature flags/experiments to any type of change to your service, not just software releases.

What Is Canarying?

The term *canarying* refers to the practice of bringing canaries into coal mines to determine if the mine is safe for humans (*http://bit.ly/2kIwYWw*). Because the birds are smaller and breathe faster than humans, they are intoxicated by dangerous gases faster than their human handlers.

Even if your release pipeline is fully automated, you won't be able to detect all release-related defects until real traffic is hitting the service. By the time a release is ready to be deployed to production, your testing strategy should instill reasonable confidence that the release is safe and works as intended. However, your test environments aren't 100% identical to production, and your tests probably don't cover 100% of possible scenarios. Some defects will reach production. If a release deploys instantly everywhere, any defects will deploy in the same way.

This scenario might be acceptable if you can detect and resolve the defects quickly. However, you have a safer alternative: initially expose just some of your production traffic to the new release using a canary. Canarying allows the deployment pipeline to detect defects as quickly as possible with as little impact to your service as possible.

Release Engineering and Canarying

When deploying a new version of a system or its key components (such as configuration or data), we bundle changes—changes that typically have not been exposed to real-world inputs, such as user-facing traffic or batch processing of user-supplied data. Changes bring new features and capabilities, but they also bring risk that is exposed at the time of deployment. Our goal is to mitigate this risk by testing each change on a small portion of traffic to gain confidence that it has no ill effects. We will discuss evaluation processes later in this chapter.

The canary process also lets us gain confidence in our change as we expose it to larger and larger amounts of traffic. Introducing the change to actual production traffic also enables us to identify problems that might not be visible in testing frameworks like unit testing or load testing, which are often more artificial.

We will examine the process of canarying and its evaluation using a worked example, while steering clear of a deep dive into statistics. Instead, we focus on the process as a whole and typical practical considerations. We use a simple application on App Engine to illustrate various aspects of the rollout.

Requirements of a Canary Process

Canarying for a given service requires specific capabilities:

- A method to deploy the canary change to a subset of the population of the service.[2]
- An evaluation process to evaluate if the canaried change is "good" or "bad."
- Integration of the canary evaluations into the release process.

Ultimately, the canary process demonstrates value when canaries detect bad release candidates with high confidence, and identify good releases without false positives.

Our Example Setup

We'll use a simple frontend web service application to illustrate some canarying concepts. The application offers an HTTP-based API that consumers can use to manipulate various data (simple information like the price of a product). The example application has some tunable parameters that we can use to simulate various production symptoms, to be evaluated by the canary process. For example, we can make the application return errors for 20% of requests, or we can stipulate that 5% of requests take at least two seconds.

We illustrate the canary process using an application deployed on Google App Engine, but the principles apply to any environment. While the example application is fairly contrived, in real-world scenarios, similar applications share common signals with our example that can be used in a canary process.

Our example service has two potential versions: *live* and *release candidate*. The live version is the version currently deployed in production, and the release candidate is a newly built version. We use these versions to illustrate various rollout concepts and how to implement canaries to make the rollout process safer.

---

2 The fraction of total service load you run on the canary should be proportional to the size of the canary population.

A Roll Forward Deployment Versus a Simple Canary Deployment

Let's first look at a deployment with no canary process, so we can later compare it to a canaried deployment in terms of error budget savings and general impact when a breakage occurs. Our deployment process features a development environment. Once we feel the code is working in the development environment, we deploy that version in the production environment.

Shortly after our deployment, our monitoring starts reporting a high rate of errors (see Figure 16-2, where we intentionally configured our sample application to fail 20% of requests to simulate a defect in the example service). For the sake of this example, let's say that our deployment process doesn't provide us the option to roll back to a previously known good configuration. Our best option to fix the errors is to find defects in the production version, patch them, and deploy a new version during the outage. This course of action will almost certainly prolong the user impact of the bug.

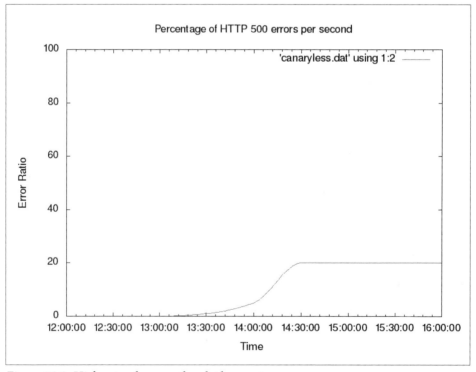

Figure 16-2. High rate of errors after deployment

To improve upon this initial deployment process, we can utilize canaries in our roll-out strategy to reduce the impact of a bad code push. Instead of deploying to production all at once, we need a way to create a small segment of production that runs our release candidate. Then we can send a small portion of the traffic to that segment of production (the canary) and compare it against the other segment (the control). Using this method, we can spot defects in the release candidate before all of production is affected.

The simple canary deployment in our App Engine example splits traffic (*http://bit.ly/2syNcVx*) between specific labeled versions of our application. You can split traffic using App Engine, or any number of other methods, such as backend weights on a load balancer, proxy configurations, or round-robin DNS records.

Figure 16-3 shows that the impact of the change is greatly reduced when we use a canary; in fact, the errors are barely visible! This raises an interesting issue: the canary evaluation is difficult to see and track compared to the overall traffic trend.

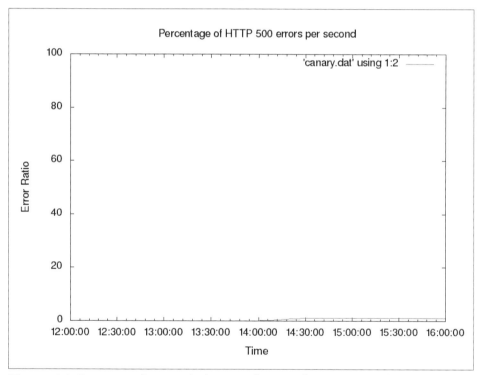

Figure 16-3. Error rate of canary deployment; because the canary population is a small subset of production, the overall error rate is reduced

To get a clearer picture of the errors we need to track at a reasonable scale, we can look at our key metric (HTTP response codes) by App Engine application version, as shown in Figure 16-4. When we look at per-version breakdown, we can plainly see the errors the new version introduces. We can also observe from Figure 16-4 that the live version is serving very few errors.

We can now tune our deployment to automatically react based on the HTTP error rate by App Engine version. If the error rate of the canary metric is too far from the control error rate, this signals the canary deployment is "bad." In response, we should pause and roll back the deployment, or perhaps contact a human to help trouble-shoot the issue. If the error ratios are similar, we can proceed with the deployment as normal. In the case of Figure 16-4, our canary deployment is clearly bad and we should roll it back.

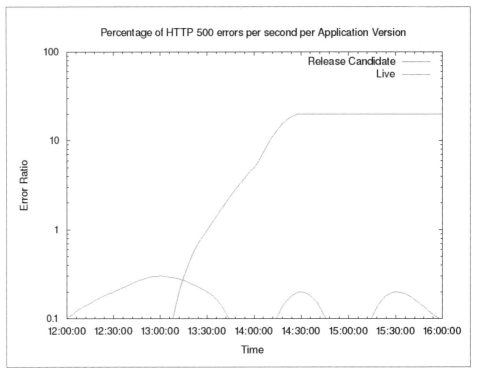

Figure 16-4. HTTP response codes by App Engine version; the release candidate serves the vast majority of the errors, while the live version produces a low number of errors at a steady state (note: the graph uses a base-10 log scale)

Canary Implementation

Now that we've seen a fairly trivial canary deployment implementation, let's dig deeper into the parameters that we need to understand for a successful canary process.

Minimizing Risk to SLOs and the Error Budget

Chapter 2 discusses how SLOs reflect business requirements around service availability. These requirements also apply to canary implementations. The canary process risks only a small fragment of our error budget, which is limited by time and the size of the canary population.

Global deployment can place the SLO at risk fairly quickly. If we deploy the candidate from our trivial example, we would risk failing 20% of requests. If we instead use a canary population of 5%, we serve 20% errors for 5% of traffic, resulting in a 1% overall error rate (as seen earlier in Figure 16-3). This strategy allows us to conserve our error budget—impact on the budget is directly proportional to the amount of traffic exposed to defects. We can assume that detection and rollback take about the same time for both the naive deployment and the canary deployment, but when we integrate a canary process into our deployment, we learn valuable information about our new version at a much lower cost to our system.

This is a very simple model that assumes uniform load. It also assumes that we can spend our entire error budget (beyond what we've already included in the organic measurement of current availability) on canaries. Rather than *actual* availability, here we consider only unavailability introduced by new releases. Our model also assumes a 100% failure rate because this is a worst-case scenario.[3] It is likely that defects in the canary deployment will not affect 100% of system usage. We also allow overall system availability to go below SLO for the duration of the canary deployment.[4]

This model has clear flaws, but is a solid starting point that you can adjust to match business needs.[5] We recommend using the simplest model that meets your technical and business objectives. In our experience, focusing on making the model as technically correct as possible often leads to overinvestment in modeling. For services with high rates of complexity, overly complex models can lead to incessant model tuning for no real benefit.

Choosing a Canary Population and Duration

When choosing an appropriate canary duration, you need to factor in development velocity. If you release daily, you can't let your canary last for a week while running

---

3 At least as far as availability is concerned. This analysis obviously does not cover the impact of incidents, such as a data leak.

4 For a sufficiently small canary, where the fraction of service equals the difference between actual availability and SLO, we can canary nonstop with confidence. This is our use of the error budget.

5 As British statistician George Box said, "Essentially, all models are wrong, but some are useful." George E. P. Box and Norman R. Draper, *Empirical Model-Building and Response Surfaces* (New York: John Wiley and Sons, 1987).

only one canary deployment at a time. If you deploy weekly, you have time to perform fairly long canaries. If you deploy continuously (for example, 20 times in a day), your canary duration must be significantly shorter. On a related note, while we can run multiple canary deployments simultaneously, doing so adds significant mental effort to track system state. This can become problematic during any nonstandard circumstances, when reasoning about the system's state quickly is important. Running simultaneous canaries also increases the risk of signal contamination if the canaries overlap. We strongly advise running only one canary deployment at a time.

For basic evaluation, we do not need a terribly large canary population in order to detect key critical conditions.[6] However, a representative canary process requires decisions across many dimensions:

Size and duration
> It should be sizeable and last long enough to be representative of the overall deployment. Terminating a canary deployment after receiving just a handful of queries doesn't provide a useful signal for systems characterized by diverse queries with varied functionality. The higher the processing rate, the less time is required to get a representative sample in order to ensure the observed behavior is actually attributable to the canaried change, and not just a random artifact.

Traffic volume
> We need to receive enough traffic on the system to ensure it has handled a representative sample, and that the system has a chance to react negatively to the inputs. Typically, the more homogeneous the requests, the less traffic volume you need.

Time of day
> Performance defects typically manifest only under heavy load,[7] so deploying at an off-peak time likely wouldn't trigger performance-related defects.

Metrics to evaluate
> The representativeness of a canary is tightly connected to the metrics we choose to evaluate (which we'll discuss later in this chapter). We can evaluate trivial metrics like query success quickly, but other metrics (such as queue depth) may need more time or a large canary population to provide a clear signal.

Frustratingly, these requirements can be mutually at odds. Canarying is a balancing act, informed both by cold analysis of worst-case scenarios and the past realistic track record of a system. Once you've gathered metrics from past canaries, you can choose

---

6 See a discussion of real-world outages at *http://bit.ly/2LgorFz*.

7 For example, consider resource contention problems, such as database write conflicts or locking in multi-threaded applications.

canary parameters based upon typical canary evaluation failure rates rather than hypothetical worst-case scenarios.

Selecting and Evaluating Metrics

So far, we have been looking at the success ratio, a very clear and obvious metric for canary evaluation. But intuitively, we know this single metric is not sufficient for a meaningful canary process. If we serve all requests at 10 times the latency, or use 10 times as much memory while doing so, we might also have a problem. Not all metrics are good candidates for evaluating a canary. What properties of metrics are best suited for evaluating whether a canary is good or bad?

Metrics Should Indicate Problems

First and foremost, the metric needs to be able to indicate problems in the service. This is tricky because what constitutes a "problem" isn't always objective. We can probably consider a failed user request problematic.[8] But what if a request takes 10% longer, or the system requires 10% more memory? We typically recommend using SLIs as a place to start thinking about canary metrics. Good SLIs tend to have strong attribution to service health. If SLIs are already being measured to drive SLO compliance, we can reuse that work.

Almost any metric can be problematic when taken to the extreme, but there's also a cost to adding too many metrics to your canary process. We need to correctly define a notion of acceptable behavior for each of the metrics. If the idea of acceptable behavior is overly strict, we will get lots of false positives; that is, we will think a canary deployment is bad, even though it isn't. Conversely, if a definition of acceptable behavior is too loose, we will be more likely to let a bad canary deployment go undetected. Choosing what's acceptable behavior correctly can be an expensive process— it's time-consuming and requires analysis. When it's done poorly, however, your results can completely mislead you. Also, you need to reevaluate expectations on a regular basis as the service, its feature set, and its behavior evolve.

We should stack-rank the metrics we want to evaluate based on our opinion of how well they indicate actual user-perceivable problems in the system. Select the top few metrics to use in canary evaluations (perhaps no more than a dozen). Too many metrics can bring diminishing returns, and at some point, the returns are outweighed by the cost of maintaining them, or the negative impact on trust in the release process if they are not maintained.

---

8 A failed user request isn't necessarily problematic. User requests can fail because the user requested something unreasonable, such as accessing a nonexistent URL. We need to be disciplined in distinguishing errors like these from problems in the systems.

To make this guideline more tangible, let's look at our example service. It has many metrics we might evaluate: CPU usage, memory footprint, HTTP return codes (200s, 300s, etc.), latency of response, correctness, and so on. In this case, our best metrics are likely the HTTP return codes and latency of response because their degradation most closely maps to an actual problem that impacts users. In this scenario, metrics for CPU usage aren't as useful: an increase in resource usage doesn't necessarily impact a service and may result in a flaky or noisy canary process. This can result in the canary process being disabled or ignored by operators, which can defeat the point of having a canary process in the first place. In the case of frontend services, we intuitively know that being slower or failing to respond are typically reliable signals that there are problems in the service.

HTTP return codes contain interesting tricky cases, such as code 404, which tells us the resource was not found. This could happen because users get the wrong URL (imagine a broken URL getting shared on a popular discussion board), or because the server incorrectly stops serving a resource. Often we can work around problems like this by excluding 400-level codes from our canary evaluation and adding black-box monitoring to test for the presence of a particular URL. We can then include the black-box data as part of our canary analysis to help isolate our canary process from odd user behaviors.

Metrics Should Be Representative and Attributable

The source of changes in the observed metrics should be clearly attributable to the change we are canarying, and should not be influenced by external factors.

In a large population (for example, many servers or many containers), we are likely to have outliers—oversubscribed machines, machines running different kernels with different performance characteristics, or machines on an overloaded segment of the network. The difference between the canary population and the control is just as much a function of the change we have deployed as the difference between the two infrastructures on which we deploy.

Managing canaries is a balancing act between a number of forces. Increasing the size of the canary population is one way to decrease impact of this problem (as discussed earlier). When we reach what we consider a reasonable canary population size for our system, we need to consider whether the metrics we have chosen could show high variance.

We should also be aware of shared failure domains between our canary and control environments; a bad canary could negatively impact the control, while bad behavior in the system might lead us to incorrectly evaluate the canary. Similarly, make sure that your metrics are well isolated. Consider a system that runs both our application and other processes. A dramatic increase in CPU usage of the system as a whole would make for a poor metric, as other processes in the system (database load, log rotation, etc.) might be causing that increase. A better metric would be CPU time spent as the process served the request. An even better metric would be CPU time spent serving the request over the window of time the serving process was actually scheduled on a CPU. While a heavily oversubscribed machine colocated with our process is obviously a problem (and monitoring should catch it!), it isn't caused by the change we're canarying, so it should not be flagged as a canary deployment failure.

Canaries also need to be attributable; that is, you should also be able to tie the canary metric to SLIs. If a metric can change wildly with no impact to service, it's unlikely to make a good canary metric.

Before/After Evaluation Is Risky

A before/after canary process is an extension of the attribution problem. In this process, the old system is fully replaced by the new system, and your canary evaluation compares system behavior before and after the change over a set period of time. One might call this process a "canary deployment in time-space," where you choose the A/B groups by segmenting time instead of segmenting the population by machines, cookies, or other means. Because time is one of the biggest sources of change in observed metrics, it is difficult to assess degradation of performance with before/after evaluation.

While the canary deployment might have caused the degradation, the degradation may very well have happened in the control system too. This scenario becomes even more problematic if we attempt to run a canary deployment over a longer period of time. For example, if we perform a release on Monday, we may be comparing behavior during a business day to behavior during a weekend, introducing a large amount of noise. In this example, users may use the service very differently over the weekend, thereby introducing noise in the canary process.

The before/after process itself introduces a question of whether a big error spike (as introduced by a before/after evaluation) is better than a small but possibly longer rate of errors (as introduced by a small canary). If the new release is completely broken, how quickly can we detect and revert? A before/after canary may detect the problem faster, but the overall time to recovery may still be quite substantial and similar to a smaller canary. During that time, users suffer.

Use a Gradual Canary for Better Metric Selection

Metrics that don't meet our ideal properties may still bring great value. We can introduce these metrics by using a more nuanced canary process.

Instead of simply evaluating a single canary stage, we can use a canary containing multiple stages that reflect our ability to reason about the metrics. In the first stage, we have no confidence or knowledge about the behavior of this release. We therefore want to use a small stage in order to minimize negative impact. In a small canary, we prefer metrics that are the clearest indication of a problem—application crashes, request failures, and the like. Once this stage passes successfully, the next stage will have a larger canary population to increase confidence in our analysis of the impact of the changes.

Dependencies and Isolation

The system being tested will not operate in a complete vacuum. For practical reasons, the canary population and the control may share backends, frontends, networks, data stores, and other infrastructure. There may even be extremely nonobvious interactions with the client. For example, imagine two consecutive requests sent by a single client. The first request may be handled by the canary deployment. The response by the canary may change the content of the second request, which may land on the control, altering the control's behavior.

Imperfect isolation has several consequences. Most importantly, we need to be aware that if the canarying process provides results that indicate we should stop a production change and investigate the situation, the canary deployment isn't necessarily at fault. This fact is true of canarying in general, but in practice, it's frequently enforced by isolation issues.

Additionally, imperfect isolation means that bad behavior of the canary deployment can also negatively impact the control. Canarying is an A/B comparison, and it's possible that both A and B can change in tandem; this may cause confusion in the canary evaluation. It is important to also use absolute measures, such as defined SLOs, to ensure the system is operating correctly.

Canarying in Noninteractive Systems

The chapter has focused on an interactive request/response system, which in many ways is the simplest and most commonly discussed system design. Other systems, such as asynchronous processing pipelines, are equally important, but have different canarying considerations, which we'll enumerate briefly. For more information on canarying as related to data processing pipelines, see Chapter 13.

First and foremost, the duration and deployment of the canary inherently depends on the duration of work unit processing. We've ignored this factor when it comes to interactive systems, assuming work unit processing will take no more than a few seconds, which is shorter than the canary duration. Work unit processing in noninteractive systems, such as rendering pipelines or video encoding, can take much longer. Accordingly, make sure the canary duration at minimum spans the duration of a single work unit.

Isolation can become more complex for noninteractive systems. Many pipeline systems have a single work assigner and a fleet of workers with the application code. In multistage pipelines, a work unit is processed by a worker, then returned to the pool for the same or another worker to perform the next stage of processing. It is helpful for canary analysis to ensure that the workers processing a particular unit of work are always pulled from the same pool of workers—either the canary pool or the control pool. Otherwise, the signals get increasingly mixed (for more about the need to untangle signals, see "Requirements on Monitoring Data" on page 349).

Finally, metric selection can be more complicated. We may be interested in end-to-end time to process the work unit (similar to latency in interactive systems), as well as quality of the processing itself (which is, of course, completely application-specific).

Given these caveats, the general concept of canarying remains viable, and the same high-level principles apply.

Requirements on Monitoring Data

When conducting canary evaluation, you must be able to compare the canary signals to the control signals. Often, this requires some care in structuring the monitoring system—effective comparisons are straightforward and produce meaningful results.

Consider our earlier example of a canary deployment to 5% of the population that runs at a 20% error rate. Because monitoring likely looks at the system as a whole, it will detect an overall error rate of only 1%. Depending on the system, this signal might be indistinguishable from other sources of errors (see Figure 16-3).

If we break down metrics by population servicing the request (the canary versus the control), we can observe the separate metrics (see Figure 16-4). We can plainly see the error rate in the control versus the canary, a stark illustration of what a full deployment would bring. Here we see that monitoring that reasons well about an entire service isn't sufficient to analyze our canary. When collecting monitoring data, it is important to be able to perform fine-grained breakdowns that enable you to differentiate metrics between the canary and control populations.

Another challenge with collecting metrics is that canary deployments are time-limited by design. This can cause problems when metrics are aggregated over specific periods. Consider the metric *errors per hour*. We can calculate this metric by summing the requests over the past hour. If we use this metric to evaluate our canary, we might encounter problems, as described in the following timeline:

1. An unrelated event causes some errors to occur.

2. A canary is deployed to 5% of the population; the canary duration is 30 minutes.

3. The canary system starts to watch the errors-per-hour metric to see if the deployment is good or bad.

4. The deployment is detected as bad because the errors-per-hour metric is significantly different from the errors per hour of the control population.

This scenario is a result of using a metric that is computed hourly to evaluate a deployment that is only 30 minutes long. As a result, the canary process provides a very muddied signal. When using metrics to evaluate canary success, make sure the intervals of your metrics are either the same as or less than your canary duration.

Related Concepts

Often, our conversations with customers touch upon using blue/green deployment, artificial load generation, and/or traffic teeing in production. These concepts are similar to canarying, so while they're not strictly canary processes, they might be used as such.

Blue/Green Deployment

Blue/green deployment maintains two instances of a system: one that is serving traffic (green), and another that is ready to serve traffic (blue). After deploying a new release in the blue environment, you can then move traffic to it. The cutover doesn't require downtime, and rollback is a trivial reversal of the router change. One downside is that this setup uses twice as many resources as a more "traditional" deployment. In this setup, you are effectively performing a before/after canary (discussed earlier).

You can use blue/green deployments more or less as normal canaries by utilizing both blue and green deployments simultaneously (rather than independently). In this strategy, you can deploy the canary to the blue (standby) instance and slowly split traffic between green and blue environments. Both your evaluations and the metrics that compare the blue environment to the green environment should be tied to traffic control. This setup resembles an A/B canary, where the green environment is the control, the blue environment is the canary deployment, and the canary population is controlled by the amount of traffic sent to each.

Artificial Load Generation

Instead of exposing live user traffic to a canary deployment, it may be tempting to err on the side of safety and use artificial load generation. Often, you can run load tests in multiple deployment stages (QA, preproduction, and even in production). While these activities don't qualify as canarying according to our definition, they are still viable approaches to finding defects with some caveats.

Testing with synthetic load does a good job of maximizing code coverage, but doesn't provide good state coverage. It can be especially hard to artificially simulate load in mutable systems (systems with caches, cookies, request affinity, etc.). Artificial load also might not accurately model organic traffic shifts that happen in a real system. Some regressions may manifest only during events not included in the artificial load, leading to gaps in coverage.

Artificial load also works poorly in mutable systems. For example, it may be downright dangerous to attempt to generate artificial load on a billing system: the system might start sending callouts to credit card providers, which would then start actively charging customers. While we can avoid testing dangerous code paths, the lack of testing on these paths reduces our test coverage.

Traffic Teeing

If artificial load is not representative, we could copy the traffic and send it to both the production system and the system in the test environment. This technique is referred to as *teeing*. While the production system serves the actual traffic and delivers responses to users, the canary deployment serves the copy and discards the responses. You might even compare the canary responses to the actual responses and run further analysis.

This strategy can provide representative traffic, but is often more complicated to set up than a more straightforward canary process. Traffic teeing also doesn't adequately identify risk in stateful systems; copies of traffic may introduce unexpected influences between the seemingly independent deployments. For example, if the canary deployment and production systems share a cache, an artificially inflated cache hit rate would invalidate performance measurements for the canary metrics.

Conclusion

You can use a number of tools and approaches to automate your releases and introduce canarying into your pipeline. No single testing methodology is a panacea, and testing strategies should be informed by the requirements and behavior of the system. Canarying can be a simple, robust, and easily integratable way to supplement testing. When you catch system defects early, users are minimally impacted. Canarying can also provide confidence in frequent releases and improve development velocity. Just as testing methodology must evolve alongside system requirements and design, so must canarying.

## PART III

Processes

SRE is more than just a collection of technical practices—it's a culture that requires consistent and logical processes. This section addresses some important elements of processes as applied in SRE: managing operations and development work, recovering from overload, structuring and managing your relationships with development partners and customers, and implementing practical change management.

If you are an SRE leader, this section is your how-to guide for creating the space and environment your teams need to successfully implement the practices covered in Part II.

## CHAPTER 17

Identifying and Recovering from Overload

By Maria-Hendrike Peetz, Luis Quesada Torres, and Marilia Melo
with Diane Bates

When an SRE team is running smoothly, team members should feel like they can comfortably handle all of their work. They should be able to work on tickets and still have time to work on long-term projects that make it easier to manage the service in the future.

But sometimes circumstances get in the way of a team's work goals. Team members take time off for long-term illnesses or move to new teams. Organizations hand down new production-wide programs for SRE. Changes to the service or the larger system introduce new technical challenges. As workload increases, team members start working longer hours to handle tickets and pages and spend less time on engineering work. The whole team starts to feel stressed and frustrated as they work harder but don't feel like they are making progress. Stress, in turn, causes people to make more mistakes, impacting reliability and, ultimately, end users. In short, the team loses its ability to regulate its daily work and effectively manage the service.

At this point, the team needs to find a way out of this overloaded state. They need to rebalance their workload so that team members can focus on essential engineering work.

Operational load (or *operational workload*) is a term that describes the ongoing maintenance tasks that keep systems and services running at optimal performance. There are three distinct types of operational load: *pages*, *tickets*, and *ongoing operational responsibilities*. Pages typically require immediate attention, and tickets related to urgent problems can have tight deadlines. Both pages and urgent tickets interrupt SREs from working on engineering projects that support the team's operational responsibilities. For that reason, we refer to them as *interrupts*. Chapter 29 (*http://bit.ly/2LQYspl*) of *Site Reliability Engineering* discusses techniques to manage the interrupts that naturally arise when a team is maintaining a complex system in a functional state.

When operational load outstrips a team's ability to manage it, the team ends up in a state of *operational overload* (also called *work overload*). A team is in a state of operational overload when it can't make progress toward key priorities because urgent issues continually preempt project work. In addition to detracting from the team's priorities and service improvements, overload can increase the chance that engineers make errors.[1]

The threshold of operational overload can vary from team to team. Google SRE teams cap operational work at 50% of an engineer's time. A successful SRE team must have confidence that over the long term, they will be able to complete the engineering projects required to reduce the operational load for the services they manage.

This chapter describes how teams at Google progressed from a difficult situation characterized by operational overload to a well-managed workload. Two case studies show the detrimental effect of operational overload on team health, and how the teams made changes to their daily tasks so they could focus on long-term impactful projects. In Case Study 1, overload results when remaining members on a shrinking team are unable to keep up with the workload. In Case Study 2, a team suffers from *perceived overload*—a state that has the same effects as operational overload, but starts as a misperception of the real workload.

While these case studies highlight specific actions that worked for two Google SRE teams, the section "Strategies for Mitigating Overload" on page 366 provides practices for identifying and mitigating overload that apply to any company or organization. Therefore, this chapter should be useful to managers of overloaded teams, or any SRE team concerned about overload.

From Load to Overload

Regardless of its origin, overload is an occupational stress that can cripple productivity. Left unchecked, it can cause serious illness (*http://bit.ly/2sozmWE*). For SRE teams, operational load is typically a combination of cognitively difficult tasks (like debugging memory leaks or segmentation faults) and many small tasks that require frequent context switches (working through quota requests, starting binary rollouts, etc.).

---

1 Kara A. Latorella, *Investigating Interruptions: Implications for Flightdeck Performance* (Hampton, VA: Langley Research Center, 1999), *https://go.nasa.gov/2Jc50Nh*; NTSB, *Aircraft Accident Report: NWA DC-9-82 N312RC, Detroit Metro, 16 August 1987 (No. NTSB/AAR-88/05)* (Washington, DC: National Transportation Safety Board, 1988), *http://libraryonline.erau.edu/online-full-text/ntsb/aircraft-accident-reports/AAR88-05.pdf*.

Work overload often happens when a team doesn't have enough time to handle all these tasks—an objective reality when the number of tasks assigned to a team can't be completed within the given deadline for each task. Perceived overload is more subjective, and happens when individuals on the team *feel* that they have too much work. This usually happens when several organizational or work changes take place over a short period of time, but the team has little opportunity to communicate with leadership about the changes.

It's never clear what problems will develop when you're on-call, or what your workload will be. On the one hand, a single, seemingly innocent ticket about running out of disk space might lead to an in-depth investigation of a recurring garbage collection job. On the other hand, a pager storm with 20+ pages might turn out to be a case of bad monitoring. When it's hard to estimate or predict your workload, you can easily fall victim to cognitive biases and misjudge your workload—for example, you might gauge a ticket queue as too large to finish during your on-call shift. Even if you can finish all the tickets quickly and the actual workload is low, you *feel* overloaded when you first look at the ticket queue. This perceived overload[2] itself has a psychological component that affects your approach and attitude toward your work. If you *don't* start your day with the preconception that there's too much work, you're more likely to dive in and start working your way through the ticket queue. Perhaps you work all day and don't finish your workload (thus facing work overload), but you make a lot more progress than if you had started your day feeling overwhelmed.

Accumulating many interrupts can lead to work overload, but it doesn't have to. But when frequent interruptions are paired with external stress factors, a large workload (or even a small workload) can easily turn into perceived overload. This stress might stem from the fear of disappointing other team members, job insecurity, work-related or personal conflicts, illness, or health-related issues like the lack of sleep or exercise.

If your work isn't properly prioritized, every task can seem equally urgent, leading to both actual and perceived overload. In the case of actual overload, the urgency of tickets and alerts might cause team members to work until they resolve the problem, even if doing so means continuous long hours. When a team faces perceived overload, reprioritizing can help decrease the amount of urgent work, creating space for them to tackle the sources of overload through project work.

---

2 Emmanuelle Brun and Malgorzata Milczarek, *Expert Forecast on Emerging Psychosocial Risks Related to Occupational Safety and Health* (Bilbao, Spain: European Agency for Safety and Health at Work, 2007), *https://osha.europa.eu/en/tools-and-publications/publications/reports/7807118*; M. Melchior, I. Niedhammer, L. F. Berkman, and M. Goldberg, "Do Psychosocial Work Factors and Social Relations Exert Independent Effects on Sickness Absence? A Six-Year Prospective Study of the GAZEL Cohort," *Journal of Epidemiology and Community Health* 57, no. 4 (2003): 285–93, *http://jech.bmj.com/content/jech/57/4/285.full.pdf*.

When analyzing your specific situation, you shouldn't necessarily assume that the workload itself needs to change. Instead, we recommend first quantifying the work your team faces, and how it has (or hasn't) changed over time. For example, you might measure workload by the number of tickets and pages the team handles. If your workload hasn't actually changed over time, the team might feel overloaded simply because they perceive the work as overwhelming. To get a more holistic view of the team's current workload, you can collect a one-time snapshot by asking every member to list all the work tasks they face. Then take a look at psychological stress factors your team faces, such as organizational changes or reprioritization. Once you've done your research, you have a stable basis for making decisions about changing the workload.

"Strategies for Mitigating Overload" on page 366 talks more about how to identify overload, both real and perceived. First, we present two case studies of teams that recognized that they were in overload and took steps to alleviate it.

Case Study 1: Work Overload When Half a Team Leaves

Background

One of Google's internal storage SRE teams was in charge of backends for multiple services, including Gmail, Google Drive, and Google Groups, and many other internal or user-facing services. We experienced a crisis in mid-2016 when two-thirds of the team—including the most senior engineer (the manager)—transferred to other opportunities within a relatively short window, for genuinely entirely unrelated reasons. This event obviously led to a huge workload management problem: fewer SREs available to cover the same operational and project work quickly resulted in overload. Our work was also bottlenecked because each team member's expertise was siloed to a different area of production. While the addition of new team members and three interns would improve our workload in the long term, ramping up those engineers would take a serious investment of time and energy.

Problem Statement

The preceding factors significantly decreased team productivity. We started to fall behind on project work, and tickets related to the many services we managed began to pile up. We didn't have the bandwidth to address this backlog, as all of our work was consumed by higher-priority tasks. It wouldn't be long before we weren't able to undertake all of the critical and urgent work we needed to. Meanwhile, our team was slated to receive more high-priority work soon.

If we didn't move some work off our plate, it was only a matter of time before we accidentally began to drop important work. However, as soon as we started offloading work, we hit some psychological barriers:

- Dropping any work that was in progress felt like we had just wasted our efforts. Most of the backlog seemed to be either critical or worth the effort to us, so it just didn't feel right to cancel or delay projects indefinitely. We didn't realize we were in the grip of a sunk cost fallacy (*http://bit.ly/2Hdgf6t*).

- Putting effort into automating processes or fixing the root cause of the workload was not as critical as immediately dealing with high-priority interrupts. When this work was added to the top of an already huge pile, all of the work felt overwhelming.

What We Decided to Do

We gathered the team in a room and listed all the team's responsibilities, including project backlog, operational work, and tickets. Then we triaged every list item. Viewing every single one of our work tasks (even though the list barely fit on the whiteboard) helped us identify and redefine our actual priorities. We were then able to find ways to minimize, hand off, or eliminate lower-priority work items.

Implementation

We identified low-effort automation that, while not critical, would significantly reduce operational load once deployed.

We also identified common problems that we could document that would enable self-service. Writing the procedures our customers needed didn't take long, and removed some repetitive work from our queue.

We closed as many of our backlogged tickets as we reasonably could. Most of these tickets turned out to be obsolete, redundant, or not as urgent as they claimed. Some tickets were monitoring artifacts that were nonactionable, so we fixed the relevant monitoring. In some cases, we were actively addressing issues that weren't critical. We set these issues aside to work on more urgent tickets, but first documented our progress so we wouldn't lose context before we were able to work on them again.

When in doubt, we dropped a task, but marked it for a second phase of triage. Once our plates were (almost) empty, we revisited this tentative list to decide what tasks to resume. It turned out that almost none of these tasks were impactful or important enough to resume.

In two days—one day of intensive triage plus one day of documenting processes and implementing automation—our much smaller team addressed a backlog of several months of interrupts. We could then deal with the few remaining interrupts, which were related to active issues in production.

Lessons Learned

Our team learned that identifying and scoping overload is the first step toward fixing it. We needed to get everyone in a room and reevaluate the backlog before we could help our team get back to a healthy state.

In order to avoid a new pile-up of interrupts, we started triaging interrupts once every two weeks. Our technical lead periodically checks the task queue and evaluates whether the team is at risk of becoming overloaded. We decided that each team member should have 10 or fewer open tickets to avoid overload. If the team lead notices that team members have more than 10 tickets, they can do one or some combination of the following:

- Remind the team to close out stale tickets.
- Sync with overloaded team members and offload tickets from them.
- Prompt individual team members to address their ticket queue.
- Organize a team-wide one-day ticket fix-it.
- Assign work to fix the sources of tickets, or operational work to reduce future tickets.

Case Study 2: Perceived Overload After Organizational and Workload Changes

Background

The Google SRE team in this case study was split between two locations, with six or seven on-call engineers at each site (for more discussion on team size, see Chapter 11 (*http://bit.ly/2JgUBU7*) of *Site Reliability Engineering*. While the Sydney team was operationally healthy, the Zürich team was overloaded.

Before the Zürich team went into overload, we were stable and content. The number of services we managed was relatively stable, and each was varied and high maintenance. While the SLOs of the services we supported were mismatched with the SLOs of their external dependencies, this mismatch hadn't caused any issues. We were working on a number of projects to improve the services we managed (for example, improving load balancing).

Simultaneous triggers sent the Zürich team into overload: we started onboarding new services that were noisier and less integrated into Google's general infrastructure, and the technical lead manager and another team member left our team, leaving it two people short. The combination of the additional workload and knowledge drain triggered more problems:

- Untuned monitoring for the new services and the migration-related monitoring resulted in more pages per shift. This buildup was gradual, so we didn't notice the uptick as it occurred.

- SREs felt relatively helpless with the new services. We didn't know enough about them to react appropriately, and often needed to ask the development team questions. While the overload perhaps warranted handing a service back to developers, our team had never handed back a service, so we didn't really consider this a viable option.

- A smaller on-call rotation of five people cut into the hours we normally spent on operational work.

- New ticket alerts were surfacing problems that existed before the recent team changes. While we had simply ignored these problems in the past, we were now required to move ignored email alerts to tickets. Project planning hadn't taken this new source of technical debt into account.

- A new ticket SLO required us to handle tickets within three days, meaning that on-callers had to resolve tickets created during their on-call shift much sooner.[3] The SLO aimed to reduce the number of tickets being added to our (mostly ignored) backlog, but created a side effect that was perhaps even worse. Now SREs felt that they couldn't get the rest they needed after a shift because they had to immediately tackle follow-up work. The higher priority placed on these tickets also meant that SREs didn't have enough time for other operational work.

During this time, our team was assigned to a new manager who also managed two other teams. The new manager was not part of the on-call rotation and therefore didn't directly feel the stress team members were experiencing. When the team explained the situation to the manager, nothing changed. Team members felt that they weren't being heard, which left them feeling distant from the management team.

The overload from tickets continued for months, making team members grumpy, until a cascade of unhappiness spread across the team.

Problem Statement

After losing two people and receiving additional and varied work, our team felt overloaded. When we tried to communicate this feeling to our direct manager, the manager disagreed. As the long hours continued, exhaustion set in. Productivity was declining and tasks started accruing faster than the team could resolve them. The perceived overload now became objective overload, making the situation worse.

---

3 For context, according to estimates, an SRE needed at least one additional day of ticket follow-up per shift.

The emotional stress caused by overload was lowering morale and causing some team members to burn out. As individuals dealt with the physical effects from overwork (illness and lower productivity), other people on the team had to pick up more work. The work assigned in weekly team meetings wasn't getting done.

We then started assuming we couldn't depend on other people to get their work done, which eroded feelings of trust and dependability within the team. As a result, we did not feel safe about *interpersonal risk taking*, an important factor in psychological safety (see Chapter 11 (*http://bit.ly/2JgUBU7*) in *Site Reliability Engineering*). Team members didn't feel accepted and respected by other team members, so they didn't freely collaborate with each other. As psychological safety diminished on the team, collaboration stopped, slowing down information sharing and causing further inefficiencies.

Team surveys also revealed a loss of psychological safety—team members said they didn't feel like they belonged on the team. They no longer cared about their own career development, and the promotion rate on the team dropped to an all-time low.

We finally hit a breaking point when upper management assigned us new mandatory company-wide projects. At this point, we renewed our conversations with management about overload with renewed vigor. A series of discussions revealed that our unhappy situation wasn't just a result of too much work—our perceptions of team safety led us to stop trusting and collaborating with each other.

What We Decided to Do

Upper management assigned our team a new manager who wasn't shared among three teams. The new manager used a participatory management style (*http://bit.ly/2kFehmx*) to improve psychological safety on the team so that we could once again collaborate. This method empowers team members to actively participate in solving team problems. The entire team, including our direct manager, engaged in a set of simple team-building exercises to improve the effectiveness of our team (some of which were as simple as drinking tea together).[4] As a result, we were able to draft a set of goals:

Short term
> Relieve stress and improve psychological safety to establish a healthy work atmosphere.

Medium term
> Build confidence of individual team members through training.

> Find the root cause of the issues that are causing overload.

---

4 We used the Google program based on Project Aristotle: *http://bit.ly/2LPemR2*.

Long term

　Resolve ongoing problems that contributed to the cascade.

In order to set these goals, we had to first achieve some kind of baseline psychological safety within the team. As morale improved, we began to share knowledge and build on each other's ideas to figure out ways to get our workload under control.

Implementation

Short-term actions

Long-term stress, whether caused by overwork or perceptions of team safety, decreases productivity and impacts people's health. Therefore, our most important short-term action was to provide stress relief and improve trust and psychological safety. Once relieved of some stress, team members could think more clearly and participate in driving the whole team forward. Within a month of identifying the overload, we implemented the following:

- **Started a semiregular round table to discuss issues.** The team released frustration and brainstormed possible causes of the overload.

- **Found a better metric for measuring load.** We decided to improve upon our original metric of number of pages. We auto-assigned tickets to on-callers, and the on-caller was responsible for these tickets even after their shift ended. Our new metric measured how much time an on-caller needed to resolve a ticket after their shift.

- **Audited and removed spamming alerts.** We reviewed alerts and removed the ones that didn't represent user-facing problems.

- **Silenced alerts generously.** The team deliberately didn't try to find the source for every single alert, but focused on relieving the stress from being paged and ticketed continuously for issues we already knew about. We used the following strategy:

  — Alerts that surfaced were silenced until they were fixed.

  — Alerts could be silenced only for a limited period of time (typically a day, sometimes up to a week). Otherwise, they might mask outages.

  — Alerts that couldn't be fixed within a few minutes were assigned to a tracking ticket.

- **Added a direct manager dedicated to a single team.** Making a well-respected team member the new manager reestablished trust in management. Rather than managing three teams, the new manager could focus more time on the individual team and its members.

- **Rebalanced the team.** We introduced a new perspective and on-call relief by adding technically experienced SREs that didn't have preconceptions about the team or organization. Finding appropriate people was by no means an easy task, but was well worth the effort.

- **Instituted team events like lunches and board game sessions.** Talking about non-work-related topics and laughing together eased tension on the team and improved psychological safety.

Mid-term actions

Short-term solutions alone wouldn't sustain a healthy atmosphere—for example, one of our short-term tactics was to silence alerts without actually fixing the cause. Within three months, we also took the following actions:

- **Limited operational work to on-call time as much as possible** (see Chapter 29 (*http://bit.ly/2LQYspl*) in *Site Reliability Engineering*) so the team could concentrate on permanent fixes and project work.

- **Returned responsibility for one service back to its development team.**

- **Trained each other (and new team members).** While training requires an investment of time and energy, disseminating knowledge meant that all team members (and future hires) could troubleshoot and fix issues more quickly in the future. Training coworkers improved our confidence, because we came to realize that we actually knew quite a bit about the services. As they gained knowledge, team members started to find new ways to manage services, improving their reliability and reducing overload.

- **Brought in SREs from the remote team to staff some of our on-call shifts and participate in training.** They noticed the strain on the team and provided some valuable new perspective.

- **Backfilled the two open roles on the team.**

- **Tackled each alert as the silences expired.** We discussed repetitive pages and pages that resulted in no action at length in the weekly production meeting, which led us to tune alerts and/or fix the underlying problems. While these were important (and obvious) actions, we only had the space to analyze and take action once the alert was silenced and not creating constant noise.

- **Organized listening events.** Management (including the skip-level manager and team leads) made a conscious effort to listen to the team's pain points and to find a team-driven solution.

- **Added perspective.** Hope is not a strategy, but it certainly helps team morale. With the promise of new members joining the on-call rotation, a shift to clearer priorities, and an end to noise-generating projects, the team's mood improved.

Long-term actions

To help maintain our newfound stability, we are currently aligning our SLOs with the SLOs of their service backends, and working toward making the services more uniform. Uniformity has a double benefit: it decreases cognitive load for SREs and makes it easier to write automation that can be used across services. We're also reviewing services that have been around for a long time and updating them to current production standards. For example, some services are operating poorly under load that's increased significantly over the years. Some services need to be updated per changes to their backend services' policies. Other services simply haven't been updated for several years.

Effects

A few months after our first brainstorming meeting, results began to surface: on-call shifts became quieter, and our team managed to quickly and efficiently deal with a difficult incident collaboratively as a group. A bit later, new team members arrived. When we discussed psychological safety during a round-table session, the new members said they couldn't imagine that the team ever had such problems. In fact, they saw our team as a warm and safe place to work. About one year after the original escalation, little of the original overload remained and an anonymous survey showed that team members now felt the team was effective and safe.

Lessons Learned

Workplace changes can have a psychological impact on the people on the team—after all, your teammates are not machines. You need to attend to the team's stress levels so that people start trusting each other enough to work together; otherwise, the team can enter a vicious cycle of overload that causes stress, which in turn prevents you from tackling overload.

Perceived overload *is*, in fact, overload, and has as much impact to a team as work overload caused by other factors. In our case, our sister team in Sydney didn't experience the same issues, and the number of pages we fielded didn't actually change very much compared to previous years. Instead, the loss of two team members, increased cognitive load, increased ticket noise, and a new three-day SLO on tickets led the team to perceive overload. In the end, the difference between objective and perceived overload didn't matter: the perceived overload of a few team members can very quickly lead to overload for the whole team.

Strategies for Mitigating Overload

An outside perspective can sometimes quite easily identify when a team is overloaded. Similarly, it's easy to comment on what actions should have been taken in retrospect. But how do you identify overload when you're in the middle of experiencing it? The path toward a healthy, friendly, and happy work atmosphere can be hard to visualize when you're mired in overload. This section describes practices for both identifying and mitigating overload on your team.

Recognizing the Symptoms of Overload

It's pretty easy to identify an overloaded team if you know the symptoms of overload:

Decreased team morale
> Overload might manifest as rants and complaints. Surveys on relevant topics (job conditions, work satisfaction, projects, peers, and managers) usually reflect team morale and yield more negative results when a team is overloaded. Regular active listening sessions with team leaders can surface issues that you weren't aware of. An essential element of active listening is to listen without judgment.

Team members working long hours, and/or working when sick
> Working overtime without compensation can be a psychosocial stressor. Leaders should set a good example: work contractual hours and stay home when sick.

More frequent illness[5]
> Overworked team members tend to get run down and sick more often.

An unhealthy tasks queue
> We recommend regularly reviewing your team's tasks queue to see how many tickets are backlogged, who is dealing with which issues, and what tasks can be delayed or dropped. If the team is missing deadlines, or if urgent matters prevent you from performing this review regularly, the team is very likely accumulating interrupts faster than it can attend to them.

Imbalanced metrics
> A few key metrics might indicate that your team is overloaded:
>
> - Long time periods to close a single issue
> - High proportion of time spent on toil
> - Large number of days to close issues originating from an on-call session

---

5 Kurt G. I. Wahlstedt and Christer Edling, "Organizational Changes at a Postal Sorting Terminal—Their Effects Upon Work Satisfaction, Psychosomatic Complaints and Sick Leave," *Work and Stress* 11, no. 3 (1997): 279–91.

The team should work together to decide what measures to use. There is no one-size-fits-all approach; every team's overload is reflected in different ways. As a manager, don't impose a measure on the team without getting an idea of each individual's workload and work habits. Team members might feel that you don't understand the work if you insist on using a specific measure. For example, if you're evaluating load by the number of days it takes to fix an issue, one person might work a full day fixing an issue, while another person might distribute the work across several days, along with other work.

Reducing Overload and Restoring Team Health

After reading through the criteria, you might think your team is already overloaded. Don't despair! This section provides a list of ideas to get your team back to a healthy state.

In general, giving team members more control and power reduces perceived overload.[6] While managers might be tempted to resort to micro-management in stressful situations, it's important to keep the team in the loop and work on prioritization together in order to increase the level of performance and job satisfaction.[7] This model assumes a baseline of a functional team (*http://bit.ly/2LPemR2*), where you have (at minimum) a somewhat healthy relationship between management and team members, and between team members.

Identify and alleviate psychosocial stressors

When it comes to fixing a dysfunctional team, first and foremost, individual team members need to regain their sense of psychological safety. A team can function only as well as its individual members.

You can start by identifying and alleviating psychosocial stressors[8] for each individual and the team as a whole. Which of these factors do you actually have control over? You can't control whether or not a team member has a major illness, but you *can* control the size of your team's backlog (as seen in Case Study 1) or silence pages (as in Case Study 2).

---

6 Robert A. Karasek Jr., "Job Demands, Job Decision Latitude, and Mental Strain—Implications for Job Redesign," *Administrative Science Quarterly* 24, no. 2 (1979): 285–308.

7 Frank W. Bond and David Bunce, "Job Control Mediates Change in a Work Reorganization Intervention for Stress Reduction," *Journal of Occupational Health Psychology* 6, no. 4 (2001): 290–302; Toby D. Wall, Paul R. Jackson, and Keith Davids, "Operator Work Design and Robotics System Performance: A Serendipitous Field Study," *Journal of Applied Psychology* 77, no. 3 (1992): 353–62.

8 Brun and Malgorzata, *Expert Forecast.*

Communicate with your partner product developer teams, and let them know your team is overloaded. They might be able to give a helping hand, provide compassion, or even take over entire projects.

When your team members rely on each other and achieve a certain level of psychological safety (*http://bit.ly/2H9Tssg*) (such that they're able to take interpersonal risks), you can give more responsibility to individual team members. Uncovering areas of expertise and assigning point people and technical leads to specific technologies increases their self-confidence and therefore enables them to take risks.

Decision making should be transparent and, if possible, democratic. Each team member should have a feeling of control over the situation. For example, the brainstorming session in Case Study 2 helped the team identify and discuss issues.

Prioritize and triage within one quarter

A healthy team can prioritize and triage issues. Case Study 1 provides a good example of this exercise: the team sat together in a room and reviewed their backlog. The review helped them realize they were overloaded. They reprioritized their work, and worked on the tasks that would quickly reduce some of the overload. The team in Case Study 2 now meets at the end of each quarter to plan and prioritize existing and future work together.

If possible, we recommend that SREs schedule *interrupt-free time* (no on-call) on their calendars, so that they have time to work on qualitatively difficult tasks like developing automation and investigating the root causes of interrupts. In Case Study 2, when the remote team gave the on-call some relief, team members then had precious time to focus on their projects.

If absolutely necessary, drop work: in Case Study 2, the team dropped on-call support for one of their services by returning this responsibility to the development team.

Protect yourself in the future

We strongly recommend establishing metrics to evaluate the team's workload. Regularly review the metrics to make sure they are measuring the right things.

Once your team emerges from overload, you can prevent future overload by taking steps to monitor or resolve the underlying problems. For example, the team in Case Study 1 now maintains a lightweight triage process to detect a growing backlog of tasks. The team in Case Study 2 is currently working on a long-term plan to align backend and service SLOs.

When your team is in overload, prioritize project work that pays down repetitive toil even more than you would if you weren't overloaded. You will profit in the future.

Finally, everyone on the team should feel responsible for the early warning signs (see "Recognizing the Symptoms of Overload" on page 366) that indicate a possible overload situation. Managers should sit down and talk with team members if they feel that the team is moving toward overload.

Conclusion

In a perfect world, SRE teams would always be able to manage interrupts with the tactics described in our first book. But we're only human, and sometimes our teams don't reach that ideal. This chapter examined some of the ways that overload can consume a team and discussed how to detect and respond when it does.

Particularly when it comes to operational work, excessive interrupts can very easily cause a team to slip from a normal workload to overload. Frequent interrupts can lead to overload, and overload negatively affects health and productivity. Overload creates psychosocial stressors for team members, which impacts work even further, causing a self-enforcing cycle.

Perceived overload is a special form of overload that can't be measured by the amount of toil or operational work. It is hard to pinpoint and to eliminate.

In order to keep a team's workload in balance, it's important to constantly monitor (perceived or nonperceived) overload. To better serve your users and do good work, you need to first show respect to yourself and your team. Maintaining a healthy balance in your daily work goes a long way in helping you and your team accomplish that goal.

## CHAPTER 18

SRE Engagement Model

By Michael Wildpaner, Gráinne Sheerin, Daniel Rogers,
and Surya Prashanth Sanagavarapu (New York Times)
with Adrian Hilton and Shylaja Nukala

Chapter 32 (*http://bit.ly/2Lc14wG*) in our first SRE book describes technical and pro‐
cedural approaches that an SRE team can take to analyze and improve the reliability
of a service. These strategies include Production Readiness Reviews (PRRs), early
engagement, and continuous improvement.

Simply put, SRE principles aim to maximize the engineering velocity of developer
teams while keeping products reliable. This two-fold goal is good for the product
users and good for the company. But there's a limit to how much even the best SRE
team can accomplish, and the SRE model is less effective when the domain is too
large and overly complex. The current microservices movement makes this dynamic
even more acute—a small company can easily have more microservices than a single
SRE team can handle. Given a large production landscape, and with the knowledge
that they can't cover every service, an SRE team must decide where to focus their
attention to achieve the best results. Product development and SRE teams can collab‐
orate to identify the correct point of focus.

This chapter adopts the perspective of an SRE team that's intending to provide sup‐
port for a new service. We look at how to engage most effectively with the service,
and with the developer and product teams who own it. Although SRE engagement
often builds around one or more services, the engagement entails much more than
the services themselves—it focuses on understanding the aims of developer and prod‐
uct teams and finding the right way to support them.

Most of this discussion is applicable regardless of your organization's scale. While we
use the word *team* frequently, a team could theoretically start off as a single person
(although that person would be quite busy). Regardless of your team's size, it's

important to proactively define the role of SRE and manage communication and collaboration with product development.

The Service Lifecycle

As described in the preface (*http://bit.ly/2LexAhJ*) to the first SRE book, an SRE team's contributions to service reliability happen throughout all phases of the service lifecycle. Their application of production knowledge and experience can substantially improve the reliability of a service well before any SRE picks up the pager for the service.

Figure 18-1 shows the ideal levels of SRE engagement over the course of a service's life. However, an SRE team might begin their engagement with a service at any stage in the lifecycle. For example, if the development team begins planning a replacement service for an SRE-supported service, SRE might be involved in the new service very early on. Alternatively, an SRE team might formally engage with a service once it has been generally available for months or years and is now facing reliability or scaling challenges. This section provides guidance on how SRE teams can effectively contribute at each phase.

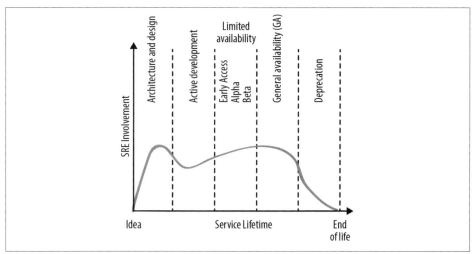

Figure 18-1. Level of SRE engagement during the service lifecycle

Phase 1: Architecture and Design

SRE can influence the architecture and design of a software system in different ways:

- Creating best practices, such as resilience to various single points of failure, that a developer team can employ when building a new product

- Documenting the dos and don'ts of particular infrastructure systems (based upon prior experience) so developers can choose their building blocks wisely, use them correctly, and avoid known pitfalls
- Providing early engagement consulting to discuss specific architectures and design choices in detail, and to help validate assumptions with the help of targeted prototypes
- Joining the developer team and participating in development work
- Codesigning part of the service

Fixing architectural mistakes becomes more difficult later in the development cycle. Early SRE engagement can help avoid costly redesigns that become necessary when systems interact with real-world users and need to scale in response to service growth.

Phase 2: Active Development

As the product takes shape during active development, SREs can start *productionizing* the service—getting it in shape to be released into production. Productionalization typically includes capacity planning, setting up extra resources for redundancy, planning for spike and overload handling, implementing load balancing, and putting in place sustainable operational practices like monitoring, alerting, and performance tuning.

Phase 3: Limited Availability

As a service progresses toward Beta, the number of users, variety of use cases, intensity of usage, and availability and performance demands increase. At this stage, SRE can help measure and evaluate reliability. We strongly recommend defining SLOs before general availability (GA) so that the service teams have an objective measure of how reliable the service is. The product team still has the option to withdraw a product that can't meet its target reliability.

During this phase, the SRE team can also help scale the system by building a capacity model, acquiring resources for upcoming launch phases, and automating turnups and in-place service resizing. SRE can ensure proper monitoring coverage and help create alerts that ideally match the upcoming service SLOs.

While service usage is still changing, the SRE team can expect an increased amount of work during incident response and operational duties because the teams are still learning how the service works and how to manage its failure modes. We recommend sharing this work between the developer and SRE teams. That way, the developer team gains operational experience with the service and the SREs gain experience with the service in general. Operational work and incident management will inform the system changes and updates the service owners need to make before GA.

Phase 4: General Availability

In this phase, the service has passed the Production Readiness Review (see Chapter 32 (*http://bit.ly/2Lc14wG*) in *Site Reliability Engineering* for more details) and is accepting all users. While SRE typically performs the majority of operational work, the developer team should continue to field a small part of all operational and incident response work so they don't lose perspective on these aspects of the service. They might permanently include one developer in the on-call rotation to help the developers keep track of operational load.

In the early phase of GA, as the developer team focuses on maturing the service and launching the first batches of new features, it also needs to stay in the loop to understand system properties under real load. In the later stages of GA, the developer team provides small incremental features and fixes, some of which are informed by operational needs and any production incidents that occur.

Phase 5: Deprecation

No system runs forever. If and when a better replacement system is available, the existing system is closed for new users and all engineering focuses on transitioning users from the existing system to the new one. SRE operates the existing system mostly without involvement from the developer team, and supports the transition with development and operational work.

While SRE effort required for the existing system is reduced, SRE is effectively supporting two full systems. Headcount and staffing should be adjusted accordingly.

Phase 6: Abandoned

Once a service is abandoned, the developer team typically resumes operational support. SRE supports service incidents on a best-effort basis. For a service with internal users, SRE hands over service management to any remaining users. This chapter provides two case studies of how SRE can hand back a service to developer teams.

Phase 7: Unsupported

There are no more users, and the service has been shut down. SRE helps to delete references to the service in production configurations and in documentation.

Setting Up the Relationship

A service does not exist in a vacuum: the SRE team engages with the developer team that builds the service and the product team that determines how it should evolve. This section recommends some strategies and tactics for building and maintaining good working relationships with those teams.

Communicating Business and Production Priorities

Before you can help someone, you need to understand their needs. To that end, SREs need to understand what the product developers expect the SRE engagement to achieve. When engaging with a developer team, SREs should build a deep understanding of the product and business goals. SREs should be able to articulate their role and how SRE engagement can enable developers to execute toward these goals.

Teams need to regularly talk with each other about business and production priorities. The SRE and developer leadership teams should ideally work as a unit, meeting regularly and exchanging views about technical and prioritization challenges. Sometimes SRE leads join the product development leadership team.

Identifying Risks

Because an SRE team is focused on system reliability, they are well positioned to identify potential risks. Gauging the likelihood and potential impact of those risks as accurately as possible is important, as the cost of disrupting regular development and feature flow is significant to the product and to engineers.

Aligning Goals

The developer and SRE teams both care about reliability, availability, performance, scalability, efficiency, and feature and launch velocity. However, SRE operates under different incentives, mainly favoring service long-term viability over new feature launches.

In our experience, developer and SRE teams can strike the right balance here by maintaining their individual foci but also explicitly supporting the goals of the other group. SREs can have an explicit goal to support the developer team's release velocity and ensure the success of all approved launches. For example, SRE might state, "We will support you in releasing as quickly as is safe," where "safe" generally implies staying within error budget. Developers should then commit to dedicating a reasonable percentage of engineering time to fixing and preventing the things that are breaking reliability: resolving ongoing service issues at the design and implementation level, paying down technical debt, and including SREs in new feature development early so that they can participate in design conversations.

Shared Goals: SRE Engagements at the New York Times

by Surya Prashanth Sanagavarapu (New York Times)

In our organization, SRE resources are in high demand when it comes to cloud migrations, production ramp-ups, and applications moving toward containers. In addition, SRE teams have their own backlogs to tackle. In the face of limited resources, these competing priorities define success for the SRE team. While hiring SREs is one obvious way to address the demand for SRE time, not every team has the luxury, experience, or time to do so.

The core mission of the SRE function at the *New York Times* is to *empower product development teams* with tools and processes to maximize reliability and resilience in applications that support our newsroom, thus enabling distribution of high-quality journalism to readers. We adopted a *shared goals model* to achieve a balance between reducing the automation backlog and engaging with other teams.

Before engaging with teams, we review our overall backlog for the current quarter/year and clearly define its work items and categories. For instance, our backlog items might include:

- Add automation to set up baseline monitoring and alerting by hitting service status endpoints for applications.
- Implement more reliable and/or faster build pipelines.

When teams approach SREs for help, one of the factors we consider when prioritizing a request is whether a joint engagement might help reduce our backlog.

Defining the Engagement

Our SREs work with product development teams according to two different models:

- A full-time basis
- A part-time basis for fairly brief and constrained projects

We define the type of engagement based upon the SRE team's bandwidth. For full-time engagements, we prefer to embed an SRE in a product development team. This helps provide focus and time to relieve some burden from the product engineering teams. The SRE and product teams have maximum time to learn about each other as the developers ramp up on SRE skills and capabilities. For long-term engagements, we prioritize applications that best fit into our company strategy.

When defining the engagement scope, we attempt to gauge the maturity of the team or the application in relation to SRE practices. We find that various teams are at different levels of maturity when it comes to thinking about SRE practices and principles. We are working on applying an application maturity model to help here.

Setting Shared Goals and Expectations

Setting the right expectations is critical for meeting deadlines and task completion. To this end, we work according to the following principles:

- We emphasize that the application owners, not SREs, are directly responsible for making changes to an application.
- SRE engagement is for company-wide benefit. Any new automation or tooling should improve common tools and automation used across the company and avoid one-off script development.
- SREs should give the developer team a heads up about any new processes the engagement might introduce (for example, load testing).
- The engagements may involve Application Readiness Reviews (ARRs) and Production Readiness Reviews (PRRs), as described in Chapter 32 (*http://bit.ly/2Lc14wG*) of *Site Reliability Engineering*. Proposed changes from ARR and PRR must be prioritized jointly by the developers and the SREs.
- SREs are not traditional operations engineers. They do not support manual work such as running a job for deployment.

When we set shared goals, we write them jointly with the development team and divide the goals into milestones. If you are an Agile-based company, you might write epics (*http://bit.ly/2LOwI4u*) or stories. The SRE team can then map those goals into their own backlog.

Our common pattern when setting goals is to:

1. Define the scope of the engagement.

   - **Example 1:** In the next quarter, I want all members of my team to handle GKE/GAE deployments, become comfortable with production environments, and be able to handle a production outage.
   - **Example 2:** In the next quarter, I want SRE to work with the dev team to stabilize the app in terms of scaling and monitoring, and to develop runbooks and automation for outages.

2. Identify the end result success story, and call it out explicitly.

   - **Example:** After the engagement, the product development team can handle our service outages in Google Kubernetes Engine without escalation.

Sprints and Communication

Any engagement with product development teams begins with a kickoff and planning meeting. Prior to kickoff, our SRE team reviews the application architecture and our shared goal to verify that the expected outcome is realistic within the given time frame. A joint planning meeting that creates epics and stories can be a good starting point for the engagement.

A roadmap for this engagement might be:

1. Review the application architecture.
2. Define shared goals.
3. Hold the kickoff and planning session.
4. Implement development cycles to reach milestones.
5. Set up retrospectives to solicit engagement feedback.
6. Conduct Production Readiness Reviews.
7. Implement development cycles to reach milestones.
8. Plan and execute launches.

We require that the teams define a feedback method and agree on its frequency. Both the SRE and development teams need feedback on what is working and what is not. For these engagements to be successful, we have found that providing a constant feedback loop outside of Agile sprint reviews via an agreed-upon method is useful—for example, setting up a biweekly retrospective or check-in with team managers. If an engagement isn't working, we expect teams to not shy away from planning for disengagement.

Measuring Impact

We have found it important to measure the impact of the engagement to make sure that SREs are doing high-value work. We also measure the maturity level of each partner team so that the SREs can determine the most effective ways to work with them. One approach we adopted from working with Google's Customer Reliability Engineering (CRE) team is to conduct a *point-in-time assessment* with leads of the product engineering team before starting the engagement.

A point-in-time assessment consists of walking through a maturity matrix, gauging the maturity of the service along the various axes of concern to SRE (as described in Chapter 32 (*http://bit.ly/2Lc14wG*) of *Site Reliability Engineering*), and agreeing on scores for functional areas such as observability, capacity planning, change management, and incident response. This also helps tailor the engagement more appropriately after we learn more about the team's strengths, weaknesses, and blind spots.

After the engagement ends and the development team is performing on its own, we perform the assessment again to measure the value SRE added. If we have a maturity model in place, we measure against the model to see if the engagement results in a higher level of maturity. As the engagement comes to an end, we plan for a celebration!

Setting Ground Rules

At Google, every SRE team has two major goals:

Short term
> Fulfill the product's business needs by providing an operationally stable system that is available and scales with demand, with an eye on maintainability.

Long term
> Optimize service operations to a level where ongoing human work is no longer needed, so the SRE team can move on to work on the next high-value engagement.

To this end, the teams should agree upon some principles of cooperation, such as:

- Definitions of (and a hard limit on) operational work.
- An agreed-upon and measured SLO for the service that is used to prioritize engineering work for both the developer and SRE teams. You *can* start without an SLO in place, but our experience shows that not establishing this context from the beginning of the relationship means you'll have to backtrack to this step later. For an example of how engineering work proceeds less than ideally in the absence of an SLO, see "Case Study 1: Scaling Waze—From Ad Hoc to Planned Change" on page 427.
- An agreed-upon quarterly error budget that determines release velocity and other safety parameters, such as excess service capacity to handle unexpected usage growth.
- Developer involvement in daily operations to ensure that ongoing issues are visible, and that fixing their root causes is prioritized.

Planning and Executing

Proactive planning and coordinated execution ensure that SRE teams meet expectations and product goals while optimizing operations and reducing operational cost. We suggest planning at two (connected) levels:

- With developer leadership, set priorities for products and services and publish yearly roadmaps.
- Review and update roadmaps on a regular basis, and derive goals (quarterly or otherwise) that line up with the roadmap.

Roadmaps ensure that each team has a long-term time horizon of clear, high-impact work. There can be good reasons to forego roadmaps (for example, if the development organization is changing too quickly). However, in a stable environment, the absence of a roadmap may be a signal that the SRE team can merge with another team, move service management work back to the development teams, expand scope, or dissolve.

Holding ongoing strategy conversations with developer leadership helps to quickly identify shifts in focus, discuss new opportunities for SRE to add value to the business, or stop activities that are not cost-effective for the product.

Roadmaps can focus on more than just improving the product. They can also address how to apply and improve common SRE technologies and processes to drive down operational cost.

Sustaining an Effective Ongoing Relationship

Healthy and effective relationships require ongoing effort. The strategies outlined in this section have worked well for us.

Investing Time in Working Better Together

The simple act of spending time with each other helps SREs and developers collaborate more effectively. We recommend that SREs meet regularly with their counterparts for the services they run. It's also a good idea for SREs to meet periodically with other SRE teams who run services that either send traffic to the service or provide common infrastructure that the service uses. The SRE team can then escalate confidently and quickly during outages or disagreements because the teams know each other and have already set expectations of how escalations should be initiated and managed.

Maintaining an Open Line of Communication

In addition to the day-to-day communication between teams, we've found a couple methods of more formal information exchange to be particularly helpful over the course of the engagement.

SREs can give a quarterly "state of production" talk to product development leadership to help them understand where they should invest resources and how exactly SRE is helping their product or service. In a similar vein, developers can give a periodic "state of the product" talk to the SRE team or involve SRE in the developer team's executive presentations. This gives the SRE team an overview of what the developer team has accomplished over the last quarter (and lets the SREs see how their own work enabled that). It also provides an update on where the product is going over the next few quarters, and where the product lead sees SRE engaging to make that happen.

Performing Regular Service Reviews

As the decision makers for the service's future, the SRE and developer team leads responsible for the service should meet face-to-face at least once a year. Meeting more frequently than this can be challenging—for example, because it may involve intercontinental travel. During this meeting, we typically share our roadmaps for the next 12–18 months and discuss new projects and launches.

SRE teams sometimes facilitate a retrospective exercise, where the leads discuss what the teams want to *stop doing*, *keep doing*, and *start doing*. Items can appear in more than one area, and all opinions are valid. These sessions need active facilitation because the best results come from full-team participation. This is often rated the most useful session in the service meeting because it yields details that can drive significant service changes.

Reassessing When Ground Rules Start to Slip

If cooperation in any of the agreed-upon areas (see "Setting Ground Rules" on page 379) begins to regress, both developers and SRE need to change priorities to get the service back in shape. We have found that, depending on the urgency, this can mean any of the following:

- The teams identify specific engineers who must drop their lower-priority tasks to focus on the regression.

- Both teams call a "reliability hackathon," but usual team priorities continue outside of the hackathon days.

- A feature freeze is declared and the majority of both teams focus on resolving the regression.

- Technical leadership determines that the reliability of the product is at acute risk, and the teams call an "all hands on deck" response.

Adjusting Priorities According to Your SLOs and Error Budget

The subtle art of crafting a well-defined SLO helps a team prioritize appropriately. If a service is in danger of missing the SLO or has exhausted the error budget, both teams can work with high priority to get the service back into safety. They can address the situation through both tactical measures (for example, overprovisioning to address traffic-related performance regressions) and more strategic software fixes (such as optimizations, caching, and graceful degradation).

If a service is well within SLO and has ample error budget left, we recommend using the spare error budget to increase feature velocity rather than spending overproportional efforts on service improvements.

Handling Mistakes Appropriately

Humans inevitably make mistakes. Consistent with our postmortem culture (*http://bit.ly/2J2Po2W*), we don't blame people, and instead focus on system behavior. Your mileage may vary, but we have had success with the following tactics.

Sleep on it

If possible, don't conduct follow-up conversations when you're tired or emotions are high. During high-stress situations, people can easily misinterpret tone in written communication like emails. Readers will remember how the words made them feel, not necessarily what was written. When you're communicating across locations, it's often worth the time to set up a video chat so that you can see facial expressions and hear the tone of voice that helps disambiguate words.

Meet in person (or as close to it as possible) to resolve issues

Interactions conducted solely via code reviews or documentation can quickly become drawn out and frustrating. When a behavior or decision from another team is at odds with our expectations, we talk with them about our assumptions and ask about missing context.

Be positive

Thank people for their positive behaviors. Doing so can be simple—for example, during code reviews, design reviews, and failure scenario training, we ask engineers to call out what was good and explain why. You might also recognize good code comments or thank people for their time when they invest in a rigorous design review.

Understand differences in communication

Different teams have different internal expectations for how information is disseminated. Understanding these differences can help strengthen relationships.

Scaling SRE to Larger Environments

The scenarios we've discussed so far involve a single SRE team, a single developer team, and one service. Larger companies, or even small companies that use a microservices model, may need to scale some or all of these numbers.

Supporting Multiple Services with a Single SRE Team

Because SREs have specialized skills and are a scarce resource, Google generally maintains an SRE-to-developer ratio of < 10%. Therefore, one SRE team commonly works with multiple developer teams in their product area (PA).

If SREs are scarce relative to the number of services that merit SRE support, an SRE team can focus their efforts on one service, or on a few services from a small number of developer teams.

In our experience, you can scale limited SRE resources to many services if those services have the following characteristics:

- Services are part of a single product. This provides end-to-end ownership of the user experience and alignment with the user.

- Services are built on similar tech stacks. This minimizes cognitive load and enables effective reuse of technical skills.

- Services are built by the same developer team or a small number of related developer teams. This minimizes the number of relationships and makes it easier to align priorities.

Structuring a Multiple SRE Team Environment

If your company is big enough to have multiple SRE teams, and perhaps multiple products, you need to choose a structure for how SRE and the product groups relate.

Within Google, we support a complex developer organization. As shown in Figure 18-2, each PA consists of multiple product groups that each contain multiple products. The SRE organization shadows the developer organization hierarchically, with shared priorities and best practices at each level. This model works when all teams in a group, or all groups in a PA, share the same or similar specific business goals, and when every product group has both a product leader and an SRE lead.

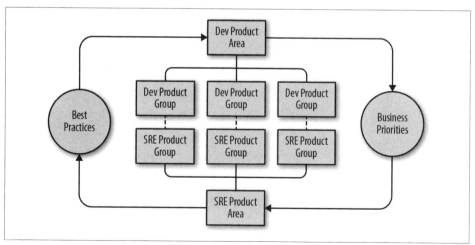

Figure 18-2. Large-scale developer-to-SRE team relationships (per product area)

If your organization has multiple SRE teams, you'll need to group them in some way. The two main approaches we've seen work well are:

- Group the teams within a product, so they don't have to coordinate with too many different developer teams.
- Group the teams within a technology stack (e.g., "storage" or "networking").

To prevent churn in SRE teams during developer reorgs, we recommend organizing SRE teams according to technology rather than developer PA reporting structure. For example, many teams that support storage systems are structured and operate in the same way. Grouping storage systems in technology-focused product groups may make more sense even if they come from different parts of the developer organization.

Adapting SRE Team Structures to Changing Circumstances

If you need to modify the structure of your SRE teams to reflect changing PA needs, we recommend creating, splitting (sharding), merging, and dissolving SRE teams based on service needs and engineering and operational load. Each SRE team should have a clear charter that reflects their services, technology, and operations. When a single SRE team has too many services, rather than building new teams from scratch, we prefer to shard the existing team into multiple teams to transfer culture and grow existing leadership. Changes like this are inevitably disruptive to existing teams, so we'd recommend that you restructure teams only when necessary.

Running Cohesive Distributed SRE Teams

If you need to ensure 24/7 coverage and business continuity, and you have a global presence, it's worth trying to distribute your SRE teams around the globe to provide even coverage. If you have a number of globally distributed teams, we recommend colocating teams based upon adjacency and upon similarity of services and shared technology. We've found that singleton teams are generally less effective and more vulnerable to the effects of reorgs outside the team—we create such teams only if clearly defined business needs call for them and we've considered all other options.

Many companies don't have the resources for full global coverage, but even if you're split only across buildings (never mind continents), it's important to create and maintain a two-location arrangement.

It's also important to create and maintain organizational standards that drive planning and execution and foster and maintain a shared team culture. To this end, we find it useful to gather the entire team in one physical location periodically—for example, at an org-wide summit every 12–18 months.

Sometimes it doesn't make sense for everyone on the team to own certain responsibilities—for example, conducting regular test restores from backups or implementing cross-company technical mandates. When balancing these responsibilities between a team's distributed sites, keep the following strategies in mind:

- Assign individual responsibilities to single locations, but rotate them regularly (e.g., yearly).
- Share every responsibility between locations, making an active effort to balance the involvement and workload.
- Don't lock a responsibility to a single location for multiple years. We've found that the costs of this configuration ultimately outweigh the benefits. Although that location will tend to become really good at executing those responsibilities, this fosters an "us versus them" mentality, hinders distribution of knowledge, and presents a risk for business continuity.

All of these strategies require locations to maintain tactical and strategic communication.

Ending the Relationship

SRE engagements aren't necessarily indefinite. SREs provide value by doing impactful engineering work. If the work is no longer impactful (i.e., the value proposition of an SRE engagement goes away), or if the majority of the work is no longer on the engineering (versus operations) side, you may need to revisit the ongoing SRE engagement. In general, individual SREs will move away from toil-heavy teams to teams with more interesting engineering work.

On a team level, you might hand back a service if SRE no longer provides sufficient business value to merit the costs. For example:

- If a service has been optimized to a level where ongoing SRE engagement is no longer necessary
- If a service's importance or relevance has diminished
- If a service is reaching end of life

The following case studies demonstrate how two Google SRE engagement models ended. The first ends with largely positive results, while the other ends with a more nuanced outcome.

Case Study 1: Ares

Google's Abuse SRE and Common Abuse Tool (CAT) teams provided anti-abuse protection for most Google properties and worked with customer-facing products to keep users safe. The Abuse SRE team applied engineering work to lower CAT's operational support burden so that the developers were able to take a direct role in supporting their users. These users were the Googlers operating the properties defended by CAT, who had high expectations about the efficacy of CAT and its response time to problems or new threats.

Efficient abuse fighting requires constant attention, rapid adaptive changes, and nimble flexibility in the face of new threats and attacks. These requirements clashed with the common SRE goals of reliable and planned feature development. CAT teams routinely needed to implement fast development and deploy new protections to properties under attack. However, Abuse SRE pushed back on requested changes, requesting more in-depth analysis of the consequences each new protection would have on the overall production system. Time constraints on consultations between teams and reviews compounded this tension.

To hopefully improve the situation, Abuse SRE and CAT leadership engaged in a multiyear project to create a dedicated infrastructure team within CAT. The newly formed "Ares" team had a mandate to unify abuse-fighting infrastructure for Google properties. This team was staffed by CAT engineers who had production infrastructure knowledge and experience building and running large services. The teams started an exchange program to transfer production management knowledge from Abuse SRE to the CAT infrastructure team members.

Abuse SREs taught the Ares team that the easiest way to launch a new service in production (when you're already running large distributed services) is to minimize the additional cognitive load that the service imposes. To reduce this cognitive load, systems should be as homogeneous as possible. Deploying and managing a collection of production services together means they can share the same release structure, capacity planning, subservices for accessing storage, and so on. Following this advice, Ares redesigned the whole abuse-fighting stack, applying modularity concepts to shift toward a microservice model. They also built a new layer that provided abstractions for developers so that they didn't have to worry about lower-level production details like monitoring, logging, and storage.

At this point, the Ares team started to act more like an SRE team for CAT by administering the new abuse-fighting infrastructure. Meanwhile, Abuse SRE focused on the production deployment and efficient day-to-day operation of the overall abuse-fighting infrastructure.

Collaboration between the Ares engineers and Abuse SRE resulted in the following improvements:

- Because the CAT team now had "in-house" production experts that were also experts in abuse fighting, Abuse SRE no longer had to vet new feature integration. This greatly reduced time to production for new features. At the same time, the CAT team's developer velocity increased because the new infrastructure abstracted away production management details.

- The Abuse SRE team now had many fewer requests from the CAT team to launch new features, as most of the requests did not require infrastructure changes. The team also needed less knowledge to evaluate the impact of a new feature, since infrastructure changes were rarely required. When infrastructure changes were necessary, Abuse SRE only needed to clarify the implications on the infrastructure rather than specific feature functionality.

- Products that needed to integrate with abuse-fighting infrastructure had a faster and more predictable turnaround time since a product integration was now equivalent in effort to a feature launch.

At the end of this project, Abuse SREs disengaged from directly supporting CAT, focusing instead on the underlying infrastructure. This did not compromise CAT's reliability or overburden the CAT team with additional operational work; instead, it increased CAT's overall development velocity.

Currently, Ares protects users across a large number of Google properties. Since the team's inception, SREs and product development have partnered to make collaborative decisions on how infrastructure will work in production. This partnership was only possible because the Ares effort created a sense of shared destiny.

Case Study 2: Data Analysis Pipeline

Sometimes the cost of maintaining an SRE support relationship is higher than the value (perceived or measured) that SREs provide. In these cases, it makes sense to end the relationship by disbanding the SRE team.[1]

When the value of a relationship declines over time, it is extremely difficult to identify a point in time when it makes sense to terminate that relationship. Two teams at Google that supported a revenue-critical data analysis pipeline had to face this challenge. Figuring out that a parting of the ways was appropriate was not a trivial task, especially after a decade of cooperation. In retrospect, we were able to identify several patterns within the team interaction that were strong indicators that we needed to reconsider the relationship between the SRE team and the product team.

The pivot

Three years before the turndown, all involved parties recognized that their primary data analysis pipeline was running into scaling limitations. At that time, the developer team decided to start planning their new system and dedicated a small number

---

1 Google HR supports employees by finding new opportunities when such transitions occur.

of engineers to the new effort. As that effort began to coalesce, it made sense to deprioritize development of large, complex, or risky features for the existing system in favor of work on the new system. This had two important effects over time:

- An informal rule was applied to new projects: if the project's complexity or the risk involved in modifying the existing system to accommodate the project was sufficiently high, then it was better to make that investment in the new system.

- As resources shifted to developing the new system, even relatively conservative changes to the existing system became more difficult. Nevertheless, usage continued to grow at an extremely high rate.

Communication breakdown

Keeping an existing system operational while a replacement system is simultaneously designed, built, and launched is challenging for any engineering team. Stresses naturally build between the people focused on new versus old systems, and teams need to make difficult prioritization decisions. These difficulties can be compounded when the teams are separated organizationally—for example, an SRE team focused on maintaining and operating an existing system and a developer team working on the next-generation system.

Regular, open, and cooperative communication is vital throughout this entire cycle in order to maintain and preserve a good working relationship across teams. In this example, a gap in communication led to a breakdown in the working relationship between teams.

Decommission

It took some time to realize that the disconnectedness between the SRE and developer teams was insurmountable. Ultimately, the simplest solution was to remove the organizational barrier and give the developer team full control over prioritizing work on old and new systems. The systems were expected to overlap for 18–24 months before the old system was fully phased out.

Combining SRE and product development functions into a single team allowed upper management to be maximally responsive to their areas of accountability. Meanwhile, the team could decide how to balance operational needs and velocity. Although decommissioning two SRE teams was not a pleasant experience, doing so resolved the continual tension over where to invest engineering effort.

Despite the inevitable extra operational load on the developer team, realigning ownership of the old system with people who had greater knowledge of service internals provided the opportunity to more quickly address operational problems. This team also had more insight into potential causes of outages, which generally resulted in more effective troubleshooting and quicker issue resolution. However, there were some unavoidable negative impacts while the developer team learned about the nuances of the operational work needed to support the service in a short amount of time. The SRE team's final job was to make the transfer of this knowledge as smooth as possible, equipping the developer team to take on the work.

It is worth noting that if the working relationship were healthier—with teams working together effectively to solve problems—SRE would have handed production work back to the developer team for a short period of time. After the system was restabilized and hardened for expected growth needs, SRE would normally reassume responsibility of the system. SRE and development teams need to be willing to address issues head on and identify points of tension that need resetting. Part of SRE's job is to help maintain production excellence in the face of changing business needs, and often this means engaging with developers to find solutions to challenging problems.

Conclusion

The form of an SRE team's engagement changes over the various phases of a service's lifecycle. This chapter provided advice specific to each phase. Examples from both the Google and the *New York Times* SRE teams show that effectively managing the engagement is just as important as making good technical design decisions. Sometimes an SRE engagement should reach a natural conclusion. Case studies from Ares and a data analysis pipeline team provided examples of how this can happen, and how best to end the engagement.

When it comes to best practices for setting up an effective relationship between SRE and product development teams, a shared sense of purpose and goals with regular and open communication is key. You can scale an SRE team's impact in a number of ways, but these principles for relationship management should always hold true. For sustaining the long-term success of an engagement, investing in aligning team goals and understanding each other's objectives is as important as defending SLOs.

## CHAPTER 19

SRE: Reaching Beyond Your Walls

By Dave Rensin
with Betsy Beyer, Niall Richard Murphy, and Liz Fong-Jones

It has been 14 years since we started practicing SRE at Google. Some of what has come in that time seems obvious in retrospect, while other developments came as something of a shock. The past two years since the publication of our first SRE book (*http://bit.ly/2kIcNYM*) have been especially interesting. The number of companies now practicing the SRE discipline and the amount of time we spend talking about it at conferences and with customers has grown beyond anything we previously imagined.

That change in particular—the rapid expansion of the non-Google ecosystem around SRE—is the most exciting development, but it makes predicting the future of the SRE profession more difficult. Still, in our own SRE work at Google we are starting to see some trends that might inform an outline of the profession's future. This chapter represents our effort to share what we, along with our SRE coworkers around the globe, have seen, and what we have concluded so far.

Truths We Hold to Be Self-Evident

The only way to make any useful sense of the future is to start with a set of principles and work forward. Some of what follows should be uncontroversial. Other bits, not so much. In every case, though, these principles are based on real things we're seeing in the world (*http://bit.ly/2JcAIKg*).

Reliability Is the Most Important Feature

People don't normally disagree much with us when we assert that "reliability is the most important feature of any system"—as long as we take care to point out that "reliability" often covers a wide area.

The argument is simple enough:

- If a system isn't reliable, users won't trust it.
- If users don't trust a system, when given a choice, they won't use it.
- Since all software systems are governed by network effects, if a system has no users, it's worth nothing.
- You are what you measure, so choose your metrics carefully.

Your Users, Not Your Monitoring, Decide Your Reliability

Since the value of a system is related to its users, it stands to reason that the only measure of reliability that matters is how your users experience reliability. If your user is worried that your platform is responsible for instability they're experiencing, then telling them "our monitoring looks fine; the problem must be on your end" won't make them any less grumpy. They're experiencing your system as unstable, and that's what they will remember when the time comes to choose between you and your competitor. (This phenomenon is called the peak-end rule (*http://bit.ly/2sy1jul*).)

Your monitoring, logs, and alerting are valuable only insofar as they help you notice problems before your customers do.

If You Run a Platform, Then Reliability Is a Partnership

If the only way for someone to use your system is via a visual user interface (e.g., a web page) *and* your system is consumed only by actual human beings (as opposed to machines), *then* the reliability your users experience is almost exclusively tied to the job you do as an SRE keeping your system healthy.

However, once you add an API and some of your "users" are actually other machines, you are running a platform and the rules change.

When your product acts as a platform, the reliability your users experience isn't limited to the choices you make. Reliability becomes a partnership. If your users build or operate a system on your platform that never achieves better than 99% availability— even if you're running your platform at 99.999% availability—then their *best-case* experience (*http://bit.ly/2HbIiDl*) is 98.99901%.

The choices these users make directly affect the experience they have and associate with your service. You might not like it, but they will hold you accountable for whatever they experience—even if it's not "your fault."

Everything Important Eventually Becomes a Platform

Since the value of your system increases with the number of people using it, you will want to find ways to reach other large established user pools. As you attract more users, other software systems will want to reach your audience, too.

This is when other companies start making their machines talk to your machines via APIs. If your system is even remotely popular, integration is an inevitable step in your evolution.

Even if you decide that you don't care about other user communities, and decide to never create a machine-consumable API, you still won't be able to avoid this future. Other people will simply wrap (*http://bit.ly/2JoZwlR*) your UI into a machine API and consume it. The only difference is that you'll have no control over the outcome.

Once your system becomes a gateway to a large collection of users, it becomes valuable. APIs—official or unofficial—will be a part of your future.

When Your Customers Have a Hard Time, You Have to Slow Down

When your customers have a hard time, their frustration turns into friction for you. Even if you don't have traditional modes of support (trouble tickets, email, phone, etc.), you will still spend time triaging questions and responding to complaints via StackOverflow, or even Twitter, Facebook, and other social platforms.

Whatever energy you put into helping users past their difficult moments is energy you can't invest in advancing your system. We have seen many teams (and companies) allow their time to be slowly absorbed by break/fix customer problems—leaving an ever-diminishing innovation budget. These teams are consumed by toil.

Once in this state, it's hard to dig out (see Chapter 6). A better plan is to get ahead of the impending toil. You might be reading this and thinking, *Gee, I'm on an internal platform team. This doesn't apply to me!*

We're sorry to inform you that this *doubly* applies to you! In your case, your customers are the consumers of your system within your company.

This leads us to the next conclusion.

You Will Need to Practice SRE with Your Customers

If you want your customers to design and operate reliable systems using your platform, you have to teach them how to do it. Yes, this includes your *internal* customers, too. Just because you work on an internal platform team doesn't mean you escape this dynamic—in fact, you're likeliest to run into it first.

Even if you could perfectly distill that information into highly scaled one-to-many forms (books, blog posts, architecture diagrams, videos, etc.), you still need a way to figure out what content and training to include. As you grow and improve your platform, those lessons will change. You will always need a way to keep these resources from getting stale.

The best way to learn these lessons is to "do SRE" with your customers.

That doesn't necessarily mean you need to take the pagers for your customers' systems, but you do need to undertake most of the work that normally leads up to pager handoff (meaning the system has met certain minimum viable reliability requirements), with at least a representative sample of your users.

How to: SRE with Your Customers

The idea of walking an SRE journey with your customers might seem a little daunting. You're probably reading this book because you're not entirely sure how to walk it yourself! No worries. It's possible to do both at the same time. In fact, the former can help you accelerate the latter.

Here are the steps we like to follow. They work pretty well for us, and we think they'll be useful for you, too.

Step 1: SLOs and SLIs Are How You Speak

You want your customers to perceive your system as reliable. Otherwise, you risk losing them. It stands to reason, therefore, that you should care a lot about *how* they form those opinions. What do they measure? How do they measure it? Most importantly, what promises (*https://oreil.ly/2snieke*) are they making to *their* customers?

Your life will be a lot better if your customers measure SLIs and alert on SLOs (*http://bit.ly/2KNCD9F*), and if they share those measurements with you. Otherwise, you will spend a lot of energy in conversations like this:

> **Customer:** API call X usually takes time T, but now it's taking time U. I think you are having a problem. Please look into it and get back to me immediately.
>
> **You:** That performance seems in line with what we expect, and everything looks fine on our end. Is it a problem if API call X takes this long?
>
> **Customer:** I don't know. It doesn't usually take this long, so obviously something has changed and we're worried about it.

This conversation will go round in circles and never reach a satisfactory answer. You will either spend a lot of time convincing your customer that they shouldn't care, or you will spend a lot of time root-causing the change so you can convince your customer they shouldn't care. In either case, you're spending a lot of effort that you could be using elsewhere.

The root cause of this problem is that the customer isn't using SLOs to figure out if they should care about the performance they're seeing. They're just noticing an unexpected change and deciding to worry about it. Remember, in the absence of a stated SLO, your customer will inevitably invent one and not tell you until you don't meet it! You'd much rather have this conversation:

> **Customer:** We're burning through our SLO for application FOO too quickly and the application is in jeopardy. SLIs X and Y seem to have fallen off a cliff. They both depend on your API X.
>
> **You:** Okay. Let me look into how API X is performing in our system and/or how it's performing specific to you.

That's a *much* more productive conversation because (a) it will happen only when the SLO is threatened, and (b) it relies on mutually understood metrics (SLIs) and targets (SLOs).

If you're running your systems using SRE practices, then you are speaking SLOs internally. Your life will be better and your customers will be happier if they are speaking SLOs, too, because it makes it easier for the two of you to talk.

We recommend a simple exercise to make your working relationship with a customer a lot better: sit down with your customer. Explain SLOs, SLIs, and error budgets—and especially how you practice them in your teams. Then help them describe the critical applications they've built on your platform in those terms.

Step 2: Audit the Monitoring and Build Shared Dashboards

Once your customers have picked some basic SLOs for their application, the next question is if they are measuring the right things (*http://bit.ly/2LgroWF*) to determine whether or not they're meeting those goals. You should help them figure out if the measurements they're using are appropriate.

In our experience, up to half of the things your customer is measuring (and alerting on) have zero impact on their SLOs. Your life will be better when you point this out to them and they turn off the offending alerting. It will mean fewer pages for them, and for you!

The remaining measurements are useful candidate SLIs. Help your customer assemble those measurements to calculate their SLOs.

Once you begin this exercise, you'll quickly find that parts of the SLOs are *uncovered*—there aren't relevant measurements in place to say anything useful about these dimensions. You should help your customer cover these parts of their SLOs, too.

Now, your customers can start to say something about their application's SLO performance on your platform.

Finally, build a set of shared SLO dashboards with your customer. You should be able to see their application SLOs, and you should share any information you have that's relevant to how they're experiencing your system performance. Your goal is that whenever your customer contacts you because their SLO seems threatened, you shouldn't have to swap much additional information. All of that information should be in the shared monitoring.

Step 3: Measure and Renegotiate

Once you sort the measurements out, you should collect data for a month or two. Be prepared for the likelihood that your customer is in for a rude awakening. The application they thought was operating at "five 9s" (99.999%; *everybody* thinks they're getting five 9s) is probably achieving only 99.5%–99.9% when measured against their shiny new SLOs.

After the initial shock wears off, this is a great time to point out that their users aren't yelling all the time, so they probably never needed the five 9s they haven't really been getting.

The key question is, how satisfied are their users with the application's performance? If their users are happy, and there's no evidence that improving performance or availability will increase user adoption/retention/usage, then you're done. You should periodically ask yourself this question to make sure that your budgets and priorities are still correct. (See Chapter 2 for a more in-depth treatment of this topic.)

If the customer thinks they still need to make things a little better, move on to the next step.

Step 4: Design Reviews and Risk Analysis

Sit down with your customer and really understand how their application is designed and operated. Do they have any hidden single point of failures (SPOFs)? Are their rollouts and rollbacks manual? Basically, conduct the same exercise you conduct for your own internal applications.

Next, rank the issues you find by how much of their error budget each item consumes. (Read more about how to do that on the Google Cloud Platform Blog (*http://bit.ly/2LOwWZo*).) Pay attention to which items your customer chooses to fix in order to "earn back the 9s" they want (e.g., to move from 99.5% to 99.9%).

What you learn from these reviews will tell you:

- How your customers consume your platform

- What reliability mistakes they make when doing so
- Which tradeoffs they choose when trying to improve

This exercise will also help your customer set realistic expectations around the reliability they should experience with their current application. Their expectations will affect their perceptions, so setting them appropriately can only be helpful in earning and keeping their trust.

Step 5: Practice, Practice, Practice

The final step is to create some operational rigor with your customer. Practice simulated problems (Wheel of Misfortune exercises, disaster and recovery testing (*http://bit.ly/2sAoKTX*), paper game days, etc.).

Develop a healthy muscle memory between the teams for effective ways to communicate during a crisis. It's a great way to build trust, lower the MTTR, and learn about weird operational edge cases that you can integrate as enhancements into your platform features.

When an incident does occur, don't just share your postmortems with your customer. Actually conduct some *joint postmortems* (*http://bit.ly/2LhcdfY*). Doing so will also build trust and teach you some invaluable lessons.

Be Thoughtful and Disciplined

It will quickly become impossible to carry out these steps with more than a small percentage of your customers. Please don't try extending this model to everyone. Instead, make some principled decisions about how you will make selections. Here are some common approaches:

Revenue coverage
> Select the minimum number of customers to account for XX% of your revenue. If your revenue is heavily weighted to a few large customers, then this might be the right choice for you.

Feature coverage
> Select the minimum number of customers to cover more than XX% of your platform features. If you run a highly diverse platform with a long tail of customers doing a lot of different things, then this approach will help you avoid surprises.

Workload coverage
> Your platform's usage may be dominated by a few distinct use cases or customer types. Perhaps no individual customer in those types is dominant, but you can easily group them into cohorts. In that case, sampling one or two customers from

each cohort is a good way to get platform coverage and discover operational differences between the use cases.

Whatever approach you choose, stick to it. Mixing and matching will confuse your stakeholders and quickly overwhelm your team.

Conclusion

Over the last few years, the SRE profession and role has spread widely outside the walls of Google. Although we never expected this, we are nonetheless thrilled by it. We might be able to say something credible about how we think the discipline will evolve inside Google, but in the wild—well, that's an "uncomfortably exciting" proposition (*http://bit.ly/2LfhBQq*).

One thing we feel pretty sure about is that as you adopt SRE principles into your organization, you will cross many of the same inflection points we did (and some we have not!)—including the need to blur the lines more between where your customers end and where you start.

Engaging with individual customers at this level of operational depth is a rewarding new frontier for us, and we're still very much on the path. (You can follow along online at the Google Cloud Platform Blog (*http://bit.ly/2xwZ2oQ*).) The further we go, however, the more certain we are that this is a journey that you, too, will need to take.

## CHAPTER 20

SRE Team Lifecycles

By David Ferguson and Prashant Labhane
with Shylaja Nukala

The Preface to this book set a goal to "dispel the idea that SRE is implementable only at 'Google scale' or in 'Google culture.'" This chapter lays out a roadmap for maturing an SRE organization from unstaffed but aspirational, through various stages of maturity, to a robust and (potentially) globally distributed set of SRE teams. Regardless of where you are in your journey as an SRE organization, this chapter will help you identify strategies for evolving your SRE organization.

We discuss the SRE principles that need to be in place at each stage of this journey. While your own journey will vary depending on the size, nature, and geographic distribution of your organization, the path we describe to successfully apply SRE principles and implement SRE practices should be generalizable to many different types of organizations.

SRE Practices Without SREs

Even if you don't have SREs, you can adopt SRE practices by using SLOs. As discussed in Chapter 2, SLO are the foundations for SRE practices. As such, they inform our first principle of SRE:

Principle #1

SRE needs SLOs with consequences.

The performance of your service relative to SLOs should guide your business decisions.

We believe that the following practices—which you can achieve without even having a single SRE—are the crucial steps toward implementing SRE practices:

- Acknowledge that you don't want 100% reliability.
- Set a reasonable SLO target. This SLO should measure the reliability that is most important to your users.
- Agree on an error budget policy that will help defend your user experience. Use the error budget to help guide:
  - Tactical actions to mitigate outages or to manage changes that return your system to a reliable state
  - Longer-term prioritization of work to make the system more reliable and use less of the error budget
- Measure the SLO and commit to following the error budget policy. This commitment requires agreement from company leadership.

Even if an organization doesn't have SRE staff, we believe that it is worthwhile to set SLOs for critical customer applications and to implement an error budget policy, if only because an implicit 100% SLO means a team can only ever be reactive. This SRE principle allows you to make data-informed decisions about how to ensure the reliability of your application.

Starting an SRE Role

Finding Your First SRE

It's possible that your first SRE employees won't have explicit experience as an SRE. We've found the following areas to be relevant to the SRE role, and therefore appropriate to cover in interviews:

Operations
Running applications in production gives invaluable insights that cannot be easily gained otherwise.

Software engineering
SREs need to understand the software they are supporting, and be empowered to improve it.

Monitoring systems
SRE principles require SLOs that can be measured and accounted for.

Production automation
Scaling operations requires automation.

System architecture
    Scaling the application requires good architecture.

Your first SRE will likely occupy a difficult and ambiguous position between velocity and reliability goals. They will need to be resilient and flexible in order to provide the right balance between enabling product development and defending the customer experience.

Placing Your First SRE

Once you've hired your first SRE, you now need to decide where to embed them in your organization. You have three main choices:

- In a product development team
- In an operations team
- In a horizontal role, consulting across a number of teams

We recommend that you evaluate the pros and cons of each of these three options after reading this chapter, taking into account:

Your own role and sphere of influence.
    If you're able to effectively influence product development team(s), then embedding an SRE in operations or horizontal work can help iron out gnarly production issues early.

The immediate challenges that you face.
    If the challenges require hands-on work to mitigate a technical problem or business risk, then embedding an SRE in an operations or product team can be advantageous. Doing so removes organizational silos and facilitates easy communication between team members.

The challenges you expect to face in the next 12 months.
    For example, if you're focusing on launches, embedding the SRE within a product development team might make sense. If you're focusing on infrastructure changes, embedding the SRE with an operations team might make more sense.

Your plan for how you want to change your organization.
    If you plan to move toward a centralized SRE organization, you might not want to embed SREs in product development teams initially—it might be hard to remove them from these teams later.

The person you have identified as your first SRE.
    Decide where this first SRE would be most productive based upon their background and skills.

It might make sense to experiment with different models as you figure out which approach works best for you. However, we strongly recommend sticking with one stable and coherent model in the long term; otherwise, the instability will undermine the effectiveness of SRE.

Bootstrapping Your First SRE

Your first SRE's initial mission is to get up to speed on the service. In order to have a positive impact, an SRE needs to understand the service's current problems, its required toil (see Chapter 6) and the engineering required to keep the system within SLOs. If your organization doesn't already have SLOs and error budgets as per Principle #1, your first SRE needs to perform the engineering required to design and implement these tools. At this point, our second SRE principle comes into play:

Principle #2

SREs must have time to make tomorrow better than today.

Without this principle, toil will only increase as service usage increases and the system becomes correspondingly larger and more complex. A healthy balance between operational responsibilities and project work is essential—if toil becomes too burdensome, talented engineers will flee the team. For more guidance on how an SRE team might obtain that balance, see Chapter 17.

Initial project work might focus on one of the following:

- Improving monitoring so you can better understand the system when things go wrong.
- Addressing any high-priority actions identified in recent postmortems (see Chapter 10).
- Implementing automation to reduce a specific element of toil required to run the service.

It is vital that the SRE has a distinctive role and that their projects benefit the whole team. Look out for signs that the SRE work is not going well:

- Their mix of work is indistinguishable from other engineering work.
- If your first SRE is on a product development team, they are doing more than their fair share of operational work, or they are the only person working on service configuration changes.

- The SLOs are not being taken seriously, and the SRE isn't making progress in measuring and defending the customer experience.

Distributed SREs

If your organization doesn't have (or doesn't plan to have) a discrete SRE team (or teams), it's important to construct a community for distributed SREs. This community should advocate the SRE's distinctive role and drive consistent changes in reliability-focused technology or practices across teams. Without a social grouping, individual SREs may feel very isolated.

Your First SRE Team

You might start an SRE team in a number of ways. Approaches we've used at Google, from least to most complex, include:

- Creating a new team as part of a major project
- Establishing a horizontal SRE team
- Converting an existing team (for example, an operations team)

The approach that's best for your organization is highly situational. A team needs enough SREs to handle the operational tasks required to run the service. Addressing that workload brings us to our third principle:

Principle #3

SRE teams have the ability to regulate their workload.

Outside of a large SRE organization, a team likely can't embrace this concept from day one. This principle is open to interpretation and can be difficult to put into practice organizationally. It's also the most subtle of our three principles, and bears some unpacking. The following sections walk through the stages of building a team, using Tuckman's performance model and stages of *forming*, *storming*, *norming*, and *performing*.[1]

---

1 Bruce W. Tuckman, "Developmental Sequence in Small Groups," *Psychological Bulletin* 63, no. 6 (1965): 384–99.

Forming

The team you assemble should have combined experience and expertise that includes the following:

- Making changes to application software to improve reliability and performance.
- Writing software to:
  - Expedite the detection and mitigation of problems in production.
  - Automate manual processes.
- Establishing and using strong software practices and standards to facilitate long-term maintainability.
- Having a methodical and careful approach to making operational changes: be able to describe why certain practices are reliable.
- Understanding system architecture (distributed systems design and operation).

Ideally, your team will be ready to adopt a new way of working, and have a balance of skills and established personal relationships with other teams. If possible, we recommend that you seed the team with internal transfers. This can reduce the time it takes your team to get up and running.

Creating a new team as part of a major project

You might create a new SRE team for a major project that is large enough to justify new headcount, and for which reliability and operational capability have been identified as project risks. Examples might include the creation of a new service or a substantial change in your technology (e.g., migration to a public cloud).

Assembling a horizontal SRE team

In this approach (well documented in Chapter 27 (*http://bit.ly/2kGWVWf*) of our first book), a small team of SREs consults across a number of teams. This team might also establish best practices and tools for configuration management, monitoring, and alerting.

Converting a team in place

You might be able to convert an existing team into an SRE team. The existing team likely isn't a product development team; typical candidates include an operations team or a team responsible for managing a popular open source component that your organization uses heavily. Be careful to avoid renaming a team from "Operations" to "SRE" without first applying SRE practices and principles! If your rebranding effort fails, your organization may be poisoned against the entire concept of SRE in the future.

Storming

Once assembled, the team needs to start working collaboratively: the team members need to work well with each other, and also with other teams.

You might employ any number of tactics to promote this type of cohesion. At Google, we've had success providing a regular forum for learning and discussing SRE practices and reflecting on how the team is performing. For example, you might hold a regular television lunch, where you show a video from SREcon, or a book club, where you all preread some relevant content and then discuss how you can apply it.

During this phase, encourage your new SRE team to stretch themselves. Your new SREs should be comfortable speaking out about SRE practices that don't fit within your organization, and whether it's worth making the change so they fit.

Risks and mitigations

During this nascent phase of the SRE journey, there are a number of ways the team might fail. Next we present some risks and possible mitigation strategies, broken down by how the new team formed. You might use one or more of the mitigation strategies for each risk.

New team as part of a major project

Risks

The team:

- Spreads itself too thin by taking responsibility for too many services at once.
  - A team that is constantly firefighting doesn't have time to address risk in a more permanent way.

- Becomes too introspective trying to understand SRE principles and how to implement them. As a result, it underdelivers.
  - For example, the team might become consumed with developing the perfect SLO definition, neglecting the needs of the service in the meantime.

- Doesn't examine its work thoroughly. As a result, service management reverts to previous behaviors.
  - The team is paged 100 times a day. Since the pages don't indicate that immediate intervention is required, they ignore the pages.

- Abandons SRE principles and practices in order to meet product milestones.
  - Reliability improvements to defend the SLO, such as architectural changes, may never be implemented because they set back development timelines.

- Gets distracted by conflict with existing teams that perceive a loss of influence or power as a result of the new SRE team.
- Does not have the necessary breadth of skills, so delivers only part of the necessary improvements.
  - Without the ability to, for example, program, SREs may be unable to instrument the product to measure reliability.

Mitigations
The team:

- Engages initially on a single important service.
- Engages as early as possible on the project, ideally at the design stage.
- Has input into the design, with a particular focus on defining SLOs and analyzing reliability risks inherent in the design.
- Partners with the product development team and works on features specific to reliability and integration with existing operational platforms.
- Is not expected to have operational responsibility on day one. Instead, this responsibility initially sits with the product development team or project team. This may be a significant cultural change that needs support from management.
- Has clear agreement on the conditions that a service must meet to be onboarded by SRE (see Chapter 32 (*http://bit.ly/2Lc14wG*) of *Site Reliability Engineering*).

In addition:

- If the project involves a migration, the team should have a solid understanding of the current and future environments. If you need to recruit team members externally, consider candidates who have knowledge of software engineering and the future environment.
- Continue to keep the number of new hires to less than a third of the team so that the training effort doesn't overwhelm existing team members.

Horizontal SRE team

Risks
The team is perceived as a new "gating" organization that does no real work or adds no real value.

Mitigations
The team:

- Is seeded with respected engineers who have relevant subject matter expertise.

- Undertakes project work that focuses on delivering tools (for monitoring, alerting, rollouts, best practices, checklists). These tools should have a short-term beneficial impact on at least two other teams.

- Communicates successes and benefits. An SRE team that makes an efficiency breakthrough, automates away toil, or permanently eliminates a source of system unreliability should be celebrated.

- Sees themselves as enablers, not gatekeepers. Focus on solutions, not just problems.

A team converted in place

Risks

The team:

- Perceives that the conversion process is the start of a slow journey to job losses as automation replaces humans.

- Doesn't support the change to an SRE team.

- Has no slack capacity they can leverage to change the team's day-to-day activities.

- Sees no benefit to their day-to-day routine after a few months.

- Works with systems that do not support scripting or automation.

- Doesn't have the software engineering skills to automate their current workload.

- Doesn't consistently have the skills needed to evolve toward SRE, or an interest in acquiring the skills.

Mitigations

The team:

- Secures senior leadership support for the change.

- Renegotiates responsibilities to create the slack needed to effect change.

- Manages communication of the change very carefully.

- Has access to robust personal and technical support throughout the transition.

- Deals with the concern about job losses head on. In a lot of environments, automation eliminates portions of work, but not jobs as a whole; while this might be a step on the path to job losses, it does at least have the virtue of freeing up time to do something better (and more sellable to a future employer) than nonautomated toil.

- Can escape operational overload and have more significant impact. If engineers reduce the volume of toil enough to necessitate a smaller team, then their experience should be highly reusable elsewhere in your organization. If their experience can't be used internally, it should provide an advantage in seeking work elsewhere.

- Receives training to acquire the skills SREs need. Your product development team can provide product training, while SRE orientation can make use of this book and other external resources.

- Changes how performance is evaluated—the metrics that assess both the team and individuals. The former should be aligned with SLOs and adoption of other SRE practices; the latter should be aligned with evidence of SRE skills.

- Adds an experienced SRE or developer to the team.

- Has the freedom (budget or time) to identify and introduce new open source or cloud-based monitoring and alerting systems to enable automation. Determining whether the existing systems are sufficient should be an early priority.

- Regularly reviews progress internally and with stakeholders.

Norming

Norming entails working past the issues raised in "Risks and mitigations" on page 405 and reaching broad agreement on best practices for the organization's SRE teams. Teams need to agree on an acceptable level of toil, appropriate alerting thresholds, and important and relevant SRE practices. Teams also need to become self-sufficient at proactively identifying the challenges ahead of the service and setting medium- and long-term goals to improve the service.

Teams should reach the following levels of maturity during the norming phase:

- SLOs and error budgets are in place, and the error budget policy is exercised following significant incidents. Leadership is interested in SLO measurements.

- On-call rotations are established and sustainable (see Chapter 8). On-call engineers are compensated for their on-call time. There is sufficient tooling, documentation (*http://bit.ly/2LPgubz*),[2] and training to support any team member during a significant incident.

---

2 Shylaja Nukala and Vivek Rau, "Why SRE Documents Matter," *ACM Queue* (May–June 2018): forthcoming.

- Toil is documented, bounded, and managed. As a result, SREs complete impactful projects that improve reliability and efficiency.

- Postmortem culture is well established. (See Chapter 10.)

- The team exhibits most of the tenets listed in Chapter 1.

- As the team solves initial issues listed in "Storming" on page 405, they capture what they learned and prevent repeating problems. The team regularly runs training exercises, such as Wheel of Misfortune or DiRT (Disaster Recovery Testing). (For more information on on-call training, see Chapter 11 (*http://bit.ly/ 2JgUBU7*) in our first book and Chapter 18 in this book.)

- The product development team benefits from remaining involved in the on-call rotation.

- The team produces regular reports (e.g., quarterly) for their stakeholders that cover the highlights, lowlights, and key metrics of the reporting period.

Transforming an Existing Team into an SRE Team

by Brian Balser, New York Times

When the *New York Times* formed its Delivery and Site Reliability Engineering department, we assembled SRE teams from engineers who had SRE-type skills, such as building tooling and operating production systems. Some teams were "greenfield": they were designed with SRE in mind with respect to talent, vision, and responsibility. Other teams had existed for several years, and had ended up running production architecture due to a combination of skill sets, interests, and chance.

Challenges

One of the existing teams transitioning into SRE was in a very challenging position. Over the years, the team had gained ownership and responsibility for managing configurations, change requests, and operations of a core component of our site-wide architecture. They effectively became a service team supporting all of our product development teams. Their work was driven by tickets and production issues, and they were in a continuous reactive mode. They didn't have time to make improvements, innovate, or do other higher-value strategic work.

While the team had many great ideas, it was overloaded with toil and a number of high-priority "blocker" service requests that were typically tied to product launches. This model was not sustainable, and the team would need to grow linearly with products to keep up with this support burden. To exacerbate this situation, the small team had a wealth of institutional knowledge that had accumulated over the years. A high volume of interrupts from teams who needed that information compounded the team's overload, and a bus factor (*http://bit.ly/2LQFqiL*) loomed over the team.

Working from First Principles

One guiding principle of our SRE organization is to remove ourselves from the critical path and to empower product development teams with self-service solutions. With that in mind, our goal became clear: invert the responsibility model to enable the product development teams to push their own changes. This strategy would both:

- Speed up delivery.
- Free SREs from managing configuration churn, allowing them to make real improvements to the system as a whole.

Process Improvement

We improved our processes through several stages of change:

1. We embedded an SRE in the development team to help relieve pressure.
2. To enable product development teams to take ownership of their service configuration in isolation, we broke out each service configuration into a team-based repo.
3. We migrated each service from the legacy CI system to our standard Drone CI/CD pipeline. The developer-friendly workflow was completely driven by GitHub events.
4. We onboarded each of the product teams to the new tooling and workflow so they could submit their own change requests without being blocked by a service ticket.

While these improvements were a big step forward, we hadn't yet reached our ideal end state. Reviewing pull requests still often required SRE expertise. To make interrupts for time-consuming reviews more manageable, we scheduled daily office hours. This consistent practice allowed us to batch questions and discussions in a more predictive manner, and also provided a venue for sharing knowledge with teams undergoing onboarding.

End Result and Next Steps

The SRE team is now meeting its initial goal of > 50% project work (versus support-related work). The team still has a wealth of institutional knowledge, but that knowledge is now being propagated more broadly, gradually improving the bus factor and reducing interrupts.

Now that we have breathing room for project work, our next steps are to focus on adding more advanced capabilities such as canary deploys, better test tooling, and observability and resilience features. Doing so will give product development teams more confidence in exercising full autonomy over their service configurations without depending on SREs for change management.

Establishing a healthy relationship with your product development team forms the basis of many of these mitigation strategies. Teams should plan work together per your organization's planning cycle.

Before moving on to the next step: pause, celebrate this success, and write a retrospective that covers your journey so far.

Performing

The SRE team's experience with production and work up to this point should have earned the respect and attention of the wider organization, and laid the foundation for strategically moving forward. In the final stage of Tuckman's performance model, performing, you should expect to:

Partner on all architecture design and change.
   From the initial design phase onward, SRE should define the patterns for how software is built and structured for reliability.

Have complete workload self-determination.
   Teams should consistently apply Principle 3 with a view toward the holistic health of the system.

Partnering on architecture

The product development team should start to reach out to its partner SRE team for advice on all significant service changes. The SRE team now has the opportunity to have some of its greatest impact.

For example, the SRE team might provide early input into the design of new service architecture to reduce the likelihood of high-cost reengineering at a later date. The product development and SRE teams can acknowledge their differences in perspective on architectural decisions to arrive at a good design process. A successful engagement can add value through:

- Improved reliability, scalability, and operability
- Better reuse of existing patterns
- Simpler migration (if required)

Self-regulating workload

Whereas architectural partnerships should emerge somewhat organically over time, an SRE team must clearly assert Principle #3 to its partners. Doing so requires strong team leadership and clear, upfront commitment from senior management. The ability to regulate its own workload secures the SRE team's position as an engineering team that works on the organization's most important services, equal to its product development team peers.

In practice, how an SRE team goes about determining its own workload depends on the teams with which SREs interface. At Google, SRE teams most commonly interact with a distinct product development team. In this case, the relationship has the following characteristics:

- An SRE team chooses if and when to onboard a service (see Chapter 32 (*http://bit.ly/2Lc14wG*) of *Site Reliability Engineering*).
- In the event of operational overload, the team can reduce toil by:
  — Reducing the SLO
  — Transferring operational work to another team (e.g., a product development team)
- If it becomes impossible to operate a service at SLO within agreed toil constraints, the SRE team can hand back the service to the product development team.
- SRE engagement is not perpetual—it feeds itself by solving problems at scale and improving the reliability of services. If an SRE team has solved all such problems for a service, you need to either:
  — Intentionally consider what other reliability challenges the SRE team needs to tackle.
  — Make an intentional decision to hand back the service to the product development team.

  Otherwise, your team risks attrition as SREs move on to more interesting opportunities. The slow bleed from attrition can put production at risk.

Not all SRE teams have partner product development teams. Some SRE teams are also responsible for developing the systems they run. Some SRE teams package third-party software, hardware, or services (e.g., open source packages, network equipment, something-as-a-service), and turn those assets into internal services. In this case, you don't have the option to transfer work back to another team. Instead, consider the following tactics:

- If the service does not conform to its SLO, stop feature-related project work in favor of reliability-focused project work.
- If it becomes impossible to operate a service at SLO within agreed toil constraints, reduce your SLOs—unless management provides more capacity (people or infrastructure) to deal with the situation.

Making More SRE Teams

Once your first SRE team is up and running, you may want to form an additional SRE team. You might do so for one of the following reasons:

Service complexity

> As a service gains users and features, it becomes more complex and harder for a single SRE team to support effectively. You might want to split the team into subteams that specialize in parts of the service.

SRE rollout

> If your first SRE team has been successful and made a clear difference, there may be an organizational interest in adopting this approach across more services.

Geographically split

> You want to split the team into two halves in different time zones and move to 12-hour on-call shifts.

When you're creating a new SRE team, we recommend that you do the following:

- Read any postmortems written after other teams were established. Identify and repeat what went well and fix and explore alternatives for things that didn't go well.

- Seed the new team with SREs from the existing team—some of your best SREs and highest-potential SREs who can rise to the challenge. In our experience, finding qualified SRE candidates is difficult, so growing a team quickly with new hires often isn't realistic.

- Standardize the framework for establishing teams and onboarding services (see Chapter 18).

- Make changes to the on-call responsibilities slowly. For example:

  — To avoid a sudden loss of skilled on-call engineers, keep team members on-call for their previous team's systems for a transitional period.

  — After the teams split, wait three to six months to split the on-call rotations.

Service Complexity

Where to split

If a service becomes too complex for a single team to manage, there are a number of ways to split the work. Consider the following options to simplify the cognitive load on team members:

Architectural splits

For example, compute, storage, and network; frontend and backend; frontend and database; client and server; frontend and pipelines.

Language splits

SRE principles are not dependent on programming languages. However, if your SREs are deeply involved in your source code, there may be some benefit in a split along these lines.

Location splits

If your organization's engineering spans multiple offices, you might want to align SRE team placement with application development.

Pitfalls

When a team splits, sometimes none of the new teams pick up responsibility for a component owned by the original team. To mitigate this risk, you can:

- Designate one team as responsible for everything not covered in the second team's charter.
- Appoint a senior SRE to an overarching technical lead role across both teams.

SRE Rollout

If your initial SRE team(s) are successful, your organization may want more of them. We recommend carefully prioritizing the services that receive SRE support. Consider the following points:

- Prioritize services for which reliability has a high financial or reputational impact. The higher the impact, the higher the priority.
- Define the minimal viable set of services that need to be up in order for the product to function. Prioritize those services and make sure that other services degrade gracefully.
- A service should not be a priority for SRE simply because it's unreliable. SRE should be applied tactically where it is most relevant for the business. You also don't want to allow your developers to ignore reliability until after SREs are engaged.

Geographical Splits

As described in Chapter 11 (*http://bit.ly/2JgUBU7*) of our first book, Google commonly staffs sister SRE teams on different continents. We do this for a number of reasons:

Service reliability
   If a major incident (e.g., natural disaster) prevents one team from operating, the other team can continue to support a service.

On-call stress
   Splitting the pager rotation into 12-hour shifts allows proper breaks for on-call engineers.

Recruiting and retaining talent
   An on-call shift that overlaps the normal working day broadens the base of engineers that we can recruit into SRE roles, and underlines the engineering part of our role.

Production maturity
   Splitting service responsibility across two offices tends to lead to an improvement in maturity as the need for documentation, training, and standardization become more important.

If your organization is lucky enough to already have engineering teams on multiple continents, we recommend staffing multisite SRE teams. It's possible to have an SRE team in a different office than the development team, but in our experience, colocation provides benefits in the form of a healthy and robust interteam dialog. Otherwise, it's harder for SREs to understand how the services evolve or how the technical infrastructure is used, and it's harder for product developers to be optimistic about infrastructure improvements.

Placement: How many time zones apart should the teams be?

Assuming you have some choice, time zone separation is an important consideration in deciding where to locate the two teams. Unfortunately, the objectives are mutually exclusive:

- Minimizing the number of hours that on-callers have to work outside of normal office hours
- Maximizing the overlap time when both teams are online so that they can interact with each other regularly

The situation is complicated by Daylight Saving Time.

In our experience, staffing teams in time zones that are six to eight hours apart works well and avoids 12 a.m. to 6 a.m. on-call shifts. You can use online resources like *https://www.timeanddate.com/worldclock/meeting.html* to visualize time zone overlaps for various locations.

People and projects: Seeding the team

When you split a team geographically, the first SRE team in a new office will set the norms for future SRE teams. Your likelihood of success will be much higher if you can identify one or more SREs who are willing to relocate from the original site on a temporary or long-term basis to establish SRE practices and recruit and train the new team. The new team should also undertake a high-value project that fosters collaboration within the team and requires interaction with their sister team.

Parity: Distributing Work Between Offices and Avoiding a "Night Shift"

Often, one of two sister SRE teams is colocated (or at least in the same time zone) with the product development team (we'll call this "Office 1"). If this is the case, be vigilant to ensure that the team that is not colocated ("Office 2") doesn't become a night shift that has little contact with the product development team, takes more than its fair share of toil, or is assigned only the less interesting or impactful projects.

The workloads of the two offices will have some natural differences:

- Your service likely has a daily peak, and one office will be on-call during that peak. As a result, the on-call experience of the two sites will differ.

- Your development process will produce new releases with a particular cadence. One office will likely take more of the burden associated with rollouts and rollbacks.

- Office 1 is more likely to be interrupted during their working day by questions from the product development team.

- It's easier for Office 1 to undertake project work associated with major releases. Conversely, it's easier for Office 2 to undertake project work decoupled from immediate product goals.

You can help maintain balance by using the following practices:

- Balance the on-call load between offices. Designate a higher percentage of tickets to the office that fields the lower percentage of pages.

- Associate development areas with SRE teams in a particular office. This could be short term (e.g., according to project) or longer term (e.g., according to service). Otherwise, the product development team will likely lean on Office 1, and not effectively engage with SREs in Office 2.

- Assign a higher percentage of internal service improvement projects (that are likely to require less involvement with the product development team) to Office 2.

- Spread the most interesting and impactful projects fairly between the two offices.

- Maintain a similar team size and seniority mix between the two offices.

- Split projects across the two sites to deliberately foster interoffice interactions between SREs. While running a major project from a single office might gain some efficiencies, splitting projects across the two sites both helps spread knowledge and builds trust between offices.

- Allow engineers to travel to the other office regularly. This enables creating better rapport and, hence, willingness to do work for the other side.

Placement: What about having three shifts?

Our attempts at splitting SRE teams across three sites resulted in various issues:

- It is impossible to have an interoffice production meeting that all SREs can attend (see Chapter 31 (*http://bit.ly/2sqRwad*) of our first book).

- It is harder to ensure parity of knowledge, capability, and operational response across three offices.

- If all on-call duties take place only during office hours, there's less of an incentive to automate low-level toil and low-value pages. Being the hero that fixes easy problems is fun during office hours. But if it has some amount of personal cost, the motivation to make sure it never happens again is sharp and immediate.

Timing: Should both halves of the team start at the same time?

You might spin up sister teams using any of the following models:

- Both halves start at the same time.

- Set up the site that is colocated with the product development team first. This allows SREs to get involved earlier in the product lifecycle.

- Set up the site that is *not* colocated with the product development team first or, if a service has been in production for some time, the SRE team and the product development team can share the pager.

- Start making changes according to where the right people are at the right time.

Finance: Travel budget

It is very important to create opportunities for high-quality interactions between the two halves of the team. Despite the effectiveness of video conferencing for day-to-day meetings, we've found that regular face-to-face interactions go a long way toward facilitating healthy relationships and trust. We recommend that:

- Every SRE, product development manager, and technical lead in Site 1 visit Site 2 annually (at a minimum), and vice versa.
- Every SRE in a management or technical leadership role at Site 1 visit Site 2 at least twice a year, and vice versa.
- All SREs convene at least once a year.

Leadership: Joint ownership of a service

If you have multiple SRE sites, you likely have decision makers in each office. These parties should meet regularly face-to-face and by video conference. Only by establishing a strong personal relationship can they:

- Debate solutions to challenges that the team faces.
- Resolve differences of opinion and agree on a joint path forward.
- Advocate on behalf of each other's team (to prevent an "us versus them" mentality).
- Support the health of each other's team.

Suggested Practices for Running Many Teams

New challenges arise as your organization accumulates more SREs and SRE teams. For example, you'll have to:

- Ensure you provide SREs with the career opportunities they need.
- Encourage consistency of practices and tooling.
- Deal with services that don't justify a full SRE engagement.

This section describes a number of the practices that we have adopted at Google to deal with these concerns. Depending on the specifics of your organization, some or many may work for you too.

Mission Control

Google's Mission Control (*http://bit.ly/2Jn48sI*) program gives engineers from product development teams the opportunity to spend six months embedded in an SRE team. We typically match these engineers to SRE teams working in a distinctly different area from their expertise. The software engineer is trained in production systems and practices and eventually goes on-call for that service. After six months, some engineers decide to stay in SRE; others return to their old teams with a much better appreciation for the production environment and SRE practices. SRE teams benefit from additional engineering resources and gain valuable insight into gaps and inaccuracies in training material and documentation.

SRE Exchange

Google's SRE Exchange program lets an SRE spend a week working alongside a different SRE team. The visiting SRE observes how the host team works and shares practices from their home team that might be useful to the host team. At the end of the exchange, the visiting SRE writes a trip report describing their week, their observations, and their recommendations for both teams. This program is useful at Google because our SRE teams are highly specialized.

Training

Training is critical to SRE's ability to operate systems. While most of this is delivered in-team (see "Training roadmap" on page 150 in Chapter 8), consider establishing a standard training curriculum for all SREs. At Google, all new SREs attend SRE EDU, an immersive weeklong training that introduces key concepts, tooling, and platforms that almost all SREs work with. This provides a baseline level of knowledge across all new SREs, and simplifies team-specific and service-specific training objectives. The SRE EDU team also runs a second series of classes a few months later that covers the common tools and processes that we use for managing major incidents. Our performance management process specifically recognizes SREs who facilitate this training.

Horizontal Projects

Because SRE teams are tightly aligned with a set of services, there is a temptation for teams to build proprietary solutions to deal with the challenges they encounter—for example, monitoring, software rollout, and configuration tools. This can lead to significant duplication of efforts across teams. While there is value in allowing a number of solutions to compete for "market" adoption, at some point, it makes sense to converge upon a standard solution that:

- Meets most teams' requirements

- Provides a stable and scalable platform upon which the next layer of innovation can be built

Google approaches these efforts by using horizontal teams, which are often staffed by experienced SREs. These horizontal teams build and run a standard solution and partner with other SRE teams to ensure smooth adoption. (For more information on horizontal software development, see "Case Study 2: Common Tooling Adoption in SRE" on page 432 in Chapter 21.)

SRE Mobility

Google does its best to ensure that engineers actively want to be part of their respective teams. To this end, we make sure that SREs are able to (and aware that they're able to) transfer between teams. Assuming there are no performance issues, SREs are free to transfer to other SRE teams with open headcount. SREs who also passed our hiring bar for software engineer roles are free to transfer to product development teams (see *http://bit.ly/2xyQ4aD*).

This level of mobility is very healthy for individuals and teams for a number of reasons:

- Engineers are able to identify and occupy roles of interest.
- If personal circumstances change and on-call responsibilities become impractical, SREs can explore opportunities on teams with less demanding on-call duties. They can obtain this information by talking to other teams and reviewing team on-call stats.
- SREs who move between teams broaden the experience of the teams they join.
- SREs who move between offices help build or maintain cultural consistency between different offices.
- SREs are not compelled to work on services that are unhealthy, or for managers who aren't supportive of their personal development.

This policy also has the side effect of keeping your SRE managers focused on healthy and happy services and teams.

Travel

In addition to the travel required to keep geographically split teams healthy (see the section "Finance: Travel budget" on page 418), consider funding for:

- Building internal company communities of interest that include SREs from a number of offices. Such groups can largely collaborate via email and video conferencing, but meet face-to-face at least annually.

- Attending and presenting at industry-wide SRE and SRE-related conferences to broaden knowledge, learn how other organizations tackle similar problems, and, hopefully, be inspired and energized.

Launch Coordination Engineering Teams

As described in Chapter 27 (*http://bit.ly/2kGWVWf*) of our first book, a Launch Coordination Engineering (LCE) team can apply SRE principles to a broader set of product development teams—teams that build services that don't require the level of attention that merits SRE engagement. Just like any other SRE team, an LCE team should be actively engaged in automating its daily operations. For example, developing standard tooling and frameworks enable product development teams to design, build, and launch their service in a production environment.

Production Excellence

As the number of SRE teams at your organization grows, a number of best practices will emerge. Every SRE team evolves differently, so evaluating them requires senior SREs with insight into multiple teams.

At Google, we run a regular service review called Production Excellence. On a regular basis, senior SRE leaders review every SRE team, assessing them on a number of standard measures (e.g., pager load, error budget usage, project completion, bug closure rates). The review both applauds outstanding performance and provides suggestions for underperforming teams.

Experienced SREs are equipped to evaluate nuanced scenarios. For example, it can be challenging to tease out a drop in project completion rate caused by a team merger or split versus genuine team performance issues. If a team is at risk of becoming overwhelmed, the reviewers can and should to use their organizational position to support the team's leadership in rectifying the situation.

SRE Funding and Hiring

At Google, we use two practices to make sure that every SRE contributes significant value:

- Much of SRE funding comes from the same source as product development team funding. Similar to testing or security, reliability is a core pillar of product development, and is funded as such.

- In our experience, the supply of SREs is always smaller than the demand for them. This dynamic ensures that we regularly review and prioritize the services that receive SRE support.

In short, you should have fewer SREs than the organization would like, and only enough SREs to accomplish their specialized work.

At Google, the ratio of SREs to engineers on product development teams ranges from around 1:5 (e.g., low-level infrastructure services) to around 1:50 (e.g., consumer-facing applications with a large number of microservices built using standard frameworks). Many services fall in the middle of this range, at a ratio of around 1:10.

Conclusion

We believe an organization of any size can implement SRE practices by applying the following three principles:

- SRE needs SLOs with consequences.
- SREs must have time to make tomorrow better than today.
- SRE teams have the ability to regulate their workload.

Since Google started talking publicly about SRE, it has grown from Google-specific production practices into a profession practiced in many companies. These principles have often proven true—both over our years of direct experience at scale, and during our more recent experience of working with our customers to adopt SRE practices. Because we've seen these practices work both within and outside of Google, we feel these recommendations should prove useful across a range of organizations of different types and sizes.

## CHAPTER 21

Organizational Change Management in SRE

By Alex Bramley, Ben Lutch, Michelle Duffy, and Nir Tarcic
with Betsy Beyer

In the introduction to the first SRE Book (*http://bit.ly/2xCtP3S*), Ben Treynor Sloss describes SRE teams as "characterized by both rapid innovation and a large acceptance of change," and specifies organizational change management as a core responsibility of an SRE team. This chapter examines how theory can apply in practice across SRE teams. After reviewing some key change management theories, we explore two case studies that demonstrate how different styles of change management have played out in concrete ways at Google.

Note that the term *change management* has two interpretations: organizational change management and change control. This chapter examines change management as a collective term for all approaches to preparing and supporting individuals, teams, and business units in making organizational change. We do not discuss this term within a project management context, where it may be used to refer to change control processes, such as change review or versioning.

SRE *Embraces* Change

More than 2,000 years ago, the Greek philosopher Heraclitus claimed change is the only constant. This axiom still holds true today—especially in regards to technology, and particularly in rapidly evolving internet and cloud sectors.

Product teams exist to build products, ship features, and delight customers. At Google, most change is fast-paced, following a "launch and iterate" approach. Executing on such change typically requires coordination across systems, products, and globally distributed teams. Site Reliability Engineers are frequently in the middle of this complicated and rapidly shifting landscape, responsible for balancing the risks inherent in change with product reliability and availability. Error budgets (see Chapter 2) are a primary mechanism for achieving this balance.

Introduction to Change Management

Change management as an area of study and practice has grown since foundational work in the field by Kurt Lewin in the 1940s. Theories primarily focus on developing frameworks for managing organizational change. In-depth analysis of particular theories is beyond the scope of this book, but to contextualize them within the realm of SRE, we briefly describe some common theories and how each might be applicable in an SRE-type organization. While the formal processes implicit in these theoretical frameworks have not been applied by SRE at Google, considering SRE activities through the lens of these frameworks has helped us refine our approach to managing change. Following this discussion, we will introduce some case studies that demonstrate how elements of some of these theories apply to change management activities led by Google SRE.

Lewin's Three-Stage Model

Kurt Lewin's "unfreeze–change–freeze" model (*http://bit.ly/2Jj4aSr*) for managing change is the oldest of the relevant theories in this field. This simple three-stage model is a tool for managing process review and the resulting changes in group dynamics. Stage 1 entails persuading a group that change is necessary. Once they are amenable to the idea of change, Stage 2 executes that change. Finally, when the change is broadly complete, Stage 3 institutionalizes the new patterns of behavior and thought. The model's core principle posits the group as the primary dynamic instrument, arguing that individual and group interactions should be examined as a system when the group is planning, executing, and completing any period of change. Accordingly, Lewin's work is most useful for planning organizational change at the macro level.

McKinsey's 7-S Model

McKinsey's seven S's (*https://mck.co/2JqEweE*) stand for structure, strategy, systems, skills, style, staff, and shared values. Similar to Lewin's work, this framework is also a toolset for planned organizational change. While Lewin's framework is generic, 7-S has an explicit goal of improving organizational effectiveness. Application of both theories begins with an analysis of current purpose and processes. However, 7-S also explicitly covers both business elements (structure, strategy, systems) and people-management elements (shared values, skills, style, staff). This model could be useful for a team considering change from a traditional systems administration focus to the more holistic Site Reliability Engineering approach.

Kotter's Eight-Step Process for Leading Change

Time magazine named John P. Kotter's 1996 book *Leading Change* (Harvard Business School Press) one of the Top 25 Most Influential Business Management Books of all time (*https://ti.me/2kIspvq*). Figure 21-1 depicts the eight steps in Kotter's change management process.

Figure 21-1. Kotter's model of change management (source: https://www.kotterinc.com/ 8-steps-process-for-leading-change/)

Kotter's process is particularly relevant to SRE teams and organizations, with one small exception: in many cases (e.g., the upcoming Waze case study), there's no need to *create* a sense of urgency. SRE teams supporting products and systems with accelerating growth are frequently faced with urgent scaling, reliability, and operational challenges. The component systems are often owned by multiple development teams, which may span several organizational units; scaling issues may also require coordination with teams ranging from physical infrastructure to product management. Because SRE is often on the front line when problems occur, it is uniquely motivated to lead the change needed to ensure products are available 24/7/365. Much of SRE work (implicitly) embraces Kotter's process to ensure the continued availability of supported products.

The Prosci ADKAR Model

The Prosci ADKAR model (*https://www.prosci.com/adkar/adkar-model*) focuses on balancing both the business and people aspects of change management. ADKAR is an acronym for the goals individuals must achieve for successful organizational change: awareness, desire, knowledge, ability, and reinforcement.

In principle, ADKAR provides a useful, thoughtful, people-centric framework. However, its applicability to SRE is limited because operational responsibilities quite often impose considerable time constraints. Proceeding iteratively through ADKAR's stages and providing the necessary training or coaching requires pacing and investment in communication, which are difficult to implement in the context of globally distributed, operationally focused teams. That said, Google has successfully used ADKAR-style processes for introducing and building support for high-level changes —for example, introducing global organizational change to the SRE management team while preserving local autonomy for implementation details.

Emotion-Based Models

The Bridges Transition Model (*http://bit.ly/2J2ssRc*) describes people's emotional reactions to change. While a useful management tool for people managers, it's not a framework or process for change management. Similarly, the Kübler-Ross Change Curve describes ranges of emotions people may feel when faced with change. Developed from Elisabeth Kübler-Ross's research on death and dying,[1] it has been applied to understanding and anticipating employee reactions to organizational change. Both models can be useful in maintaining high employee productivity throughout periods of change, since unhappy people are rarely productive.

The Deming Cycle

Also known as the Plan-Do-Check-Act (or PDCA) Cycle, this process from statistician Edward W. Deming is commonly used in DevOps environments for process improvements—for example, adoption of continuous integration/continuous delivery techniques. It is not suited to organizational change management because it does not cover the human side of change, including motivations and leadership styles. Deming's focus is to take existing processes (mechanical, automated, or workflow) and cyclically apply continuous improvements. The case studies we refer to in this chapter deal with larger, organizational changes where iteration is counterproductive: frequent, wrenching org-chart changes can sap employee confidence and negatively impact company culture.

---

1 Elisabeth Kübler-Ross, *On Death and Dying: What the Dying Have to Teach Doctors, Nurses, Clergy and Their Own Families* (New York: Scribner, 1969).

How These Theories Apply to SRE

No change management model is universally applicable to every situation, so it's not surprising that Google SRE hasn't exclusively standardized on one model. That said, here's how we like to think about applying these models to common change management scenarios in SRE:

- *Kotter's Eight-Step Process* is a change management model for SRE teams who necessarily embrace change as a core responsibility.

- The *Prosci ADKAR model* is a framework that SRE management may want to consider to coordinate change across globally distributed teams.

- All individual SRE managers will benefit from familiarity with both the *Bridges Transition Model* and the *Kübler-Ross Change Curve*, which provide tools to support employees in times of organizational change.

Now that we've introduced the theories, let's look at two case studies that show how change management has played out at Google.

Case Study 1: Scaling Waze—From Ad Hoc to Planned Change

Background

Waze is a community-based navigation app acquired by Google in 2013. After the acquisition, Waze entered a period of significant growth in active users, engineering staff, and computing infrastructure, but continued to operate relatively autonomously within Google. The growth introduced many challenges, both technical and organizational.

Waze's autonomy and startup ethos led them to meet these challenges with a grassroots technical response from small groups of engineers, rather than management-led, structured organizational change as implied by the formal models discussed in the previous section. Nevertheless, their approach to propagating changes throughout the organization and infrastructure significantly resembles Kotter's model of change management. This case study examines how Kotter's process (which we apply retroactively) aptly describes a sequence of technical and organizational challenges Waze faced as they grew post-acquisition.

The Messaging Queue: Replacing a System While Maintaining Reliability

Kotter's model begins the cycle of change with a *sense of urgency*. Waze's SRE team needed to act quickly and decisively when the reliability of Waze's message queueing system regressed badly, leading to increasingly frequent and severe outages. As shown in Figure 21-2, the message queueing system was critical to operations because every component of Waze (real time, geocoding, routing, etc.) used it to communicate with other components internally.

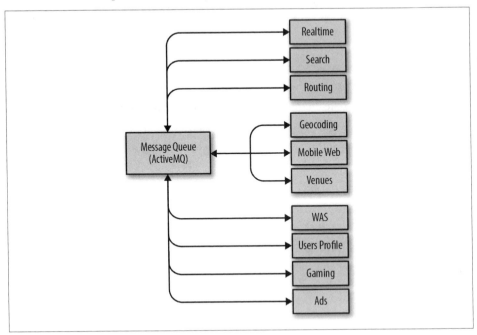

Figure 21-2. Communication paths between Waze components

As throughput on the message queue grew significantly, the system simply couldn't cope with the ever-increasing demands. SREs needed to manually intervene to preserve system stability at shorter and shorter intervals. At its worst, the entire Waze SRE team spent most of a two-week period firefighting 24/7, eventually resorting to restarting some components of the message queue hourly to keep messages flowing and tens of millions of users happy.

Because SRE was also responsible for building and releasing all of Waze's software, this operational load had a noticeable impact on feature velocity—when SREs spent all of their time fighting fires, they hardly had time to support new feature rollouts. By highlighting the severity of the situation, engineers convinced Waze's leadership to reevaluate priorities and dedicate some engineering time to reliability work. A *guiding coalition* of two SREs and a senior engineer came together to form a *strategic vision* of a future where SRE toil was no longer necessary to keep messages flowing. This small team evaluated off-the-shelf message queue products, but quickly decided that they could only meet Waze's scaling and reliability requirements with a custom-built solution.

Developing this message queue in-house would be impossible without some way to maintain operations in the meantime. The coalition removed this *barrier to action* by enlisting a *volunteer army* of developers from the teams who used the current messaging queue. Each team reviewed the codebase for their service to identify ways to cut the volume of messages they published. Trimming unnecessary messages and rolling out a compression layer on top of the old queue reduced some load on the system. The team also gained some more operational breathing room by building a dedicated messaging queue for one particular component that was responsible for over 30% of system traffic. These measures yielded enough of a temporary operational reprieve to allow for a two-month window to assemble and test a prototype of the new messaging system.

Migrating a message queue system that handles tens of thousands of messages per second is a daunting task even without the pressure of imminent service meltdown. But gradually reducing the load on the old system would relieve some of this pressure, affording the team a longer time window to complete the migration. To this end, Waze SRE rebuilt the client libraries for the message queue so they could publish and receive messages using either or both systems, using a centralized control surface to switch the traffic over.

Once the new system was proven to work, SRE began the first phase of the migration: they identified some low-traffic, high-importance message flows for which messaging outages were catastrophic. For these flows, writing to both messaging systems would provide a backup path. A couple of near misses, where the backup path kept core Waze services operating while the old system faltered, provided the *short-term wins* that justified the initial investment.

Mass migration to the new system required SRE to work closely with the teams who use it. The team needed to figure out both how to best support their use cases and how to coordinate the traffic switch. As the SRE team automated the process of migrating traffic and the new system supported more use cases by default, the rate of migrations *accelerated significantly.*

Kotter's change management process ends with *instituting change.* Eventually, with enough momentum behind the adoption of the new system, the SRE team could declare the old system deprecated and no longer supported. They migrated the last stragglers a few quarters later. Today, the new system handles more than 1000 times the load of the previous one, and requires little manual intervention from SREs for ongoing support and maintenance.

The Next Cycle of Change: Improving the Deployment Process

The process of change as a *cycle* was one of Kotter's key insights. The cyclical nature of meaningful change is particularly apparent when it comes to the types of technical changes that face SRE. Eliminating one bottleneck in a system often highlights another one. As each change cycle is completed, the resulting improvements, standardization, and automation free up engineering time. Engineering teams now have the space to more closely examine their systems and identify more pain points, triggering the next cycle of change.

When Waze SRE could finally take a step back from firefighting problems related to the messaging system, a new bottleneck emerged, bringing with it a renewed *sense of urgency*: SRE's sole ownership of releases was noticeably and seriously hindering development velocity. The manual nature of releases required a significant amount of SRE time. To exacerbate an already suboptimal situation, system components were large, and because releases were costly, they were relatively infrequent. As a result, each release represented a large delta, significantly increasing the possibility that a major defect would necessitate a rollback.

Improvements toward a better release process happened incrementally, as Waze SRE didn't have a master plan from square one. To slim down system components so the team could iterate each more rapidly, one of the senior Waze developers created a framework for building microservices. This provided a standard "batteries included" platform that made it easy for the engineering organization to start breaking their components apart. SRE worked with this developer to include some reliability-focused features—for example, a common control surface and a set of behaviors that were amenable to automation. As a result, SRE could develop a suite of tools to manage the previously costly parts of the release process. One of these tools incentivized adoption by bundling all of the steps needed to create a new microservice with the framework.

These tools were quick-and-dirty at first—the initial prototypes were built by one SRE over the course of several days. As the team cleaved more microservices from their parent components, the value of the SRE-developed tools quickly became apparent to the wider organization. SRE was spending less time shepherding the slimmed-down components into production, and the new microservices were much less costly to release individually.

While the release process was already much improved, the proliferation of new microservices meant that SRE's overall burden was still concerning. Engineering leadership was unwilling to assume responsibility for the release process until releases were less burdensome.

In response, a small *coalition* of SREs and developers sketched out a *strategic vision* to shift to a continuous deployment strategy using Spinnaker (*http://spinnaker.io/*), an open source, multicloud, continuous delivery platform for building and executing deployment workflows. With the time saved by our bootstrap tooling, the team now was able to engineer this new system to enable one-click builds and deployments of hundreds or thousands of microservices. The new system was technically superior to the previous system in every way, but SRE still couldn't persuade development teams to make the switch. This reluctance was driven by two factors: the obvious disincentive of having to push their own releases to production, plus change aversion driven by poor visibility into the release process.

Waze SRE tore down these *barriers to adoption* by showing how the new process added value. The team built a centralized dashboard that displayed the release status of binaries and a number of standard metrics exported by the microservice framework. Development teams could easily link their releases to changes in those metrics, which gave them confidence that deployments were successful. SRE worked closely with a few *volunteer* systems-oriented development teams to move services to Spinnaker. These *wins* proved that the new system could not only fulfill its requirements, but also add value beyond the original release process. At this point, engineering leadership set a goal for all teams to perform releases using the new Spinnaker deployment pipelines.

To facilitate the migration, Waze SRE provided organization-wide Spinnaker training sessions and consulting sessions for teams with complex requirements. When early adopters became familiar with the new system, their positive experiences sparked a chain reaction of *accelerating adoption*. They found the new process faster and less painful than waiting for SRE to push their releases. Now, engineers began to put pressure on dependencies that had not moved, as *they* were the impediment to faster development velocity—not the SRE team!

Today, more than 95% of Waze's services use Spinnaker for continuous deployment, and changes can be pushed to production with very little human involvement. While Spinnaker isn't a one-size-fits-all solution, configuring a release pipeline is trivial if a new service is built using the microservices framework, so new services have a strong incentive to standardize on this solution.

Lessons Learned

Waze's experience in removing bottlenecks to technical change contains a number of useful lessons for other teams attempting engineering-led technical or organizational change. To begin with, change management theory is not a waste of time! Viewing this development and migration process through the lens of Kotter's process demonstrates the model's applicability. A more formal application of Kotter's model at the time could have helped streamline and guide the process of change.

Change instigated from the grass roots requires close collaboration between SRE and development, as well as support from executive leadership. Creating a small, focused group with members from all parts of the organization—SRE, developers, and management—was key to the team's success. A similar collaboration was vital to instituting the change. Over time, these ad hoc groups can and should evolve into more formal and structured cooperation, where SREs are automatically involved in design discussions and can advise on best practices for building and deploying robust applications in a production environment throughout the entire product lifecycle.

Incremental change is much easier to manage. Jumping straight to the "perfect" solution is too large a step to take all at once (not to mention probably infeasible if your system is about to collapse), and the concept of "perfect" will likely evolve as new information comes to light during the change process. An iterative approach can demonstrate early wins that help an organization buy into the vision of change and justify further investment. On the other hand, if early iterations don't demonstrate value, you'll waste less time and fewer resources when you inevitably abandon the change. Because incremental change doesn't happen all at once, having a master plan is invaluable. Describe the goals in broad terms, be flexible, and ensure that each iteration moves toward them.

Finally, sometimes your current solutions can't support the requirements of your strategic vision. Building something new has a large engineering cost, but can be worthwhile if the project pushes you out of a local maxima and enables long-term growth. As a thought experiment, figure out where bottlenecks might arise in your systems and tooling as your business and organization grow over the next few years. If you suspect any elements don't scale horizontally, or have superlinear (or worse, exponential) growth with respect to a core business metric such as daily active users, you may need to consider redesigning or replacing them.

Waze's development of a new in-house message queue system shows that it is possible for small groups of determined engineers to institute change that moves the needle toward greater service reliability. Mapping Kotter's model onto the change shows that some consideration of change management strategy can help provide a formula for success even in small, engineering-led organizations. And, as the next case study also demonstrates, when changes promote standardizing technology and processes, the organization as a whole can reap considerable efficiency gains.

Case Study 2: Common Tooling Adoption in SRE

Background

SREs are opinionated about the software they can and should use to manage production. Years of experience, observing what goes well and what doesn't, and examining the past through the lens of the postmortem, have given SREs a deep background coupled with strong instincts. Specifying, building, and implementing software to automate this year's job away is a core value in SRE. In particular, Google SRE recently focused our efforts on horizontal software. Adoption of the same solution by a critical mass of users and developers creates a virtuous cycle and reduces reinvention of wheels. Teams who otherwise might not interact share practices and policies that are automated using the same software.

This case study is based on an organizational evolution, not a response to a systems scaling or reliability issue (as discussed in the Waze case study). Hence, the Prosci ADKAR model (shown in Figure 21-3) is a better fit than Kotter's model, as it recognizes both explicit organizational/people management characteristics and technical considerations during the change.

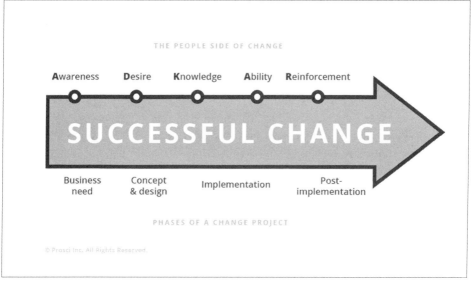

Figure 21-3. Prosci ADKAR model of change management

Problem Statement

A few years ago, Google SRE found itself using multiple independent software solutions for approximately the same problem across multiple problem spaces: monitoring, releases and rollouts, incident response, capacity management, and so on.

This end state arose in part because the people building tools for SRE were dissociated from their users and their requirements. The tool developers didn't always have a current view of the problem statement or the overall production landscape—the production environment changes very rapidly and in new ways as new software, hardware, and use cases are brought to life almost daily. Additionally, the consumers of tools were varied, sometimes with orthogonal needs ("this rollout has to be fast; approximate is fine" versus "this rollout has to be 100% correct; okay for it to go slowly").

As a result, none of these long-term projects fully addressed anyone's needs, and each was characterized by varying levels of development effort, feature completeness, and ongoing support. Those waiting for the big use case—a nonspecific, singing-and-dancing solution of the future—waited a long time, got frustrated, and used their own software engineering skills to create their own niche solution. Those who had smaller, specific needs were loath to adopt a broader solution that wasn't as tailored to them. The long-term, technical, and organizational benefits of more universal solutions were clear, but customers, services, and teams were not staffed or rewarded for waiting. To compound this scenario, requirements of both large and small customer teams changed over time.

What We Decided to Do

To scope this scenario as one concrete problem space, we asked ourselves: What if all Google SREs could use a common monitoring engine and set of dashboards, which were easy to use and supported a wide variety of use cases without requiring customization?

Likewise, we could extend this model of thinking to releases and rollouts, incident response, capacity management, and beyond. If the initial configuration of a product captured a wide representation of approaches to address the majority of our functional needs, our general and well-informed solutions would become inevitable over time. At some point, the critical mass of engineers who interact with production would outgrow whatever solution they were using and self-select to migrate to a common, well-supported set of tools and automation, abandoning their custom-built tools and their associated maintenance costs.

SRE at Google is fortunate that many of its engineers have software engineering backgrounds and experience. It seemed like a natural first step to encourage engineers who were experts and opinionated about specific problems—from load balancing to rollout tooling to incident management and response—to work as a virtual team, self-selected by a common long-term vision. These engineers would translate their vision into working, real software that would eventually be adopted across all of SRE, and then all of Google, as the basic functions of production.

To return to the ADKAR model for change management, the steps discussed so far—identifying a problem and acknowledging an opportunity—are textbook examples of ADKAR's initiating *awareness* step. The Google SRE leadership team agreed on the need (*desire*) and had sufficient *knowledge* and *ability* to move to designing solutions fairly quickly.

Design

Our first task was to converge upon a number of topics that we agreed were central, and that would benefit greatly from a consistent vision: to deliver solutions and adoption plans that fit most use cases. Starting from a list of 65+ proposed projects, we spent multiple months collecting customer requirements, verifying roadmaps, and performing market analysis, ultimately scoping our efforts toward a handful of vetted topics.

Our initial design created a virtual team of SRE experts around these topics. This virtual team would contribute a significant percentage of their time, around 80%, to these horizontal projects. The idea behind 80% time and a virtual team was to ensure we did not design or build solutions without constant contact with production. However, we (maybe predictably) discovered a few pain points with this approach:

- Coordinating a virtual team—whose focus was broken by being on-call regularly, across multiple time zones—was very difficult. There was a lot of state to be swapped between running a service and building a serious piece of software.
- Everything from gathering consensus to code reviews was affected by the lack of a central location and common time.
- Headcount for horizontal projects initially had to come from existing teams, who now had fewer engineering resources to tackle their own projects. Even at Google, there's tension between delegating headcount to support the system as is versus delegating headcount to build future-looking infrastructure.

With enough data in hand, we realized we needed to redesign our approach, and settled on the more familiar centralized model. Most significantly, we removed the requirement that team members split their time 80/20 between project work and on-call duties. Most SRE software development is now done by small groups of senior engineers with plenty of on-call experience, but who are heads-down focused on building software based on those experiences. We also physically centralized many of these teams by recruiting or moving engineers. Small group (6–10 people) development is simply more efficient within one room (however, this argument doesn't apply to all groups—for example, remote SRE teams). We can still meet our goal of collecting requirements and perspectives across the entire Google engineering organization via videoconference, email, and good old-fashioned travel.

So our evolution of design actually ended up in a familiar place—small, agile, mostly local, fast-moving teams—but with the added emphasis on selecting and building automation and tools for adoption by 60% of Google engineers (the figure we decided was a reasonable interpretation of the goal of "*almost* everyone at Google"). Success means most of Google is using what SRE has built to manage their production environment.

The ADKAR model maps the *implementation* phase of the change project between the people-centric stages of *knowledge* and *ability*. This case study bears out that mapping. We had many engaged, talented, and knowledgeable engineers, but we were asking people who had been focused on SRE concerns to act like product software development engineers by focusing on customer requirements, product roadmaps, and delivery commitments. We needed to revisit the implementation of this change to enable engineers to demonstrate their abilities with respect to these new attributes.

Implementation: Monitoring

To return to the monitoring space mentioned in the previous section, Chapter 31 (*http://bit.ly/2sqRwad*) in the first SRE book described how Viceroy—Google SRE's effort to create a single monitoring dashboard solution suitable for everyone— addressed the problem of disparate custom solutions. Several SRE teams worked together to create and run the initial iteration, and as Viceroy grew to become the de facto monitoring and dashboarding solution at Google, a dedicated centralized SRE development team assumed ownership of the project.

But even when the Viceroy framework united SRE under a common framework, there was a lot of duplicated effort as teams built complex custom dashboards specific to their services. While Viceroy provided a standard hosted method to design and build visual displays of data, it still required each team to decide what data to display and how to organize it.

The now-centralized software development team began a second parallel effort to provide common dashboards, building an opinionated zero-config system on top of the lower-level "custom" system. This zero-config system provided a standard set of comprehensive monitoring displays based on the assumption that a given service was organized in one of a handful of popular styles. Over time, most services migrated to using these standard dashboards instead of investing in custom layouts. Very large, unique, or otherwise special services can still deploy custom views in the hosted system if they need to.

Returning to the ADKAR model, the consolidation of monitoring tools at Google began as a grassroots effort, and the resulting improvements in operational efficiencies provided a quantifiable basis (*awareness* and *desire*) to initiate a broader effort: SRE self-funded a software development team to build production management tooling for all of Google.

Lessons Learned

Designing a migration of interdependent pieces is often more complicated than a blank-sheet design. But in real life, the hardest engineering work ends up being the evolution of many small/constrained systems into fewer, more general systems— without disturbing already running services that many customers depend on. In the meantime, alongside the existing systems, new small systems are added—some of which eventually surprise us by growing into large systems. There is an intellectual attraction to starting anew with the big design, only backing into constraints that are really necessary, but the migration of systems and teams turns out to be the most difficult work *by far*.

Designing horizontal software requires a lot of listening to prospective end users, and, in many ways, the tasks of building and adoption look much like the role of a product manager. In order for this effort to achieve success, we had to make sure that we absorbed and prioritized priorities. Meeting customer needs—of both SREs and other production users—was also a critical element of success. It is important to acknowledge that the move toward common tooling is still a work in progress. We iterated on the structure and staffing of the teams building our shared technologies to better enable meeting customer needs, and we added product management and user experience talent (addressing missing *knowledge*).

In the past year or two, we have seen uptake of these SRE-designed and -built products across a broad swath of teams at Google. We have learned that to achieve success, the cost of migration (from older, fragmented but specialized solutions) needs to be small relative to the net benefits of the new common solution. Otherwise, the migration itself becomes a barrier to adoption. We continue to work with the individual teams building these products to *reinforce* the behaviors needed to delight customers with the common solutions the teams are delivering.

One common theme we discovered across horizontal software development projects was that no matter how good new software and products were, the cost of migration —away from something that was already working to something new—was always *perceived* as very high. Despite the allure of easier management and less specific deep knowledge, the costs of migrating away from the familiar (with all its warts and toil) were generally a barrier. In addition, individual engineers often had a similar internal monologue: "I'm not improving or changing the system; I'm swapping out one working piece for another working piece." ADKAR describes this resistance as the "knowledge-to-ability gap." On the human side, in order to recognize and embrace change, people need time, coaching, and training in new tools and skills. On the technical side, implementing change requires understanding adoption costs and including work to minimize these costs as part of the launch process.

As a result, migration costs need to be nearly zero ("just recompile and you pick up new $thing") and the benefits need to be clear ("now you're protected from $foo vulnerability") to the team, to individuals, and to the company.

SRE commonly used to build products that we committed to in a "best effort" way, meaning that the amount of time we gave the product fit into the cracks between everything else we were doing (managing primary services, capacity planning, dealing with outages, etc.). As a result, our execution was not very reliable; it was impossible to predict when a feature or service would be available. By extension, consumers of our products had less trust in the end result since it felt perpetually delayed and was staffed by a rotating cast of product managers and individual engineers. When individual SREs or SRE teams built tools for their own use, the focus was on solving individual problems to reduce the cost of maintaining SLOs for supported systems. In endeavoring to build common tooling for most use cases at Google, we needed to shift the focus to measuring the success of this effort in terms of product adoption.

Owing to both our organizational culture and our wealth of resources, we approached this project in a bottom-up, rather than top-down, fashion. Instead of mandating that users migrated to our new monitoring system, we sought to win over users by demonstrating that our new offering was better than existing solutions.

Over time, we learned that how we conducted our development process would inform how potential internal users perceived the end result. These projects gained real traction only when staffed by production-experienced engineers 100% dedicated to building software, with schedules and support identical to the rest of Google's software development. Building common software transparently, like clockwork, with great communication ("We'll have X done by Y date"), greatly improved the speed of migration to the new system. People already trusted the new system because they could observe how it was developed from an early stage. *Perceptions of how the sausage is made turned out to be more important than we anticipated from the get-go.* Our initial thought that "if you build something great, people will naturally flock to it" didn't hold true. Rather, these projects had to be clearly defined, well advertised in advance, evaluated against a multitude of user cases (targeted to the grumpiest adopters first), leaps and bounds better than existing options, and adoptable with little to no effort.

The more consumers you have for common tooling and adoption, the more time you actually have to spend doing things other than writing code. This may sound obvious in retrospect, but clear end goals, believable dates, regular updates, and constant contact with consumers is paramount. Often skeptical consumers will ask, "If my current one-off shell script works okay, do I really need this?" Adoption of common software or processes is analogous to reliability as a feature—you may build the best thing in the world, but if people don't adopt it (or can't use it if it's not reliable), it's not useful to anyone. Having a plan for adoption—from champions to beta testers to executive sponsors to dedicated engineers who understand the importance of minimizing barriers to adoption—is both the end goal and the starting point when it comes to building and adopting common tools and practices.

This is because adoption drives a network effect: as the scale and reach of common software tools increases, incremental improvements to those tools are more valuable to the organization. As the value of the tools increases, development effort dedicated to them also tends to increase. Some of this development effort naturally goes toward further reducing migration costs, incentivizing greater adoption. Broad adoption encourages building organization-wide improvements in a consistent, product-like fashion, and justifies staffing full teams to support the tools for the long term. These tools should be characterized by rapid development, feature stability, common control surfaces, and automatable APIs.

When it comes to measuring the impact of such efforts, we can ask questions similar to the following:

- How quickly can a new product developer build and manage a world-scale service?

- Enabled by common tools and practices, how easily can an SRE in one domain move to another domain?

- How many services can be managed with the same primitives, as end-to-end user experiences versus separate services?

These are all possible and highly valuable ways to measure impact, but our first measurement must be adoption.

Conclusion

As demonstrated by the Waze and horizontal software case studies, even within a single company, SRE change management may need to tackle a variety of problem spaces and organizational context. As a result, there's likely no single formal model of change management that will neatly apply to the spectrum of changes any given organization may tackle. However, these frameworks, particularly Kotter's eight-step process and the Prosci ADKAR model, can provide useful insights for approaching change. One commonality across any change necessary in an environment as dynamic as SRE is constant reevaluation and iteration. While many changes may start organically in a grassroots fashion, most can benefit from structured coordination and planning as the changes mature.

Conclusion

By Dave Rensin, Betsy Beyer, Niall Richard Murphy,
Stephen Thorne, and Kent Kawahara

Onward...

The American economist Edgar Fiedler used to say that "[h]e who lives by the crystal ball soon learns to eat ground glass." Predicting the future is dangerous.

Nonetheless, we're going to risk the broken glass and try to say a few useful words about what we think comes after this book.

The Future Belongs to the Past

Our experiences since the publication of the first SRE book (*http://bit.ly/2kIcNYM*) and the process of assembling this volume have clearly demonstrated a huge pent-up demand for SRE from enterprises both large and small. From this, some interesting observations emerge.

First, large enterprises tend to have correspondingly large appetites to adopt SRE practices in a robust way. The familiar meme that large enterprises are slow to change is decidedly not true in this case. We expect to see a lot of interesting innovation in the SRE space from these firms over the next year, and that's really exciting.

Next, smaller firms are finding ways to adopt SRE practices regardless of whether or not they can staff a full-blown, globally distributed SRE team. We've long speculated that although the substance and sequence of the dishes are vitally important, people don't have to eat the whole SRE meal at once. We are now seeing that notion put into good practice, and that's also really exciting because it allows everyone to participate.

Finally, if you are reading this book and wondering if there's a market opportunity for you to offer services or build products that help firms adopt SRE, then the answer is a resounding yes. In fact, if that's something you decide to do, please let us know through O'Reilly at *bookquestions@oreilly.com*. We'd like to keep up with your progress.

SRE + <Insert Other Discipline>

We heard from many thoughtful people that SRE principles and practices seem like they should also apply to other disciplines—particularly security. We didn't cover the SRE/security overlap in the first book (or this book), but this is clearly a quickly burgeoning area of focus. If you're wondering why we didn't cover it in any depth in this volume, it's because we're not sure what we want to say about it (yet).

At the time of this writing (early spring 2018) we're already seeing the emergence of the term *DevSecOps*—a recognition that development, security, and operations are all interdependent—in the marketplace. If you're an SRE looking for a useful and unexplored space in which to spend some time, that's a really good candidate!

In general, we think this is the start of a trend toward asking, "How would SRE be applied to <insert other discipline>?" It certainly stands to reason that some SRE principles and practices could have value in other domains.

We're pretty excited to see where that leads…

Trickles, Streams, and Floods

The number of people offering to contribute content to this volume was much larger than the previous volume. That seems easy enough to explain—the first book was pretty popular, so people were keen to contribute to the second one. However, the *variety* of people offering to pitch in has been interesting. The types and range of the content proposals we evaluated surprised us. For example, a team of lawyers approached us about how they might incorporate error budgets into nontechnical legal agreements. How SRE applies to the legal profession is a topic clearly out of scope for this book, but is probably really interesting to a whole other professional population.

Because of this variety, we decided that this volume will not just be an implementation companion to the previous book. It will also be a launching point for whole new streams of SRE-related content. That means more books, articles, podcasts, videos, and who knows what else. This volume is a beginning, not an end.

SRE Belongs to All of Us

When we started work on the first book, our primary motivation was to explain SRE—this interesting thing we do to make Google work well for our users. It seemed useful to spread that knowledge around.

In our enthusiasm to explain our view of the world, we anchored on our direct experiences. As a result, we unintentionally alienated some in the larger DevOps community and beyond, who felt we ignored other organizations' contributions to the field. This volume aims to correct that mistake by devoting considerable space to discussing DevOps and SRE and why they are not at odds.

To our great joy, SRE is a growing community of practitioners that now extends very far outside of Google. In fact, it's likely that the number of non-Google SREs will significantly outnumber Google SREs by the time you read this.

Whatever its history, SRE is now a global community of which Google is one member. It belongs to all of us, and that's a good thing. It's already abundantly clear, via conferences like SREcon, meetups, and other publications, that we all have a lot to share with and learn from each other. To that end, we hope this book further expands that ongoing conversation.

On Gratitude

This volume has been a labor of love for us, and we are deeply grateful that you decided to read it. This process has taught each of us some surprising lessons about what SRE has become and made us all very excited to see what comes next.

(And since we are SREs, we'll be starting a lengthy postmortem on this process. Who knows, maybe you'll even see it in a blog post one of these days…)

> *May your queries flow and your pagers stay silent.*
> —Dave, Betsy, Niall, Stephen, and Kent

Example SLO Document

This document describes the SLOs for the Example Game Service.

Status	Published
Author	Steven Thurgood
Date	2018-02-19
Reviewers	David Ferguson
Approvers	Betsy Beyer
Approval Date	2018-02-20
Revisit Date	2019-02-01

Service Overview

The *Example Game Service* allows Android and iPhone users to play a game with each other. The app runs on users' phones, and moves are sent back to the *API* via a REST API. The *data store* contains the states of all current and previous games. A *score pipeline* reads this table and generates up-to-date league tables for today, this week, and all time. League table results are available in the app, via the API, and also on a public *HTTP server*.

The SLO uses a four-week rolling window.

SLIs and SLOs

Category	SLI	SLO
API		

Availability	The proportion of successful requests, as measured from the load balancer metrics. Any HTTP status other than 500–599 is considered successful.
	
	`count of "api" http_requests which`
	`do not have a 5XX status code`
	`divided by`
	`count of all "api" http_requests`
		97% success

Latency	The proportion of sufficiently fast requests, as measured from the load balancer metrics.
	"Sufficiently fast" is defined as < 400 ms, or < 850 ms.
	
	`count of "api" http_requests with`
	`a duration less than or equal to`
	`"0.4" seconds`
	`divided by`
	`count of all "api" http_requests`
	
	`count of "api" http_requests with`
	`a duration less than or equal to`
	`"0.85" seconds`
	`divided by`
	`count of all "api" http_requests`
		90% of requests < 400 ms
		99% of requests < 850 ms

HTTP server		

Availability	The proportion of successful requests, as measured from the load balancer metrics. Any HTTP status other than 500–599 is considered successful.
	
	`count of "web" http_requests which`
	`do not have a 5XX status code`
	`divided by`
	`count of all "web" http_requests`
		99%

Latency	The proportion of sufficiently fast requests, as measured from the load balancer metrics.
	"Sufficiently fast" is defined as < 200 ms, or < 1,000 ms.
	
	`count of "web" http_requests with`
	`a duration less than or equal to`
	`"0.2" seconds`
	`divided by`
	`count of all "web" http_requests`
	
	`count of "web" http_requests with`
	`a duration less than or equal to`
	`"1.0" seconds`
	`divided by`
	`count of all "web" http_requests`
		90% of requests < 200 ms
		99% of requests < 1,000 ms

Category	SLI	SLO
Score pipeline		

Freshness	The proportion of records read from the league table that were updated recently. "Recently" is defined as within 1 minute, or within 10 minutes. Uses metrics from the API and HTTP server:
	
	`count of all data_requests for`
	`"api" and "web" with freshness`
	`less than or equal to 1 minute`
	`divided by`
	`count of all data_requests`
	
	`count of all data_requests for`
	`"api" and "web" with freshness`
	`less than or equal to 10 minutes`
	`divided by`
	`count of all data_requests`
		90% of reads use data written within the previous 1 minute. 99% of reads use data written within the previous 10 minutes.

Correctness	The proportion of records injected into the state table by a correctness prober that result in the correct data being read from the league table. A correctness prober injects synthetic data, with known correct outcomes, and exports a success metric:
	
	`count of all data_requests which`
	`were correct`
	`divided by`
	`count of all data_requests`
		99.99999% of records injected by the prober result in the correct output.

Completeness	The proportion of hours in which 100% of the games in the data store were processed (no records were skipped). Uses metrics exported by the score pipeline:
	
	`count of all pipeline runs that`
	`processed 100% of the records`
	`divided by`
	`count of all pipeline runs`
		99% of pipeline runs cover 100% of the data.

Rationale

Availability and latency SLIs were based on measurement over the period 2018-01-01 to 2018-01-28. Availability SLOs were rounded down to the nearest 1% and latency SLO timings were rounded up to the nearest 50 ms. All other numbers were picked by the author and the services were verified to be running at or above those levels.

No attempt has yet been made to verify that these numbers correlate strongly with user experience.[1]

---

1 Even if the numbers in the SLO are not strongly evidence-based, it is necessary to document this so that future readers can understand this fact, and make their decisions appropriately. They may decide that it is worth the investment to collect more evidence.

Error Budget

Each objective has a separate error budget, defined as 100% minus (–) the goal for that objective. For example, if there have been 1,000,000 requests to the API server in the previous four weeks, the API availability error budget is 3% (100% – 97%) of 1,000,000: 30,000 errors.

We will enact the error budget policy (see Appendix B) when any of our objectives has exhausted its error budget.

Clarifications and Caveats

- Request metrics are measured at the load balancer. This measurement may fail to accurately measure cases where user requests didn't reach the load balancer.
- We only count HTTP 5XX status messages as error codes; everything else is counted as success.
- The test data used by the correctness prober contains approximately 200 tests, which are injected every 1s. Our error budget is 48 errors every four weeks.

Example Error Budget Policy

Status	Published
Author	Steven Thurgood
Date	2018-02-19
Reviewers	David Ferguson
Approvers	Betsy Beyer
Approval date	2018-02-20
Revisit date	2019-02-01

Service Overview

The *Example Game Service* allows Android and iPhone users to play a game with each other. New releases of the backend code are pushed daily. New releases of clients are pushed weekly. This policy applies both to backend and client releases.

Goals

The goals of this policy are to:

- Protect customers from repeated SLO misses
- Provide an incentive to balance reliability with other features

Non-Goals

This policy is not intended to serve as a punishment for missing SLOs. Halting change is undesirable; this policy gives teams permission to focus exclusively on reliability when data indicates that reliability is more important than other product features.

SLO Miss Policy

If the service is performing at or above its SLO, then releases (including data changes) will proceed according to the release policy.

If the service has exceeded its error budget for the preceding four-week window, we will halt all changes and releases other than P0[1] issues or security fixes until the service is back within its SLO.

Depending upon the cause of the SLO miss, the team may devote additional resources to working on reliability instead of feature work.

The team *must* work on reliability if:

- A code bug or procedural error caused the service itself to exceed the error budget.
- A postmortem reveals an opportunity to soften a hard dependency.
- Miscategorized errors fail to consume budget that would have caused the service to miss its SLO.

The team *may* continue to work on non-reliability features if:

- The outage was caused by a company-wide networking problem.
- The outage was caused by a service maintained by another team, who have themselves frozen releases to address their reliability issues.
- The error budget was consumed by users out of scope for the SLO (e.g., load tests or penetration testers).
- Miscategorized errors consume budget even though no users were impacted.

Outage Policy

If a single incident consumes more than 20% of error budget over four weeks, then the team must conduct a postmortem. The postmortem must contain at least one P0 action item to address the root cause.

---

1 P0 is the highest priority of bug: all hands on deck; drop everything else until this is fixed.

If a single class of outage consumes more than 20% of error budget over a quarter, the team must have a P0 item on their quarterly planning document[2] to address the issues in the following quarter.

Escalation Policy

In the event of a disagreement between parties regarding the calculation of the error budget or the specific actions it defines, the issue should be escalated to the CTO to make a decision.

Background

 This section is boilerplate, intended to give a succinct overview of error budgets to those unfamiliar with them.

Error budgets are the tool SRE uses to balance service reliability with the pace of innovation. Changes are a major source of instability, representing roughly 70% of our outages, and development work for features competes with development work for stability. The error budget forms a control mechanism for diverting attention to stability as needed.

An error budget is 1 minus the SLO of the service. A 99.9% SLO service has a 0.1% error budget.

If our service receives 1,000,000 requests in four weeks, a 99.9% availability SLO gives us a budget of 1,000 errors over that period.

---

2 At Google, quarterly planning is public, and teams are held accountable to their plans.

Results of Postmortem Analysis

At Google, we have a standard postmortem template that allows us to consistently capture the incident root cause and trigger, which enables trend analysis. We use this trend analysis to help us target improvements that address systemic root-cause types, such as faulty software interface design or immature change deployment planning. Table C-1 shows the breakdown of our top eight triggers for outages, based on a sample of thousands of postmortems over the last seven years.

Table C-1. Top eight outage triggers, 2010–2017

Binary push	37%
Configuration push	31%
User behavior change	9%
Processing pipeline	6%
Service provider change	5%
Performance decay	5%
Capacity management	5%
Hardware	2%

Table C-2 presents the top five contributing root-cause categories.

Table C-2. Top five root-cause categories for outages

Software	41.35%
Development process failure	20.23%
Complex system behaviors	16.90%
Deployment planning	6.74%
Network failure	2.75%

Index

A

abandoned phase (service lifecycle), SRE engagement in, 374

Abuse SRE and Common Abuse Tool (CAT) teams, Ares case study, 385-387

access control policies for data processing pipelines, 277

accidents, view in DevOps, 3

ACM Queue article on Canary Analysis service, 313

action items in postmortems, 200
- gamification of postmortem action items, 216
- in good postmortem example, 212
  - blamelessness of, 213
    - concrete action items, 213
  - monitoring tool for, 222
  - rewarding closeout of, 215

active development phase (service lifecycle), SRE engagement in, 373

ADKAR, 426, 433
- (see also Prosci ADKAR model)

AdMob and AdSense systems, 137

AdWords NALSD example, 246-259
- design process, 246
- distributed system, 251-259
  - LogJoiner, 252
  - MapReduce, evaluating, 251
- initial requirements, 247
- running application on one machine, 248
- scaling resources for parsing logs, 249

alerts
- alert suppression, 64
- alerting on SLOs, 75-91

burn rate for error budgets, 80
- considerations in, 75
- increased alert window, 78
- incrementing alert duration, 79
- low-traffic services and error budget alerting, 86-89
- making sure alerting is scalable, 89
- multiple burn rate alarms, 82
- multiwindow, multi-burn-rate alerts, 84
- services with extreme availability goals, 89
- target error rate SLO threshold, 76

contributors to high pager load, 158

paging alerts, defining thresholds for, 163

provided by monitoring system, 64
- in metrics-based and logs-based systems, 65

separating alerting in monitoring systems, 69

testing alerting logic in monitoring system, 72

using good alerts and consoles to identify cause of pages, 161

analysis of postmortems, 222, 453

animated (undesirable) language in postmortems, 201

anycast, 226
- stabilized, implementation of, 227

APIs
- availability and latency for API calls, Home Depot case study, 52
- availability and latency SLIs, 25
- case study, end-to-end API simplicity, 134
- machine consumable, 393

external dependencies and incident
response, 183
in data processing pipeline, causing failures,
286
modeling, 40
monitoring system metrics from, 70
planning for failure in data processing pipelines, 270
deployments
automated, 336
blue/green, 350
continuous, 3
(see also continuous integration and
continuous delivery)
deploying data processing pipeline to production, 275
partial, performing for data processing
pipelines, 274
roll forward deployment vs. simple canary
deployment, 340-342
small, 336
deprecation phase (service lifecycle), SRE
engagement in, 374
depth in postmortems, 213
design phase (service lifecycle), SRE engagement in, 372
design process (NALSD), 246
destructive testing or fuzzing, 159
detection time (SLO alerts), 76
development
development process in Spotify case study,
296
mapping data processing pipeline development lifecycle, 272-275
partnership with SRE, critical importance
of, 12
placing your first SRE in development team,
401
setting up relationship between SRE and
development team, 375-380
aligning goals, 375-378
communicating business and production priorities, 375
identifying risks, 375
planning and executing, 379
setting ground rules, 379
SRE teams having responsibility for, 412
SRE-to-developer ratio and support of multiple services by single SRE team, 382

SREs sharing ownership with developers, 7
sustaining an effective ongoing relationship
between SRE and development teams,
380-382
DevOps
about, 2
accidents, view of, 3
comparing and contrasting with SRE, 8
elimination of silos, 2
gradual change, 3
implementation by SRE, 4
interrelation of tooling and culture, 4
measurement as crucial, 4
organizational context and fostering successful adoption, 9-12
disaster and recovery testing, practicing with
customers, 397
disaster recovery testing (DiRT) at Google, 193,
271
diskerase, 196
Display Ads Spiderweb, simplification of (case
study), 137
distributed SRE teams, running, 384
distributed SREs, 403
documentation
creating and maintaining for data processing pipelines, 271
Spotify case study, customer integration and
support, 294
domain-specific languages (DSLs) for configuration, 319
domain-specific optimization (excessive) in
configurations, 318
draining requests away from buggy system elements, 162
drills (incident management), 193
dropping work, 368
durability SLI, 25
duration parameter (alerts), incrementing, 79

E

ease of implementation and transparency
for data processing pipeline, 283
emergency response, practicing, 161
emotion-based models for change management, 426
end-to-end measurement for data processing
pipeline SLOs, 270
ending SRE engagements, 385-389

case study, Ares, 386-387
case study, data analysis pipeline, 387
Equal-Cost Multi-Path (ECMP) forwarding, 227
error budgets, 47
(see also service level objectives)
addressing missed SLO caused by a dependency, 41
adjusting priorities according to, 381
agreed-upon by SRE and development teams for a service, 379
alerting on burn rate, 80
multiple alarms, 82
multiwindow, multi-burn-rate alerts, 84
calculating, 20
dashboard showing error budget consumption, 34
decision making using, 37-38
documenting error budget policy, 32
establishing error budget policy, 31
example policy, 449-451
for example game service, 448
low-traffic services and error budget alerting, 86-89
combining services, 87
generating artificial traffic, 87
lowering the SLO or increasing the window, 88
making service and infrastructure changes, 87
minimizing risk to by canarying releases, 343
prerequisites for adopting as SRE approach, 18
reliability targets and, 19
rolling back recent changes and, 162
support tickets per day vs. measured loss in budget, 35
errors
alerting for target error rate over SLO threshold, 76
debugging in different monitoring systems, 65
defining SLOs for in Home Depot case study, 53
errors per hour metric in canary deployment, 349
increased alert window for SLO errors, 78
measurement in Home Depot case study, 51

evangelism, SLOs at Home Depot, 51, 54
events
event delivery in Spotify case study, 288
event processing to order or structure data, 265
Evernote, SLO case study, 43-49
current state of SLO use and practice, 49
introduction of SLOs, journey in progress, 45-47
why Evernote adopted SRE model, 44
extract, transform, load (ETL) model, 264
ETL pipelines, 264
in Spotify case study, 290

F
failures, 3
data processing pipeline, prevention and response, 284-287
potential causes, 286
potential failure modes, 284
dependency failure in data processing pipeline, 270
failure tolerance in data processing pipeline, 282
handling mistakes appropriately, 382
not passing off blame for, 10
reducing cost of, 6
feature isolation, 162
features
feature coverage in SRE with customers, 397
planning for data processing pipelines, 278
separating feature launches from binary releases, 338
tradeoffs between feature velocity and reliability, 19
feedback from users, toil management with, 105
finger pointing in postmortems, 201
follow-up to pager alerts, rigor in, 164
follow-up to postmortems, 222
forming your first SRE team, 404
Four Golden Signals, 51, 70
freshness
data freshness SLOs for data processing pipeline, 269
of data in monitoring system, 62
freshness SLI, 24
implementation for pipeline freshness, 26
funding and hiring (SREs), 421

future protection from overload, 368

G

H

example machine learning data processing pipeline, 266
Maglev, 226
    implementing stabilized anycast with, 227
    packet delivery using consistent hashing and connection tracking, 228
major incident response at PagerDuty, 188
manual overrides and kill switches in autoscaling, 238
MapReduce, evaluating for use in AdWords distributed system, 251
maturity matrix for data processing pipeline, 281-284
McKinsey's 7-S change management model, 424
mean time to repair (MTTR), 6
measurements
    decision on what/how to measure for SLOs at Evernote, 46
    effectiveness of automated tasks, 105
    end-to-end measurement for data processing pipeline SLOs, 270
    importance in DevOps, 4
    in DevOps and SRE, 8
    in SRE with customers, 396
    measurability in action items in postmortems, 213
    measuring the SLIs, 26-28
    measuring toil, 96-98, 101
    metrics for Home Depot services, 51
    sources of, for API and HTTP sever availability and latency SLI, 25
    with service level indicators (SLIs), 20
meeting in person to resolve issues, 382
metrics, 64
    (see also measurements)
    choosing between metrics-based and logs-based monitoring systems, 65
    collecting in canary deployments, time limits on, 349
    establishing to evaluate team workload, 368
    indicating work overload, 366
    metric-based monitoring system, 65
    quantifiable, in good postmortem example, 213
    restructuring at Evernote for cloud datacenters, 154
    selecting and evaluating for canary deployments, 345-348

selection for canarying in noninteractive systems, 349
    visible and useful, from monitoring system, 69-72
    dependencies, 70
    implementing purposeful metrics, 72
    intended changes to your service, 70
    on resource usage saturation, 71
    status of served traffic, 72
microservices
    combining for low-traffic services and error budget alerting, 87
    limiting how much an SRE team can accomplish, 371
    running hundreds on a shared platform, case study, 139
    using microservice approach to creating data processing pipelines, 280
migrations, 99
    automation in filer-backed home directory decommissioning, 126
Mission Control program (SRE teams), 419
mistakes, handling appropriately, 382
mitigation delays, reducing, 162
mitigation in incident response, 184
    prioritizing mitigation above all else, 185
mobility for SREs, 420
Moira portal, 125
monitoring, 61-74
    auditing and building shared dashboards in SRE with customers, 395
    calculating SLOs from data, 46
    choosing between monitoring systems, examples, 65
    covering in interviews with SREs, 400
    data collection for causes of on-call paging, 165
    decisions on reliability and, 392
    desirable features of monitoring strategy, 62-64
    alerts, 64
    calculations support, 62
    interfaces for data display, 63
    speed of data retrieval, 62
    for data processing pipeline, 282
    implementation in common tooling adoption in SRE case study, 436
    managing monitoring systems, 67-69
    encouraging consistency, 68

Learn from experts.
Find the answers you need.

Sign up for a **10-day free trial** to get **unlimited access** to all of the content on Safari, including Learning Paths, interactive tutorials, and curated playlists that draw from thousands of ebooks and training videos on a wide range of topics, including data, design, DevOps, management, business—and much more.

Start your free trial at:

oreilly.com/safari

(No credit card required.)